NEW STUDIES IN BIBLICAL THEOLOGY 63

'EGYPT MY PEOPLE . . . AND ISRAEL MY INHERITANCE'

'The Latter Prophets continually bear witness to a God whose ways with the nations both highlight his sovereignty and surprise us. Timmer's impressive study brings what the prophets have to say about the nations to the foreground and explores how this relates to the gospel and contemporary politics.'
Andrew Abernethy, Professor of Old Testament, Wheaton College, Illinois

'In this volume, Timmer takes us on a journey through the prophetic books attentive to one of its key topics. His priority is the message of the text, but this is placed initially within the ideological context of the nations which surrounded Israel and Judah. The prophetic message is regularly traced into its ultimate biblical-theological context, which opens the way to addressing the challenges of the present generation of faithful followers of the God of the text. Here one finds the value of decades of patient study on Scripture, a significant achievement.'
Mark J. Boda, Professor of Old Testament, McMaster Divinity College, Hamilton, Ontario

'What a fine, learned and timely book. An excellent example of exegesis, theology and cultural critique! We have few examples where a book combines all three in a thorough and learned way on a topic of universal relevance. There is much here for both the preacher, the apologist and the historian/cultural analyst. This is one of the most thorough books I have read on the topic of the nations in the prophetic oracles, and it is unique in working from a biblical-theological and canonical perspective. Timmer shows, in the end, not just the view of the foreign nations within each prophetic book, but their place within the trajectory of the biblical canon. There is not only divine judgment for nationalistic idolatry and arrogant overreach but also a concern for the salvation of the nations (and in particular individuals within the nations) and their purification to live in the presence of God as his people in a new creation. Thus the resurrected Christ's command for his disciples to go into the entire world and to preach to the nations the good news is but a logical consequence of this prophetic message. I enthusiastically recommend this book!'
Stephen G. Dempster, Emeritus Professor of Religious Studies, Crandall University, New Brunswick

'This helpful study clarifies how Yahweh's writing prophets confronted the misguided practices and perspectives of foreign nations yet also celebrated the inclusion of an international remnant among God's people in the eschatological messianic age. Thoughtful, thorough and theological, Timmer not only highlights how the fifteen Latter Prophets address the sins and salvation of Israel's neighbours but also shows how the New Testament develops these themes.'
Jason S. DeRouchie, Research Professor of Old Testament and Biblical Theology, and Rich and Judy Hastings Endowed Chair of Old Testament Studies, Midwestern Baptist Theological Seminary, Missouri

'In his timely book, Daniel Timmer unfolds the rich and diverse ways in which the Old Testament prophets depict the nations in God's sovereign purposes of judgment and salvation. He skilfully shows us how to do biblical theology by weaving together ancient imperial contexts, the prophets' countercultural engagement with their world, and the contemporary relevance of their unique view of power. Look no further for help if you've ever had the (mis)impression that the God of the prophets is ethnocentric and xenophobic!'
Jerry Hwang, Associate Professor of Theology, Trinity Christian College, Illinois

'Daniel Timmer has given more attention to the non-Israelite nations in the prophets than most. In *'Egypt My People . . . and Israel My Inheritance'*, he brings his breadth of research to bear in a fresh way. Beginning by setting the messages of the individual prophetic books in conversation with the national ideologies of the ancient Near East, Timmer evinces the underlying threads of what the prophets critique and how they frame their oracles of salvation. Through chapters chock-full of exegetical and biblical-theological insight, Timmer's redemptive-historical survey compellingly demonstrates the biblical vision for the one people of God in Christian Scripture. Timmer's final chapter on the relevance of the prophetic books for considering the gospel's challenge to contemporary world-view issues is a much-welcomed inclusion. I trust many will find this book a helpful resource not only for the study of Christian Scripture but also for the motivation to spread the word and ways of the triune God to the ends of the earth.'
Andrew M. King, Assistant Professor of Biblical Studies, Midwestern Baptist Theological Seminary, Missouri, and Spurgeon's College, London

'Standing at a crossroads of redemptive history, Israel's prophets spoke into the world of ancient Israel with a multinational vision of what God *will do* to restore his people and his world. With unique clarity, the Latter Prophets speak to the Lord's sovereignty over some of the greatest empires in human history, and Daniel Timmer masterfully walks us through the ideologies of these ancient kingdoms and the message of the true King who reigns over them. Yet Timmer's theological vision does not end with the Old Testament. With the skill and intuition that only comes from decades of research and reflection, Timmer guides us through a biblical-theological picture of the nations in the Latter Prophets and how it shapes our understanding of the work of God in the New Testament. Historically accurate, carefully articulate, and theologically rich . . . *tolle lege*!'
William R. Osborne, Professor of Biblical and Theological Studies, College of the Ozarks, Missouri

'Dan Timmer has provided an invaluable resource by tracing God's purposes for the nations throughout the books of the prophets and offering an adept biblical-theological exploration of this theme. Particularly enlightening is his analysis of the ideologies promoted within the different non-Israelite nations mentioned in the prophets, the prophetic critiques of these ideologies, and how they are seen in our world today (e.g. materialism, political liberalism, imperialism and decolonization). This book is essential reading for missiology students, pastors looking to apply the messages of the prophets to the modern world, and anyone seeking a deeper understanding of God's glorious plan to include people from all nations in the blessed kingdom of his Son.'
Anthony R. Petterson, Lecturer in Old Testament and Biblical Hebrew, Morling College and Australian College of Theology, Sydney

'Daniel Timmer, one of our most insightful interpreters of the prophets (among other things), here offers a one-stop shop on the non-Israelite nations in Isaiah to Malachi. All of Timmer's many gifts are on display here: his characteristic erudition, keen insight, wide command of the literature (both primary and secondary) and sound judgment – all captured within a biblical-theological framework that pays particular attention to questions of ideology. The final chapter is alone worth the price of the book, as Timmer contemplates how the prophetic word bears upon the ideologies that rule our own world, lives and hearts.'
Brent A. Strawn, D. Moody Smith Distinguished Professor of Old Testament and Professor of Law, Duke University, North Carolina

'Why does God often seem to overlook the violence, arrogance and idolatry of power of empires and political forces? Should not a God of justice protect the weak and defend those who serve him? The prophetic oracles about the non-Israelite nations of the Old Testament are often perceived as dark and difficult texts. Daniel Timmer, however, demonstrates how concretely and compassionately these biblical passages address these pressing issues. His careful reading of passages from Isaiah, Jeremiah, Ezekiel and the Book of the Twelve reveals that God not only makes use of the nations. Instead of condemning entire nations, his judgment of violence and injustice also exposes and convicts those who do not recognize him as the Lord of history. In this way, Timmer translates his expertise in social-scientific and redemptive-historical biblical interpretation for a wider audience. More importantly, he encourages readers to trust in God in times of upheaval and to look forward to new heavens and a new earth in which righteousness dwells.'

Koert Van Bekkum, Professor and Department Chair of the Old Testament, and Vice Dean of Research, Evangelical Theological Faculty, Leuven

NEW STUDIES IN BIBLICAL THEOLOGY 63

Series editors: D. A. Carson and Benjamin L. Gladd

'EGYPT MY PEOPLE . . . AND ISRAEL MY INHERITANCE'

The non-Israelite nations in the Latter Prophets

Daniel C. Timmer

Published in Great Britain by APOLLOS (an imprint of Inter-Varsity Press)
SPCK Group, Studio 101, The Record Hall, 16–16A Baldwin's Gardens, London
EC1N 7RJ, England
Email: ivp@ivpbooks.com
Website: www.ivpbooks.com

Published in the USA by B&H Academic®, Brentwood, Tennessee

First published 2025

British Library Cataloguing-in-Publication Data
A catalogue record for this book is available from the British Library.

Apollos ISBN: 978–1–78974–578–8
eBook ISBN: 978–1–78974–275–6

Library of Congress Cataloging-in-Publication Data is on file at the Library of Congress, Washington, DC

B&H Academic ISBN 979–8–3845–3092–3
eBook ISBN 979–8–3845–3093–0

30 29 28 27 26 25 VP 1 2 3 4 5 6 7 8 9 10

Typeset by Fakenham Prepress Solutions, Fakenham, Norfolk NR21 8NL
Printed in the USA

Produced on paper from sustainable sources

Inter-Varsity Press publishes Christian books that are true to the Bible and that communicate the gospel, develop discipleship and strengthen the church for its mission in the world.

IVP originated within the Inter-Varsity Fellowship, now the Universities and Colleges Christian Fellowship, a student movement connecting Christian Unions in universities and colleges throughout Great Britain, and a member movement of the International Fellowship of Evangelical Students. Website: www.uccf.org.uk. That historic association is maintained, and all senior IVP staff and committee members subscribe to the UCCF Basis of Faith.

Contents

Series preface xvii
Author's preface xix
Abbreviations xxii

1 The prophets, the nations and biblical theology 1
The prophets and the nations 1
The focus of this book: the nations in the prophets 2
Why do Israel's prophets talk about the nations? 2
What do the prophets say about the nations? 3
What is biblical theology? 6
Definition, key assertions and methods 6
Biblical theology and the nations 7
Tracing the nations through the prophets 9
Concepts and distinctions 9
A focus on individual books 11
Chronological (diachronic) order 13
The contemporary significance of the prophets' treatment of the nations 13

2 Ancient Near Eastern nations and their ideologies 17
Egypt 18
Neo-Assyria 25
Neo-Babylonia 30
Achaemenid Persia 34

3 Isaiah 43
The nations as the object of Israel's misplaced trust 43
The nations as God's means for punishing his covenant people 45
The nations under judgment 46

Assyria's imperial mission: gods, king, war, order – all for Assyria's glory (Isa. 10:5–19) 47
The world and Babylon (Isa. 13:1–22) 49
Babylon in Sheol (Isa. 14:3–23) 51
The nations under judgment with salvation as a possibility 54
Moab and its refugees (Isa. 15:1 – 16:14) 54
The nations under judgment *and* salvation 57
Old and new Egypt (Isa. 19:1–25) 57
Tyre and Sidon: from worship of wealth to worship of Yahweh (Isa. 23:1–14, 15–18) 62
The judgment of the old, the creation of the new (Isa. 24 – 25) 64
The nations and salvation 66
The Servant, Israel and the nations (Isa. 42:1–12; 49:1–7) 66
Contribution to and participation in Zion's eschatological restoration (Isa. 60 – 62) 69
Full integration of non-Israelites into renewed Israel and its worship (Isa. 56:1–8; 66:18–24) 71
Summary and New Testament developments 73

4 Jeremiah 77
The nations prior to Judah's exile 78
The nations as God's means for punishing Judah – and God's subsequent punishment of the nations 79
Babylon as God's primary means for punishing Judah – and God's subsequent punishment of Babylon 81
Babylon and the nations during Judah's exile 86
Babylon as Judah's 'home away from home' 87
Babylon as Yahweh's temporary vice-regent over the Levant 90
The end of exile and beyond: Judah and many nations restored 92
'The nations' in general 92
Egypt (Jer. 46:26b) 95
Moab (Jer. 48:47) 96
Ammon (Jer. 49:6) 97
Edom (Jer. 49:11) 97

Elam (Jer. 49:39) 98
Summary and New Testament developments 99

5 Ezekiel 101
The nations in the context of God's discipline of Israel (Ezek. 1 – 24) 102
Non-Israelite nations as the stage on which Yahweh's relationship with Israel takes place 102
Non-Israelite nations not responsible for inducing Israel to sin 103
Non-Israelite nations as the adversarial audience of Judah's judgment and salvation 104
Non-Israelite nations, especially Babylon, as God's means for punishing unfaithful Judah 105
Non-Israelite nations as God's means for punishing other nations 107
The nations as enemies of Yahweh and his people 108
Ammon (Ezek. 21:28–32; 25:1–7) 109
Moab and Seir (Ezek. 25:8–11) 110
Edom (Ezek. 25:12–14; 35:1–15) 111
Philistia (Ezek. 25:15–17) 112
Tyre and the quest for dominion and divine glory (Ezek. 26:1 – 28:19) 113
Egypt and the violent quest for domination and glory (Ezek. 29 – 32) 119
Gog and his allies as the last enemies of Yahweh and restored Israel (Ezek. 38 – 39) 127
Salvation for some from the nations 128
Sodom adopted as a daughter by superlatively restored Judah (Ezek. 16:49–63) 129
Egypt shares a common eschatological restoration with Judah (Ezek. 29:13–16) 130
Sojourners worship God and inherit the land alongside Israelites (Ezek. 47:22–23) 130
Summary and New Testament developments 132

6 Hosea 135
Covenant beginnings: no nations, no idols 135
Covenant infidelity and rupture: the nations as lethal idols 136
Sources of protection and provision: idols 137
Enemies: lethal idols 138
Covenant discipline: nations as witnesses or masters 138
Covenant restoration: no nations, no idols 139
Summary and New Testament developments 140

7 Joel 143
The nations in the past and present: foes, threats, antagonists 143
The nations in the future: life through the Spirit or death through judgment 145
Salvation for those who call on Yahweh, Israelite and non-Israelite alike 146
Destruction for those who militate against Yahweh and his people 147
A renewed earth with Jerusalem at its centre 148
Summary and New Testament developments 148

8 Amos 151
Secondary roles: witnesses, comparisons and instruments of God's covenant discipline 151
Past offences and imminent punishment 152
The remnant of Israel and the remnant of the nations 154
Summary and New Testament developments 156

9 Obadiah 157
Edom (Obad. 1–14) 157
'All the nations', including 'Edom' (Obad. 15–21) 159
Summary and New Testament developments 160

10 Jonah 163
The non-Israelite sailors 163
Nineveh 166

Background: Neo-Assyrian imperialism 166
Foreground: non-Israelites' repentance, Yahweh's compassion and deliverance 167
Summary and New Testament developments 168

11 Micah 171
The nations in negative roles in non-eschatological settings 171
Non-Israelites in negative roles in eschatological settings 172
Non-Israelites in positive roles in eschatological settings 174
Summary and New Testament developments 177

12 Nahum 179
Global, individual, definitive judgment and salvation of humanity (Nah. 1:2–8) 179
Selective, limited judgment of Assyria (Nah. 1:9 – 3:19) 181
What is 'Assyria' in Nahum? 181
Yahweh versus Assyria: God as supremely important 182
Rejection of the monarch as the personification of empire and omnipotent defender and provider 182
Deconstruction of Nineveh's impregnability and splendour 184
What of the others? 186
Summary and New Testament developments 188

13 Habakkuk 191
Babylon as God's instrument for punishing sinful Judah 191
Babylon as God's enemy 192
Babylon in the dialogue of Habakkuk 1 192
Babylon's imperialism and idolatry will be punished (Hab. 2) 194
The Divine Warrior's present–future battle against the wicked (Hab. 3) 197
Summary and New Testament developments 198

14 Zephaniah 201
The world as part of a supra-ethnic whole to be judged (Zeph. 1:2–3, 14–18; 3:8) 201

Some Judeans and some among the nations will be judged (Zeph. 1:4–13; 2:4–10, 12–15) 202
Some among the nations will be saved (Zeph. 2:11; 3:9, 14–20) 204
Summary and New Testament developments 207

15 Haggai **209**
The transformative shaking of the nations and Yahweh's temple (Hag. 2:1–9) 210
The destructive shaking of the nations and Yahweh's kingdom (Hag. 2:20–23) 212
Summary and New Testament developments 213

16 Zechariah **217**
Judgment of nations, restoration of Jerusalem, integration of non-Israelites (Zech. 1:7 – 2:13; 6:1–8; 8:20–23) 217
Judgment and destruction of the enemies of God's people 218
The restoration of Jerusalem/Zion 218
The integration of foreigners into restored Israel *as Yahweh's people* 218
Judgment, transformation and integration of foreigners (Zech. 9:1–17) 220
Retribution against God's enemies among the nations 220
Integration of some non-Israelites into renewed Israel *as Israelites* 221
Transformation or judgment of non-Israelites 222
Judgment *and* deliverance of Jerusalem *and* the nations, integration of foreigners (Zech. 14:1–21) 222
Judgment of God's people (punishment) and their enemies (deliverance) 223
Restoration of Jerusalem and integration of non-Israelites *as worshippers of Yahweh* 223
Summary and New Testament developments 224

17 Malachi **227**
Some non-Israelites as God's opponents: Edom (Mal. 1:2–5) 227
Some non-Israelites as God's worshippers (Mal. 1:11, 14) 229

Ideal worshippers of God 229
An identity that overlaps with that of Israel's repentant, restored remnant (Mal. 3:16–18) 230
Transcending the Israelite–non-Israelite distinction in the Day of Yahweh (Mal. 4:1–3) 231
Summary and New Testament developments 233

18 The nations, contemporary ideologies and the gospel 235
The main elements of ancient imperial ideologies 239
Some contemporary expressions of ideology 240
The human being 242
The material world 245
Politics 247
Ideology and individuals 251
Salvation as God-given, gracious, non-ideological restoration 253
Reading, preaching and hearing the oracles concerning the 'nations' 255

Bibliography 259
Index of authors 297
Index of Scripture references 303
Index of ancient sources 315

Series preface

New Studies in Biblical Theology is a series of monographs that address key issues in the discipline of biblical theology. Contributions to the series focus on one or more of three areas: (1) the nature and status of biblical theology, including its relations with other disciplines (e.g. historical theology, exegesis, systematic theology, historical criticism, narrative theology); (2) the articulation and exposition of the structure of thought of a particular biblical writer or corpus; and (3) the delineation of a biblical theme across all or part of the biblical corpora.

Above all, these monographs are creative attempts to help thinking Christians understand their Bibles better. The series aims simultaneously to instruct and to edify, to interact with the current literature and to point the way ahead. In God's universe, mind and heart should not be divorced: in this series we will try not to separate what God has joined together. While the notes interact with the best of scholarly literature, the text is uncluttered with untransliterated Greek and Hebrew, and tries to avoid too much technical jargon. The volumes are written within the framework of confessional evangelicalism, but there is always an attempt at thoughtful engagement with the sweep of the relevant literature.

The Old Testament prophetic books have a great deal to say about the nations, and Daniel Timmer wisely charts how Gentiles fit into God's plan of redemption. The strength of this project lies in an overview of the historical, political and ideological context of the nations. Timmer also traces the New Testament writers' appropriation of the Old Testament prophetic hopes, revealing that the nations find their ultimate identity in Christ and his work.

D. A. Carson
Trinity Evangelical Divinity School

Benjamin L. Gladd
The Carson Center for Theological Renewal

Author's preface

This book's rather immodest goal is to make reading the Old Testament's oracles concerning the nations a fruitful and edifying experience for ordinary readers of the Bible. Several decades of listening to sermons in a variety of settings in the United States and Canada, as well as ample anecdotal evidence, have led me to believe that this part of the Old Testament is among the most neglected. While this state of affairs is lamentable, the reasons for it are understandable, and the present volume was written precisely to help readers explore this material, which is no less rich and rewarding than it is unfamiliar and intimidating. To that end, the first two chapters lay the foundation for a Christocentric, historically situated and ideologically attuned reading of the prophets, while the final chapter shows how these oracles help Christians illuminate and critique contemporary ideologies that have very significant effects on concrete dimensions of our daily existence. It also explores how the gospel can counter such ideologies and strengthen the reader's love for and satisfaction in the God who, as creator and redeemer, is the only one able to give us 'all things' in his Son (Rom. 8:32). The intervening chapters explore, book by book, the ways in which the prophets themselves practised inspired, theocentric, gospel-oriented, incisive and ultimately constructive critique of the ideologies that were promulgated in the cultures around them.

The process of writing this volume was a joy, even though its conclusion consumed a large part of last year's Christmas holidays (appropriately enough). I thus owe a first debt of gratitude to my wife, Andreea, and our sons, Nathan and Felix, who graciously accommodated my occasional unavailability and patiently awaited the volume's completion. I have benefited immensely from interaction with the students with whom I have explored the Old Testament's prophetic books over the years, first at Institut Farel in Montreal; then Reformed Theological Seminary (RTS) in Jackson, Mississippi; the University of Sudbury (Ontario); the Evangelical Theological Faculty (Leuven); China Reformed Theological Seminary (Taiwan); Alexandria School of Theology; and now for a decade or more at the Faculté de théologie évangélique (FTE) in Montreal and Puritan

Reformed Theological Seminary (PRTS) in Grand Rapids, Michigan. During the same period I have also had the pleasure of teaching some of this material at l'Église réformée St-Jean in Montreal and l'Église réformée St-Paul in Repentigny (Quebec). Reaching further back in time, I remain grateful for my introduction to biblical theology with Dr Jerry Bilkes at PRTS and to the prophets with Dr Willem VanGemeren at Trinity Evangelical Divinity School (Deerfield, Illinois).

In God's good providence, a number of influences and interests converged over the last decade in ways that helped me better appreciate the theological and practical value of the prophetic oracles concerning the nations. The Book of the Twelve Group of the Institute for Biblical Research and the Israelite Prophetic Literature group of the Society of Biblical Literature were excellent contexts for sharpening my thinking, and my peers helped me get a better grasp on the various roles of non-Israelites in the prophetic books. The work of Tim Keller (and, through him, Lesslie Newbigin), Christopher Watkin, Carl Trueman, Richard Bauckham, John Webster, Oliver O'Donovan, Iain Provan and others has been extremely helpful in navigating contemporary thought and articulating clearly the epistemological, ethical and other issues that are inevitably hidden under the trappings of cultural discourse. My colleagues at RTS, the FTE and PRTS have also enriched my thinking in many ways, whether by conversation, by example or by their publications, and I am grateful for their fellowship in the gospel. I am especially thankful for conversations with Chris Hanna that helped me to think critically about aspects of contemporary culture. Last but not least, David Firth's *Including the Stranger: Foreigners in the Former Prophets* appeared in the NSBT series at just the right moment, and prompted me to propose a complementary volume focused on foreigners in the Latter Prophets.

The writing of this volume and some related articles as well as the research behind them were facilitated by the generous and multifaceted support that PRTS accords me. President Adriaan Neele and Academic Dean Jonathon Beeke continue to foster a context in which the inseparability of learning and the personal dimension of theological knowledge is valorized and in which faculty members have ample time to conduct research and to write. In this connection I also gratefully acknowledge the excellent access to resources that I enjoyed in the William Perkins Library, directed by Laura Ladwig. Other digital resources recently adopted by the FTE and put in place by Dr Jean Maurais also proved to be wonderful tools for research. Kevin Wang, my research assistant, cheerfully and efficiently helped me bring order and consistency to the bibliography and footnotes and also helped to produce the indexes.

Finally, I thank the editors of this series, Dr D. A. Carson and Dr Ben Gladd, as well as IVP publishing director Tom Creedy, for their helpful feedback and assistance. I am equally grateful to Mollie Barker for her patient and expert editing of the manuscript, and to Dr Rima Devereaux for overseeing the production process. Whatever weaknesses or errors remain are mine alone. My deepest debt, and one I joyfully acknowledge, is to the Lord, who graciously and patiently continues to teach and form me and has blessed me beyond my reckoning. He is likewise the one who brought my wife Andreea and me together, and it is to her, as a fellow labourer in the gospel, that I dedicate this work. Her determination, generosity, love, wisdom and humility are daily blessings that I receive with joy and gratitude.

Abbreviations

AB — Anchor Bible
ABD — *Anchor Bible Dictionary*, ed. D. N. Freedman, 6 vols., New York: Doubleday, 1992
ABG — Arbeiten zur Bibel und ihrer Geschichte
ABRL — Anchor Bible Research Library
ABS — Archaeology and Biblical Studies
AIL — Ancient Israel and Its Literature
ANEM — Ancient Near Eastern Monographs
ANET — *Ancient Near Eastern Texts Relating to the Old Testament*, ed. J. B. Pritchard, 3rd edn with supplement, Princeton: Princeton University Press, 1969
AOAT — Alter Orient und Altes Testament
AOTC — Apollos Old Testament Commentary
AYB — Anchor Yale Bible
BBR — *Bulletin for Biblical Research*
BBRSup — Bulletin for Biblical Research Supplement Series
BCOTPB — Baker Commentary on the Old Testament Prophetic Books
BETL — Bibliotheca Ephemeridum Theologicarum Lovaniensium
BHQ — Biblia Hebraica Quinta
Bib — *Biblica*
BibInt — *Biblical Interpretation*
BibInt — Biblical Interpretation Series
BSac — *Bibliotheca Sacra*
BST — Bible Speaks Today
BWANT — Beiträge zum Wissenschaft vom Alten (und Neuen) Testament
BZAW — Beihefte zur Zeitschrift für die alttestamentliche Wissenschaft
CANE — *Civilizations of the Ancient Near East*, ed. J. M. Sasson,

	4 vols., New York, 1995; repr. in 2 vols., Peabody: Hendrickson, 2006
CBOTS	Coniectanea Biblica Old Testament Series
CBQ	*Catholic Biblical Quarterly*
CC	Continental Commentaries
CCT	Contours of Christian Theology
CEB	Commentaire évangélique biblique
CHANE	Culture and History of the Ancient Near East
COS	*The Context of Scripture*, ed. William W. Hallo and K. Lawson Younger Jr, 4 vols., Leiden: Brill, 1997–2016
CSMS Journal	*Canadian Society for Mesopotamian Studies / La Société canadienne des études mésopotamiennes Journal*
CTJ	*Calvin Theological Journal*
DANE	*Dictionary of the Ancient Near East*, ed. P. Bienkowski and A. Millard, Philadelphia: University of Pennsylvania Press, 2000
EBR	*The Encyclopedia of the Bible and Its Reception*, ed. H.-J. Klauck et al., Berlin: De Gruyter, 2002–
ECC	Eerdmans Critical Commentary
ESV	English Standard Version
EuroJTh	*European Journal of Theology*
ExAud	*Ex Auditu*
FAT	Forschungen zum Alten Testament
FOTL	Forms of Old Testament Literature
FRLANT	Forschungen zur Religion und Literatur des Alten und Neuen Testaments
HB	Hebrew Bible
HBAI	*Hebrew Bible and Ancient Israel*
HBT	*Horizons in Biblical Theology*
HCOT	Historical Commentary on the Old Testament
HSM	Harvard Semitic Monographs
HTKAT	Herders Theologischer Kommentar zum Alten Testament
HTS	*HTS Teologiese Studies/Theological Studies*
ICC	International Critical Commentary
IDS	*In die Skriflig*
IEJ	*Israel Exploration Journal*
Int	*Interpretation*

JANEH	*Journal of Ancient Near Eastern History*
JAOS	*Journal of the American Oriental Society*
JARCE	*Journal of the American Research Center in Egypt*
JBL	*Journal of Biblical Literature*
JBQ	*Jewish Bible Quarterly*
JETS	*Journal of the Evangelical Theological Society*
JHebS	*Journal of Hebrew Scriptures*
JNES	*Journal of Near Eastern Studies*
JNSL	*Journal of Northwest Semitic Languages*
JRAS	*Journal of the Royal Asiatic Society*
JSOT	*Journal for the Study of the Old Testament*
JSOTSup	Journal for the Study of the Old Testament Supplement Series
JTS	*Journal of Theological Studies*
LHBOTS	Library of Hebrew Bible/Old Testament Studies
LNTS	Library of New Testament Studies
LPhThB	Linzer Philosophisch-Theologische Beiträge
LSAWS	Linguistic Studies in Ancient West Semitic
LXX	Septuagint
MT	Masoretic Text
NAC	New American Commentary
NAU	New American Standard Bible (1995)
NBf	*New Blackfriars*
NCBC	New Cambridge Bible Commentary
NICNT	New International Commentary on the New Testament
NICOT	New International Commentary on the Old Testament
NIDOTTE	*New International Dictionary of Old Testament Theology and Exegesis*, ed. Willem A. VanGemeren, 5 vols., Grand Rapids: Zondervan, 1997
NIGTC	New International Greek Testament Commentary
NIV	New International Version
NSBT	New Studies in Biblical Theology
NSKAT	Neuer Stuttgarter Kommentar, Altes Testament
NT	New Testament
NTM	New Testament Monographs
NTT	New Testament Theology
OBO	Orbis Biblicus et Orientalis
OIS	Oriental Institute Seminars

OLA	Orientalia Lovaniensia Analecta
Or	*Orientalia*
ORA	Orientalische Religionen in der Antike
OT	Old Testament
OTE	*Old Testament Essays*
OTL	Old Testament Library
OTT	Old Testament Theology
PRSt	*Perspectives in Religious Studies*
RB	*Revue Biblique*
ResQ	*Restoration Quarterly*
RevExp	*Review and Expositor*
RIMA	The Royal Inscriptions of Mesopotamia, Assyrian Periods
RINAP	Royal Inscriptions of the Neo-Assyrian Period
RINBE	Royal Inscriptions of the Neo-Babylonian Empire
SB	Sources Bibliques
SBLABS	Society of Biblical Literature Archaeology and Biblical Studies
SBLSymS	Society of Biblical Literature Symposium Series
SBS	Stuttgarter Bibelstudien
SHBC	Smyth & Helwys Bible Commentary
SJC	Studies in Jewish Civilization
SJOT	*Scandinavian Journal of the Old Testament*
SJSJ	Supplements to the Journal for the Study of Judaism
SNT	Studien zum Neuen Testament
SOTSMS	Society for Old Testament Studies Monograph Series
TBN	Themes in Biblical Narrative
TDOT	*Theological Dictionary of the Old Testament*, ed. G. J. Botterweck and H. Ringgren, tr. J. T. Willis et al., 16 vols., Grand Rapids: Eerdmans, 1974–2018
Them	*Themelios*
THOTC	Two Horizons Old Testament Commentary
ThTo	*Theology Today*
TOTC	Tyndale Old Testament Commentary
TrinJ NS	*Trinity Journal* (New Series)
TSTS	Toronto Semitic Texts and Studies
TynBul	*Tyndale Bulletin*
TZ	*Theologische Zeitschrift*

UF	*Ugarit Forschungen*
VT	*Vetus Testamentum*
VTSup	Supplements to Vetus Testamentum
WBC	Word Biblical Commentary
ZAW	*Zeitschrift für die alttestamentliche Wissenschaft*
ZDPV	*Zeitschrift des deutschen Palästina-Vereins*
ZECOT	Zondervan Exegetical Commentary on the Old Testament

1

The prophets, the nations and biblical theology

The prophets and the nations

The Old Testament prophetic books (Isaiah–Malachi, excluding Lamentations and Daniel) are not an easy corpus for the Bible's readers to navigate. There are many reasons for this: one might mistakenly think that their message was addressed only to the original audience (but cf. 1 Pet. 1:10–12), or find their many condemnations of Israel, Judah and the nations repetitive, or simply discover that they are not an easy form of literature for contemporary readers.[1] Whatever the reason, a number of considerations encourage all who value God's Word to make the effort necessary to understand these books as part of Christian Scripture. After all, the fifteen prophetic books make up nearly one-fifth of the entire canon,[2] so one can hardly justify passing them by. More importantly, whether one simply tallies up the relatively clear cases in which the New Testament quotes or alludes to the Old Testament, or probes deeper into the relation between the Old and New Testaments, it soon becomes clear that the prophetic books are deeply interwoven into the theology of the New Testament.[3] As a result, we need to understand the prophets in order to understand the New Testament, and vice versa.

---

[1] It is reassuring to read Luther's statement that anyone who reads the prophets will likely conclude 'that they observe no order but ramble along from one subject to another . . . It is indeed very irritating to read a book that observes no order, in which statements are so disconnected that they do not fit together and therefore lack proper coherence' (Luther 1974: 152). It is important to note, however, that Luther goes on to exhort readers to develop the necessary skills! Sandy (2002) is a valuable aid in this area.

[2] See <https://overviewbible.com/bible-length-infographic> (accessed 8 March 2024). The prophetic books total roughly 110,350 words in the original languages, while the Bible as a whole contains about 611,000 words in the original languages.

[3] For quotations and allusions, see the tables in B. Aland et al. 1994: 887–901. For more

The focus of this book: the nations in the prophets

This book is intended to lead readers through the prophetic corpus by exploring one of its most prominent themes, that of non-Israelites or foreigners ('Gentiles' in many New Testament texts). In the prophets, non-Israelites typically appear as groups, whether bearing a specific identity (for example, Cushites) or being referred to more generally as 'nations' or 'peoples'.[4] A glance at any prophetic book shows that the nations figure largely in this part of the canon even though its original intended audience was exclusively Israelite (whether in the northern or southern kingdom, or in exile). This sustained interest in non-Israelites may well strike us as odd: why do prophets who address only Israel and Judah, two nations in a unique covenant relationship with Yahweh, give so much attention to *foreign* nations who are not covenant partners with them?

Why do Israel's prophets talk about the nations?

A quick survey of some programmatic texts in earlier parts of the Old Testament will remind us that the nations are hardly an afterthought or a secondary interest of the biblical writers. On the contrary, the history of redemption begins long before the call of Abram in Genesis 12, and includes all of humanity in its scope even as it follows two lines of descent, Eve's and the serpent's (Gen. 3:15).[5] After passing through Seth (Gen. 5:1–32) and later Shem (Gen. 11:10–26), the line of promise does eventually issue in Terah's three sons, with Abram mentioned first (Gen. 11:26). Despite this selectivity, the calling of Abram itself puts remarkable emphasis on those outside his line, and Abram is blessed in order that God might bless 'all the families of the earth' through him (Gen. 12:3). The change of his name to Abraham, in view of his becoming the 'father of

---

synthetic treatments of the Old Testament in the New Testament, see the thematic study of Porter 2016 and the extensive analyses in Beale and Carson 2007.

[4] The few individual non-Israelites who appear in the Latter Prophets usually have a direct connection to an empire or nation whose ideology figures largely in their role (they are most often kings or their representatives), and are therefore presented in terms of that relationship (e.g. Sennacherib's spokesman in Isa. 36, or the Babylonian envoys in Isa. 39). This creates an interesting difference with the Former Prophets, which include a fair number of individuals without such ideological connections, such as Caleb, Shamgar and Achish; see Firth 2019.

[5] See Mathews 1996: 246–247.

a multitude of nations' (Gen. 17:5), makes this point in the most obvious way possible.

The same emphasis appears when God formally constitutes the nation of Israel under the Sinai covenant. Insofar as its people obey Yahweh, they will be a 'kingdom of priests' (Exod. 19:5–6). Since priests by definition facilitate or mediate access to God for others, Israel's role among the nations was to demonstrate by her actions (cf. Deut. 4:6) and convey by her words (frequently commanded in the Psalms) God's gracious character, beneficent will and sovereign rule over the world.[6] While the blessing element of Genesis 12:3 is prominent in the prophetic oracles concerning the nations, the curse that it threatens against those who curse or disdain Abram's line (and, indirectly, the God who has committed to blessing it) is no less prominent, and plays an important role in many of the prophets' condemnations of the nations.

What do the prophets say about the nations?

The prophetic books, the earliest of which were written in the eighth century BC, pick up this theme of Israel's calling to be a light to the nations, and their potential resistance to God's work through Israel, at a critical juncture.[7] In the biblical storyline, the nations are often aligned with the forces of opposition to God's purposes first seen in the devil's appearance in the serpent. Most clearly in Egypt's oppression, enslavement and genocidal campaign against the rapidly multiplying Israelites in the book of Exodus, and with increasing frequency in Judges–Kings, the Old Testament historical narrative demonstrates that non-Israelite groups become increasingly dangerous for the people of Israel, not least as a source of temptation to adapt their worship of Yahweh to pagan patterns or to abandon it altogether. The prophetic books give equal attention to another danger that the nations pose: that Israel and Judah would look to them rather than to God for safety amid the unpredictable geopolitical currents of the ancient Near East.

In addition to exemplifying condemnable religious practices and welcoming Israel's and Judah's misplaced trust on the political scene,

[6] Timmer 2011: 30–37. Note the commands to speak of Yahweh and his deeds to the nations in Pss 9:11; 18:49; 33:8; 46:10; 49:1; 57:10; 66:1–4; 67:1–7; 72:8, 11, 17; 83:18; 96:3, 10; 105:1; 108:3; 117:1; 119:46; 145:6, 12, 21.

[7] Robertson 2004: 195–196. Since the book of Daniel is not part of the Latter Prophets, it is not treated in this volume, but is ably explored in Hamilton 2014.

the nations also treat Israel and Judah as mere pawns in their own self-serving plans. This recurrent reality presented God's people with two very different problems: God seemed to overlook the violence, arrogance and idolatry of the nations, while the obvious power and success of these foreigners surely made many Israelites wonder if their gods were not, in fact, greater than Yahweh.[8] The oracles against the nations address both these concerns. First, in them God promises that his justice will see the surrounding peoples punished for their mistreatment of Israel and Judah in the near term. Oracles that announce judgment against these nations are emphatic affirmations that God is aware of their idolatrous and violent behaviour, that in his wisdom he uses them for his own purposes and that in due time they will be punished for their misdeeds.[9] Second, in doing so, Yahweh would also demonstrate his radical superiority over the pagan gods. Furthermore, the fact that Israel and Judah were privy to God's plans to judge the nations that persisted in opposition to him and his saving purposes for faithful Israelites encouraged God's people to wait patiently for him to deal with those groups. The eschatological fulfilment of the punishment of the 'nations' is presented in bold colours in Revelation, where Babylon represents not a single nation but 'the *systems* – political, economic and religious – which oppose God and his righteousness and are symbolized by the beast, the false prophet, Babylon and the kings of the earth'.[10]

Yet the nations' negative role with regard to Israel and Judah is not simply due to their greed, pride and disregard for Yahweh. The sins of both the northern and the southern kingdoms repeatedly obliged God to exercise corrective and eventually punitive action against them, and in such cases the surrounding peoples are the disciplinary instrument God most often uses (see Isa. 10:5–6). The aggressive posture of the nations during the divided monarchy is thus inseparable from the second dynamic that drives much of the prophets' preaching: an almost uninterrupted spiritual decline in Israel and Judah, leading to large-scale apostasy and the final covenantal punishment of exile. This penalty was imposed against both countries, with Assyria taking Israel into exile in 722 BC and Babylon deporting much of Judah's population in 586 BC.

---

[8] Ben Zvi 1993.

[9] Raabe 1995.

[10] Bauckham 1993: 102, emphasis original.

The writing prophets therefore arrive on the scene at a crucial moment in the history of redemption. They announce and explain exile, the fracture of the Sinai covenant, the interruption of the Davidic line (2 Sam. 7; cf. Pss 2; 45; 110), and the loss of the land promised to Abraham and of the presence of God in the Jerusalem temple. But alongside their explanation of the end of the theocracy and most of its trappings, they announce a radically new future in which God's people, purified and renewed, will enter a new covenant with him (Jer. 31) and will know divine blessing in unprecedented ways. The renewal of Israel, moreover, will involve radically transformed relationships with some non-Israelites, who, like renewed Israel, will turn to Yahweh. The near-term fulfilment of this aspect of the prophetic message is evident only in limited ways in the history of Israel prior to Christ's coming (see Ezra 6:19–21; Neh. 10:28–29), but its eschatological fulfilment bursts into view in the New Testament. Paul's use of Jeremiah 31:31–34 exemplifies the way in which the apostle to the Gentiles saw Israel's renewal in relation to the integration of non-Israelites into the renewed people of God,[11] as does his use of Isaiah 11:10–11 in Romans 15:12.[12]

Another way to view the contribution of the prophets to biblical theology is to contrast them with the 'Former Prophets' (Joshua–Kings, excluding Ruth). Both parts of the Old Testament take their fundamental orientation from God's plan to establish fully his kingdom, fulfilling not only his promises to Abraham, Israel and David but also his intentions for the cosmos as a whole, as sketched in Genesis 1 – 3. But although Israel's history as presented in the Former Prophets has an overall upward, progressive movement from Joshua to Solomon, what follows is largely the loss of these gains. The Davidic monarchy is interrupted, the land promised to Abraham is lost to invaders, and the people fall under the curses of the Sinai covenant. The last word of this section of the canon is rather gloomy, to say the least, and the only spark of hope is the hint that God's covenant with David and his descendants has not been forgotten (2 Kgs 25:27–30).[13]

[11] Shead 2000.

[12] Wagner 2002: 317–327.

[13] Although the Former Prophets end with Kings, the book of Chronicles, which was completed at least several decades later than Kings, concludes with Cyrus's command for as many exiled Judeans as so wish to return to Jerusalem to rebuild the temple (2 Chr. 36:22–23). Yet, as described by Ezra and Nehemiah, the following century and more were hardly the realization of the massive restoration predicted by the prophets.

While the prophets also recognize the grave state of affairs in Israel/Judah and regularly call their audience to repent, their inspired visions of the future take the reader beyond the dark cloud of exile. Their oracles develop and extend in many different ways the upward trajectory sketched by God's commitment to crush the serpent's head, to bless Abraham and through him the world, to deal fully with his people's sin, and to bring the entire creation under God's just and good rule through a descendant of David.[14]

What is biblical theology?

Definition, key assertions and methods

The points outlined in the previous section bring us full circle, and demonstrate that a solid grasp of the theme of foreigners in the Old Testament prophetic books is essential to their proper interpretation and to a robust understanding of how the nations-theme functions in both Testaments. For these and other reasons, what this book undertakes can be described as 'biblical theology'. Among the various sorts of biblical theology practised at present,[15] our 'redemptive-historical' approach assumes that God is the ultimate Author of all Scripture but reveals himself and accomplishes his plan to save his people and establish his kingdom gradually. The divine origin of Scripture means that it is essentially a unified whole, but one that develops over time and sometimes involves discontinuity. Its full meaning is clear only in the light of the whole canon.[16] We also recognize that Scripture is self-interpreting, meaning that as much as possible we take our interpretative cues, norms and methods from Scripture itself. Accepting that the canon is unified on its own terms, our goal is to understand how the significant diversity that we see in the prophets' treatment of foreign nations, and secondarily in the New Testament's reuse of that material, contributes to the rich, multicoloured fabric of biblical

[14] See the helpful image that captures these dynamics of redemptive history across the canon in Goldsworthy 2000: 109. Watts (2004) is an excellent example of such an approach focused on Isa. 40 – 55.

[15] Klink and Lockett (2012) helpfully analyse and summarize the differences between five versions of 'biblical theology'. Here I follow primarily their 'BT2', entitled 'History of Redemption'.

[16] Watson 1997: 181. The explanation of the canonical dimension of a text's meaning by Vanhoozer (2018) is particularly helpful.

revelation.[17] The emphasis on the historical nature of revelation and of the accomplishment of redemption means that we will trace this theme chronologically, giving attention to the historical contexts of the books that present it and to the various future contexts in which these prophecies situate foreigners. We will also endeavour to analyse the biblical text, and to present our findings, using terms and concepts that are native to the texts themselves rather than introducing categories or classifications that derive from other sources.[18]

Biblical theology and the nations

Finally, the fulfilment of the Old Testament as presented in the New Testament, where it is grounded in the saving work of the triune God revealed and realized in Jesus Christ, authorizes and even obliges us to set our findings in that context.[19] In order to do so, it is important to recognize that while the Old Testament material that deals with the foreign nations genuinely refers to states such as Moab, and empires such as Assyria, it *does not usually present those groups as simple political entities with homogeneous populations that are equally implicated in the sins for which the prophets condemn them.* Rather, the prophets' oracles of judgment in particular almost always focus on a small fraction of the nation's population that is defined, in those contexts, by its trust in false gods, its adherence to political–religious ideologies, and its sinful implementation of such ideologies.[20] Nahum, for example, essentially defines the Assyrian

[17] Vos (1980: 13–14) notably argued that the 'striking multiformity of teaching employed for the same purpose' leads to the conclusion that 'individual coloring . . . and a peculiar manner of representation are not only not detrimental to a full statement of the truth, but directly subservient to it'.

[18] Rosner 2000: 5–6.

[19] The approach sketched here is presented in detail by Goldsworthy (2006).

[20] I develop this approach in Timmer 2025. Weinfeld (1986: 171) suggests that such prophetic material be called 'prophecies concerning empires' in which empires are condemned because they all 'subdue nations, exploit them, and plunder them'. By (political) ideology I mean a network of ideas 'of a particular kind. Ideologies are ideas whose purpose is not epistemic, but political. Thus an ideology exists to confirm a certain political viewpoint, serve the interests of certain people, or to perform a functional role in relation to social, economic, political and legal institutions', as explained by Sypnowich (2019). In the ancient Near East, these ideologies involve interconnected beliefs about the origin of the cosmos, the gods, human beings, the king, and the nation's divinely mandated mission in the world (see chapter 2 of this volume). 'Imperialism' is thus shorthand for such ideologies and their implementation by an empire or a smaller, less organized state or political entity. The definition of ideology by Chan (2017: 150) is similar: 'the foundational and mythological claims that individuals or groups create and perpetuate about themselves, especially regarding their relationships to deity/deities, their status in the cosmos, and their purpose in the world'.

Empire as its king, elites, diplomats and soldiers, all of whom were committed to pursuing its project of world domination under the aegis of its gods. Accordingly, the fall of Assyria as predicted by Nahum did not involve the Medo-Babylonian forces killing the entire Assyrian population (in any case, until that point in time Babylon had been an Assyrian province), but rather destroying its military–political–religious apparatus and exposing the emptiness of its religious–political ideology.[21] The end result was in accord with what Nahum had prophesied: God demonstrating his absolute supremacy over the arrogant, God-dishonouring and ultimately impotent Assyrian monarch (Nah. 1:10–12), the various power structures he directed (2:11–14; 3:4, 12, 16, 17–19) and the gods he served (esp. 1:14) through the fall of Nineveh, a few other key cities and ultimately the whole empire to Babylon.

The prophets' presentation of foreign nations as religiously defined states that characteristically manifested a structured, intentional pursuit of their own power and glory with the help of their gods also helps us recognize *later* manifestations of such opposition to God, whether connected to a nation-state or not, as continuations of what those ancient Near Eastern polities embodied.[22] This understanding of the nations lies behind the use of 'Babylon' in Revelation, which builds on Isaiah's presentation of that empire as oppressive, violent and pompous, and of its king as self-deifying.[23] In Revelation, 'Babylon' continues to symbolize 'avaricious power, the evil influences of sin and idolatry, and all anti-God predilections',[24] making it a fitting symbol for Rome and its often violent religious–ideological opposition to God and his purposes.[25] The last

---

[21] The nearly exclusive focus on pitched battles between armies, to the exclusion of the general populace, is clear in Babylon's own records; see Grayson 2000: chronicle 3, and the OT-focused observations of Raabe (2018: 247). Hauser (2017: 229) notes that the 'conquest of the Assyrian cultic and political capitals Ashur and Nineveh in 614/612 . . . sent shock waves through the entire former Assyrian realm and far beyond'.

[22] Both modernism and postmodernism recapitulate this fundamental sin in various ways; Desmond (2013: 549–550) observes that modernism 'turns to the human being as its own measure of self-determination uncoupled from any mysterious God who cannot be quite univocally factored in any equation of immanent autonomy'. Harvey (2000: 5) observes of postmodernism that '[t]he absolute relativism and romantic nihilism that often characterize postmodernism as a cultural style should be viewed as inverted images of modern culture's arrogant longing for godlike powers'.

[23] See the exposition of Isa. 14 in Beuken 2007: 105–109.

[24] Arnold 2000: 394.

[25] See Beale 1999: 25. Bauckham (1993: 153) notes that this interpretative 'principle allows prophetic oracles to transcend their original reference, without supposing that somehow when Jeremiah [or Isaiah] referred to Babylon he really meant Rome'. K. J. Vanhoozer, building on

chapter of this volume explores a number of contemporary ideologies with an eye to critiquing them along the same lines as the prophets.

Tracing the nations through the prophets

Keeping in mind our commitment to understanding and interpreting the foreign nations in the prophetic books using categories and concepts that arise from the texts themselves, the following concepts and distinctions will be of help.

Concepts and distinctions

1. A remnant/part exists in opposition to the whole. Bipartite or multipart identities are possible for all groups, and may themselves change over time. Grammar often requires the reader to distinguish between 'nations' and 'all nations' (sometimes allowing for hyperbole in the latter case), while a 'remnant' is more precisely part of a larger whole.
2. Apart from explicit indications to the contrary, the way in which the prophets typically characterize non-Israelite nations makes it preferable to see behind those references an ideological, religious and military–political complex that vaunts itself and opposes God rather than a homogeneous, fixed population of ethnically or politically united citizens without theological significance. H. C. P. Kim explains this tendency in terms of a shift from 'concrete historical referents' to more abstract, universal referents that apply 'to different audiences across generations and geography'.[26]
3. To expand on the previous point, attention to characterization, that is, the way in which the text presents a person or group, is essential to good interpretation. Because a group's characterization is determined in and by individual contexts, it is possible that the same group, especially if divided into multiple parts or set in earlier and later situations, may be described in different ways. And indeed, the prophetic books sometimes present different characterizations of the same nation or 'the nations' as they trace the radical effects of God's

---

insights of Willem VanGemeren, offers a clear explanation of the shift in referent that is made possible by the progressively widening redemptive-historical frame of reference that later parts of the canon provide for earlier parts; see Vanhoozer 2018.

[26] Kim 2020: 71.

saving and judging work on the international scene (e.g. Isa. 19; Ezek. 29). This typically involves the modification of the group as initially described in terms of judgment (surviving or avoiding judgment instead of perishing under it), moral traits (poor, needy, revering Yahweh, submitted to Yahweh, etc., instead of wicked, sinful, proud, violent, etc.), cultic status and activities (purity, sabbath observance, serving as priests and so on instead of the contrary), and recognition of Yahweh's supremacy (subjugation, vassal-like submission, bringing gifts, and the like) rather than rejection of it and grasping at autonomy.[27]

4 Attention to characterization is especially important when it helps the reader see that a non-Israelite group shares with Israel/Judah or its remnant a characteristic that is so important that it establishes a fundamental religious unity between the two groups. Such a 'criterion of identity' can be formally defined as 'that which *x* must be to be *y*'.[28] These shared traits are especially significant because they show that the prophets often do more than simply affirm that good things will happen to the nations in the future. They not infrequently foretell that many among the nations will have in common with renewed Israel defining, positive spiritual traits whose importance far outweighs the ethnic, linguistic and other characteristics that distinguish them. In other words, criteria of identity allow the prophets to identify non-Israelites with eschatological Israel by means of key religious categories without effacing their distinct ethnic identity (see, e.g., Zech. 2:11–12; it is less common for non-Israelites to be explicitly integrated into Israel). Such texts are very potent predictions of the unity that characterizes the global Christian community (or should!), while they also make clear that whatever features distinguish one group of believers from another are of far lesser importance.[29]

Likewise, the following inductive categories will be useful as we classify the different ways, both negative and positive, in which the nations relate to Israel/Judah and to Yahweh.[30]

---

[27] Raabe (2018: 246) may overlook this when he suggests that 'an entire nation or city-state can be characterized in certain ways' in the oracles concerning the nations.

[28] Gibson 2001: 140.

[29] The use of criteria of identity in several prophetic passages is explored in Timmer 2021b.

[30] See the more detailed list in Schultz 2009: 123.

1 Most negatively, the nations assume divine prerogatives, dismiss Yahweh's exclusive claims to deity, violate his norms, treat his land and his people as they wish, or abuse other nations.
2 Less negatively (although the absence of condemnation is not equivalent to vindication), the nations are sometimes God's agent for punishing Judah or other nations.
3 In a neutral role, the nations are sometimes witnesses of God's work in the world, especially when God punishes or restores Israel/Judah.
4 Positively, the nations sometimes facilitate Israel's restoration, serve it as vassals or celebrate its renewal.
5 Most positively, the nations are identified with Yahweh's people either outright or by means of a criterion of identity such as election, worship of Yahweh, sharing in Israel's salvation, coming to Jerusalem, celebrating Israel's feasts, and so on.

A focus on individual books

A biblical-theological approach as defined above entails dealing with each book individually. This is enormously helpful given our goal of capturing the biblical material on its own terms. While it goes without saying that we will take up Isaiah, Jeremiah and Ezekiel as individual books, adopting this approach for the Minor Prophets requires some explanation in the light of the interest in the 'Book of the Twelve' that has arisen over the last few decades.[31] The approach most commonly practised in recent study of the Minor Prophets is indebted primarily to secular, historical-critical convictions.[32] These pre-interpretative commitments lead their practitioners to assume that the very modest level of unity they find in a biblical book, or between biblical books, arises primarily from post-authorial additions and redactions that themselves are unified. Thus a redactor who held dear the simple belief that God's grace was classically demonstrated at Sinai after Israel built and worshipped the gold calf (Exod. 34:6–7) is thought by some to have stitched together the otherwise quite unrelated and disharmonious books of the Twelve by means of a 'grace redaction'

[31] For a brief history of research, see Schart 2012. For more detail, see the related essays in Tiemeyer and Wöhrle 2020, the methodologically focused discussion of Ben Zvi and Nogalski (2009), and Timmer 2024d.

[32] I describe in more detail what I mean by 'historical-critical' methods and convictions in Timmer 2018, parts of which I adapt here.

that appears in Joel 2:12–14; Jonah 3:9; 4:2; Micah 7:18–20; Nahum 1:2b, 3a; and Malachi 1:9a.[33]

It bears repeating that the unity of the Minor Prophets on such views is limited either to redactions (which necessarily run contrary to the rest of the book in which they appear) or to very basic building blocks of Israelite faith that are common to all Old Testament books: monotheism, Israel's election, and the like. It is a serious shortcoming that these approaches typically exclude the possibility of a single divine Author inspiring various prophets and so producing a coherent collection of diverse books. It is also problematic that many interpreters are satisfied with a minimal level of unity that is overshadowed by the immense diversity that they claim to find in the theology of the various authors and redactors. On such views, the only source of unity for the Book of the Twelve as a whole would be history in the most abstract sense of the term. The various conflicting views on God, Israel, the nations, grace, human nature and so on that historical-critical readings typically find in the Book of the Twelve can all be tied to different situations at different points on the historical spectrum. Beyond that bare and almost meaningless baseline, the Twelve are a unity in name only.[34]

The approach taken here recognizes that the twelve Minor Prophets are all unique compositions, arising within particular circumstances and composed by different authors. Indeed, the superscriptions that appear as part of some of the minor prophets' books, internal evidence bearing on their dates of composition, and their distinct literary and theological profiles compel readers who accept the truthfulness of the text to recognize their historical, literary and theological diversity. Similarly, their varying perspectives on the same topic (e.g. Jonah and Nahum on Nineveh) and their selection of different subjects and emphases require substantial work on the part of the interpreter if he or she is to make sense of it all. But the reality of historically, literarily and theologically diverse books is precisely what biblical theology recognizes in the canon of Scripture. The task of preserving the canon's diversity while demonstrating the coherence of the whole is the task that biblical theology has set for itself, following the lead of Scripture. In the chapters that follow, therefore, each of the Minor Prophets will also be studied as an individual composition. Links between

[33] See Wöhrle 2008: 363–420.

[34] See in more detail Timmer 2020b.

adjoining books of the Twelve will receive neither more nor less attention than links with other prophetic books or with books elsewhere in the canon in the light of its ultimate unity.[35]

Chronological (diachronic) order

Because our commitment to a biblical-theological approach entails attention to chronological sequence, this study will attend to the chronological placement of the individual books. However, because our focus on individual books is more important than the correlation of the different messages of books situated or composed in the same historical period, and because the dates for Joel, Obadiah and Malachi cannot be determined with confidence, the books will not be treated in concert with their contemporaries. That being said, it is important to note that we can situate books such as Joel, Obadiah and Malachi redemptive-historically even when a precise date of composition eludes us.

The prophetic books range over roughly four centuries and follow Israel and Judah across an extremely turbulent period. Beginning with Hosea and Amos, who prophesied before the resurgence of Assyria in the Levant that began around 735 BC, the prophets accompanied God's people through the subsequent fall of the northern kingdom of Israel in 722, the eventual collapse of Assyrian power tied to the rise of Babylon in the late seventh century BC and the fall of Judah to Babylon shortly thereafter, and the Persian king's policy of granting permission to Judean exiles to return to their former homeland after his armies conquered Babylon in the second half of the sixth century BC. Through all these changes, the post-exilic prophets directed the people's hopes beyond the very limited restoration of the sixth and fifth centuries to something much greater.

The contemporary significance of the prophets' treatment of the nations

The prophets' teaching on the nations and foreigners is presented against the backdrop of humanity's fundamental unity as God's created

[35] James Nogalski was the first to propose a large-scale interpretation of the Book of the Twelve on the basis of catchwords that he sees linking the closing section of one book with the opening of the following book; see Nogalski 1993a; 1993b; and Ben Zvi's critique of his approach in Ben Zvi and Nogalski 2009. The effect of the different canonical order of the prophetic books in the Masoretic and Greek traditions on interpretation of the Twelve is explored by Sweeney (2012).

image-bearers. It also is fully cognizant of the universal penchant to sin from Genesis 3 onward that only divine transformation and reconciliation can remedy. This latter point highlights the necessity of situating the prophets' message in the context of the gospel, with which the prophetic books are inseparably united (1 Pet. 1:10–12).

As later chapters will show, the prophetic books address a wide range of issues that are of critical importance to the Christian church worldwide. The unity of the people of God not only makes racism and nationalism abominable but also calls every member of the body of Christ to manifest in his or her everyday interactions, choices and attitudes the profound unity that the Holy Spirit creates among believers. The prophets' frequent deconstruction of nations as organized expressions of self-sufficiency, autonomy and the pursuit of power and glory is both a comfort to persecuted Christians living under authoritarian control and a warning to Christians who put their hope in governments, legislation, terrestrial power or material clout to protect or advance the gospel (or worse, to promote pseudo-Christian causes or nationalism). The spiritual focus of the prophets' descriptions of the nations also prevents us from assuming that 'mission' is something that must be pursued outside one's own nation, for one's non-Christian neighbour is no less in the 'nations' category than an unbeliever on the other side of the globe.

The church, by its very nature, is not a political, national or military group, and its most aggressive opponents are not 'flesh and blood' (see John 18:36; Eph. 6:10–12), even though the powers of evil may well make use of various forms of earthly power. The prophets' rich and bold depictions of Yahweh's triumph over evil and the consummation of his saving work are thus sources of immense comfort and confidence for believers as they wage spiritual warfare in this life. The prophets' poetic and aesthetic beauty can help their words take root in our minds, while their truth defends us against the onslaught of day-to-day trials and false, God-defying ideologies and world views by reminding us of the end of the story and the perfect reliability of its Author.

It is perhaps only a slight oversimplification to say that the essence of the prophets' development of the theme of non-Israelites in relation to Israel is, for both those groups, a recasting of their *identity*. In both cases, the prophets insist that one's ultimate identity, then as now, is determined individually and primarily in relation to God. This cautions us against assuming that individuals are almost automatically Christian by virtue of baptism, church membership, or some other rite or status that is only superficial and external.

Finally, the consistently theocentric vision of the prophets makes their books a corrective against insipid views of God that domesticate his holiness, discount our absolute dependence on his grace, consider our abilities so highly that his almighty aid and blessing are unnecessary, or reduce sin to a mere pattern of behaviour that can be solved without his radical intervention.[36] God's grandeur and majesty call us to humble ourselves before him, while his amazing condescension makes him ready and willing to help those who begin to recognize how great he really is (Isa. 57:15). His power, wisdom and faithfulness invite us to trust his good plan and protection even when all might seem lost (Hab. 2:1; 3:17–19). Finally, his salvation, righteousness and grace, as consummately revealed in Jesus Christ, demonstrate that the pardon, righteousness and eternal life that he promises to his people are beyond reckoning, and call for our praise now and always (Isa. 12; 62; Jer. 33:1–9; Ezek. 37:24–28; Zeph. 3:17).

[36] Webster 2003: 79–84.

2
Ancient Near Eastern nations and their ideologies

A crucially important feature of prophetic oracles concerning the nations, whether they announce judgment or salvation, is that the nations are usually *not* presented as simple political entities with clearly defined borders, populations and political structures.[1] As noted in chapter 1, the majority of oracles against the nations focus only on *part* of the population of the nation being discussed (a sort of negative 'remnant') and on the *ideology* that the same segment of the population promotes and enacts. (By ideology I mean, in political contexts, a network of interconnected beliefs that are intended to legitimate and motivate participation in a state or empire and its self-assigned role or mission in the world.[2]) In a similar way, oracles of salvation typically focus on another part of the nation in question – essentially a remnant in the positive sense of the term – and describe its transformation and deliverance in terms of its rejection of the ideology which it formerly held and its unqualified acceptance of God's saving mercy and beneficent rule in its place. This chapter will explore the relation between the political ideologies of the empires that played a role in the history of Israel and Judah and the theological, moral and related dimensions of the prophetic oracles concerning them. Our survey of the ideologies of the Egyptian, Neo-Assyrian, Neo-Babylonian and Achaemenid Persian empires will focus on how each ideology was *presented* to the citizens of the respective empires and to the world at large, and how each empire *implemented* its ideology. Although smaller states such as Moab and Edom typically created fewer structures

[1] Throughout this volume I use the term 'nation' as roughly equivalent to 'state', but recognize the 'structural antagonism of state and local community that characterized most or perhaps all premodern states other than microstates' noted by Scheidel (2013: 8).

[2] See the fuller discussion of political ideology in chapter 1 of the present volume.

and texts that bear witness to their ideologies (and the vagaries of time have not preserved all that they did produce), prophetic descriptions of them perceive in their attitudes and actions similar hubris, violence and self-glorification, and they will be discussed in connection with particular oracles in the chapters that follow.

Egypt

Egypt had played a prominent role in the life of the people of Israel during the second millennium BC, but in the first millennium BC it was often rather divided and weak compared to the halcyon days of the New Kingdom period (c.1550–1070). Near the end of the tenth century, Shoshenq I (c.945–924) attempted to restore Egypt's presence in the Levant (note his raids in Palestine [1 Kgs 14:25–28]), but much of the 'kingdom gradually dissolved into a veritable mosaic of Libyan-dominated fiefdoms'.[3] After suffering several Assyrian invasions, Egypt was sporadically unified during the eighth and seventh centuries BC, and intervened more or less directly in Judean affairs a few times near the end of the seventh century. It sought to keep the Levant as a sort of buffer zone between itself and Babylon, and in one such case, in 616 BC, Egypt under Psamtik I supported Assyrian resistance to Babylonian presence in the middle Euphrates region. Less than a decade later, however, in 609, Necho II felt compelled to again resist Babylon's steady progress through the Levant. For reasons that are not clear, Josiah led a Judean attempt to repulse Egypt at this juncture, but failed and lost his life in the process. Necho replaced King Jehoahaz with Eliakim, changing his name to Jehoiakim and making Judah a vassal state of Egypt until Babylon took control of Judah in 605.[4] Following Babylon's failed attempt to invade Egypt in 601, Judah shifted its loyalty back to Egypt, only to be forced to submit to Babylon again in 597. Egypt tried unsuccessfully to form an alliance with Levantine states to resist further Babylonian aggression around the year 592 and opposed Babylon's campaign in Judah without success a few years later, but was eventually able to establish control over some of the eastern Mediterranean during the reign of Amasis (570–526).[5]

---

[3] Lloyd 2014: xlii–xliii, which I follow throughout this section.

[4] Redford 1992: 448–449.

[5] Perdu 2014: 146–148.

Egypt's independence came to an end when it fell to Persia in 525, immediately after the death of Amasis. It eventually regained its independence one last time from 404 to 343, but came under the control of Persia in 343, then of Greece in 332 and finally of Rome in 30 BC.[6]

This rather unimpressive chapter in Egypt's history contrasts sharply with the ideologies that many of its elite put forward as establishing the magnificence of Egypt and its rulers throughout most of its history. Regardless of the condition of the empire at a given point in time, these beliefs showed surprising consistency over millennia, and endured from Egypt's very beginning in the late fourth millennium BC until the fourth century BC.[7] Although there are significant differences between the four empires discussed in this chapter, their ideologies show remarkable consistency in establishing the empire's and the ruler's legitimacy and roles. This was done by appealing to a wide variety of foundational beliefs, including cosmogony (how the world and universe came to be), ontology (what exists), theology (the nature and roles of the gods), anthropology (the nature, value and role of human beings), ethics (what should be done, what is proper behaviour) and how the world can be made right (what might loosely be termed soteriology and eschatology, although in these contexts both concepts are geopolitical and do not involve the radical spiritual renewal of the individual that is at the heart of biblical soteriology and eschatology).

'Cosmogony', meaning the consideration of how the cosmos began, is a rather unusual term in much biblical interpretation due to Scripture's strong emphasis on God's free, monergistic creation, from nothing, of all that exists. And in point of fact, the concept of creation is very difficult to apply to the vast majority of ancient Near Eastern accounts of how the world came to be because of the prominence of pre-existent (that is, eternal) matter or stuff; both the gods and the world they *formed* consisted of such pre-existing material. Even the few apparent exceptions to this pattern, such as the Memphite Theology and the idea of 'creation' by Ptah's 'heart and tongue', connect the god(s) involved and what they produce to primal waters or the like.[8] Although John Walton and others are essentially correct that for ancient Egyptians '[m]aterial substance

---

[6] Lloyd 2014: xliii–xlv.

[7] While I often refer to these beliefs as comprising an ideology, these ideologies and the related beliefs were rooted in and expressed elements of what one might call a world view.

[8] Hasel and Hasel 2015; Allen 2003: 22.

had relatively little importance or relevance to their understanding of the world', this is because the existence of primordial material was taken for granted.[9] 'Creation' in these texts is thus more accurately defined as 'the process through which the One became the many', and ancient Egyptian cosmologies portray a world of which the gods are literally part.[10] A deity that exists within the immanent world that he or she *forms* makes impossible any clear distinction between creature and 'creator'. This scenario threatens to make the deity contingent, being acted upon, and acting within, a closed system of cause and effect – and thus not freely.[11] This point may seem arcane, but it explains why the goal of history in such paradigms remains immanent, with an ideal end point arrived at through material, personal or environmental changes that are produced by human effort or natural causes.[12] By the same token, the inherence of evil in the world-as-formed makes evil primordial.[13]

Despite the immanent framework in which Egyptian and most other ancient Near Eastern cosmogonies are set, the gods are clearly superior to human beings and wield significant power. Some of them are involved in the formation of the cosmos (actors and specifics vary among the many cosmogonies), while others are especially active in the world as it now is. Divine activity after the formation of the world focuses on the Egyptian king, who from the Old Kingdom period onward (c.2700–2150) bore royal titles that tied him to Horus, a god associated with the domination of foreigners even before the 'official unification' of Egypt. Moreover, the king was named 'The Son of Re-', with the royal name completing the hyphenated title.[14] Due to his involvement in the ordering of the cosmos, the solar deity Re is an archetype or role model for the pharaohs who embodied or represented him.[15] This is of great significance for Egyptian royal ideology:

[9] Walton 2018: 146, 148.

[10] Allen 1988: 57.

[11] Contrast monotheistic *ex nihilo* creation, in which '[e]verything that exists was brought into being by God; this was a free act of God's will, not an emanation from his being, and there was no preexisting material. Consequently, all that is not God is contingent, dependent upon him for its existence and continuation' (Letham 2019: 271).

[12] Bauckham 2007.

[13] Ricoeur 1967: 177.

[14] Leprohon 2006: 276. On Horus's significance for the pharaoh, see Morris 2014.

[15] Janák and Coppens 2017: 131.

> Since the pharaoh was the embodiment of the sun god, he was described as re-enacting these powerful cosmic moments [especially the battle of Re-as-Osiris versus Seth – DCT] in the historical sphere. Thus, just as Re repelled Apep, the pharaoh is said to repel *isfet* [chaos – DCT] from his borders by appearing as the god Atum himself, the form that Re takes at sunset.[16]

Other gods also played roles in the imperial project that they collectively conferred upon the king. Despite his Nubian origins, the foreign-born Piankhy (c.751–720) unhesitatingly identified himself in terms of the Egyptian pantheon:

> I the King, image of god,
> Living likeness of Atum! . . .
> The good god, beloved of gods,
> The son of Re, who acts with his arms,
> Piye [i.e. Piankhy – DCT] beloved-of-Amun[17]

Because the primordial battle against chaos has cosmic significance, the rule of the Egyptian kings who represent the gods was similarly not limited to Egypt. The global domain of the world-forming and world-governing gods of Egypt legitimated an imperial ideology that was to be extended as far as possible beyond Egypt's borders:

> According to the Egyptian worldview, the Pharaoh inherits 'everything [the] gods have created' at his coronation, and his purpose is to keep it in balance. The world itself is considered harmonious and the property of the Pharaoh . . . However, there was that part of the world outside Egypt, which was . . . ruled by chaos . . . As a result, one of the duties of the Pharaoh was to expand the territory of mAat [sic] as much as he could, essentially by expanding the borders of his country.[18]

The gods' close association with the pharaoh thus entailed a royal ideology that promoted the expansion of Egypt far beyond its current borders, a belief attested across much of ancient Egypt's history. In the Middle

[16] Noegel 2007: 23.

[17] Lichtheim 2003: 42. Used by kind permission of Brill.

[18] Xekelaki 2021: 3944.

Kingdom period (c.2040–1674), the Prophecy of Neferti ostensibly foretold that during the reign of Amenemhet I (c.1985–1956):

> The Asiatics will fall to his slaughter,
> The Libyans will fall to his flame,
> The rebels to his wrath, the traitors to his might.[19]

In the same spirit, a hymn to Sesostris III (c.1870–1831) associates him with Horus, 'extender of his borders', and describes the king as an international ruler (the terms 'Bowmen' and the 'Nine Bows' are shorthand for all foreign territories and persons[20]):

> Land's protector who widens its borders,
> Who smites foreign countries with his crown . . .
> [Who subdues foreign] lands by a motion of his hands.
> Who slays Bowmen without a blow of the club,
> Shoots the arrow without drawing the string.
> Whose terror strikes the Bowmen in their lands,
> Fear of whom smites the Nine Bows.[21]

During the New Kingdom period, Thutmose III (1481–1425) asserted that Re had enabled him to dominate all those outside Egypt's borders, with those populations being the pharaoh's rightful possession and witnessing to his unequalled power:

> There is no opponent of mine in the southern lands, northerners come bowing because of my awe. It was Re who ordained it concerning me, I having surrounded that which his eye has encircled. He gave to me the length and breadth of the land, I having bound together the Nine Bows, the islands in the midst of the sea, the Aegean and rebellious foreign lands[22]

---

[19] Shupak 2003: 109. Used by kind permission of Brill.

[20] Bestock 2018: 161.

[21] Lichtheim 2006: 198. Used with permission of University of California Press, from *Ancient Egyptian Literature, vol. 1: The Old and Middle Kingdoms* by M. Lichtheim, 2006; permission conveyed through Copyright Clearance Center, Inc.

[22] Hoffmeier 2003a: 15. Used by kind permission of Brill.

As the late fourth-millennium Narmer Pallet shows, violence was a necessary element of Egyptian ideology from the very beginning, symbolizing the 'pharaoh's Re-like victory over chaos' (see Fig. 1).[23]

A millennium later, an image from the Eleventh Dynasty (c.2040–1991) that reuses the classic image from the Narmer Pallet of the pharaoh about to strike a subdued foreigner with a mace is accompanied by the following inscription: 'subduing the chiefs of the Two Lands, reorganize Upper and Lower Egypt, the foreign lands, the two banks, the nine [bows], the towns'.[24] Royal violence could even be exercised against unruly populations within the empire,[25] and its perennial relevance is evident from the use of the scene from the Narmer Pallet in reliefs 'even when no true campaign, conquest, or military encounter had really taken place'.[26]

The royal–imperial ideology that motivated and legitimized ancient Egypt's military involvement and was conveyed to surrounding nations in diverse ways was arguably the primary factor that drove Egypt's extensive military undertakings on the international scene. Chosen and empowered by the gods, the pharaohs undertook concrete steps towards extending

Figure 1 **The Narmer Pallet (late fourth millennium BC) showing an example of the violence inherent in ancient Egyptian royal ideology**

[23] Noegel 2007: 23. The image, by Heagy1, is 'self-published work' on Wikimedia Commons, licence at <https://commons.wikimedia.org/wiki/File:Narmer_Palette_verso.jpg> (accessed 29 March 2024).

[24] Bestock 2018: 164.

[25] Ibid. 168–169.

[26] García 2021: 39.

Egyptian domination, piously recognizing the help of the gods as they did so.[27] The ideal world would see all Egypt's enemies submit to the pharaoh and contribute to the empire's well-being, which Piankhy sees as the outcome of his victories against foreigners in the Nile Delta: 'The west, the east, and the islands in the midst are on their bellies in fear of him, and are sending their goods to where his majesty is, like the subjects of the palace.'[28]

Notably, García's summary of Egyptian imperial ideology underlines a divergence between this elite–royal ideal and the realities of daily life for most non-Egyptians in and around the empire:

> Egyptian self-representation was that of *the* center of prosperity and cosmic order, in sharp contrast with the poverty, chaos, and danger prevailing abroad. Consequently, the cosmic mission of the pharaohs consisted in preserving and extending the realm of the *maʾat* (order) by destroying any menace or enemy. Foreign populations were thus required to recognize the authority of the pharaoh in order to survive, but their beliefs, ways of life, and social organization were usually respected in the absence of a true policy of 'Egyptianization.' In fact, while foreign populations were usually depicted in stereotyped, negative terms, beyond the restricted domain of artistic and literary conventions, foreigners could apparently easily integrate into Egyptian society and even rise to eminent positions.[29]

Finally, all this is not to imply that Egypt never pursued peace in other ways. Assmann notes, for example, that after the battle of Qadesh in 1274 Ramesses II 'eschewed further military exploits in favor of a policy of peace and rapprochement.'[30] Unsurprisingly, though, it was Egyptian imperial aggression, and especially the ideology, values and attitudes driving it, that drew the critical gaze of the Israelite prophets.

[27] David 2007: 72.

[28] Lichtheim 2003: 50. Naunton (2014: 124) notes the influx of Libyans in the western delta at this time.

[29] García 2021: 38.

[30] Assmann 2003: 270.

Neo-Assyria

Unlike Egypt, Neo-Assyria's imperial ambitions frequently affected Israel and Judah in concrete ways during the period of the divided monarchy in Israel and Judah. Shalmaneser III (858–824 BC) opposed a variety of Levantine kings, including Ahab, at the battle of Qarqar in 853, Judah became the vassal of Tiglath-Pileser III in exchange for his help in breaking up an Israelite–Aramean attempt to force Judah to join a coalition against Assyria in 733–732 (2 Kgs 16:7–10), and the northern kingdom of Israel was eventually conquered and absorbed into the Assyrian Empire in the closing decades of the eighth century BC. Assyria's prominent role in the history of Israel and Judah was driven by a potent and relatively well-known ideology, and Israelite prophets engaged with it directly. Here we will again note the ways in which Assyria's imperial and royal ideologies involve cosmogony, ontology, theology, anthropology, and a vision for how the world in its current imperfect condition can be set right, in order to understand the prophets' critical responses to them.

Like their Egyptian analogues, Mesopotamian cosmogonies begin with primordial matter from which the gods and the cosmos emerge or are formed, respectively.[31] In some cases this involves conflict between the gods, which, once resolved, produces a stable hierarchy among them and is followed by the formation of humankind.[32] Among the Mesopotamian examples of this literary genre, the Babylonian 'Epic of Creation' (*Enūma Elish*) was exceptionally influential.[33] Most likely composed in Babylon following the return of a captured cult statue of Marduk from Elam under Nebuchadnezzar I (1125–1104 BC), its cosmogony recounts the elevation of Marduk to the head of the Babylonian pantheon.[34] This elevation follows a battle between Marduk, a junior god, and Tiamat, the primordial ocean/goddess, who had mixed with the primordial fresh water/god, Apsu, to produce the first few generations of deities. The battle is sparked by a conflict between the older gods and the younger gods, whose noise

[31] Pongratz-Leisten 2012: 964.

[32] Andrew George summarizes the key elements of Mesopotamian cosmogonies as follows: 'watery chaos; heavens and earth; generation of many gods therein; separation of heavens and earth; release of sunlight; conflicts of the gods with one another; slaying of monster; creation of mankind; civilization through mediation of wisdom; Flood; postdiluvian age' (George 2016: 18, my translation).

[33] Foster 2012: 20.

[34] Millard 2000.

disturbs them. In response to Apsu's plan to kill the younger gods, the younger deity Ea uses magic to overcome and kill Apsu. Marduk's boisterous behaviour upsets the older gods a second time, and in response to their petition to bring them rest, Tiamat agrees to reduce the younger god 'into nothingness'. The younger gods implore Marduk to face her in battle and promise to recognize him as supreme if he emerges victorious. Once the battle is joined, Marduk kills and then dismembers Tiamat, ultimately forming various parts of the cosmos from her remains:

> He [Marduk] shot off the arrow, it broke open her [Tiamat's] belly,
> It cut to her innards, it pierced the heart.
> He subdued her and snuffed out her life,
> He flung down her carcass, he took his stand upon it . . .
> Then [Marduk] turned back to Tiamat whom he had captured.
> The Lord trampled upon the frame of Tiamat,
> With his merciless mace he crushed her skull.
> He cut open the arteries of her blood,
> He let the North Wind bear (it) away as glad tidings . . .
> He calmed down.
> Then the Lord was inspecting her carcass,
> That he might divide(?) the monstrous lump and fashion artful things.
> He split her in two, like a fish for drying,
> Half of her he set up and made as a cover, heaven.
> He stretched out the hide and assigned watchmen,
> And ordered them not to let her waters escape.[35]

The element of conflict in *Enūma Elish* is central to Marduk's role as the one who destroys evil and establishes cosmic order.[36] As a result of his victory, he is recognized as the king of the gods, who then build Babylon and its Esagil temple in his honour. The correspondence between the divine and human realms is such that the world-building motif of 'warfare, kingship, order'[37] presented in *Enūma Elish* provides the pattern for human kingship. However, because the older version of *Enūma Elish*

[35] Foster 2003: 398; I have added several verbal subjects or objects in brackets for clarity. Used by kind permission of Brill.

[36] Foster 2012: 20.

[37] Crouch 2009: 27.

was focused on Marduk and his rule in Babylon, long-standing tensions between Assyria and the province of Babylon that came to a head in Sennacherib's destruction of Babylon in 689 BC prompted a religious reform that involved a reworking of the myth. Sennacherib's scribes replaced 'Babylon' with 'Batlil', 'a ceremonial designation of the city of Assur, and the name of Marduk by that of the national deity Aššur', allowing Assyrian royal ideology to integrate the myth's 'doctrine of absolute rule' without reference to Babylon.[38] This brought the myth's message into line with Assyrian ideology from the late second millennium BC and gave it new relevance in the seventh century BC.

Central to the king's rule was the responsibility of enlarging the empire:

> From the Middle Assyrian period onward . . . the basic 'mission' of the Assyrian king is that of extending . . . the land under his domain: the king is constantly to advance the frontiers of his realm and to establish order, justice, and peace. Implicit in this mission is the distinction between an orderly and peaceful center . . . and a periphery that will be made like the center when the imperial frontiers extend to include it.[39]

This obligation to extend the empire's boundaries to the ends of the earth is explicit in an inscription of Tiglath-Pileser I (1114–1076):

> The god Aššur (and) the great gods who magnify my sovereignty, who granted as my lot power and strength, commanded me to extend the border of their land. They placed in my hands their mighty weapons, deluge in battle . . . I added territory to Assyria (and) people to its population. I extended the border of my land and ruled over all their lands.[40]

Another inscription of Tiglath-Pileser I integrates all of the elements noted so far with typical gusto, stressing the approbation and support of key deities:

[38] Frahm 2010: 8.

[39] Liverani 2017: 13.

[40] RIMA 2 #87.1, I 46–61, cited in Liverani 2017: 15.

> At that time, by the exalted might of Ashur, my lord, with the authoritative consent of Shamash, the warrior, with the support of the great gods by which I have just authority in the four quarters and have neither competitor in battle nor rival in combat, Ashur, my lord, commissioned me to march to the Nairi lands, whose distant kings on the Upper Sea coast in the west, have not known submission . . . I crossed the Euphrates. The king of . . . [twenty-three city-states are named – DCT] . . . advanced in order to wage warfare, battle and combat. I attacked them with the fury of my fierce weaponry. I brought about the slaughter of their troops like a deluge of Adad.[41]

In this text, the role of the gods in legitimating the imperial project and the sharp contrast between the empire's orderly, submissive core and the disorderly, uncontrolled periphery/Other are central. The element of violence that – on the monarch's reckoning – is justifiably exercised against those who are not Assyria's subjects is rather muted by comparison. Yet, in keeping with the tone of Marduk's complete destruction of Tiamat, other Assyrian royal inscriptions frequently indulge in graphic descriptions of violence against the king's enemies. In one such example, detailing eight of his military campaigns undertaken between 694 and 691,[42] Sennacherib recounts his actions in the battle of Ḫalulê, in which he opposed Babylonian and Elamite enemies:

> I slit their throats like sheep (and thus) cut off their precious lives like thread. Like a flood in full spate after a seasonal rainstorm, I made their blood flow over the broad earth. The swift thoroughbreds harnessed to my chariot plunged into the floods of their blood . . . The wheels of my war chariot, which lays criminals and villains low, were bathed in blood and gore. I filled the plain with the corpses of their warriors like grass. I cut off (their) lips and (thus) destroyed their pride. I cut off their heads like the *stems* of cucumbers in season.[43]

---

[41] Greenwood 2006: 157–158.

[42] Grayson and Novotny 2012: 167.

[43] Ibid. 183, emphasis original.

Similarly, as part of his conquest in 677 BC of the city-states of the kings Sanda-uarri and Abdi-Milkūti (the latter being king of Sidon) due to the danger their alliance posed to his 'lordship', Esarhaddon relates how he dealt with Sanda-uarri:

> I . . . besieged him, caught him like a bird . . . and cut off his head . . . To show the people the might of the god Aššur, my lord, I hung (the heads) around the necks of their nobles and I paraded them in the squares of Nineveh with singer(s) and lyre(s).[44]

As a final example, in the context of Ashurbanipal's campaigns against Egypt (667, 663 BC), Assyria punished the rebels in the most public and gruesome way imaginable: 'Their bodies they hung up on stakes. They flayed their skins and clad the city wall with (them).'[45]

Alongside this violence, more mundane goals were also pursued, including the acquisition, as spoils of war, of the material and human resources that the empire needed. Tiglath-Pileser III provides an extensive list of spoils taken from various rulers:

> From Rezin [...] x talents of gold, 300 talents of silver, 200 talents of [...], 20 talents of ladanum, 300 . . . 30 [...] . . . Kuštašpi . . . iron, elephant hides, elephant tusks (ivory), red-purple wool, [...] . . . multi-colored garments, linen garments – numerous clothes of their lands, [...] weapons, spindle(s) . . .[46]

A few decades later, Esarhaddon recounts that in the course of tearing down an armoury in Nineveh to make space for a larger one, he used forced labour: 'I made the people of the lands plundered by my bow take up hoe (and) basket, and they made bricks.' Revealingly, the rest of the section continues in the first person: 'I razed that small place . . . I laid its foundations with limestone . . . and raised the terrace.'[47] In a related text, Esarhaddon makes a similar statement after a successful campaign to suppress rebellious kings on the Mediterranean coast, capped off with the

[44] Leichty 2011: 17.

[45] Melville 2006: 364.

[46] Younger 2003: 284–285.

[47] Leichty 2011: 23.

destruction of Sidon: 'I gathered the kings of Ḫatti (Syria-Palestine) and the seacoast, all of them, and had (them) build a city in another place.'[48]

Finally, passages that laud the king as rightful ruler of the world are very common, appearing as part of the introduction to nearly every royal annal. That of Tukulti-Ninurta is typical:

> I am Tukulti-Ninurta, king of the world, the mighty king, king of the land of Assyria, king of the land of Sumer and Akkad, king of the four quarters, chosen by the gods Ashur and Shamash, reverent prince, the king who is the favorite of the god Enlil . . . the one who in his fierce heroism subdued princes and all kings . . . the one who established his names over the four quarters in victory . . . the one who has encircled all quarters with his mighty power, . . . the one who has received tribute from lands east and west.[49]

In summary, Neo-Assyrian royal ideology held that the king, as 'the "perfect image" of Assur', was designated and empowered to expand Assyria's borders and so establish a form of dominion on earth that reflected Ashur's dominion in the sphere of the gods.[50] States that could not be coaxed into harmonious relations were subjugated by violence, and such violence was morally justified as the expression of the gods' will while also serving to control or eliminate chaos. These claims of global dominion, the theology that lay behind them, and the violence and exploitation to which they led meant that Yahweh's critique of them, expressed through Israel's prophets, was inevitable.

Neo-Babylonia

Babylon had a long and proud history, beginning as a city in the third millennium BC, then slowly developing into the empire that Hammurabi ruled in the eighteenth century BC.[51] After several hundred years under foreign control, Babylon had its sovereignty restored by Nebuchadnezzar I (1125–1104). Around this time, the elevation of Marduk to which *Enūma*

---

[48] Ibid. 48.

[49] Morgan 2006: 155.

[50] Noegel 2007: 21.

[51] Dalley 2021: 60. In this paragraph I draw on the discussion of Babylon's history in Timmer 2024f: 118–121.

Elish bears witness gave rise to a royal ideology in which Marduk and Babylon, his city, were 'at the center of a world empire'.[52] But just as this ideology took form, Babylon's star waned under pressure from Assyria and 'successive waves of Aramean immigration' from the west.[53] Over the next few centuries, Babylon existed in the shadow of Assyria and occasionally suffered at the hands of invaders before it regained enough stability and strength to repeatedly seek independence from Assyrian control.[54] This tension eventually drove Sennacherib to destroy the city of Babylon in 689 BC, only to have Esarhaddon rebuild it shortly thereafter. In the final chapter of this saga, a sustained rebellion by Babylon (652–648) failed to bring about its immediate independence, but managed to weaken Assyria permanently. By the year 625, the Babylonian king Nabopolassar claimed independence for Babylonia, and his son Nebuchadnezzar II (604–562) had put the empire on a solid footing by the end of the seventh century.

Neo-Babylonian kings, particularly in their inscriptions and building projects, bore eloquent witness to an imperial ideology that grew out of *Enūma Elish* and assumed a form very similar to that seen in Neo-Assyria. Of course, this unmodified version preserved Marduk as the dominant deity and Babylon as his chosen residence. Marduk's restoration of moral order by killing Tiamat and her co-conspirator Kingu,[55] like his establishment of cosmic order by setting in place the sky, stars and moon, and creating human beings as slaves so that the gods might rest, traces the main lines of the dynamic of 'warfare, kingship, order'[56] that guided Babylonian monarchs. In addition to setting the example for the king by their actions, the gods supported and participated in his military campaigns as the most direct means by which to establish on earth an order that mirrored the divine realm, such that 'all battles are cosmic battles'.[57] For example, in one of his inscriptions, Nabopolassar asserts his identity as 'the king of justice' by stating:

[52] Arnold 2004: 83.

[53] Vanderhooft 2016: 122.

[54] Arnold 2004: 90.

[55] Tiamat's plans to do away with some of the other gods make her an 'evildoer' and prompt Anshar, another primordial god, to recruit Marduk to fight her; Kingu is 'guilty' of unjustified 'war' according to Foster (2003: 393, 400).

[56] Crouch 2009: 27.

[57] Noegel 2007: 21.

> [Marduk] called me to the lordship over the country and the people . . . He let (me) succeed in everything I undertook. He caused Nergal, the strongest among the gods, to march at my side; he slew my foes, felled my enemies.[58]

This excerpt summarizes a good deal of Babylonian imperial ideology: the divine vocation of the king to rule over Babylon and subdue enemies outside it; the gods' empowerment of the imperial mission; and the violence that was the primary means for establishing order and enlarging the empire. Similarly, after an introduction that details his piety, Neriglassar (561–560) states: 'Marduk . . . declared (my) gracious name to be king in the land . . . he gave me a just scepter that widens the land . . . let my hands grasp a staff that subdues enemies'.[59] Validated and graced with divine power on the battlefield, Neriglassar recounts how he fulfilled his role as the servant of the gods of Babylon: 'I killed foes, slaughtered enemies, (and) suppressed all of the unsubmissive. I constantly established justice in the land (and) peacefully shepherded my widespread people.'[60]

Both of these kings speak with relative restraint compared to Nebuchadnezzar, who evidently 'paid greater attention to propagandistic communication of Babylon's rule as a preeminent power than Nabopolassar did'.[61] Consequently, Nebuchadnezzar's inscriptions bring Neo-Babylonian imperial ideology to its most forceful expression. An inscription that recounts some of his most impressive building projects and their significance for the gods begins thus:

> I am Nabû-kudur-uṣur (II), king of Babylon; the pious prince, the favorite of Marduk . . . When Marduk, the great lord, elevated me to kingship and entrusted me with the rulership of all these peoples, Nabû, who cares for all of heaven and earth, caused me to take hold of a just scepter to lead the people aright.[62]

The text is more explicit than usual regarding the divine accompaniment of the king on his military campaigns:

---

[58] Beaulieu 2003: 307.

[59] Weiershäuser and Novotny 2020: 37.

[60] Ibid.

[61] Vanderhooft 1999: 34.

[62] Wallenfels 2008: 289–290.

> Upon his [Marduk's] august trust, he repeatedly escorted me in remote lands, distant mountains . . . and I slew the unsubmissive. I captured the enemy, I put right the land and I made the people flourish; the evil one and the wicked one I drove away from the people. Precious silver (and) gold, choice stone, copper . . . everything precious, golden fruit, the produce of the mountains . . . a heavy tribute, lavish presents, I had brought before him in my city Babylon, and I have taken care of E-sagil, the palace of his beloved lordship.[63]

The contrast between those who submit and give 'heavy tribute' to the empire and those who are 'evil' and 'wicked' reveals the binary perspective in which this ideology understood the empire's mission. Either one submits and provides whatever material or human resources are required, or one suffers violent punishment as an enemy of the empire and its gods. Claims that the Babylonian monarch's rule over the world was beneficent – '(As for) the widespread peoples whom Marduk, my lord, gave into my hand . . . I continually strove for their welfare . . . I assembled all the people for their good'[64] – are thus relevant (if not convincing) only for those who recognize the empire's absolute supremacy and submit themselves and their possessions to its will.

The empire's expansion and establishment of order point to its ultimate goal. With the cosmogony of *Enūma Elish* in the background, the world has been established by Marduk for his glory, and human beings exist to serve the gods (those who refuse to serve Babylon and its gods should be done away with, as was Tiamat). The empire as the earthly reflection of Marduk's irresistible rule should bring all peoples under its dominion, and is to be sustained by the necessary material and human resources, which are to be taken by force from those the empire conquers. If all this is done consistently, one can hope that the entire world will soon reach quasi-perfection, in keeping with Nebuchadnezzar's prayer:

> O compassionate Marduk, may I enjoy the splendor of the palace I built: within it, may I become old, may I attain very old age; may I

[63] Ibid. 290.

[64] Vanderhooft 1999: 42.

> receive therein from the kings of the entire world the heavy tribute of all people . . . may there be no enemy of mine . . . (and) therein may my descendants rule mankind forever![65]

The book of Daniel presents a vision of Babylon which corresponds very closely to this world view, and the earlier prophets are clearly familiar with it as well. Needless to say, Babylon's imperial ideology stands in direct opposition to Yahweh's claim to be the world's only creator, judge and reconciler. The largely negative attention that the prophets give to Babylon, including their foretelling of its fall, which came about in 539 BC, reveals the importance of critiquing such beliefs in the light of Yahweh's unique deity and ability to reconcile human beings with him and with one another.

Achaemenid Persia

Apart from rare mentions in pre-exilic prophecy (Isa. 44:28; 45:1), the Persian Empire enters the biblical storyline rather late, during the Babylonian exile. Unlike Egypt, Assyria and Babylon, Persia enjoys a comparatively positive presentation in Scripture, orchestrating the return of many Judean exiles to their former homeland (Ezra 1) and ultimately funding the reconstruction of the Jerusalem temple there. This at least superficially conciliatory posture was itself part of Persia's imperial strategy, which seems to have been calculated to present the empire as pacific and beneficent whenever possible. In the same vein, Persia never developed a society-wide ideology that 'might have replaced regionally or locally constructed solidarities', and was 'able to make cultural diversity serve the needs of imperial unity'.[66] All the same, its royal ideology was no less developed than that of Egypt, Assyria or Babylon.[67]

Like the other empires discussed here, Persia set its ideology in the context of cosmogony: some 70% of extant Achaemenid inscriptions more than two paragraphs in length begin 'with an account of the world's

[65] Wallenfels 2008: 293.

[66] Wiesehöfer 2009: 86.

[67] Lincoln 2013.

creation'.[68] These abbreviated, formalized mini-narratives identify the deity ('A great god is the Wise Lord') and four or five of his creative acts: 'who created this earth, who created that sky, who created people, who created all abundance for people, who made Darius king'.[69]

As noted earlier, the term 'create' here is not an exact parallel for the biblical concept.

> The idea that the spiritual creations descend from Ahura Mazdā and thus consist of the very stuff from which the god is made, is of the utmost importance for Zoroastrian cosmology. For it is these spiritual beings . . . that ultimately give rise to the material world . . . Via the spiritual beings, the material thus also derives from Ahura Mazdā . . . Zoroastrianism therefore entails the concept of *creatio ex deo*.[70]

Ahura-Mazda, however, is clearly supreme among the gods, and 'all worship, both ritual and devotional, is focused on him, albeit on occasion indirectly'.[71] His prominence presumably explains the relatively high degree of unity that characterized the cosmos at the beginning. As Bruce Lincoln explains, Persian sources affirm that '[d]iversity . . . enters only at a later stage of cosmic history, when the demonic force the Achaemenians referred to as "the Lie" . . . assaulted the world and caused its fragmentation'.[72]

Persian royal ideology promoted the idea that the world apart from Persian hegemony was disordered and chaotic by advancing negative accounts of how other states or empires had (mis)treated their citizens before Persia came to their rescue. In the Cyrus Cylinder, for example, Cyrus affirms that by conquering Babylonia he had delivered its populace from the reign of an 'incompetent person' who had angered the gods by interrupting temple rites and attempting to end 'the worship of Marduk'.[73] Cyrus then establishes himself within the Neo-Babylonian world view by recounting that Marduk, Babylon's god, 'surveyed and looked throughout

[68] Lincoln 2008: 223.

[69] Drawing on one example in ibid. 224–225.

[70] Hintze 2014: 243–244.

[71] Ibid. 227.

[72] Lincoln 2008: 224.

[73] Cogan 2003: 315.

all the lands, searching for a righteous king whom he would support. He called out his name: Cyrus, king of Anshan; he pronounced his name to be king over all (the world).'[74]

Since, according to this view, the Lie has divided humanity 'into multiple groups, each of which produces its own leaders' who pursue their own purposes and bring about violence, war and suffering, the Lie's destructive work can be undone only if 'the many' peoples are 'encompassed by the one, as all other kings (and all other peoples)' submit to 'the leadership of God's chosen: the Achaemenian monarch'.[75] It was precisely with the goal of vanquishing such manifestations of the Lie and restoring global unity that Ahura-Mazda granted supremacy to the Persian monarch: 'Darius the king proclaims: Auramazda, when he saw this earth in commotion, thereafter bestowed it [i.e. kingship – DCT] upon me, made me king; I am king.'[76] This ideology was affirmed at the investiture of the Persian king, who 'received a divine sanction from the god Auramazda, to whom the king offered a sacrifice and celebrated with a banquet'.[77] In the light of their purportedly magnificent accomplishments, as promulgated by inscriptions and reliefs, Darius and his successors were the only ones able to achieve 'the restoration of primordial happiness and the accomplishment of God's will for humanity'.[78] Once humanity's unity was restored by the integration of these disparate states and nations into the Persian Empire, perfect peace would ensue:

> At that moment, the state of wholeness, totality, and 'happiness for mankind' that the Wise Lord made the crown of his original creation will have been restored, at least in the imperial center . . . Later, as surplus of all goods accumulates at the center, this can be returned to the peripheries. At that point, the entire state becomes happy, prosperous, peaceful, and whole once again, as history ends and a state of eschatological perfection opens into eternity.[79]

---

[74] Ibid.

[75] Lincoln 2008: 226.

[76] Kuhrt 2007: 503 (from the inscription of Darius at Naqsh-i Rustam A).

[77] Brosius 2023: 983.

[78] Lincoln 2008: 229.

[79] Ibid. 233.

To reinforce the self-evident wisdom of participating submissively in the Persian Empire's mission, many of the reliefs that adorned massive royal structures

> reminded the royal subjects of the rulers' extraordinary qualities and achievements, as well as their duty of loyalty to these kings. Second, both the inscriptions and the palace and tomb reliefs emphasize the royal idea of the *pax Achaemenidica*, that is, the god-given and universal state of peace that was guaranteed by the kings and desired by their subjects. Opposition to this arrangement, in terms of the Great Kings' announcements, would have seemed nothing short of irresponsible.[80]

The bas-relief from the tomb of Darius at Naqsh-i Rustam eloquently portrays this ideal status quo (see Fig. 2).[81]

Figure 2 **Bas-relief from the tomb of Darius depicting the universal state of peace prevailing under Achaemenid rule**

[80] Wiesehöfer 2009: 67.

[81] Adapted from Kohler 1879, 'posted publicly for all uses as a work in the public domain' at <www.flickr.com/photos/psulibscollections/5833058665> (accessed 29 March 2024).

Amélie Kuhrt's explanation of the image reveals how well it depicts the key features of Persian imperial ideology:

> The king stands on a stepped podium with a bow resting on the tip of his foot . . . He raises his hand in a gesture of salutation to a divine figure who hovers above a winged disc. The god faces the king and raises one hand in an identical gesture of greeting; with his other hand he holds out a ring, an old symbol of kingly power . . . The podium and the fire altar are set on a kind of throne; its struts are supported by representatives of the different subject-peoples, all carefully differentiated by their clothing and labeled; the viewer is exhorted to look at them in order to be awed by the Persian achievement. Wars have been fought by Persians at the distant boundaries of the earth, and, with Ahuramazda's help, have delivered the people here depicted into the Persian king's hand. Although they retain their individual character, they are now united in service to the king, whose mastery they uphold and whose law they obey.[82]

Although this pacific perspective is attested in many Persian sources, it is not the whole picture. Despite the peaceful face of the Persian Empire and its calculated strategy of avoiding violence when other means were more expedient, it was nonetheless established by violence and maintained by threats of the same. Persia burst on to the scene of history by military conquest when 'the petty king Cyrus of Anshan/Fars in southwestern Iran and his son Cambyses conquered the mighty Medes and the empires of Lydia, Babylonia, and Egypt'.[83] A cylinder seal from Cyrus's royal complex at Persepolis depicts him (apparently early in his rise to power) hurling a spear at unidentified enemies, two of whom lie fallen under his horse while a third has already been transpierced by another spear.[84] A lack of sources makes it impossible to trace in detail the events that led to Cyrus's conquest of Babylon in 539 BC. The little that we know involves Cyrus's victory at Opis, 'the subsequent massacre of the Babylonian soldiers, and the conquest of Sippar', after which the Persian commander Ugbaru was welcomed without resistance by Babylon's population and the last

[82] Kuhrt 2001: 105.

[83] Wiesehöfer 2009: 66. Cyrus's conquest of the Medes is described in Nabonidus's Sippar Cylinder.

[84] Waters 2023: 391.

Babylonian king, Nabonidus, was captured.[85] The Nabonidus Chronicle gives a rare official account of imperial violence, although it is unclear whether it is a Babylonian or Persian account:[86] 'In the month Tashritu (27th September–26th October) when Cyrus did battle at Opis on the [bank of] the Tigris against the army of Akkad, the people of Akkad retreated. He carried off the plunder (and) slaughtered the people.'[87]

The maintenance of the empire in the face of occasional revolts, like its ongoing expansion, was also accomplished by violence. Cambyses (530–522) conquered Egypt in 525 BC, and Darius (522–486) suppressed a significant number of revolts across the empire several decades later.[88] The Behistun relief depicts the nine rulers who spearheaded these revolts, notably associating each of them with the Lie that subverts legitimate order and unity by stating of each: 'This is [name], who lied.'[89] While in some cases Darius instructed those responsible for bringing new areas under control to show restraint – for example on the Greek island of Samos they were ordered '[n]ot to kill or capture any Samian, but to hand the island over . . . intact'[90] – in other situations he called for his troops 'to take men and women captive.'[91] According to Herodotus, the Ionians conquered by Persia revolted under Darius, only to be violently subdued and 'reduced . . . to slavery' yet again.[92] In the decades after Darius, the subsequent history of the Persian Empire continues the oscillation between expansion, revolt and attempts to regain control.

In the main, Persian imperial ideology differs at only a few points from the pattern we have traced thus far. Its emphasis on the originally perfect world formed *ex deo*, its desire to depict political (but not cultural) unity as an ideal and the absence of a clear primordial conflict between the gods distinguish it somewhat from the ideologies of Egypt, Neo-Assyria

[85] Wiesehöfer 2009: 70. Cyrus's peaceful entry into Babylon is described in detail in the Cyrus Cylinder.

[86] Waters 2023: 395–396.

[87] Kuhrt 2007: 51, citing the Nabonidus Chronicle iii.12–14. Lincoln (2013) discusses the extraordinarily gruesome (but also exceptional) punishment allotted to (or postulated of) two soldiers who disputed Cyrus's claim that he had killed the human instantiation of the Lie, thus undermining the king's *primary* task.

[88] Briant 2002: 114–119.

[89] See ibid. 125.

[90] Ibid. 140.

[91] Ibid. 143, citing Ctesias, *Persica*, §§16–17.

[92] *Histories* 6.62, cited in Briant 2002: 156.

and Neo-Babylonia. Yet the essence of Persia's imperial ideology closely resembles the others surveyed here: a primary deity chooses and equips the king to subdue the forces of chaos by violence in order to restore order and justice and to glorify the god(s) who make the imperial mission possible. As is typically the case, justice and order are defined by the empire rather than by those it seeks to integrate so as to serve its purposes, including the exploitation of material and human resources and the glory of the king.[93]

The post-exilic prophets seem to recognize that Persian ideology was somewhat less prominent and, more importantly, that Persia treated Jews quite well, even supporting the rebuilding of the Jerusalem temple. Ezra 1 interprets Cyrus's decree to that effect as the fulfilment of Jeremiah's promise of return from exile, and Ezra–Nehemiah generally presents the Persian kings in a positive light. Yet Malachi, writing during the Persian period, subtly relativizes Persia's claim to global dominion with repeated assertions that the name of Yahweh, the 'great King', will be 'great among the nations, and in every place incense will be offered to [his] name, and a pure offering' (1:11; similarly, 1:14).

The complex nature of the empires around Israel/Judah is especially evident in the case of Persia, but nearly every foreign state that is not simply mentioned in passing by the prophets is characterized in similarly complex ways that repay careful attention, as our exploration of the prophetic books will show. The prophets' rejection of these ideologies and condemnation of those who hold them is fundamentally a theological argument. Rather than the uncreated cosmos being managed 'from the inside', as it were, by immanent gods and their human representatives, the cosmos was created *ex nihilo* by the God of Israel so that human beings made in his image might enjoy life, blessing and happiness in communion with him. This supra-ethnic world view accounts for the prophets' focus on internal transformation, a process that sees sinful Israelites and non-Israelites alike turn to a transcendent deity who is uniquely able to change human hearts and sovereignly bring all of creation to the goal he has set for it. Warfare is not the means for extending God's rule, nor does God inevitably accompany the king every time he goes to war. Perhaps most strikingly, the prophets foresee that the nations will come to Jerusalem

[93] Yamauchi (1996: 274) notes that immense quantities of gold gathered through taxes and tribute were taken by Alexander the Great at Susa and elsewhere.

not as slaves or conscripts, but as worshippers of Yahweh who – given the priority of that relationship over every other – are essentially one with his people. This vision, finally, is realized in a world in which evil is not inherent, and which can therefore be made a suitable place for God to live in perfect fellowship with his redeemed and reconciled people.

3
Isaiah

Isaiah includes an extensive series of oracles against foreign nations in Isaiah 13 – 23, but the theme of the nations is present throughout the rest of the book as well. In Isaiah's prophecies (and also in the few narrative sections), the histories and destinies of Israel and the nations are intertwined to an unprecedented degree, yielding a perspective that is immense in scope and unsurpassed in beauty.[1] The nations-theme in Isaiah is especially noteworthy for its attention to non-Israelite groups in relation to God's acts in history, reflected in the different sections of the present chapter. As we will see, Isaiah often uses the juxtaposition of judgment *and* salvation for the same nation to demonstrate the rich complexity of God's plans for his people, and offers – with evident delight – a kaleidoscope of perspectives on the mission of Israel and its eschatological Servant to bring salvation to the nations. Although it is sometimes difficult to distinguish the multiple horizons often present in these oracles and their fulfilment,[2] this chapter's survey of the theme will show that its significant diversity does not militate against the coherence of the theme or of the book as a whole, but rather demonstrates the rich unity of both.[3]

The nations as the object of Israel's misplaced trust

Israel's and Judah's habitual dependence on foreign powers for security

[1] Oswalt 2006: 41.

[2] Schultz 2005: 338.

[3] Although multiple-author redactional approaches to Isaiah are still quite common, a significant fraction of contemporary Isaiah scholarship presents a variety of challenges to the long-standing division of the book into three or more parts. On Isa. 40 – 66, see Tiemeyer and Barstad 2014; on the book as a whole, see Rossi, Irudayaraj and Hens-Piazza 2023; Block and Schultz 2015. For a collection of generally historical-critical approaches, see Stromberg and Hibbard 2021.

serves as an ironic preface to the nations' adversarial role, discussed in the next section. Although this tendency receives greater attention later in the book of Isaiah, in historical terms it often precedes the nations' aggression against God's people and is a prominent feature of their infidelity to him and his covenant, especially when faced with an external threat.[4] For example, when faced with the threat by Aram (Syria) and Israel to join their anti-Assyrian coalition or face invasion, King Ahaz of Judah prefers to ask Assyria for help rather than to trust Yahweh's promises (Isa. 7). The outcome of this unwise decision is that Judah becomes Assyria's vassal, and Ahaz gives at least lip service to the supremacy of Assyria's gods in contracting such an arrangement. Later in the book, King Hezekiah fares better in the face of direct Assyrian aggression (chs. 36 – 37), and his trust in Yahweh is vindicated when God decimates the Assyrian forces outside Jerusalem. But at another point in time Hezekiah shows that he is all too ready to impress a Babylonian delegation in the hopes of making Babylon a potential ally against Assyria.[5] The irony that is generally evident in Judah's deleterious relations with the nations is presaged here as well, since Babylon eventually becomes not a potential ally against Assyria but the very entity that will destroy Jerusalem and bring an end to the kingdom of Judah.

The dependence of Judah's leaders on other nations brings consequences that are painfully evident in the nations' exploitation of them, but this misplaced trust also poses a far greater danger: Judah's lack of faith distances it from Yahweh, the only source of genuine security and well-being. This covenantal breach is clear in the opening lines of the description of the Day of Yahweh in Isaiah 2:6–22, where Judah's dependence on foreign alliances is inseparable from divination and other efforts to discern the future apart from Yahweh and his revelation through his prophets (2:6–7). The danger of this turning away from Yahweh also explains, in part, the oracles against the nations in chapters 13 – 23, which demonstrate that 'Zion's security is to be found not in foreign alliances, but in reliance upon Yahweh'.[6] In his only attested sign-act, Isaiah's three years of walking 'naked and barefoot' as a portent of the imminent fall of Egypt and Cush to Assyria also demonstrated the futility of trusting in

[4] Schultz 2005: 339.

[5] So Oswalt 1986: 694–695; Wildberger 1997: 472–473, 474–475; Beuken 2010: 452–453. Childs (2001: 286) is more sceptical of a political dimension here.

[6] Webb 1990: 71; similarly, Oswalt 2006: 45.

other states' military power (20:1–6). Yet, despite the efforts of Isaiah and earlier Judean prophets, the placement of Isaiah 31 suggests that Judah's leaders failed to learn this fundamental lesson.

> Woe to those who go down to Egypt for help and rely on horses, who trust in chariots because they are many and in horsemen because they are very strong, but do not look to the Holy One of Israel or consult Yahweh! . . . The Egyptians are humans, and not God! Their horses are flesh, not spirit! When Yahweh stretches out his hand, the helper will stumble and the one who is helped will fall – they will all perish together!
> (Isa. 31:1, 3, my translation)

This is the problem in its starkest form: if Judah perceives the nations as stronger, more dependable and safer than its other options, it has *utterly failed to know Yahweh*. This leads to the other reason behind Isaiah's many oracles against the nations: these states' self-glorification, violence and far-reaching claims infringe on the glory of the Creator by whose will, and for whose glory, they exist.

The nations as God's means for punishing his covenant people

The role of some nations as Judah's adversary is hinted at in the book's opening segment, where Yahweh's analysis of Judah's penchant for rebellion (Isa. 1:2) is that it has not even been slowed by the nearly total destruction of its land by 'foreigners' (*zārîm* [1:7]). This role becomes more pronounced in Isaiah 5:26–30, where the prophet announces that God, angered by his people's rejection of his word and covenant love, will summon 'nations far away' to attack them like lions attacking their prey (5:29), with no one to rescue them. Judah's imminent exile, mentioned earlier in the same chapter, is also part of this judgment (5:13). A very similar scenario is presented in response to Ahaz's lack of faith in chapter 7, where Egypt and Assyria are identified as the instruments by which Yahweh will reduce the kingdom of Judah to a land of uncultivated fields where only livestock can graze and only bees can flourish amid wild vegetation (7:18–25; similarly, 8:5–10, with Assyria alone; against Israel, 9:8–12, with Arameans and Philistines). The increasing severity of God's punishments of Judah testify to the profound estrangement from him that its sins have produced, an estrangement that Isaiah captures in a striking way by referring to his Judean audience as 'rulers of Sodom' and 'people of Gomorrah' (1:10). No less remarkably, an oracle against Jerusalem (22:1–25) is included in the otherwise uninterrupted string of oracles against foreign nations in chapters 13 – 23.[7]

The covenantal discipline and punishments that God brought on his people were not simply destructive, however. Promises of salvation appear regularly for 'the remnant of Israel', which will be characterized by a new-found trust in and submission to Yahweh (10:20–21; note also 1:24–31). God's promises of future deliverance allow those who take Isaiah's oracles seriously to avoid being overwhelmed with fear at the prospect of violence at the hands of Assyria in particular. God reassures those who accept his word in faith that just as he will summon Assyria against Judah, he will free his people from its yoke, ultimately cutting Assyria down to the ground (10:24–34; also 10:16–19; 29:1–14; 33:1, 18–19). This outcome, quite counter-intuitive considering Assyria's immense power and massive expansion in the second half of the eighth century BC, hints at the long-range purposes of Yahweh's covenantal discipline. The violence of the nations will indeed serve as God's means of punishment for Judah's and Israel's protracted covenant infidelity. But beyond judgment and the creation of the remnant lies a radical restoration that can only be produced by Yahweh's grace.[8]

The nations under judgment

While some passages in Isaiah show Yahweh using non-Israelite states (more precisely, their military forces) to punish Judah but do not include explicit condemnation of their actions, other passages tie such aggression against Judah to imperial ideologies and related beliefs and so condemn a number of different states on those grounds. Indeed, such passages exceed, in both number and size, those that simply describe the nations' pursuit of their agendas without any negative evaluation. This penchant for critique of foreign states that goes beyond condemnation of their

[7] The array of nations that this chapter envisages coming against Judah is 'figurative' rather than literal, as noted in Oswalt 1986: 410.

[8] Webb (1990) offers a helpful discussion of the remnant.

violence reveals the importance of ideology for understanding the oracles concerning the nations in Isaiah.

Assyria's imperial mission: gods, king, war, order – all for Assyria's glory (Isa. 10:5–19)

Excessive violence

In Isaiah's first sizable oracle against a foreign nation, Yahweh addresses Assyria (the proper noun refers to the monarch, as 10:8 makes clear) as 'the rod of [his] anger' and refers to Judah as the object of his wrath (10:5–6).[9] God's intentions for Assyria's troops as they bring military action against Judah are presented in bold terms: they are to spoil, plunder, and 'tread them down like the mire of the streets', that is, to deeply shame them.[10] However, Assyria is overzealous in its implementation of this mandate. Whereas the terms in 10:6 imply subjugation of Judah and the appropriation of its material resources, Assyria's imperial mission clearly exceeds these limits. It will 'destroy' and 'cut off nations not a few' (10:7), transgressing Yahweh's remit in terms of both degree (destroy rather than subjugate) and scope (many nations rather than one).

Pride

As grave as this lust for blood and plunder is, the heart of the oracle (10:9–15) shifts its focus to the proud beliefs that drive Assyria's appetite for destruction. The monarch puts his commanders on par with other states' kings (10:8), past victories are taken as guarantees of future ones (10:9), and his supposed legitimacy as the weapon in the hands of Assyria's gods leads him to believe that Yahweh is as powerless as the gods of the states that he has already vanquished (10:10–11).[11] The arrogance that drives these overly optimistic predictions is mentioned twice in 10:12 before it is unfurled further in a flurry of egocentric claims reminiscent of the self-glorifying rhetoric of Assyrian royal inscriptions:

[9] For other oracles against Assyria in Isaiah, see 14:24–27; 37:22–29. Aster (2017: 108) shows that this passage contains the same ideological elements as the letter of Sargon II to the gods, which was 'a sort of "official statement" of imperial ideology, even more so than the standard royal inscriptions'.

[10] Wolff 1990: 223; Schnittjer 2021: 418–419; cf. Mic. 7:10; Zech. 10:5.

[11] McConville (2023: 164–165) explains well the outrageous tone of the Assyrian's 'provocation' of Yahweh here.

By the strength of my hand I have done it . . .
my wisdom . . . I have understanding;
I remove the boundaries . . .
[I] plunder . . .
I bring down . . .
My hand . . .
I have gathered all the earth . . .
(Isa. 10:13–14)[12]

Yahweh's response, which bluntly rejects the monarch's boasting and self-adulation (10:15), underlines a fundamental reality the Assyrian has overlooked: God is his creator, and the proud magnate is completely under divine control. As grave as the empire's excessive violence is against those created in God's image, the theological dimensions of the Assyrian monarch's actions are even more objectionable, since they directly contradict Yahweh's claims about himself and so seek to reinterpret reality in the most radical way possible.

The inevitable end of (imperial) pride

As the language of this passage shows, Yahweh's response to this imperial hubris is limited to the Assyrians involved in the imperial mission, that is, the monarch and his army (10:16). Described as trees that Yahweh's wrath will burn until only a few are left (10:19), the imposing warriors will be reduced to almost nothing, revealing the groundless nature of the emperor's boasting.[13] The certainty of Assyria's future demise means that God's people can live without fear in the present, although they must trust in Yahweh if they are to survive (10:20–22). This oracle was most likely fulfilled (at least in the non-eschatological short term) in the destruction of Assyria's army at Jerusalem in 701 BC (Isa. 37).[14]

[12] Machinist (2016: 201) notes a number of literary and other connections between this text and Assyrian royal texts. Eck (2021: 424) suggests that 'the arrogance of the King of Assyria in 10:5–15 refers forward to the universal Day of YHWH announced in Isa 13 to the world of the nations. It can therefore be assumed that the punishment of the King of Assyria belongs to the context of the Day of YHWH in Isa 13.'

[13] See Beuken 2003: 287–289.

[14] Webb 1990: 70.

The world and Babylon (Isa. 13:1–22)

The long collection of oracles against the nations in Isaiah 13 – 23 develops a much wider perspective on the nations, one that frequently extends far beyond the horizon of the eighth and seventh centuries BC. Babylon's pride of place in this large unit reflects its importance for understanding Yahweh's judgment of 'the nations' in general in Isaiah. As a sort of introduction to chapters 13 – 23, Isaiah 13 is particularly significant for several reasons. First, the oracles against the nations follow the powerful presentation of the Messiah's rule in Isaiah 11, and so should be seen in the light of that overarching perspective. Isaiah 11 also announces both judgment and salvation for the nations, a subtheme that runs through the following chapters. Second, the oracles against particular nations are case studies, as it were, of God's declaration of judgment against a sinful world that will be realized in the Day of Yahweh (13:6–16). The impressive number of nations that figure among these oracles and the role of chapters 24 – 27 in closing this section show that these chapters form a mosaic of universal judgment against those who take human plans, power and purposes to be determinative of history.[15] Only once that global context is in place do 13:17–22 and the bulk of Isaiah 14 focus on the punishment and ultimate fate of Babylon, which is the archetypal manifestation of 'human glory' that opposes Yahweh himself.[16] This encourages readers to see the nations under judgment as limited or focused examples of the negative aspect of the Day of Yahweh in which the guilt–condemnation–punishment logic is applied to *particular* manifestations of the *general* phenomenon of opposition to Yahweh, his plans and his people.

It is crucially important to notice that non-Israelite groups have several distinct identities and roles in Isaiah 13:1 – 14:2. First, 13:2–5 presents an international perspective in which Yahweh summons a group of anonymous 'kingdoms' and 'nations' (13:4) and designates them as the means to execute his wrath on an unidentified enemy.[17] Since their target is Babylon (13:1, 19), 'nations' as used here is not an absolutely inclusive

[15] Oswalt 1986: 299; Beuken 2007: 51; Williamson 2021: 545–546.

[16] Oswalt 1986: 299.

[17] 'Consecrated' (Isa. 13:3) here should be taken to mean only that God has set them apart as those who (unwittingly) fight for him; they are thus 'his' warriors who carry out 'his' wrath. Similarly, God's use of Assyria as the 'rod of [his] anger' (10:5) and of Cyrus as his 'anointed' (45:1) does not suppose those agents' volitional alignment with every aspect of the divine will.

category. Furthermore, whatever their motives, these nations and kingdoms act in accord with God's sovereign purposes, having been summoned as Yahweh's weapons to destroy 'the whole land' (13:5).[18] Despite their imposing strength, these nations are nothing more than Yahweh's instrument for punishing others.

By contrast, 13:6–16 presents every 'people' and 'land' as part of the *world* that will be judged in the Day of Yahweh. The fall of Babylon is thus part of (or a prelude to) the eschatological project of global divine judgment and deliverance frequently referred to as the Day of Yahweh.[19] This 'destruction from the Almighty' (13:6) will be universal in scope, affecting every human being (13:7) but destroying only 'sinners' (13:9), while leaving a small remnant (13:12). The presentation of the world's population as individuals who are evaluated solely in terms of their guilt or innocence before God makes possible their definitive judgment, and transcends the nations-paradigm for the same reason – those who are judged are condemned without reference to any other characteristic or identifier. References to the guilty or their actions in moral or judicial terms ('evil', 'wicked' and full of 'iniquity' [13:11]) give way to descriptions of anti-God attitudes and actions: 'the pomp of the arrogant' and 'the pompous pride of the ruthless' (13:11; cf. 2:12).[20]

The final section of Isaiah 13 leaves behind this global perspective and returns to the narrower focus on Babylon (13:17–22) as a microcosm of the Day of Yahweh. Notably, the only sins alleged against Babylon here are those involved in its self-ascribed 'glory', 'splendour' and 'pomp' (13:19), claims that will be exposed as false when it falls.[21] Babylon's pride, like that of all human things that are 'proud and lofty' in Isaiah (cf. 2:12), makes it ripe for judgment and humiliation, and the passage presents an extensive description of Babylon's end. Four lines predict that it will be perpetually without human inhabitants (13:20), and six lines foretell its repopulation by wild animals (13:21–22b). Babylon's removal by God from the ordered, just world that his righteousness will establish contrasts sharply with the destiny of restored Jerusalem, whose population

[18] The Hebrew noun *ʾereṣ* can be translated as 'land' or 'earth'. 'Land' is better here, since the nations come against a specific territory, whereas 'earth' is a better translation in Isa. 13:9 as part of the global Day of Yahweh described in 13:6–16 (note the parallel with *tēbēl* in 13:11, a term for which the only sense is 'world').

[19] Sweeney 1996: 223.

[20] This is also noted by Wildberger (1997: 37–38).

[21] Childs 2001: 125.

will grow beyond all expectation, and which constitutes the centre of the world later in the book (Isa. 60 – 62).[22]

Isaiah 13 is indeed a fitting introduction to the theme of the nations in Isaiah. It presents both focused (Babylon) and global perspectives on non-Israelites, interweaves judgment and salvation, and shows that human pride, self-determination and the headlong pursuit of one's goal by any means necessary are at the heart of what the 'nations' are in Isaiah. These emphases and perspectives will reappear frequently, in many different configurations, in the other passages we will consider in this chapter.

Babylon in Sheol (Isa. 14:3–23)

Isaiah 14 begins with a brief but potent description of the restoration of Jacob and Israel in which Yahweh's compassion will liberate them and return them to their land. There, quite surprisingly, non-Israelite 'sojourners' will 'join' and 'attach themselves' to God's renewed people. Their integration into restored Israel reveals that they too are fully committed to Yahweh as their God and will walk in his ways (cf. 56:1–8). In the same context, other non-Israelites who also live harmoniously with God's people are described as either facilitating their return from exile or serving them once they have returned to the land (14:2; cf. the same variety of roles for non-Israelites in Isa. 60 – 62).[23]

Yahweh's superlative restoration of Israel and pacification of the nations form the backdrop for the taunt against the king of Babylon in chapter 14 that complements the prediction of Babylon's destruction in chapter 13.[24] The focus on this royal figure is another example of the selective nature and ideological focus of many prophetic references to non-Israelite nations.[25] In connection with the end of Judah's 'hard service' under the Babylonian yoke, the Babylonian monarch is presented as an oppressor driven by 'insolent fury' (14:4–5) who habitually exercises violence against a string of people groups, relentlessly subjugating and dominating

[22] Beuken 2007: 78.

[23] See Timmer 2024e.

[24] Abernethy (2016: 194) notes in connection with 14:1–2 that God's judgment of the nations is 'part of YHWH's gracious act in restoring Israel'.

[25] The identity of the Babylonian king in this context remains debated, probably because the description cannot easily be limited to any particular Babylonian king; see Van Keulen 2010. Vanderhooft (1999: 129) tentatively suggests that Nebuchadnezzar is in view, but his observation that 'the biblical prophets perceived . . . continuity in the imperial worldviews and institutions' of various empires corroborates the point being made here.

them (14:6). Babylon's imperial corps has 'perverted the divine world order' by imposing its 'totalitarian system of violence and chaotic fury' on many nations, and this sets the stage for its precipitous fall from ruling over the world to inhabiting the underworld.[26]

The taunt then delves deeper into the pride, self-entitlement and God-defying claims to supremacy that were at the heart of Babylonian imperialism.[27] The voices of the monarch's former victims, including both the cedars of Lebanon (14:8) and the kings of the nations that Babylon battered (14:9–11), celebrate the end of its violence against them and the proof that, in death, it is as 'weak' as they are.[28] This section is a pointed critique of Babylonian imperialism's penchant for connecting its military endeavours with the will of the empire's gods, Marduk in particular.[29] This link is rooted, it was believed, in the gods' choice and empowerment of the king, a theme that appears frequently in Neo-Babylonian royal inscriptions. For example, Nabopolassar (r. 625–605 BC) speaks of himself as the 'shepherd chosen by the god Marduk, creation of the goddess Ninmenna . . . protégé of the god Nabû and the goddess Tašmētu, beloved prince of the god Ninšiku'.[30] Even in his youth he 'sought out the shrines of the gods Nabû and Marduk' and was eventually 'called' by Šazu 'for dominion over the land and people'.[31] In the pursuit of the imperial mission, he attests to divine help: 'Nergal . . . march[ed] at my side; he killed my enemies (and) cut down my opponents.'[32]

Similarly, Nebuchadnezzar II (605–562 BC) affirmed his piety by stating that his attention was 'fixed [o]n the god Nabû' and that he faithfully brought gifts to the temples of his gods. Once Marduk raised him up as king, Nebuchadnezzar undertook the task of conquest: he 'mustered [... in all] lands everywhere . . . from the Upper Sea [to the Lo]wer [Sea, the fa]r-off [lands, the widespread people of the inhabited wor]ld' whom Marduk placed 'in [my ha]nd t[o pu]ll [his] chariot pol[e], and I imposed

[26] Eck 2021: 409.

[27] Franke (1996: 109) notes that Isa. 14 parodies a typical lament, especially by presenting a negative picture of the deceased and so replacing a lament's sympathy with scorn and its grief with celebration.

[28] Gordon 2010: 48–49.

[29] So Scurlock 2022: 407. I am grateful to Tom Underhill for pointing me to this article.

[30] Nabopolassar 03, cited from <https://oracc.museum.upenn.edu/ribo/babylon7/Q005362> (accessed 5 January 2024).

[31] Nabopolassar 03, <https://oracc.museum.upenn.edu/ribo/babylon7/Q005362>.

[32] Nabopolassar 03, <https://oracc.museum.upenn.edu/ribo/babylon7/Q005362>.

(the carrying of) bask[et(s)] on the workmen of the gods Šamaš and [Marduk]' to build their temples.[33] The same god–king–conquest script is used by later kings such as Neriglassar (559–556):

> When the god Marduk . . . looked upon me and declared (my) gracious name to be king in the land . . . he gave me a just scepter that widens the land . . . let my hands grasp a staff that subdues enemies . . . I killed foes, slaughtered enemies, (and) suppressed all of the unsubmissive.[34]

Isaiah's taunt perceives behind the ostensible distinction between the gods and the king (which, due to the immanent nature of Babylonian cosmologies, is not absolute) the king's appropriation of the gods' relatively untrammelled sovereignty and supernatural status.[35] Robert P. Gordon captures this imperial fantasy well: 'The arrogance of Babylonian power is hyperbolized in this passage into an attack on the mount of the gods, and the monarch's preoccupation with the heights generates the detailed account of the descent into the underworld.'[36] This pride, which drives the king to imagine that he will 'conquer for himself the absolutely highest position above all gods', engenders the monarch's fatal misunderstanding of his place in Yahweh's world and so leads to his downfall.[37] Eck puts this well: 'Devoid of wisdom, his attempted ascent to heaven must ultimately result in his fall from the incommensurable heights of his hubris.'[38] The fall of the Babylonian is paired with his humiliation, and he finds himself mocked by the other denizens of the underworld in whose eyes his death without burial and the end of his dynasty (Isa. 14:16–21) constitute the ultimate dishonour. In Sheol, his glory no longer exists, and in sharp contrast to the Babylon king's 'delusions of grandeur' in 14:12–15, 'in the tyrant's own presence the kings in Sheol . . . refer to him . . . simply as "the man" (v. 16)!'[39] Yahweh's words close the section no less emphatically

---

[33] Nebuchadnezzar II 001, cited from <https://oracc.museum.upenn.edu/ribo/babylon7/Q005472> (accessed 5 January 2024).

[34] Weiershäuser and Novotny 2020: 36–37.

[35] Bartholomew 2022: 366.

[36] Gordon 2010: 49.

[37] Eck 2021: 424. Scurlock (2022: 397) notes that in official texts 'no Assyrian or Babylonian king could ever have been described as appearing in the heavens'.

[38] Eck 2021: 411.

[39] Holladay 1999: 642.

by pronouncing the end of Babylon as an empire. God will 'cut off from Babylon name and remnant, descendants and posterity' and transform it into uninhabitable swampland that cannot even be used for agriculture (14:22–23).[40] The greatest empire (by human standards) is also the most flagrant offender against Yahweh's glory. Therefore, Babylon's specious imperial pretensions will be shown to be as insubstantial as the empire itself when Yahweh brings his just judgment against it.

The nations under judgment with salvation as a possibility

This section draws attention to one aspect of Isaiah's detailed and nuanced presentation of the nations. While some oracles announce only negative fates (see the previous section) and others are entirely positive (see the following section), still others include various combinations of salvation and judgment. Here we consider an oracle that leaves the nations in a liminal situation, with judgment already a reality and deliverance a possibility.

Moab and its refugees (Isa. 15:1 – 16:14)

The lengthy oracle against Moab shows that the pride at the heart of ancient Near Eastern imperialism was also evident in smaller and less powerful states such as Moab. Moab's earlier history with Israel/Judah was fraught, as it was subjected to Israel during the reigns of Omri (884–873 BC) and Ahab (873–852 BC) but regained its independence shortly thereafter.[41] Despite its brevity and imperfect state of preservation, an inscription in which Mesha, king of Moab, recounts how Moab regained its independence from Israel is similar in tone and content to royal inscriptions authored by rulers of much larger states. In that inscription, Mesha asserts that he had a cultic site built in honour of the deity Chemosh in recognition of the latter's role in delivering him 'from all kings' and elevating him over 'all [his] enemies', including Israel, which Mesha claims – quite prematurely – 'has gone to ruin for ever!'[42] The rest of the text recounts royal building projects and a number of military

[40] Beuken 2007: 100.

[41] The Moabite king Mesha recounts that he unilaterally ended Moab's vassal relationship to Israel following Ahab's death in 852 BC; see Smelik 2003.

[42] Ibid. 137.

campaigns in which whole populations bore the brunt of Mesha's ambitions for conquest, with Chemosh being either the recipient of the spoils or the one who called for military action and then brought about Moab's victory.

God's judgment of Moab

The oracle in Isaiah 15 – 16 reflects on a calamity that will be brought upon Moab by its enemies ('the lords of the nations' [16:8]).[43] This foreign aggression will destroy its vineyards (a prominent sector of its economy), cause bitter grief (15:2–5) and drive some Moabites to flee (15:7).[44] The ultimate cause of Moab's hardship is presented in 16:6 in the context of the state's inflated self-estimation.[45] There its 'eminence' (my translation of *gā ʾôn*, used of Yahweh in 2:10, 19, 21) is mentioned twice and is in parallel with a host of related terms: 'pride' (*ga ʾăwâ*; cf. 9:9; 13:11; 25:11), 'insolence' and 'idle boasting'. Moab's inflated self-perception is essentially identical to the 'glory' that, per 16:14, will become an object of contempt. Since the sin of pride is sufficient by itself for Moab's condemnation, the theological significance of pride, which emboldens nations to disregard Yahweh, cannot be overstated. The affirmations that Moab seeks help from its deities in its time of trouble (15:2; 16:12) reveal the theological dimension that pride inevitably involves. Yahweh is sovereign over the nations, whereas the gods of the nations are false claimants to deity and so can safely be ignored, yet Moab pursues the very opposite course of action.[46]

Possibilities beyond judgment

The elements noted so far in this passage are often the only ones present in oracles of judgment: God brings charges against the nation in question, a sentence is announced, and the outcome of the sentence is described. Here, however, several additional elements add further depth to the oracle. First, the prophet himself is deeply saddened at the Moabites' suffering and the destruction of their fields and vineyards (15:5; 16:9–11).[47]

---

[43] Isa. 16:13–14 was apparently appended to the preceding oracle prior to its fulfilment; see Couey 2015: 30–31.

[44] Couey (2015: 22–26) notes the prominence of Moab's grief.

[45] The voice is most likely that of the prophet and his Judean audience; cf. Beuken 2007: 137. In any case, apart from the enemy, no other group is mentioned in these two chapters.

[46] Scolnic 2023: 104–105.

[47] Landy 2021: 111. This is presumably because Moabites were related to Judeans through Lot,

Second, Isaiah calls for his Judean audience to welcome Moab's refugees when they enter Judean territory (16:3–4a).[48] Third, the identification of the group of people who flee Moab clearly distinguishes them from the 'Moab' that Yahweh will destroy (cf. 16:14), and this distinction is complemented by the potential for significant proximity to Israelites should they seek refuge in Judah (16:4).[49] Finally and climactically, the prophet's insistence that Judah is obliged to protect and care for the fleeing Moabites is immediately followed by a prediction of the Davidic kingdom's superlative re-establishment by Yahweh.[50] In contrast to Moab's destroyer, the Davidic dynasty is characterized by 'steadfast love', 'faithfulness', the performance of 'justice', and 'righteousness' (16:5). It is to that Davidic king and his God, rather than to its deities, that Moab should direct its trust.[51]

Whether this is indeed how Moab reacted to its hardship is unknown, and in any case the oracle is not an outright announcement of deliverance for those Moabites who flee their homeland. Still, the passage makes several important points: the neighbouring nations are not so secure as to merit Judeans' trust; non-Israelites who are not involved in their state's belligerence and pride should find welcome and protection in Judah; and Judah itself will become the only source of hope for the *nations'* deliverance when Yahweh brings the Davidic line to its apogee (cf. Amos 9:11).[52] The ambiguity of this oracle as to whether Moabites will manifest such a change of heart draws attention to the clear contrast between the violent domination that the nations pursue and the just, gracious and peaceful nature of the kingdom into which God invites the fleeing Moabites and all who come to see that their trust in the security and goodness of lesser things is badly misplaced.

had received their land from Yahweh's hand (Deut. 2:9) and occasionally had positive interaction with Israelites. Wildberger (1997: 149) notes Ruth and the shelter afforded to David's parents by Moab in 1 Sam. 22:3–4.

[48] It is unlikely that this section is sarcastic, if for no other reason than that it complements the prophet's anguish and flows smoothly into the following oracle concerning the Davidic line; see Aspray 2021: 430–431 for further arguments of this nature.

[49] Ibid. 434.

[50] Goswell (2014: 96) notes various ties between 2 Sam. 7 and clearly messianic passages in Isaiah, e.g. 9:7; 11:4. Isa. 16:1 is probably not sarcastic in the light of 16:3–5, and is apparently a tardy proposal to seek protection from Judah by requesting 'vassal status', according to Smothers (1996: 80). Note also Moab's earlier vassal payment to Ahab (2 Kgs 3:4).

[51] Following Goswell 2014: 101.

[52] On the latter point, see ibid. 102–103.

The nations under judgment *and* salvation

In Scripture, judgment and hope are interwoven almost from the very moment that sin enters the world (Gen. 3:14–21), and the same pair reappears throughout the canon at key moments (e.g. Gen. 12:1–3). It is also prominent in the book of Isaiah, both in its overall message and with respect to foreign nations.[53] This section examines a few oracles in which salvation *and* judgment are experienced by the same nation or group, an apparent tension that highlights the decisive role of individuals' adherence to, or rejection of, the ideology of a particular political entity (Isa. 19; 23) or, in a broader optic, of the pattern of sinful autonomy that characterizes humanity as a whole (Isa. 24 – 25).

Old and new Egypt (Isa. 19:1–25)

This oracle stands out within chapters 13 – 23 thanks to its sharp juxtaposition of forceful messages of condemnation and salvation for Egypt. This complexity forces the reader to recognize that 'Egypt' in this passage is not a static or monolithic entity.

Judgment of Egypt (Isa. 19:1–15)

The oracle of judgment in 19:1–15 with which this passage begins focuses on three aspects of Egypt's identity that ostensibly guaranteed its security and stability: its many gods (19:1–4), the River Nile as a perennial source of irrigation and nourishment (19:5–10), and Egypt's wisdom (19:11–15). Like some other judgment oracles, chapter 19 does not present formal accusations, but instead links the fall of Egypt to phenomena that are tied to self-evident causes. When Egypt's false gods (*ʾĕlîlîm*) 'tremble' at Yahweh's majestic arrival, their inability to protect Egypt from his judgment is inseparable from Egyptians' culpable worship of things that in reality are not gods (19:1).[54] Similarly, their attempts to avoid divine punishment by divination (19:3) reveal their dependence on pseudo-revelation, which will not help them. The punishment for these particular actions, which will see Egypt serve a 'harsh' king (19:4), is not

[53] Oswalt 1996.

[54] The very multiplicity of Egypt's gods may also lie behind the social disintegration foreseen in 19:2, since each nome (administrative district) had its own god(s).

eschatological and probably refers (at least in the first instance) to Egypt's progressive subjugation by Assyria from 673 to 663 BC.[55]

Further along in the passage, the Nile is presented as the basis of Egypt's economy and much more (19:5–10). The massive river nourished aquatic plants used for the production of papyrus and supplied water for irrigation and fish for consumption, but also had immense religious significance. 'The Nile of Egypt found its mirror image in the celestial Nile whereon sailed the sun-barque' of the deity Re,[56] and it was considered 'the great efflux of Osiris', who had gifted Egypt with it.[57] The annual inundation of the Nile 'ensured fertility', and Egyptians' worship 'of Hapy (god of the inundation) specifically honored his blessings'.[58] Sobek, a crocodile god, also represented 'the Nile floods and fertility' and was 'a symbol of royal power' during the Middle Kingdom period.[59] Yahweh's announcement that he would dry up the Nile is thus nothing less than the complete disruption of Egypt economically, religiously and even cosmically, for according to Egypt's founding myths, the Nile's desiccation would imply Osiris's defeat at the hands of Seth and the consequent descent of Egypt into chaos.[60]

The third pillar of Egypt's stability, its wisdom, is the target of a biting critique in 19:11–15.[61] The affirmations that Zoan's 'rulers' (my translation) are 'utterly foolish' and Pharaoh's 'wisest counsellors . . . give stupid counsel' (19:11a–b) are followed by two rhetorical questions (19:11c–12) that are sharpened by the ominous assertion that these savants are unaware of Yahweh's purposes concerning their own country! Indeed, the very inability of these sages to give good counsel – despite Egypt's impressive contributions to international wisdom since the third millennium BC – is the result of Yahweh's intervention, which will culminate in the complete undoing of Egypt (19:14–15).[62]

In summary, the 'Egypt' against which Isaiah announces judgment is

---

[55] Other options have been suggested, including Piankhy's conquest of Upper Egypt in 730 BC and Shabaka's establishing Ethiopian control over the Nile Delta in 716–712; see Watts 1985: 253.

[56] Redford 2002: xvi.

[57] Tobin 2002: 242.

[58] Griffiths 2002: 256.

[59] Doxey 2002: 336.

[60] Lesko 1991: 93.

[61] Sweeney 1996: 265–266.

[62] Hollis 2009: 101.

characterized as being idolatrous, polytheistic and dependent on divination for knowledge. It trusts the gods responsible for the Nile's inundation to maintain agriculture and the economy as a whole, and too easily trusts in its own wisdom. Notably, the pharaoh is the only individual specifically referred to, and the section limits its focus to government leaders and those who provide them with guidance. In short, 'Egypt' in this oracle *is* those who follow gods other than Yahweh and trust in their sources of knowledge and stability rather than in him.

The spiritual transformation of Egypt (and Assyria) (Isa. 19:16–25)

Rather than destroying the Egyptians who correspond to the description given immediately above, Yahweh's purposes in this oracle are better described as transformative, without implying that every Egyptian will be transformed (note that a number of cities, rather than the entire nation, will swear allegiance to Yahweh [19:18]). This new and very positive theme begins to appear even in 19:16–17, which announces that fear and trembling will seize the population when Yahweh 'shakes' his hand (cf. 11:15) over them and they realize the extent of his purposes against them, but stops short of announcing further destruction.[63]

The four remaining oracles in this chapter (19:18, 19–22, 23, 24–25) present several dimensions of the amazingly positive divine intervention that will follow the disintegration and collapse of Egypt announced in 19:11–17. In verse 18, the conversion of five cities to the worship of Yahweh surely represents a swelling number of Yahwistic converts among a non-Yahwistic majority, but may involve more than that. In the light of the geographically and metaphorically central role of the worship of Yahweh later in the passage, the suggestion of Israelit-Groll that '[t]he five cities apparently represent the major "theologies" of Egypt', with the number five being simply symbolic, is plausible.[64] This possibility receives further support from the assertion that 'one of these will be called the

[63] The link between Judah's and Egypt's terror should be attributed to the Yahweh–Judah connection, so that the focus remains on Yahweh and thus on Egypt's response to him; see Wildberger 1997: 267.

[64] Israelit-Groll 1998: 302. This suggestion is perhaps strengthened by the prominence of groups of five in Egyptian cultic or royal contexts. Note the formal identification of four or five priestly positions, with the highest-ranking priest at Hermopolis Magna bearing the title 'Greatest of the Five' (Spencer 2014: 257) and the number of regnal titulary reaching five during the Old Kingdom period (Morris 2014: 205).

City of the Sun' (reading *ḥeres* [signifying the sun] rather than *heres* ['Destruction', 19:18 ESV]).[65] If the proposed reading is correct, '[t]he theological point thus appears to be that even in the city of Re, the Egyptian sun god, the "language of Canaan" is spoken by those professing loyalty to the God of Israel'.[66] If such a change is evident in the city dedicated to the worship of one of Egypt's greatest deities, it is surely evident elsewhere in Egypt.

The oracle in verses 19–22 presses further in the direction of a large-scale conversion of Egyptians to faith in the God of Israel. In verses 19–20a, a Yahwistic altar and pillar at the centre and the periphery of the kingdom, respectively, symbolize 'open and official'[67] worship of Yahweh across the land.[68] The altar is a cultic element that allows legitimate worship of God, including forgiveness of sins, and 'implies sacrifice and a priesthood'.[69] The pillar most likely has the same function as those built by Israel when it solemnized or renewed a covenant (Exod. 24:4–8; Josh. 24:26–31), suggesting that Egypt is now Yahweh's by covenant[70] and providing the theological context for the altar and the worship it symbolizes. This understanding seems to be confirmed by the link between 'it' (the altar and/or pillar) being 'a sign and a witness' to Yahweh of Hosts and his deliverance of Egypt from its oppressors by means of his 'saviour and defender' (19:20; the various echoes from Exod. 2:23; 3:9 and elsewhere make this a 'first exodus' for Egypt!).[71]

The covenantal aspect is developed even further in 19:21, where Yahweh reveals himself to the Egyptians so that they 'will know Yahweh in that day'. This is perhaps the strongest affirmation in the entire passage of the definitive nature of the Egyptians' new relationship with God.[72] To this are added other characteristics of faithful followers of Yahweh, 'serving' him (cf. Exod. 3:12; 4:23; and throughout Exod. 7 – 12) by means of sacrifices, offerings and vows that are paid (cf. Pss 50:14; 66:13; 76:11;

[65] Hibbard (2015) discusses the text-critical issues.

[66] Childs 2001: 144.

[67] Watts 1985: 258.

[68] See Oswalt 1986: 379.

[69] Watts 2015: 315.

[70] Beuken (2007: 194–195) notes the patriarchs' construction of altars (Gen. 12:6–7; 26:25) or pillars (Gen. 35:14) in recognition of Yahweh as their God.

[71] Ibid. 195; Wildberger 1997: 276.

[72] Watts (1985: 258) asserts that '[a] more complete statement of the full mutual relation of Yahweh and Egypt cannot be imagined'.

etc.). The summary of Yahweh's intervention in terms of 'striking and healing' captures the transformation that resolves the apparent tension in Isaiah 19 between Egypt as an enemy whom God judges and Egypt as part of his people whom he saves (19:22).

To this already stunning description of Egypt's spiritual transformation the short oracle of 19:23 adds the image of a highway between Egypt and Assyria along which Assyria travels to Egypt, not to invade it (as it would do several times in the seventh century BC) but to serve (*ʿābad*) Yahweh alongside it! This laconic statement assumes that the same spiritual transformation that turned Egypt as a collective into worshippers of Yahweh also has taken place among Assyria (also a collective), since only this can explain how the two can worship Yahweh together.

Finally, although there is no doubt as to Israel's primordial position in the history of redemption (19:24b), the last oracle stresses that non-Israelites who come to faith in Yahweh are not second-rate citizens in his kingdom.[73] 'In that day Israel will be the third with Egypt and Assyria, a blessing in the midst of the earth' (19:24). Even more astonishingly, God himself assigns titles previously reserved for Israel – in the same order as the previous verse – to transformed non-Israelites in Egypt and Assyria: 'Blessed be Egypt my people, and Assyria the work of my hands, and Israel my inheritance' (19:25).[74] This is more than simply drawing non-Israelites into Israel's blessing mandate (Gen. 12:1–3), although it surely includes that: Egypt and Assyria share Israel's titles and thus its very identity as Yahweh's people![75] This is the strongest possible affirmation of their religious identity with Israel. The supernatural growth of Israel 'in the midst of the earth' also echoes Jacob's prayer for Israel's multiplication (Gen. 48:16), a theme developed intensively in later chapters of Isaiah.

---

[73] The *atnach* (a verse divider in the MT) under 'Assur' ends the first phrase there, and the absence of any verbal element in v. 24b makes it necessary to understand 'Israel will be' as the presumed subject and verb. Beuken (2007: 199) similarly argues that v. 24b is in apposition with 'Israel' in v. 24a.

[74] For 'my people', see Exod. 3:7 and frequently in Isaiah; for Israel as 'the work of my hands', see Isa. 29:23; 45:11; 60:21; for Israel as 'my inheritance', see Deut. 4:20; 9:29; Ps. 28:9; Isa. 29:23; 63:17; 64:18; etc.

[75] McConville (2023: 246) notes the significance of this passage for understanding Israel's election.

Tyre and Sidon: from worship of wealth to worship of Yahweh (Isa. 23:1–14, 15–18)

A satirical city-lament (Isa. 23:1–14)

Tyre, along with Sidon and sometimes in competition with it, dominated trade between the Near East and countries around the Mediterranean for the better part of a millennium. As the references to Tarshish in Isaiah 23 suggest, this trade network extended to the coast of Spain, and included Tyrian colonies at Carthage (in modern Tunisia) and on Cyprus.[76] The expansion of Phoenicia's international trading network in the early first millennium BC was driven by several internal factors, among which expanding its 'sphere of economic influence' was certainly central.[77]

This oracle's narrow focus on Tyre as a key node of international commerce implies that the city-state as a whole is not in view, for Tyre was more than its maritime trade. Indeed, it is not even maritime trade per se that forms the object of Isaiah's critique. While Tyre as portrayed here was clearly the hub of commerce on the Levantine coast, Isaiah's critique focuses on its self-understanding as incompatible with Yahweh and his purposes (23:9). God's purposes are, first, larger than Tyre: 'to defile the pride of all glory, to dishonour all the honoured of the earth'.[78] All honour that is not accorded by Yahweh or consistent with his incomparable and original glory is corrupt.

It is, second, in that radically theocentric context that Tyre's impressiveness, whether ascribed to it by its trading partners or by itself, reveals its idolatrous origins. The city is exultant, its origins in ancient times imply its stability and permanence, its reach extends beyond the horizon to its colonies, it confers rule and status on selected subordinate entities, its merchants enjoy elevated standing, and its traders receive the world's 'glory' (23:7–9). The city-state's *extension* in time (from ancient days until now), space (from Tyre across the Mediterranean) and status (from unremarkable to exalted, glorious, princely and 'crowning' others[79]) makes clear its unequalled status.

[76] Bryce 2009: 728.

[77] Woolmer 2017: 177.

[78] Van der Kooij 1998: 26.

[79] Wildberger (1997: 429) plausibly suggests that this refers to Tyre designating rulers for its colonies.

Crucially, however, Tyre's supposedly unparalleled importance and glory are expressed without reference to Yahweh, and for that reason are diametrically opposed to him.[80] Yahweh 'fills all the recesses of creation, and there is no place left for any other being except as a medium for reflecting the divine glory'.[81] It is this misallocation of glory that motivates God's judgment and spells the doom of Tyre.[82] Isaiah's 'bitter, sarcastic' tone in this section reflects the pitiful nature of its self-glorification, highlighted by the call to 'howl' (23:1, 6, 14, my translation), the imposition of shame through metaphorical childlessness (23:4) and the climactic fall of Tyre's fortress (23:14).[83]

Transformational salvation (Isa. 23:15–18)

The quite unexpected oracle of salvation in 23:15–18, especially its final lines (23:17–18), succinctly presents Tyre's *restoration* after a period of humiliation. Tyre's far-reaching trade, presented under the metaphor of prostitution, will begin again, and on an even larger scale than before: 'with all the kingdoms of the world on the face of the earth' (23:17). The description of this trading activity as metaphorical prostitution might lead one to conclude that the activity is as illegitimate as it was in 23:1–14 (cf. Deut. 23:18), meaning that it still has the same motives and goals as those that justified its downfall. But, like Tyre itself, the metaphor is radically transformed. Rather than serving the satisfaction of its own desires, the city's riches are not hoarded but are given without hesitation to supply generously those 'who dwell before [Yahweh]' (Isa. 23:18). Not only does the idea of ill-gotten gain clash with its purposes of filling and equipping those who are perpetually in God's presence, but God himself will accept and sanctify that wealth for his own use!

This profound change in the nature of Tyre's material wealth draws attention to the transformative nature of God's 'intervention' or 'visiting' of the city (see 23:17). Rather than being dedicated to its own glory and exaltation and so leading to its condemnation, Tyre's commercial activity

[80] This is well argued by Beuken (2007: 308).

[81] Vos 1980: 275.

[82] The comparison with the Chaldeans in 23:13 likely has in view the explicitly divine and thus theological nature of Tyre's unmatched standing; see Beuken 2007: 308. Van der Kooij (1998: 30) suggests that it refers to those who inhabited it after Assyria 'destined it for the wild beasts' by destroying it.

[83] These points are drawn from Lessing 2003.

and generation of wealth will one day contribute to *Yahweh's* glory and equip and beautify those who worship him. Although this radical change is not presented in terms of the instantaneous conversion of Tyrians from worship of other deities to worship of Yahweh, the transformation of a self-serving commercial power focused exclusively on material goods into one that glorifies God by its activities displays the re-creating power and grace of a God who brings the nations and their wealth to himself in his temple (cf. 45:14; 60:5–11, 13; 61:6; etc.). It also closes the series of oracles 'against' the nations with the prediction of a surprising fulfilment of the Abrahamic covenant.[84]

The judgment of the old, the creation of the new (Isa. 24 – 25)

Isaiah 24 follows, quite naturally, the series of oracles concerning the nations in 13 – 23.[85] Chapter 24 makes the international and supra-ethnic dimensions that appear frequently in chapters 13 – 23 its dominant perspective as it announces a worldwide judgment for which the only criterion is whether or not one has 'transgressed the laws, violated the statutes, [and] broken the everlasting covenant' (24:5). In the judgment that unfolds across the rest of the chapter, most but not all of earth inhabitants are 'scorched' (24:6), caught (24:18, 22) and finally punished along with 'the host of heaven' (24:21–22). Even the earth itself is scarred by these judgments (24:4, 13, 19–20) and 'falls' as if never to rise again (24:20).

Building on the existence of a remnant that is delivered from this judgment (24:6) and the praise of Yahweh by voices that are raised from all directions (24:14–16a), the statement that Yahweh of Hosts will reign 'on Mount Zion and in Jerusalem' and that his elders will see his glory (24:23) reveals that God's work of salvation runs parallel to his devastating judgment. Zion, presented here as being free of sin, the location of God's presence, and the only stable location in the universe – even 'the centre of the universe' – contrasts with the 'wasted city' and 'earth' that fell under judgment in 24:1–22.[86]

This same contrast appears in the groups mentioned in chapter 25. On

[84] Kim 2020: 61.

[85] In this section I occasionally draw on Timmer 2022b.

[86] Beuken 2015: 48.

the one hand, the wasted city and the citadel of the foreigners[87] (*zārîm*) are for ever ruined (25:2), and God subdues the 'foreigners' and the 'ruthless' (25:5). On the other hand, 'strong peoples will glorify you; cities of ruthless nations will fear you' (25:3). This second depiction of non-Israelites (*ʿam ʿaz* and *gôyîm ʿārîṣîm*) is as positive as the references to other non-Israelites in 25:2 are negative. Having survived the judgment that Yahweh sent against sinners, these 'strong peoples' and these nations glorify Yahweh for his justice and revere him just as faithful Israelites do. God's deliverance of the 'poor' and 'needy' from judgment (25:4) underscores the fact that his salvation is granted without reference to the nationality or ethnicity of those whom he delivers.[88]

The parallels between the scene in 24:23 and the covenant meal described in Exodus 24 suggest that Yahweh's relationship with the international group that survives the judgment of chapter 24 has reached a new stage, but even so, the feast announced in 25:6–8 is completely unprecedented (cf. Exod. 15:17–18). It will be set on Mount Zion, where God's glory is now revealed (24:23; contrast 1:21–24), and those welcomed at the meal are described as 'all peoples', 'all nations' and 'his [Yahweh's] people'. Since these groups are presented exclusively in terms of their relationship with Yahweh, whom they 'glorify' and 'revere' (25:3, my translation), their national or ethnic identity is inconsequential. To this diverse group Yahweh serves an unparalleled feast that symbolizes his gift of superlative life. Even this image pales somewhat before the statement that God 'will swallow up death for ever' (25:8) and wipe tears 'from all faces' so that suffering, death and every other cause for sadness will be no more. The eternal life and flourishing of those on Yahweh's mountain is contrasted with the fate of Moab, presented here as symbolizing a proud opposition against God that resists his rule.[89]

It is quite in keeping with Isaiah's theology that the book's clearest presentation of the consummation of redemptive history does away almost entirely with the Israel–nations distinction in favour of spiritual–relational characteristics that correlate with the diametrically opposed

[87] Beuken (2007: 341–342) argues that 'foreigners' should not be emended to 'arrogant', attested by the LXX, whereas Wildberger (1997: 515, 519) favours the emendation and Oswalt (1986: 457) is ambivalent.

[88] Dekker 2021: 160.

[89] Bürki 2013: 56–57; Dekker 2021: 161–162.

outcomes of eternal life or destruction.[90] In place of humankind's broken covenant (24:5), God establishes in ways the text does not directly address a means by which sinful human beings from all nations can survive his judgment and sit eternally at his table in perfect joy and security (Matt. 8:11).[91]

The nations and salvation

Although other Old Testament prophetic books sometimes portray the involvement of the remnant in the salvation of the nations or evoke the Abrahamic covenant and foresee that Israel will be a blessing to the nations, Isaiah gives more attention to Israel's role in relation to the nations' salvation than any other prophetic book.[92] He does so especially by including the nations in the Servant's mission (Isa. 42:1–9; 49:1–6; note also the sprinkling of 'many nations' in 52:15) and by developing the image of the peaceful coming of the nations to Zion.[93] In this section we will consider how salvation comes to the nations through these two movements in passages that announce no judgment against non-Israelites and so emphasize as strongly as possible the inclusion of non-Israelites in Yahweh's work of salvation.[94]

The Servant, Israel and the nations (Isa. 42:1–12; 49:1–7)

Israel and the nations form one people (Isa. 42:1–12)

The nations appear in three contiguous sections in chapter 42: the presentation (42:1–4) and commissioning (42:5–9) of Yahweh's Servant, and

[90] So also Dekker (2021: 158–161), who is careful to preserve Israel's unique role in redemptive history.

[91] Hagelia (2001: 198–199) argues for the covenantal nature of this meal.

[92] Oehler 1883: 517.

[93] Isaiah also applies the term 'servant' to the nation of Israel (41:8–9; 42:19; 44:21; etc.), which by the seventh century BC had failed to fulfil that role, and Cyrus, who serves in a quite different capacity. See Watts 1990: 41–44, 50–56, on Cyrus and the Servant, respectively.

[94] Space constraints oblige us to bypass many oracles which address the redemptive-historical dynamics that appear in the passages treated here: the nations rebuild Zion (45:13), worship Yahweh (45:14), trust in Yahweh (51:5), pay tribute to Yahweh as his vassals (Isa. 18), are born as Zion's children (45:22–25; 49:14–26), follow the eschatological Davidic king (11:10; 55:4–5), and much more.

the hymn of praise that these divine actions evoke (42:10–12). Although Isaiah has repeatedly announced deliverance for Zion from Isaiah 40 onward, it is still remarkable that in terms of literary order, the messianic Servant's *first* sphere of saving activity is the nations (42:1; similarly, 42:6). The description of the Servant in Isaiah 42 begins by presenting him as one who receives, to an unprecedented degree, Yahweh's support, delight and Spirit for his task of bringing justice to 'the nations' (42:1). Koole summarizes the outcome of this task as 'the realization of God's rule, the advent of the kingdom in which God is recognized, obeyed, and praised'.[95] The international dimension of the Servant's commission includes his establishing 'justice in the earth' and bringing his teaching to distant islands or coastlands (42:4).

The second half of the commission continues the same trajectory, with only slight changes. Subsuming Israel and Judah in the global perspective defined by Yahweh as the creator of 'the people' who inhabit the earth (42:5), Yahweh commits to give his Servant as a covenant to or for 'people' (*'am*, most likely referring to Israel, or perhaps to people in general) as well as 'a light to nations' (*gôyîm* [42:6, my translation]).[96] The Servant thus establishes a (new) covenant that binds Yahweh to members of *both* groups, and the light he brings symbolizes the deliverance, justice and righteousness in which this covenant relationship culminates (Isa. 9:2; 30:26; 42:16; 58:8, 10; 59:9). Notably, the last verse of the commission (42:7) sets aside any ethnic or national designators in favour of descriptors that are limited to the needs addressed by the Servant's mission: metaphorical blindness and imprisonment. These concepts emphasize the transformative, spiritual deliverance that lies at the heart of the Servant's mission and establish a sharp contrast between this Servant's role and that of Cyrus.[97] The profuse use of nations-terminology in the hymn of

[95] Koole 1997: 208.

[96] In favour of 'people' referring to non-Israelites, see Fischer 1995: 87; Van Winkel 1985: 456. Many exegetes favour seeing Israel as the people in view; cf. Koole 1997: 230.

[97] Schultz 2005: 341. Although God uses Cyrus to free the exiles and permit the rebuilding of Jerusalem (45:13 and context), the work of the Servant presented in Isa. 49 is of an entirely different nature. Cyrus and the messianic Servant have radically different relationships with Yahweh (Cyrus does not know Yahweh, whereas the Servant trusts him resolutely); their actions affect different groups (the exiles in Babylon versus Jacob/Israel and the 'preserved ones of Israel') and bring them to different destinations (Yehud versus Yahweh), and they produce different outcomes (Cyrus's military success allows the exiles to return and rebuild Jerusalem but nothing more, whereas the Servant manifests Yahweh's glory, is glorified by Yahweh and participates in bringing Yahweh's salvation to the end of the earth). The arguments of Nguyen (2021: 491) falter principally because Cyrus is never presented in the OT or in Persian sources as recognizing Yahweh as

42:10–12 forms the climax of the passage and the ultimate outcome of the Servant's mission as people in every conceivable location celebrate Yahweh's new work of salvation and give him glory. What Yahweh does, through his Servant, for the nations (not to the exclusion of Israelites) in Isaiah 42:1–12 and what he does for his people in Isaiah 41:8–20 establishes an extremely significant criterion of identity between these two groups.

Despite its brevity, Isaiah 42:1–12 summarizes beautifully the main elements of Yahweh's work of salvation. Taking account of his covenant people's inability to fulfil the role of servant, Yahweh brings from among them another Servant who will achieve all his purposes with astonishing meekness and compassion, in contradistinction to the approach of the empires in which Judah often hoped, whose rulers used other means to accomplish their goals. This work of salvation is correlated with God's creation of the cosmos at the beginning (42:5), and culminates in his praises being sung by those whom he has liberated, transformed and made suitable for the perfectly just world created through the Servant's work. The salvific mission of God's Servant also stands in sharp opposition to the immanent, material focus of the deliverance that Israel and Judah hoped to receive by means of alliances with other states.

The inclusion of Israelites and non-Israelites in the Servant's saving mission (Isa. 49:1–7)

As was the case in chapter 42, the Servant's speech in Isaiah 49 begins by addressing the 'coastlands' and 'peoples from afar'. But whereas 42:1–9 describes especially the nature of the Servant's mission, the present passage focuses on its scope. This Servant, identical to the figure introduced in Isaiah 42, embodies or epitomizes the ideal identity of 'Israel' and is designated and prepared by Yahweh. His initial mission, in which Yahweh was to glorify himself (49:3), consisted of bringing 'Jacob . . . Israel' back to him, that is, renewing Israel. However, the Servant's work or mission is anticipated to be too limited in scope (49:4, 6a). In response to the Servant's dissatisfaction with the limited results of his anticipated work, Yahweh *expands* the scope of his mission to include being 'a light

---

supreme and because the Cyrus Cylinder is less relevant for the messianic Servant's identity than is the rest of the OT. Assuming that Cyrus is described as 'righteous' in 41:2 (Sweeney 2016: 70; for discussion, see Goldingay and Payne 2006: 1:142–144), this elevated title is comparable to the honorific descriptions used of Nebuchadnezzar in Jer. 27.

to nations' so that Yahweh's salvation 'may reach the end of the earth' (49:6, my translations). Although the Servant's mission involves his humiliation, its accomplishment will ultimately lead to his elevation and the prostration of kings and princes before him (49:7). These rulers are 'urged to recognize him (49:7, 22–23), to render homage to Yahweh, and to bring the exiles of his people to Zion with them as they themselves come in pilgrimage'.[98] The passage thus follows a sequence that is evident across the Old Testament, in which Israel is restored and (some) non-Israelites subsequently participate in that salvation.[99] This sequence is clear throughout Isaiah 40 – 55, where 'God's mission to restore desolate Zion and Israel will coincide with and even be the means through which all nations find blessing under the rule of YHWH in glorious Zion'.[100] It is also central in the third major section of Isaiah's book (chs. 56 – 66), to which we now turn.

Contribution to and participation in Zion's eschatological restoration (Isa. 60 – 62)

The final portion of the book of Isaiah, chapters 56 – 66, shifts its focus to Zion-in-transformation while maintaining a very positive secondary focus on the nations. The anticipated audience's setting is post-exilic, and in that context the prophet foresees that the 'Zion' to whom he addresses his message is far from being fully restored. The following chiastic structure makes clear the tension between 'now' and 'not yet' that runs through these chapters. This tension coincides, strikingly if only roughly, with a contrast between the dire straits in which Israelites are often presented and the general positive condition of non-Israelites.[101] All the same, the nations still come to salvation through Israel, and its final condition will be glorious indeed, as the central chapters of Isaiah 56 – 66 show.[102]

A (56:1–8) Faithful non-Israelites in God's service after salvation

[98] Köstenberger and O'Brien 2001: 48.

[99] Zehnder 2005: 499.

[100] Abernethy 2016: 195.

[101] Oswalt (2006: 50) speaks of 'the apparent inability of Zion to live out the kind of obedience the foreigners and eunuchs are offering' in chs. 56 – 66.

[102] Here I follow the structure in Abernethy 2016: 84, with some changes.

B (56:9 – 59:8) Confronting faithless Israelites with judgment, comforting the faithful with salvation

C (59:9–15a) Prayer for forgiveness and restoration

D (59:15b–21) The warrior king judges the wicked and redeems the repentant

E (60 – 62) Zion's international renown amid Yahweh's glory and his messenger

D′ (63:1–6) The warrior king judges and saves the nations

C′ (63:7 – 64:12) Prayer for forgiveness and restoration

B′ (65:1 – 66:17) Confronting faithless Israelites with judgment, comforting the faithful with salvation

A′ (66:18–24) Faithful non-Israelites in God's service after salvation and judgment

We will consider Zion's restoration first since it is arguably antecedent, logically if not chronologically, to the fully consummated horizon sketched in Isaiah 56:1–8 and 66:18–24.[103] Despite the diversity of roles attributed to non-Israelites in these chapters, they are best taken as complementary and positive (excepting the possible refusal of some to serve [60:12]).[104] Although the nations' roles are typically presented in images drawn from Israel's historical experience (suzerain–vassal relationship, etc.), the element of spiritual transformation that predominates in all of them and the figural nature of the images themselves caution against a woodenly literal understanding of these roles in the new epoch of salvation sketched in these chapters.[105]

The opening verses of Isaiah 60 foretell how the 'glory of Yahweh' that will characterize superlatively restored Zion as 'the peaceful capital of YHWH's kingdom' will draw the nations to Zion *as part of their coming to Yahweh.*[106] As former enemies of Zion and her God (60:14; cf. Isa. 2:4), these non-Israelites are irresistibly attracted to and transformed by his glory, now made visible in his rule over and presence with his people, whom they come to join. Similarly, in Isaiah 62:2, the righteousness that Zion receives from Yahweh (61:1–3; cf. 59:14–21) is the source of the

[103] Oswalt (2006: 50) concludes that the 'submission of the nations to Zion' is 'partial and not final'.

[104] Tiemeyer 2017: 15.

[105] Richelle 2012.

[106] Abernethy 2016: 102; McConville 2023: 665.

glory that the nations perceive and to which they come (60:3).[107] Non-Israelites also recognize Zion's blessedness (60:14; 61:6, 9) and covenantal priority (61:6; cf. the background of creation for Israel's election in 51:16) as they come to join its citizens in worship of Yahweh.

As participants in and contributors to God's exaltation of his people, non-Israelites bring their wealth to Zion (60:5–7, 11, 13; 61:6), participate in its rebuilding (60:10, 13, a task shared with Israelites [61:4]),[108] tend its flocks and fields (61:5), serve it in an 'eminent' capacity (60:10), and nourish and nurture it as a nursing mother (60:16).[109] Although presented largely in terms of submission to Zion, the non-Israelites in these chapters *share Zion's most fundamental criterion of identity*: the worship of Yahweh (60:6), in whom they 'hope' (60:9) and to whom their contributions are ultimately offered.[110] This identity is all the more evident if the 'sons' and 'daughters' of Zion are non-Israelites (60:4; cf. 49:8–21; 54:1–4; 66:7–9), as seems most likely. But even if the children in 60:4 are Israelites, both Israelites and non-Israelites come to Zion to live and worship there permanently (60:4–7), a reality that represents nothing less than the consummation of all of Scripture's redemptive covenants (Gen. 12:3; 15:1–21; 17:1–21; Exod. 15:17–18; 31:12–17; 40:38; 2 Sam. 7:1–16; Pss 2; 45; 72; 110).[111]

Full integration of non-Israelites into renewed Israel and its worship (Isa. 56:1–8; 66:18–24)

As suggested by the chiastic structure presented above, these two units form a bracket around Isaiah 56 – 66.[112] They present with unsurpassed power and clarity Isaiah's message of salvation for non-Israelites, asserting that non-Israelites will participate fully in cultic worship of Yahweh and even serve as his priests. While both passages are extremely positive in this regard, they are not at odds with the other positive treatments of

---

[107] Isa. 61:1–3 is most likely another speech by the messianic Servant; see Oswalt 1998: 562–563.

[108] Webb (1990: 79) refers to the nations' participation in Zion's rebuilding as making 'reparation for past wrongs'.

[109] Koole (2001: 238) notes the elevated status of the verbal subjects of the Hebrew root *š-r-t*, notably in relation to the temple (cf. 61:5–6), as does Paul (2012: 526).

[110] 'Hope' is supported by the majority of the versions; see the discussion in Koole 2001: 235–236. A reading like that proposed by Paul (2012: 525–526), 'The vessels of the coastlands shall assemble', requires more than a little textual emendation.

[111] Koole 2001: 226; similarly, Paul 2012: 520.

[112] Sweeney 2016: 297; Schuele 2014: 97–103.

non-Israelites.[113] As we have seen, similarly positive predictions regarding non-Israelites abound in chapters 60 – 62, which describe the nations' multifaceted peaceful relations with and participation in renewed Zion.

The call for Isaiah's (Judean) audience to 'keep justice, and do righteousness' (56:1) that begins the unit sets what follows in the context of Yahweh's immanent revelation of his righteousness, which will be saving for those who faithfully observe the sabbath as the sign of the Sinai covenant and as representing the holistic obedience that the covenant's stipulations require.[114] Although set in the context of Israel's long-standing national covenant with Yahweh, Isaiah 56:2 promises blessing to a generic person or human being, opening the door to what follows.[115] The metaphor of an open door is well-suited to describe the message of 56:3–8, since Yahweh announces that groups formerly excluded from temple worship, notably foreigners (56:3a, 6–7), will now be fully included.[116] This openness is all the more remarkable in the light of the prohibition in Deuteronomy 23:1–8, elements of which Isaiah develops and clarifies in order to radically widen access to the worship of Yahweh.[117] These centre on any 'foreigners' who, presumably on the basis of their non-Israelite descent, fear being 'totally separated' from Yahweh's people (see 56:3). To this Yahweh replies that any foreigners who commit to following him from the heart (to 'join themselves' to Yahweh) by serving and loving him in keeping with his covenant will be brought to his temple, where God will make them joyful and accept the sacrifices they offer (cf. Isa. 2:1–4). This level of access to the temple is as complete as that offered to the Israelite eunuchs whom the passage also addresses – again, in contradistinction to Deuteronomy 23.

This unfettered access to Yahweh's presence and cultic worship is complemented by the book's final passage, in which Yahweh announces that he will send non-Israelites to distant places where they will 'declare [his] glory' and bring *Israelites* as a metaphorical 'offering to [Yahweh] . . . to [his] holy mountain Jerusalem' (66:19–20). The emphasis on non-Israelites' unrestricted access to the most sacred tasks pertaining to the temple

---

[113] Contrast the arguments of Tiemeyer 2017: 15–20.

[114] See Timmer 2009: 53–55, 98–99.

[115] Schulmeister 2012: 42.

[116] See Timmer 2024c, on which I occasionally draw in this section.

[117] Ibid. 42–43, 45, 51–52. It is also possible to interpret Isa. 56 as an abrogation of the restrictions in Deut. 23.

reaches its peak in God's promise that he will take 'some of them . . . for priests and for Levites' (66:21), indicating that they share in all of the privileges and roles formerly reserved for Israelites, *even those formerly based on genetic descent*.[118] This international group of worshippers, defined by their fidelity to Yahweh and his gift of righteousness to them (59:15b–21; 63:1–6; cf. 52:13 – 53:12; 60:21), constitute the 'all flesh' of 40:5 – those who worship him without interruption in the new heavens and new earth that form the book's most distant and most glorious horizon.[119]

Summary and New Testament developments

The non-Israelite nations appear at all points of the judgment–salvation spectrum that structures much of Isaiah's theology and at all points in redemptive history. They are always seen in relation to Israel, which typically manifests the same penchant for idolizing earthly things and powers even as it remains the vehicle through which Yahweh will bring his salvation to the ends of the earth. Isaiah's most focused treatment of the nations, in the oracles of Isaiah 13 – 23, deconstructs their ideologies and, while also announcing salvation, often spells out its effects in terms of their embrace of radically different beliefs and behaviours in which Yahweh's grace and righteousness are central. Isaiah's Servant is uniquely prominent as the one through whom Yahweh's saving word and works reach the 'peoples' and 'nations', most notably in his suffering for the sins of 'many nations', a group that Isaiah includes in the group whose griefs and sorrows he carried (Isa. 52:15; 53:4). This allows Israelites and non-Israelites alike, finally, to enjoy eternal life in Yahweh's presence and to unite their voices in praise of his glory (Isa. 24:14–16; 25:9; 26:19).[120]

Isaiah is frequently drawn upon by the authors of the New Testament as they explain the progress of redemption in the light of Christ's incarnation, earthly ministry and universal reign.[121] As far as the nations are concerned, following Simeon's prophecy based on Isaiah 42:6 that Jesus

[118] Wodecki 1982: 251.

[119] Oswalt 1997.

[120] Kim (2020: 67–73) conveniently summarizes the primary functions of the oracles in Isaiah; Oswalt (2006: 42) concisely summarizes the nations' roles.

[121] See, beyond the literature cited here, Raabe 2013; Timmer 2019a.

will be 'a light for revelation to the Gentiles' (Luke 2:32) and the nations as part of 'all flesh' (Isa. 40:3–5) that will see God's salvation (Luke 3:4–6), Jesus' announcement in Luke 4:17–22 that he has come to fulfil Isaiah 61:1–2 proves to be 'programmatic' for Luke's presentation of the Christ's work in Luke–Acts, even though the same context anticipates that widespread rejection of Jesus by Jews will lead to the gospel being brought to Gentiles (Luke 4:23–27).[122] Luke's presentation of the Ethiopian eunuch in Acts 8 may well intend to evoke the promise in Isaiah 56 that eunuchs will be fully integrated into the eschatological people of God, a reality signified by his baptism.[123] The apostles' assumption of the Servant's role as 'a light for the Gentiles' in Acts 13:47, where Paul and Barnabas redirect their ministry to the Gentiles, is a striking use of Isaiah 49:1–12.[124] Not only do the apostles take on the Servant's ministry as their own, but also their words echo Luke 24:47 and Acts 1:8, tying this new phase of mission to Jesus' commission of the apostles.[125] The book of Acts closes with the citation of another key passage from Isaiah that ties Israel's temporary hardening to the rapid extension of the gospel into the Gentile world.[126]

The letter to the Romans provides a microcosm of Paul's use of Isaiah's rich presentation of non-Israelites in relation to salvation. Although Paul cites Isaiah 52:5 in Romans 2:24 as part of his argument for Jews (and Gentiles) being 'under the power of sin', the context in Isaiah 52 follows this with God's commitment to bring salvation to Zion, and Paul 'places himself among' the messengers of Isaiah 52:7–10 who bring the news of 'the salvation of our God' to 'the ends of the earth'.[127] In the discussion of Israel's place in redemptive history in Romans 9 – 11, Paul includes 'us . . . not only from among the Jews, but also from the Gentiles' among those who will receive God's mercy (Rom. 9:23–24).[128] In Romans 10:20–21, Paul contrasts Israel's temporary rejection of the Messiah with God's being 'found by those who did not seek [him]', but integrates the salvation of the nations into God's one work of salvation for Jew and Gentile alike (Rom. 11:25–32), citing Isaiah 59:20–21. Towards the end of the epistle,

[122] Rosner 1998: 220; Koet 2005: 81–83; Angers 2018: 172–173; Bock 2012: 292, 297.

[123] Seccombe 1998: 360.

[124] Koet 2005: 99.

[125] Bock 2012: 299.

[126] Koet 2005: 95–97.

[127] Wagner 2005: 119.

[128] Ibid. 120, citing an unknown translation of Rom. 2:24.

Paul argues that the confirmation of the promises made to the patriarchs, specifically that 'the Gentiles might glorify God for his mercy' (Rom. 15:9), is the fulfilment of the promise in Isaiah 11:10–11 that the 'peoples' and 'nations' will come to the royal Messiah (Rom. 15:12). In both Isaiah 11 and Romans 15, God's saving mercy comes to the Gentiles through Israel and its Messiah, tying the two groups together as the one people of God. Indeed, some of Isaiah's clearest statements of the integration of non-Israelites into the eschatological people of God (e.g. Isa. 56:1–8; 66:18–21) underlie Paul's assertion that this unity has now become reality 'through faith alone in Christ, the embodiment of true Israel, and not by identifying with the externals of the Mosaic covenant'.[129] The unexpected children that 'Zion *did not bear*' in Isaiah 49:21 are another striking example of the organic relationship between Jewish and Gentile believers, both Zion's children by the Spirit.[130]

Finally, the book of Revelation makes frequent use of Isaiah in its description of judgment in Revelation 14 – 19.[131] These chapters draw on Isaiah's oracles against Babylon and Edom in Isaiah 21, against Tyre in Isaiah 23, against Babylon again (Isa. 47; 52:11) and against the 'nations' as a collective in Isaiah 34. The echo of Isaiah 23:17 in Revelation 17:2 and 18:3, 9, for example, implies that Babylon is the culmination of Tyre's impressive but self-satisfied, luxury-sated and God-dishonouring self-glorification, and its sudden and irreparable ruin at God's hand is thus inevitable. The idolatrous dimension of Tyre's practice is emphasized in Revelation's repeated use of 'sexual immorality' as a metaphor for putting one's trust in some facet of the creation rather than in the Creator.[132] John places Rome and its ideology within the purview of Isaiah's oracles because he perceived in its desire to control creation by whatever means were most effective for satisfying its ambition and pride the same rejection of God that Tyre manifested in pursuing its own glory as its highest good. At the end of his work, John also draws on several of Isaiah's oracles of salvation to describe the eschatological renewal of the cosmos, including the allusion to Isaiah 25:8, where death is destroyed, in Revelation 21:4. This is connected, in turn, with the statement 'Behold, I am making all

[129] Gladd 2023: 554.

[130] Blocher 2002: 7, emphasis original; Richelle 2012: 112–113.

[131] Here I follow Mathewson 2005: 198. It is also notable that Isaiah's second-exodus theology is drawn upon repeatedly at key points in Rev. 15:1; 16:1–14, as noted by Piotrowski (2023: 239).

[132] Mathewson 2005: 199.

things new', which draws on the new-creation theme in Isaiah 43:19 and 65:17–20 to form 'the climax of' Revelation 21:1–5.[133]

[133] Ibid. 203.

4
Jeremiah

'Who would not fear you, O King of the nations?' (Jer. 10:7). This rhetorical question, nestled in one of the short doxologies scattered across the book of Jeremiah, hints at the very close connection between God as universal king and the turbulent geopolitical scene that is both the backdrop and the subject matter of the book of Jeremiah.[1] Perhaps no other period of biblical Israel's history was as chaotic as the final decades of Judah's existence, in which Assyria fell to Babylon, Egypt attempted in vain to impede Babylon's subjugation of the Levant, and a number of smaller states there struggled to survive amid the confrontations entailed by these shifts of power. Yet it was in the very midst of this maelstrom that Jeremiah announced to Judah Yahweh's sovereign, unqualified control over the nations (Jer. 1:10).[2] Unlike the gods of the surrounding kingdoms (10:8–9), Yahweh is peerless and unchangeably committed to his plan to save his people in justice and mercy. Despite the nations' self-centred plans for survival, the acquisition of resources, dominion and glory – exemplified above all by Babylon – God's wisdom and sovereignty show in surprising ways 'that empire is not what it is usually thought to be'.[3] It is neither an uncontrolled mortal danger to Judah (as many Judeans feared), nor is it an unstoppable, autonomous power protected by its gods (as Babylonian imperial ideology would have it).

The nations are at the centre of Jeremiah's message, whether negatively in God's repeated commands to Judah and its leaders to submit to covenant discipline by surrendering to Babylon, or positively in the close connection between Babylon's fall and Judah's ultimate salvation in Jeremiah 50 – 51. This chapter surveys the main contours of the theme

[1] Fischer 2012: 95.

[2] Kessler 2004: 61. Hwang (2021: 483–488) carefully traces the international dimensions of Jeremiah's call and ministry.

[3] Brueggemann 1991: 15.

of the nations (including their relation to Judah) in three overlapping chronological phases: (1) prior to Judah's exile, when the nations, especially Babylon, serve as God's means for bringing increasingly severe punishments on Judah; (2) during Judah's exile, when Babylon's role shifts radically from aggressor to host; and (3) at the end of exile and beyond, with a complex mix of judgment and salvation determining the fates of the nations.

The nations prior to Judah's exile

In keeping with the covenant that God established with Abraham and Israel's calling to be a nation of priests at Sinai several hundred years later, the theme of the nations in Jeremiah is interwoven with the life and destiny of God's covenant people. In the very first vision recounted in Jeremiah 1:13, the activity of the enemy from the north (Babylon) serves God's purpose of declaring his 'judgments against [the people of Judah], for all their evil in forsaking [him]' (1:16), making the punitive role of the nations with respect to Judah prominent from the very beginning of the book.

In the following chapters, ancient Israel's initial fidelity to Yahweh long ago (2:2–3) contrasts with its present 'forsaking' of him in favour of 'broken cisterns' (see 2:13) that fail to satisfy its thirst for security. Judah's misdirected dependence on the nations reveals a pragmatic *Realpolitik* that set its leaders' political calculus above God's unparalleled commitment to his people as their creator, redeemer and king. By the time of Jeremiah, this was a centuries-old problem. The northern kingdom's appeal to Assyria (Hos. 5:13; 7:11) and Egypt (Hos. 7:11), Ahaz's plea to Assyria to neutralize the threat posed by Aram and Israel (2 Kgs 16:1–9), Hezekiah's imprudent openness to Babylonian envoys (2 Kgs 20:12–19), and Judah's desire to secure help from Egypt and Assyria against Babylon in Jeremiah's day (Jer. 2:18, 36) all reveal a preference among some of God's people – often its leaders – for human help over covenant fidelity and blessing. This inevitably occurs in the context of their own disobedience and involves a desire to overlook their pursuit of 'lovers' (4:30) as the possible (indeed, all too likely) cause of these same crises.[4] In this section we will consider 'the nations' other than Babylon separately in the light of Jeremiah's much more extensive treatment of the latter. Because of the

[4] Ortlund 1996: 83–84.

close connection that the book makes between these nations' actions on the geopolitical scene and God's responses, these sections reach beyond the pre-exilic timeframe to include announcements of the nations' future punishment.

The nations as God's means for punishing Judah – and God's subsequent punishment of the nations

Ironically, Judah's misguided attempts to secure its future apart from repentance and dependence on God bring it harm rather than benefit. The southern kingdom's earlier involvement with Assyria had brought it into the very unfavourable role of being the empire's vassal, and Egypt too had proven and would prove to be an erstwhile ally (2:36).[5] Insisting that self-destructive attempts to enlist the aid of the nations instead of turning to God in repentance are 'evil' and amount to 'apostasy' (2:19), Jeremiah warns that those same groups will be the means by which God punishes his people's sin. In this role, the nations are presented as beasts of prey who oppress Judah (2:15), lurking like a lion, wolf and leopard (5:6) as they wait for an opportune moment to attack. These 'others' will take possession of the Judeans' homes (6:12), and these 'conquerors' will take over their fields (8:10).

The theological and moral tenor of God's word 'over' the nations comes fully into view in the identification of 'the nations that know you not' as 'the peoples that call not on your name' and who have 'devoured Jacob . . . devoured him and consumed him, and have laid waste his habitation' (10:25). Again, in 12:14, Yahweh threatens to 'pluck up' from their lands (the same verb as in Jeremiah's commission in 1:10) the 'evil neighbours' who have harmed his inheritance. Even when God insists that all the nations to whom he sends Jeremiah must drink the 'cup of the wine of wrath' (25:15), roughly half of the twenty-two cases mentioned limit the cup's recipients to the kings or leaders of the groups named (25:17–26). More significantly, the following oracle in 25:31 limits divine judgment, at least in its severest form (the sword), to 'the wicked' (25:31; the same holds for the divine storm of wrath that will strike Judah in 23:19; 30:23). In all these cases, God directs his judgment against those whose guilt is

[5] The temporal setting envisaged in Jer. 2:16 may be future; so Goldingay 2021a: 121; Craigie, Kelley and Drinkard 1991: 32–33; cf. 2 Kgs 23:33–35. Redford (1992: 448–449) helpfully sketches the international background of Egypt's renewed involvement in the Levant from about 610 BC onward.

unforgiven, although the precise identity of those affected and the nature of their offences is not always clear.

In the so-called Book of Consolation (Jer. 30 – 33) that focuses on Judah's future restoration, God promises: 'I will make a full end of all the nations among whom I scattered you' (30:11). Judah's enemies will 'go into captivity', and justice will be done to those who plundered it and made it their prey (30:16). The 'full end' announced there almost certainly does not refer to the annihilation of these states, but to the end of the states in question *as Judah's oppressors*. This is confirmed by the inclusion of many of these groups in restoration passages elsewhere in Jeremiah (see below).

Much of what Jeremiah says about the nations (other than Babylon) is confined to the oracles in Jeremiah 46 – 49. Notably, all the nations mentioned in chapters 46 – 49 were (apart from overt rebellion) vassals of the Babylonian Empire from about 600 BC onward,[6] such that Yahweh's claim of sovereignty over them relativizes Babylon's. These oracles, which differ in order and placement in the Hebrew and Greek textual witnesses,[7] reveal the inner workings of these states' aggression against Judah, and on that basis God accuses them of moral offences and corrupt beliefs that justify the punishment announced in these oracles.[8] While the distinction between those involved in aggression against Judah and the general population of the respective state is perhaps not as clear as it is in Nahum, for example, the precision and specificity of the charges mean that they are only relevant to a portion of the state in question, especially its military and administrative corps. There is also a strong theological critique of many of these nations for their opposition to Yahweh or aggression against his people.[9]

At the beginning of the collection, God asserts that Egypt's gods are involved in its imperial designs to dominate the world (46:2, 8, 15) and that they will be shamed when it falls to Babylon at his command (46:25–26a).[10] Moab (48:1–46) will be punished because it trusted in its 'works'

[6] Smothers 1988: 551. The Chronicles that recount Nebuchadnezzar's first ten years document his subjugation of these nations and city-states.

[7] See Peels 2007 for discussion, and Graybill 2021 (390–393) for a convenient overview.

[8] Raabe (2018: 242) notes the predominance of God as 'the textual speaker', one of many ways in which the oracles show that 'the God of Israel is in charge of the entire sequence' of oracles.

[9] There are several exceptions. The oracles against the Philistines (47:1–7) and Kedar and Hazor (49:28–33) mention neither religious (false gods, etc.) nor moral offences such as violence. The oracle against Damascus/Aram (49:23–27) is similarly vague, but since 49:27 is reused from Amos 1:5, violence may be inferred.

[10] The Septuagint reads 'Why has Apis fled?' in 46:15a, and this may well be the better reading. The MT has a singular verb with a plural subject, and the consonants of the verbal form, if

and 'treasures' (48:7), took pride in its military might (48:14, 29–30), 'magnified' itself against Yahweh, derided Israel (48:26–27, 42) and practised idolatry (48:35). The theological significance of its idolatry is emphasized in the prediction that Moab's chief god Chemosh (48:46) will be exiled along with his priests and officials (48:7, 13). God's accusation of Ammon (49:1–6), purportedly under the aegis of its chief god Milcom, follows similar lines: it has 'dispossessed Gad' (49:1, territory that God had allocated to Israel), boasted in its valleys, trusted in its wealth and imagined that it was beyond danger (see 49:4). The religious nature of the 'Ammon' that is referred to here is evident in the statement that Milcom will be exiled along with his priests and officials (49:3). For its part, Edom (49:7–22) 'inspired horror' by means of violence, was proud, and sought to put itself beyond danger (see 49:16). Finally, Elam (49:34–38) is defined in terms of its 'bow' (49:35) and its 'king and officials' (49:38), references to the military and royal corps that directed its autonomous political strategy and aggression.

These carefully focused portrayals of the nations in God's condemnations of them (Babylon excepted, for the moment) have nothing to do with hatred for the ethnic 'other',[11] but rather focus selectively on those within the groups named who arrogantly reject Yahweh's supremacy and will as their creator, give their allegiance to false gods who underwrite their nationalist projects, and pursue security apart from God. Yahweh's punishment of them is therefore morally necessary, and curtails violence on the geopolitical level while imposing the inevitable consequences of rebellion against God. However, as we will see, God's mercy makes it possible even for these enemies to be transformed by his grace.

Babylon as God's primary means for punishing Judah – and God's subsequent punishment of Babylon

Serving as the instrument of God's discipline of Judah is one of the few roles that Babylon shares with the other non-Israelite nations in Jeremiah, and in that role it dwarfs them. In historical terms, Judah's dealings with Babylon are limited to the last few decades of the empire's existence, but

revocalized, read '. . . did Apis flee?' Because Apis was represented as a bull, this reading aligns well with the bovine imagery in 46:20 as well. See Lundbom 2004: 209–210 for discussion.

[11] Contrast Graybill's 'extreme nationalist sentiments' (2021: 389) and the reference by Sharp (2015: 99) to 'boundaries between insiders and outsiders'.

they were of unprecedented significance for Judah and for biblical theology. In 604 BC, following Babylon's rout of Egypt in the battle of Carchemish in 605, Jehoiakim of Judah became a vassal of Babylon (2 Kgs 24:1), before switching his allegiance back to Egypt in 601 (Jer. 46:14–28). In the short term, a variety of enemies launched small-scale attacks against Judah (2 Kgs 24:2), until Babylon laid siege to Jerusalem and Jehoiachin wisely capitulated, early in 597 (2 Kgs 24:10–17).[12] The last Judean king, Zedekiah (597–586), apparently summoned envoys from the surrounding states to discuss how they might resist Babylon, arousing Nebuchadnezzar's suspicion (Jer. 51:59).[13] Notably, the letter that Jeremiah sent to these states at this time was clearly in favour of *submission* to Babylon rather than rebellion (Jer. 27:4–11), an example of the diametrically opposed understandings of the Judah–Babylon relationship held by the prophet on the one hand and Judah's leaders on the other. Whatever plans Zedekiah and his putative allies might have made, and despite Egypt's abortive last-minute attempt to help (Jer. 37:5, 11), Babylon laid siege to Jerusalem late in 588 BC, and the city fell some eighteen months later.[14]

These events were clear fulfilment of Jeremiah's prophecy that God would send an army from the north that would be as fatal to Judah as 'serpents' and 'adders' (8:16–17; note also the leonine metaphor in 4:7) and would interrupt the Davidic monarchy (22:1–7). The narrative of Jeremiah 39:1–10 describes the capture of the king, the killing of his sons and other nobles, and the destruction of the palace and the city walls. The narrative that closes the book completes this picture by recounting those same events (52:1–11) and adding a lengthy section that focuses on Babylon's destruction of the temple (52:12–23) and on some of the most prominent items taken from it.

Much more clearly than in the case of other nations, Jeremiah highlights the asymmetric involvement of God and Babylon, with the latter being merely his instrument for punishing Judah. God wields Babylon as his hammer (50:23; 51:20) and directs it as a cup of divine wrath (51:7) to destroy Judah (albeit not completely [4:27; 5:18]) and the surrounding nations. The Babylonian emperor is even called Yahweh's 'servant' (25:9; 27:6), the only time that this title, which underlines both the importance

[12] This event is recounted in the Babylonian Chronicles; see Wiseman 1961: 72.

[13] Redford (1992: 465) suggests that by 589, 'Zedekiah had formally renounced any allegiance to Babylon', apparently in the hope of regaining renewed independence from Babylon.

[14] Redford 1992: 466–467.

(32:1–16) continues this focus on Egypt's claim to unlimited power and self-determination by citing the pharaoh's self-attributed leonine image. The lion had long been a symbol of invincibility and unmatched power (and not a little violence) across the ancient Near East, and the metaphor captures the pharaoh's confidence in his ability to defend his empire against any threat.[79]

Yahweh's responses to these hubristic and self-adulatory expressions of ideology are diverse. In chapter 30, God announces that he will demonstrate the futility of Egypt's military pride in the Day of Yahweh, as part of which the Babylonian king as a divine instrument of judgment will destroy Egypt's military 'from Migdol to Syene' (30:6, a north–south merism for all Egypt).[80] To this he adds the threat that he will destroy Egypt's 'idols and images', referring to the so-called gods rather than simply to their physical representations. In the same vein, the drying up of the Nile (30:12) would put an end to the resurrection of Osiris, symbolized by the river's annual flooding, and so deconstruct the beliefs that the land would be perpetually rejuvenated and that the dead pharaoh would receive the status of deity through association with Osiris.[81]

The metaphorical comparison of 'Pharaoh and his multitude' with Assyria in chapter 31 moves very naturally towards the ultimate consequence of the pride that defines Egypt: death. For its pride, Egypt will be cut down, 'given over to death' and brought 'down to the pit' by Yahweh (31:14–17). Revealing the flawed interpretations of reality produced by dizzying hubris, *God's* evaluation of Egypt's self-attributed 'glory and . . . greatness' differs radically from the empire's (31:18). Despite its great height, the Egypt-tree descends to the pit at the very bottom of the cosmos, and finds itself on the same level as those over whom it had earlier cast its shade. Its place among the uncircumcised reinforces its condemnation and permanent alienation from Yahweh, who in his mercy will nonetheless shower his goodness upon Egyptians who are characterized by humility (cf. 29:13–16).

garden of Eden, waters, many waters, and rivers), although the evidence for chaos in the same images is less evident here than Crouch (2011: 482) suggests. Geyer (2004) carefully examines evidence for seeing this tree as the 'Cosmic Tree' in combination with other elements from the *Epic of Gilgamesh*. The more one sees mythological overtones in these elements, the harder the tree falls, so to speak, as Nevader (2015b: 173–175) observes.

[79] Strawn 2005.

[80] Greenberg 1997: 606.

[81] See Hoffmeier 1997: 149–150; Silverman 1991: 55–56.

of his role and his (involuntary) submission to Yahweh in it, is given to a non-Israelite.[15] Lest the success and power of Babylon be misinterpreted in immanent, military–political terms, God repeatedly states that he superintends all of Babylon's actions. As the grammatical subject of dozens of verbs, *he* gives captured Judeans and their fields to their foes (8:10), *he* will 'give all Judah into the hand of the king of Babylon' (20:4; with variations, 20:5; 21:4, 7, 10; 22:25; 27:5, 6; 28:14; 29:21; 32:4, 28; 34:2–3, 20–21; 44:30), and *he* will send Judeans into exile (29:4).

The theological significance of these details is self-evident. There is indeed overlap between Nebuchadnezzar's purposes and Yahweh's punishment of Judah, but the significance of that very rare intersection nonetheless makes Yahweh's sovereignty determinative of all that happens.[16] Hill captures this point nicely with respect to the key passage in Jeremiah 25: 'Babylon is both the agent of YHWH's judgment and the subject of it. While enjoying a special status via the figure of Nebuchadnezzar, Babylon is still completely subordinate to the God who has power over all the nations'.[17] Seen in this light, even kings who deny Yahweh's existence or significance are used by him for his purposes – *and* will be punished for their excesses and godlessness as they sinfully pursue their self-serving goals in the process. As a case in point, Babylon's violence is linked to the purification of Judah's remnant (6:6–9; 5:10, 15–18), yet its conquest of Judah involves significant 'iniquity', which God will punish (25:12–14). As Amesz observes:

> Babylon's hegemony would last as long as YHWH thought he needed it as an instrument (cup/hammer) for the execution of his plan. After that, his [Babylon's ruler's] kingdom would be totally destroyed and his god Marduk would be put to shame (50:2), as opposed to the Creator of all things, the God of Israel and Judah (51:19).[18]

The oracle against Babylon in Jeremiah 50 – 51 is much more extensive, incisive and definitive than the condemnations against other nations in

[15] Cyrus, in a similar role, receives an equally exceptional title, 'anointed', in Isa. 45:1. Smothers (1988: 552) suggests that 'the empire of Babylon, with Yahweh as suzerain, and with Nebuchadnezzar as Yahweh's servant, is the central reality which can explain the oracles against the nations in Jeremiah' and speaks of 'Yahweh's imperium'. Smelik (2014) concludes similarly.

[16] See Hill 2004; Peels 2007.

[17] Hill 2004: 154.

[18] Amesz 2004: 114.

Jeremiah 46 – 49.[19] It is also remarkable for including several oracles concerning Judah in 50:4–8, 17–20, 28, 33–34, clear evidence of the interwoven fates of the two states.[20] Because this oracle justifies Yahweh's punishment of Babylon by reference to its military violence, it is not a blanket condemnation of all Babylonians, many of whom had become subjects of the empire only recently when it conquered Assyria. This selective focus is further clarified by the extensive description of the beliefs, attitudes and actions that constitute Babylon's imperialism and by the mention of specific members of Babylon's military and administrative corps ('young men' and 'soldiers' [50:30; 51:3]; 'officials . . wise men . . . governors . . . commanders . . . warriors' [51:57]) .

The oracle begins at the theological heart of Babylonian imperialism with a prophecy that its gods, Bel/Marduk in particular, will be shamed (50:2). This directly contradicts the Babylonian creation epic *Enūma Elish*, which ends with Marduk's elevation to the top of the Mesopotamian pantheon amid the praise of the lesser gods.[21] Babylon's aggression against Judah is interpreted in the light of the crucially important fact that Judah is *Yahweh's* people and heritage (2:11; cf. 10:16), such that Babylon has plundered (50:11) and 'gnawed [the] bones' of God's elect people (50:17).

As the oracle unfolds, it becomes increasingly clear that opposition to God is at the heart of Babylon's imperial project. Its larger project of subjugating the Levant is summarized as *sin against God* (50:14), again with an emphasis on what Babylon 'has done' to others (50:15; similarly, 50:29). Because Babylon has 'opposed Yahweh' (50:24), God imposes the 'ban' (*ḥerem*) against it (see 50:21) and identifies himself as its opponent: 'I am against you' (50:31; also 51:25). God also condemns the empire's pride (50:32), refusal to release Judean captives (50:33) and full-orbed idolatry (50:36; 51:17–18, 47, 52). Revealing both his transcendence and his radical holiness, Yahweh declares that Babylon is 'full of guilt against the Holy One of Israel' (51:5) for 'all the evil . . . done in Zion' (51:24), having crushed, emptied, swallowed and rinsed out Jerusalem and its inhabitants (51:34–35, 47).[22] This mountain of guilt shows that the time

[19] Kessler (2004: 64) notes that Jer. 50 – 51 is 'by far the longest oracle of the collection' and 'also the fiercest in tone and the most absolute in its destructive tendency'.

[20] Allen 2008: 510.

[21] See Foster 2005; the composition ends with an exhortation to 'sound abroad the song of Marduk, how he defeated Tiamat and took kingship' (485).

[22] The comparison of Nebuchadnezzar to Tannin in 51:34 adds mythological overtones to the king's actions; see Vanderhooft 1999: 148–149; Lundbom 2004: 474–475. Similar uses of the term

has indeed come for divine 'repayment' (51:6; 'vengeance' [51:11]) of Babylon's culpable conquest of 'all the earth' (51:7), a blanket condemnation of its global ambitions (51:25, 49).

The latter sections of the oracle continue the deconstruction of the religious elements that underlie Babylon's project of conquest and self-aggrandizement. Jeremiah foresees the symbolic inundation of the city of Babylon, reminiscent of Sennacherib's destruction of the city and subsequent dissipation of its soil in the River Euphrates as proof of its definitive destruction in 689 BC (51:42).[23] He also foresees the fall of Babylon's wall, which Nabopolassar described as 'the fortification ground of the great gods, whose foundations the Igigi and the Anunnaki had (originally) established in the jubilation of their hearts' (see 51:44, 58).[24] Bel/Marduk will be forced to give up what he has swallowed (most notably the wares from Yahweh's temple [51:44; cf. 51:51]), and Yahweh will render to Babylon's gods, represented by their cult images, their due by destroying them (51:47, 52). The final outcome of this barrage of judgments will see Babylon-as-empire dragged down to destruction (51:53–56) when the 'King, whose name is [Yahweh] of Hosts' (51:57), destroys it once and for all. Nothing will remain of Babylon (50:26), its imperial corps will 'sleep a perpetual sleep' from which it will never awake (51:39, with *ʿôlām*), and the scroll on which Babylon's downfall is written is to be tied to a stone and sunk in the Euphrates 'to rise no more' when Yahweh's word against Babylon is fulfilled (51:64).

Despite God's use of Babylon as the instrument of covenantal discipline against his people, Jeremiah portrays Babylon's judgment in more detail and in more vivid colours than that of other nations. The fundamental issues are the same in both cases: excessive violence, pride that knows no bounds and which drives an imperial project that is similarly limitless, and – most fundamentally – the refusal to recognize Yahweh as creator, king and judge. These negative traits are complemented by the tragically misguided attempt to secure unlimited authority, power and perpetuity by human means. Due to its comprehensive, unqualified

are evident in Job 7:12; Ps. 74:13 (destroyed by God); Isa. 27:1; 51:9 (destroyed by God in both passages); Ezek. 29:3; 32:2.

[23] Galter 2007: 533. This section of the oracle against Babylon apparently reuses the oracle against Judah in 6:22–24; see Crouch 2011: 492.

[24] Beaulieu 2003: 307. See on this point Van De Mieroop 2003: 9. Nebuchadnezzar focused much of the empire's building capacity on making Babylon spectacular per Kuhrt 1995: 593.

opposition to Yahweh, Babylon-as-empire is one of very few states in Jeremiah for which there is no promise of restoration after judgment. The oracle against Babylon thus brings to a peak God's condemnation of the empire as an impressively organized, strategic and powerful expression of self-glorification and domination.

However, as other sections in Jeremiah show, this judgment is only one side of God's saving plan for his people, one that is realized in both profound weakness (Phil. 2) and stunning, fearsome power (Jer. 50 – 51; Revelation). The selective, focused nature of God's opposition to evil and those who enact it does reveal a sort of 'ideology', if we borrow Graybill's term, but it is a radically subversive one that inevitably confronts autonomous human beings and their self-centred ideologies.[25] God alone, in perfect righteousness and surprising mercy, brings an end to human sin and violence, establishes perfect justice, and restores peace between human beings and between God and those whom he has rescued from their headlong pursuit of life apart from him.

Babylon and the nations during Judah's exile

Babylon appears first in the title of this section for the simple reason that it plays a key role, geographically and politically, in Jeremiah's interpretation of Judah's exile and related events. As we have seen, Babylon in Jeremiah is both a highly effective tool in God's hand for punishing Judah and a resolute enemy of Yahweh and his absolute sovereignty over the world. To this twofold understanding of Babylon Jeremiah adds a third dimension, that of Babylon as a sort of 'home away from home' for the Judean exiles. Rather than seeing this diversity as the result of 'strongly divergent voices at work' in Jeremiah or concluding that 'the Babylonian oracles do not comport well with the contention that the Babylonians had done God's work, indeed that Nebuchadnezzar was God's servant (27:6)', giving attention to the ways that *this* Babylon (not Babylon-as-empire) is described and to the roles it plays will show that Babylon is indeed a multifaceted character in the drama of Yahweh's redemptive and restorative work.[26]

[25] Graybill 2021: 403.

[26] For the first opinion, see Claassens 2019. The second is advanced by Biddle (2021: 239). Sals

Babylon as Judah's 'home away from home'

At first glance it is hardly surprising that many Judeans would balk at the idea of leaving Jerusalem for Babylon. Not only had Babylon already forcibly deported Judeans on two separate occasions by the time Jeremiah sent his letter (29:4–23), but it had done so as a pagan nation that was motivated not by a concern for Judah's well-being but by a desire to exercise control over the entire ancient Near East. Despite these realities, God's good purposes for his people required that they reckon with the gravity of their sin, which was so grave that the final covenantal sanction of exile had become unavoidable. Yet even in that challenging situation, God instructed them through Jeremiah to make Babylon their home: 'Build houses and live in them; plant gardens and eat their produce. Take wives and have sons and daughters . . . that they may bear sons and daughters; multiply there, and do not decrease' (29:5–6). Strikingly, several of these phrases are standard expressions for the 'good life' under God's blessing, always used (until now) of life in the land of Canaan (Deut. 6:11; 20:5–8; 28:30; Josh. 24:13; cf. Gen. 1:28; Exod. 1:7) or of Israel's eschatological restoration (Amos 9:14; Ezek. 28:26) and consummation (Isa. 65:21–22). Their application to the exiles living in Babylon is not evidence that Babylon is now equivalent to the Promised Land, if for no other reason than the fact that some Judeans were drafted into administrative service (for example, Daniel and his companions).[27] But that seems to have been the exception rather than the rule, and the exiles' experience of blessing while in Babylonia would be proof that God's plans for his people *even in exile* were for their good and would benefit non-Israelites around them.[28]

Jeremiah 24 is particularly important for understanding the role of Babylon as a temporary host for God's displaced people. Against the backdrop of God's condemnation of Judah's leaders in 23:1–8, part of the justification for God's command to leave Judah for Babylon is the hiatus of the Davidic monarchy and the stark reality that Zedekiah, who ignored God's words through Jeremiah (Jer. 37:1–2), could not provide for the people's safety (cf. 21:1–10; 29:16).[29] This latter point is beyond

(2014: 306) speaks more plausibly of 'two trends' in Babylon's depictions in Jeremiah: as 'a divine tool' and as 'YHWH's adversary'.

[27] Oded 1995.

[28] Delorme 2019.

[29] Allen 2008: 277.

doubt in the light of God's irrevocable pronouncement that he would give Jerusalem and all it contained into the hand of the king of Babylon (20:5). If we add to this the rejection by many Judeans of Jeremiah's repeated commands to accept the covenantal punishment of exile and to go to Babylon in the confidence that God would bring back their descendants (29:19),[30] the 'judicial differentiation' between good and bad figs in Jeremiah 24 reflects opposing views concerning what is ultimately best for Judah and whether God's intentions can be thwarted.[31] Exile is not meant to decimate Yahweh's people; on the contrary, God affirms that they can thrive while in Babylon, indeed, *only by going to Babylon*. There, contrary to their expectations, they will be spared the 'sword, famine, and pestilence' that God will send against those who remain in Judah and do not 'pay attention' to his words (29:17, 19). In short, temporary residence in Babylon was more conducive to their long-term well-being than remaining in a quasi-deserted land with very little social structure or security and without a king, in direct opposition to God's good plans for them.[32] To draw on the fig metaphor in chapter 24, the vision shows that those who persist in disobedience to God cannot possibly become good, even if they stay in the land, whereas those who obey God and depart will thrive regardless of where they are planted.[33]

The unique nature of Babylon as a temporary 'home away from home', a phrase that recognizes its practical role as well as its non-identity with the Promised Land, is most evident in God's command that the exiles are to 'seek' and 'pray for' the welfare of Babylon (see 29:7).[34] This brings the contrast between Babylon as home away from home and Babylon-as-empire to its peak: are there, after all, 'strongly divergent voices' behind these radically different understandings of Babylon? Babylon's roles and

[30] When Jeremiah's calls to repentance went largely unheeded, he 'shifted his focus' to 'the inevitability of the covenant curse sanctions', according to P. Y. Lee (2016: 285), who summarizes Unterman's interpretation of Jeremiah's ministry.

[31] The phrase in quotations marks is from Plant 2008: 89. Harrison (1973: 127) sees a similar distinction, but too hastily connects it to the unqualified participation of those who go to Babylon in the renewal promised in Jer. 24:7 to those who seek God with all their heart.

[32] God would protect those whom he commanded to stay in Judah after Gedaliah's murder from Babylon's retribution (42:11–12); this includes Babylon's conquest of Egypt, signified by Jeremiah in 43:8–13; 44:30.

[33] Hayes 2009: 101. Harrison (1973: 127) similarly observes that 'fellowship with God and the blessings of divine grace need have no connection with cultic forms, national institutions or geographical locations'.

[34] Contra Hill (1999: 146–153), who argues for the identity of Judah and Babylon as the Promised Land. Thelle (2009: 200) properly stresses the 'temporary' nature of this role for Babylon.

identity in Jeremiah are certainly complex. On the one hand, Babylon as empire *remains* the militant, self-glorifying entity that Jeremiah elsewhere condemns, and would never harbour Judean exiles *in that role*. On the other hand, in its role as temporary home to Judah's exiles, Babylon has no imperial dimension, and is *merely* a city or region that is a suitable place to live. In the same vein, the exiles are not to pray to Yahweh for the *empire's* expansion and victory, but for peace in 'the city' of Babylon (29:7).[35] It is thus not a question of the exiles' 'loyalty to their surrounding [Babylonian] society' but rather of their trust in God's providential wisdom in using the homeland of the empire that served as his hammer against his disobedient people to shelter his obedient people until the time of restoration.[36] This distinction is also conveyed by the text's references to the exiles as distinct from the other residents of Babylon, and Jeremiah 29 refers to the exiles in Babylonia as a 'clearly defined and separated' entity that does not overlap with Babylonians.[37] Yet Babylon as host-city is also a tool in Yahweh's hands, and will serve his saving purposes as a shield for his people for as long as he so wills.

These textual nuances reflect, or are borne out by, historical realities. Until its very end, there was no change in Babylon-as-empire, which continued to pursue its imperial designs nearly until the Persian conquest in 539 BC. Alongside – but quite separate from – its role as empire, Babylonia welcomed thousands of exiled Judeans as displaced people who lived within its borders. Study of the domestic, familial and legal dimensions of these Judeans' lives in Babylonia reveals that their experience was generally positive. To begin with the most salient contrast with Babylon-as-empire, Babylon-as-temporary-home made no attempt to impose its official religion on the Judean deportees, whose names not infrequently explicitly revealed their Yahwistic culture or beliefs.[38] More generally, there is significant evidence to support the conclusion that the exiles 'were in fact able to live a quiet and undisturbed life in southern Babylonia, while Judean identity thrived and prospered' thanks to Babylonian policies that 'favored the survival of small ethnic

[35] Kähler 2021: 112.

[36] Contrast the essentially sociopolitical interpretation of this perspective in ibid. 105, 112.

[37] Ibid. 107.

[38] On the former point, see Oded 1995: 209; on the latter, see Beaulieu 2011. In this paragraph, I draw on the discussion of the Judean exiles' life in Babylonia in Timmer 2024f: 143–144.

communities' and a variety of ties between the exiles' settlements and their Judean origin and identity.[39]

Babylon as the exiles' home away from home exists as part of Yahweh's plan to help his chosen people pass through the covenant sanction of exile with trust in his ongoing care and confidence that he will bring back and restore those who turn to him in repentance (Deut. 30). The city itself is dissociated from Babylon-as-empire by its lack of anything resembling imperialism and, conversely, its being a suitable way-station for the exiles. For these reasons, Jeremiah instructs Judeans to seek its welfare in keeping with Yahweh's will to protect his displaced people until the exile ends. If God is committed to the well-being of the Judean exiles, and if their well-being depends for now on that of Babylon (29:7), then God will ensure the well-being of Babylon as long as the exiles remain there (the logic of Gen. 12:3 is congenial to this scenario). This holds true even when the Babylon Empire fell to Persia, since only Opis and perhaps a few other major cities fell to the Persians. Even as the *empire* of Babylon falls, God continues to use the *city* of Babylon to harbour his people until their restoration.

Babylon as Yahweh's temporary vice-regent over the Levant

Compared to Babylon's role as the temporary home for Judah's exiles, its hegemony over the Levant for 'seventy years' (25:11–12) is essentially the continuation of its military dominance as evident in the conquest of Judah, with one crucial exception: its violence against Judah has come to an end, at least as far as Jeremiah is concerned (Babylon remained active militarily in Egypt and elsewhere).[40] Here we will briefly consider the significance of Babylon's temporary supremacy in the Levant, with special attention to the sometimes extravagant language used to describe it.

Jeremiah 27 recounts a divine oracle instructing the prophet to put on a yoke and send a related message from Yahweh to the kings of Edom, Moab, Ammon, Tyre and Sidon advising them of his decision: 'I have given all these lands into the hand of Nebuchadnezzar, the king of Babylon, my servant' (Jer. 27:6). The message also states that God will grant to the Babylonian king control of 'the beasts of the field to

[39] Delorme 2019: 72.

[40] Kuhrt 1995: 593.

serve him', and that '[a]ll the nations shall serve him and his son and his grandson' until Babylon falls to an anonymous enemy (27:7). As he had done with Judah, God warned that he would punish any nation that refused to put on the vassal-yoke of Babylon by means of sword, famine and pestilence until it was 'consumed' by Babylon (27:8).

One might wonder why it was important not only for Judeans but also for all the states of the Levant to submit to Babylon (chs. 24; 27; 29). The presence of envoys from the five neighbouring nations at a meeting convened by Zedekiah (27:3; cf. 51:59) makes it likely that Yahweh's warning was intended to deter the Judeans from banding together with these states in order to resist Babylon's advance. But whatever the geopolitical optics of such a plan, the theological element remains primary in Jeremiah's messages. Allying itself with other states to resist Babylonian control would be for Judah 'to sell its soul' to them, putting its confidence in human power while continuing to refuse the word of Yahweh through his prophet (whatever Judah's false prophets might be saying [27:9–10]).[41]

Perhaps the most remarkable dimension of Babylon's role during Judah's exile involves its king. Noting the exalted title of 'servant' (25:9; 27:6) that God gives him and the divine grant of 'all these lands'[42] and 'the beasts of the field to serve him', John Hill has argued that Nebuchadnezzar is a 'new Adam'.[43] Although Jeremiah's descriptions have loose conceptual connections to the granting of lands to Abraham (Gen. 26:3–4) and of authority over the animals to Adam in Genesis 2, Hill's proposal does not adequately account for several other considerations. As was the case with Babylon's status as the exiles' new home, Nebuchadnezzar's role here is temporary, lasting only two generations, as Hill goes on to note. The comparison of the land grant to the patriarchs also falters in the light of the permanent nature of that grant over against Babylon's short-lived tenure of the Levant. Further, the reception of the faint echo of Genesis 2 here (if such is indeed the case) may be limited to the violence of wild animals in the context of war-torn societies (Deut. 7:22; Ezek. 39:4),[44] and in any case is limited to the Levant (contrast Gen. 1:26; Ps. 8:6–7) and

[41] This point is made well by Goldingay (2021a: 575), whose apt figure of speech I borrow.

[42] Thelle (2009: 198) is probably mistaken when she conflates 'the earth' in 27:5 with 'all these lands' that Yahweh cedes to Babylonian control in 27:6, since the context makes Babylon's control relevant to the five states named in 27:3. The Septuagint (Jer. 34:6–7 LXX) has 'earth' in both cases.

[43] Hill 2004: 156.

[44] Keown, Scalise and Smothers 1995: 50.

further curtailed by the certainty that this 'service' is morally compromised by Babylon's 'iniquity' (Jer. 25:12).[45] Finally, the closing statement that Babylon's supremacy will end when the nations who served it will make it *their* servant does not see this event as the fall of a primordial king but simply as a transfer of power and status from weaker to stronger.[46] It thus seems best to recognize the rhetorical nature of God's description of Nebuchadnezzar and the possibility that it echoes in limited ways God's grants of land and power to the patriarchs and Israelite kings without elevating Nebuchadnezzar into a class of his own. Yahweh's utterly unique deity, manifested in his work of creation and rule (27:5), makes it inevitable that the figure of Nebuchadnezzar is made entirely of clay.[47]

The end of exile and beyond: Judah and many nations restored

Having already examined the punishment of the nations (including Babylon), here we return to the eschatological horizon of the oracles concerning the nations and related material elsewhere in the book of Jeremiah to consider the alternative outcome, that of deliverance.

'The nations' in general

Not surprisingly, in the light of Israel's priority in redemptive history by virtue of election and covenant (Gen. 12; 15; 17; Exod. 19; etc.), the restoration of the nations sometimes follows upon that of Judah in the book of Jeremiah. In Jeremiah 3, Yahweh first promises to gather a remnant of the northern kingdom of Israel that 'returns' to him and to bring this group to Zion, where he will provide ideal rulers who will feed his renewed people

[45] Rather than introducing 'considerable tension' into this oracle, as Pannkuk (2021: 66) suggests, the oracle makes clear that Yahweh is able to make use of the actions of a very objectionable figure, and to punish that person appropriately, in pursuance of his plans. Pannkuk's observation (68) that 'YHWH and the Babylonian king remain independent agents' in this servant–master arrangement is helpful, as is his observation (75) that in the passages in which the Babylonian monarch is described as Yahweh's servant, 'the imperial ambitions of the Babylonians and the actual motives behind Nebuchadnezzar's retributive actions against Jerusalem . . . never enter the discursive frame'.

[46] Collins and Collins (1993: 227) speak of 'status' in connection with Jer. 27:5–6 and Dan. 4:12. Contrast the suggestion of Pannkuk (2021: 87) that the Babylonian king is 'YHWH's elected representative over the created order'.

[47] Against Sals's conclusion (2014: 306) that Yahweh's destruction of Babylon entails the comparability of its power with his.

with 'knowledge and understanding' (see 3:12–15). As restored Israel flourishes in Yahweh's presence, which transcends the ark and the temple, 'all the nations will be gathered to Yahweh's name' and will no longer stubbornly follow 'their evil heart' (3:17, my translation). This idyllic scenario is completed by the reunification of the northern and southern kingdoms in the land (3:18).

In a similar call to repentance in 4:1–2, Israel's return to and newfound fidelity towards Yahweh are followed by the nations blessing 'themselves in him' (or 'invoking blessings by him' [cf. NIV]) and glorying in him in fulfilment of Genesis 22:18; 26:4, and similar texts. Again, Jeremiah announces in 16:14–21 that God will purify and restore his people, demonstrating his 'power' and 'might' (Jer. 16:21). As the nations witness Israel's stupendous restoration, Jeremiah foretells that

> to you [Yahweh] shall the nations come
> from the ends of the earth and say:
> 'Our fathers have inherited nothing but lies,
> worthless things in which there is no profit.
> Can man make for himself gods?
> Such are not gods!'
> (Jer. 16:19–20)

The nations' comprehensive rejection of idolatry and unqualified commitment to Yahweh as the only God, cast in terms that echo the words prepared for repentant Judah in 3:22–24, constitute a relationship that is summarized as knowing him (16:21).[48]

In other contexts, the apparent order of events is different, or at least has different emphases. For example, God states in Jeremiah 12:14–17 that the nations that seized Israel and which he therefore exiled from their lands would be brought back to their lands because of his mercy (a term used positively of non-Israelites only here in Jeremiah).[49] But in this case, return is not equivalent to salvific restoration. Rather, it leaves the nations in a *liminal position*, faced with the choice of committing unreservedly to

[48] Allen (2008: 194) properly stresses the 'divine self-revelation' that drives the conversion of these non-Israelites. Yates (2018: 72) notes the similarity between 3:22–24 and 16:19–20.

[49] Piel of *r-ḥ-m* (12:15). The same verb is used positively elsewhere in Jeremiah only of Israelites: restored Jacob (30:18); Ephraim (31:20); all Israel (33:26); and those who stay in the land with divine permission (42:12).

Yahweh as God. If they 'truly learn the ways of my people' and 'to swear by my name, "As Yahweh lives"', rather than following other gods, 'then they shall be built among my people' (12:16, my translation). In the event that the nations turn to God, they will become part of his restored people by sharing in the same holistic, saving restoration, and any remaining distinctions will be of far lesser importance.[50] This scenario also involves the removal of geographical separation between renewed Israel and the renewed nations, making both groups residents of the same territory.[51]

The Book of Consolation contains several brief but potent references to the nations. The oracle that begins in Jeremiah 31:10 commands 'nations' to hear Yahweh's promise to restore Israel and to 'declare it in the coastlands far away'. An obedient response to this command would entail the nations' submission to God, following the model seen in Jeremiah 12 and 16. This response is presumed in the oracle in Jeremiah 33:1–13, according to which Jerusalem and its forgiven and spiritually purified inhabitants will 'be a name of joy, a praise and a glory before all the nations of the earth who shall hear of all the good that I do for them' (33:9a). As witnesses to Israel's restoration, the nations will 'fear and tremble' (33:9b) because of God's amazing deeds on behalf of his people (contrast their negative appraisal of Judah in 25:9; 30:17). Although elsewhere Jeremiah uses the verbs 'fear' and 'tremble' as results of divine punishment, here these reactions are caused by a phenomenal display of God's goodness, and their significance is therefore quite different. At a minimum, these reactions suggest a link between 'the restoration of Israel and Judah' and 'a larger harvest of people to enter the family of God', and probably involve their coming to know Yahweh as the one true God.[52]

Yahweh's freedom to rescind his threat of judgment against 'a nation or a kingdom' in the event that it 'turns from its evil', as spelled out in Jeremiah 18:7–8, provides a fitting entry to the announcements of restoration that appear here and there in the oracles against the nations in

[50] Yates (2018: 70) also notes the similarity of the salvation of the nations and of Judah here.

[51] Raabe (2018: 250) concludes that either 'restored Israel will incorporate the foreign nations' or 'restored Israel's land will be considered as including the lands of the foreign nations', with reference to Ps. 87; Isa. 19:24–25; Zech. 2:11.

[52] Citing Hwang 2013: 502. See Wright 2006: 127, 241; and note what Brueggemann (1997: 500) writes with reference to Pss 67; 86; 126: 'these characteristic actions of Yahweh are so compelling and so overwhelming that the nations will want to join Israel in praise, on the basis of actions done for Israel'. Note also Pss 22:27, 30–31; 40:3.

chapters 46 – 51 (none are present in the oracles against the Philistines, Aram, and Kedar and Hazor). There are five such instances, all quite brief.

Egypt (Jer. 46:26b)

'Afterward she will settle as long ago, utterance of Yahweh' (46:26b, my translation). This somewhat cryptic line closes the lengthy oracle against Egypt in Jeremiah 46. The oracle presents Egypt as Yahweh's enemy (46:10) even as it affirms Babylon's subordinate involvement in Egypt's defeat at Carchemish (46:2, 13) and its subsequent exile, both of which are ultimately brought about by Yahweh (46:15, 19). The culminating element of Egypt's fall is the defeat of several of its most prominent gods, including Amon/Amun of Thebes (one of Egypt's oldest and most significant deities), as well as the pharaoh and 'those who trust in him' (46:25).[53]

It is against this chaotic backdrop of an empire undone that God announces that Egypt will again 'settle' or 'dwell' in its land after being exiled. Davidson proposes that 'the combination of self-exile (46:16), forced exile (46:19, 26), and annihilation (46:14) wipes the space [Egypt – DCT] clean of its otherness to enable its rehabilitation (46:26)'.[54] Indeed, as seen from God's point of view, this otherness captures the primary emphasis of the judgments announced in response to Egypt's trust in its gods and king (46:25; similarly 46:8, 10, 15). At the same time, however, Egypt is not absolutely other, for Yahweh will bring the Egyptians back to their homeland. This is where the oracle leaves Egypt: returned, but committed neither to its past imperialism nor to Yahweh's service. Having been undone as an empire and re-established in a much humbler, peaceful form (so also Ezek. 29:13–16), Egypt's population is in a *liminal* situation like that attributed to other nations in 12:15. Should some or all of these Egyptians turn to Yahweh (cf. Jer. 12:16), their future would be identical to that of the other nations who come to know God in Jeremiah.[55]

---

[53] On Amun-Re, see Silverman 1991: 39.

[54] Davidson 2021: 201. 'Egypt' and other terms referring to it are sometimes masculine and sometimes feminine in ch. 46, but the verses immediately preceding 46:26 refer to Egypt's population as a heifer (46:20) and as 'the daughter of Egypt' (46:24, both grammatically feminine), and pronominal references to Egypt are also feminine. Hence it is the Egyptians as a feminine singular entity that will 'settle' (third-person singular feminine) in 46:26b.

[55] Keown, Scalise and Smothers (1995: 295) seem to equate too quickly this qualified restoration with the more substantial 'restoration of fortunes' in the oracles regarding Moab, Ammon and Elam (and, similarly, Edom).

Moab (Jer. 48:47)

As we saw earlier in this chapter, God announces in Jeremiah 48 that Moab will be punished for putting its confidence in its material resources and accomplishments (48:7, 14), exalting itself against Yahweh while denigrating his chosen people (48:26–27, 29–30, 42), and practising idolatry (48:7, 13, 35, 46). A very different Moab, exiled, dishevelled, humiliated (48:2–4, 39, etc.), and abandoned by its god Chemosh, is the subject of Yahweh's surprising promise that he will restore it: 'But I will restore the fortunes of Moab at the end of the days, utterance of Yahweh' (48:47a, my translation).[56] It is highly unlikely that this restoration would involve God simply making Moab what it was prior to his judgment, since to do so would be to nullify his verdict and so undermine the oracle as a whole. In the light of the semantics of the phrase 'restore the fortunes', which describes Judah's radical restoration earlier in the book (30:3, 18–19; 31:20–25; 32:37–44; 33:7–26), and Jeremiah's repeated 'leveling of Yahweh's dealings with the nations and Israel',[57] it is much more likely that the phrase involves the *transformation* of those involved.[58] So understood, this brief promise of restoration predicts that (some) Moabites, characterized quite differently from those whose beliefs and actions brought divine punishment, will be the objects of divine mercy and superlative restoration in the eschatological future in the same way as the faithful in Judah, establishing a strong criterion of identity between them.[59] This interpretation receives additional support from God's unprecedented lament over

[56] In favour of the coherence of an oracle that involves both judgment and salvation, see Cox (2013: 85), who observes that 'hoped-for restoration' was essential to the Sumerian city-laments. Millard (2012) notes the same phenomenon with respect to other texts. For an example, see the prayer that concludes the 'Lamentation over the Destruction of Ur' in Kramer 1969: 463.

[57] Yates 2018: 72. He elsewhere describes this 'equating of Judah and the nations' in terms of condemnation and judgment (74–75).

[58] Schmid and Steck (2001: 52), who note the dual emphasis in many of the prophets on restoration of the land and the people. As used of Judah/Israel in Jeremiah, the phrase 'restore the fortunes of' is used of Judah, which 'will be found by YHWH' (see 29:14); involves return and repossession of its territory (30:3); and happens because God will 'have compassion on [Judah's] dwellings', leading to the rebuilding of city and palace and the raising of praise to Yahweh (30:18–22; similarly 31:20–25). Jer. 32:37–44; 33:6–22 add forgiveness of sin, an internal transformation that ensures permanent fidelity to God, a new covenant, restoration of the Davidic monarchy, and more. Uses of the phrase in Ezek. 39:25 and Joel 3:1 and their contexts are comparable.

[59] This close correspondence is noted by Yates (2018: 70). Following Peterson 1992: 575, I consider as 'eschatological' future circumstances that are sufficiently discontinuous with the present to allow one to 'speak of an entirely new state of reality'. Talmon (2001) notes some examples of superlative restoration (i.e. beyond the return from exile) in late Second Temple Judaism.

(some of) Moab in 48:31–32.[60] Those from Moab whom Yahweh will restore will, like restored Judeans, experience a radical shift from status 'A' (about to be punished) through a post-punishment 'non-A' to the ideal status 'B'.[61] The fact that Jeremiah portrays both Judah/Israel and many of the nations as passing through the same process is another point in favour of seeing Moab's restoration as identical to that of Israel/Judah, and thus as reconciling it with Yahweh.

Ammon (Jer. 49:6)

Yahweh's oracle against Ammon condemns it for taking over territory that had belonged to Gad (49:1), acting proudly and believing itself to be beyond danger. The prominence in this oracle of Milcom, Ammon's chief deity, reveals that the 'Ammon' that is condemned is defined by its affiliation with a false god no less than by its pride and disdain for Yahweh's people. As was the case with Moab, God's announcement that he will 'restore the fortunes of the Ammonites' is surprising, even if the movement from status 'A' to 'non-A' that the oracle foretells means that Ammon has lost its territory (49:2) and has experienced widespread destruction. Furthermore, Milcom and his cultic attendants have gone into exile, indicating either his abandonment of the Ammonites or his impotence before their enemies. In either case, God's promise to restore the Ammonites' fortunes involves the radical movement from destruction (status 'A') to superlative restoration (status 'B'). Some Ammonites will be characterized by affiliation with Yahweh rather than with Milcom, humility rather than pride, and salvation rather than judgment.

Edom (Jer. 49:11)

The brief promise of deliverance in the oracle against Edom (Jer. 49:7–22) appears in the midst of announcements of judgment (cf. Zeph. 2:11). Despite its brevity, it is quite clear. First, the *survival of a remnant* composed of orphans and widows is explicit. Conversely, those whom Yahweh will punish (Jer. 49:8) are closely associated with 'Esau', although the statement that his 'children' of an unspecified age will perish (49:10, 20) is qualified or clarified by the survival of orphans (exceptionally vulnerable

[60] Hwang 2013: 505.

[61] This simplified explanation is adapted from Ben Zvi 1992: 325–329.

and dependent children) in verse 11.[62] Second, God himself encourages Esau (his opponent!) to entrust to his care his orphans, promising to 'keep them alive', and calls for Edom's widows to 'trust in [him]' (49:11; cf. Ps. 68:5).

These directives presume massive shifts in the *beliefs and attitudes* of Edom's survivors that go to the heart of the binary opposition of Yahweh and Esau. God is undoubtedly committed to eradicating Esau-as-enemy, meaning the violent, proud nation-state that shed the blood of others (Jer. 49:16), but he is no less committed to preserving the lives of those who would have had no part in Edom's violence, especially women and children.[63] The command to Edom to leave its children in Yahweh's care would be plausible only if the Edomites addressed were convinced that Yahweh, even though he has brought punishment on Edom, is both just and merciful. Taking him to be so, one can be sure that Edom's orphans would be safe in his care. The same epistemic change is presumed or encouraged on the part of Edom's widows, who should 'trust in [Yahweh]'. Prior to being judged, Edom 'trusted' (same Hebrew term) in its material wealth (49:4), but having seen that wealth cannot buy security and that Milcom cannot deliver, its widows are now encouraged to trust in the God of Israel. Even as Yahweh delivers other nations from Edom's violence, he graciously preserves a remnant within it and calls for these people to trust him because of their vulnerability. The oracle leaves Edom's survivors in this liminal position.

Elam (Jer. 49:39)

The oracle against Elam (49:34–39) focuses entirely on the state's military and royal corps ('bow', 'might' [49:35]; 'king and officials' [49:38]). This selectivity requires understanding the 'Elam' that is the target of God's 'fierce anger' (49:37) as a small subset of the general population. The image of God setting up his throne in Elam likewise presumes that there is a surviving population over which he will rule. As with the other states in the book of Jeremiah, the prominence of military and administrative actions suggests that autonomous self-preservation and aggression had characterized Elam in the past. The collapse of the state and the exile

[62] Mattingly 2000a: 72.

[63] The distinction between elect, non-elect and anti-elect is clearly articulated by Kaminsky (2007, esp. 107–110).

of (some of) its citizens would thus bring an end to 'Elam' as a violent state that merits divine punishment. Consequently, it is a humbled Elam, dispersed and having abandoned its militant disposition, whose fortunes Yahweh graciously promises to restore. As with the other uses of this phrase, spiritual and moral transformation is central to God's good plans for such Elamites, and by turning to him they will share a superordinate criterion of identity with his restored covenant people.

Summary and New Testament developments

God's commission to Jeremiah, recorded in Jeremiah 1:4–12, holds the key to understanding the prophet's wide-ranging and diverse pronouncements regarding the nations. God sets his prophet 'over nations and over kingdoms' to both dismantle and rebuild (1:10). The themes of God's authoritative speech through Jeremiah (he is 'King' in 46:18), his sovereignty over every nation and kingdom (25:9), and his just and gracious realization of his twofold plan of judgment and salvation run throughout this magnificent book and give coherence to its treatment of the nations.[64] Amid the chaos and violence of Judah's final decades, Jeremiah's assertions of God's omnipotence and sovereignty over even his people's most imposing enemy foster faith in God's good plans for those who trust in him and obey his commands. Even when that involved submitting to the devastation of Yahweh's land, the glory of the promised restoration far surpassed the sorrow and hardship of defeat and exile (50:19–20).

In the New Testament, the main contours of the nations-theme in Jeremiah are visible in the various ways in which Jews and non-Jews respond to God's actions in and through Jesus Christ and the apostolic proclamation that accompanied them.[65] Even during Jesus' earthly ministry, which largely preserved the priority of Israel in the history of salvation (Matt. 10:6; 15:24), some non-Israelites were drawn to him (Matt. 8:10 // Luke 7:9; Mark 7:24–30 // Matt. 15:28; Mark 15:39) while many Jews were not (Jer. 9:26; Rom. 2:25). Evoking the liminal location of several of the nations in Jeremiah's oracles, ambiguous responses to

[64] On God's word in Jeremiah and in biblical theology, see Shead 2013.

[65] For inner-biblical reflections that go beyond the nations-theme which is our focus, see P. Y. Lee 2016: 299–301; Mazurel 2004: 181–189.

the gospel among various groups of non-Israelites (Acts 17:32; 26:28–29; etc.) show some Gentiles to have been non-committal, at least for the moment. Nevertheless, the Babylon-as-empire in Jeremiah that 'ultimately embodies the relentless presence of evil in the world that must be destroyed by God' aligns well with the treatment of the same symbolic entity in Revelation, per which the nations 'with their idolatrous ways are presently in subjection to unseen powers that work themselves out in the habitual practices' of the Roman Empire.[66]

Finally, the New Testament's attribution of salvation or judgment to individuals or collectives solely in conjunction with their response to God's claims upon them as fully revealed in the gospel echoes Jeremiah's consistent focus on one's relationship with God regardless of ethnicity or nationality.[67] The prophet's emphasis on salvation coming to the nations through Israel also implies that ethnic or national identity is of no consequence (Rom. 1:16; Gal. 3:28; Col. 3:11), while showing that renewed Israel is the one people of God into which the nations are integrated (Rom. 9 – 11; Gal. 6:16), 'a new pot made from the old lump of clay . . . a new Israel into which the Gentiles are grafted'.[68] Seeing God's grace poured out on his people (cf. Jer. 33:9) and abandoning their idols to serve the living God (1 Thess. 1:9), they share in the same salvation as believing Jews (Eph. 3:6), in fulfilment of the mystery of God now revealed in that very reality (Eph. 3:3–10). In sum, Jeremiah's promise that Yahweh will save a people from among all nations and bring a definitive end to opposition to him – exemplified by Babylon –makes that empire's historical fall a 'typological foreshadowing not just of Christ's historical victory over death and calling into being of his church, but of the eschatological consummation of his work'.[69]

[66] Hwang 2021: 499; McNicol 2011: 121.

[67] Soza 2000: 227.

[68] Shead 2023: 371.

[69] Ibid.

5
Ezekiel

The structure of the book of Ezekiel strongly implies that the nations are directly connected to the judgment and restoration of Israel that form the twofold theme of the book. However, their roles vary widely: Babylon serves as God's instrument of punishment for his people and as his weapon against Tyre and Egypt but is never condemned for its actions. Most of the other nations, by contrast, are condemned in the oracles of Ezekiel 25 – 32 for their 'disdain' of Yahweh, his people and his land. These eight chapters of oracles follow the death of Ezekiel's wife in chapter 24, which symbolizes Judah's imminent destruction (Ezek. 23:22–24), and are followed by the second divine call to Ezekiel to serve as a watchman in chapter 33, which introduces God's gracious, superlative restoration of Israel that will follow upon its punishment and exile (chs. 33 – 48). Here, too, non-Israelite states appear at key points. The oracles of chapter 35 announce the destruction of Mount Seir (Edom) as a counterpart to the restoration of the 'mountains of Israel' in 36:1–15, and chapters 38 – 39 announce the destruction of Gog and all other enemies of Israel prior to the culminating description of Yahweh's eschatological temple in the restored land of Israel (chs. 40 – 48).

In addition to serving as God's means for punishing Israel and falling under divine judgment themselves for other (sometimes related) sins, the nations also have a minor role as beneficiaries of God's restoration of his people (limited to Sodom [16:49–63] and Egypt [29:13–16]) and as 'sojourners' integrated into restored Israel (47:22–23).[1] This very small number of positive depictions of non-Israelites does not mean that 'Ezekiel did not believe that there was hope for blessings for the foreign nations', but rather affirms that 'these blessings would come to the nations

[1] Crouch (2023: 289) notes this role in relation to Ezek. 29:14–16 but does not discuss the case of the sojourner in 47:22–23.

by means of Israel'.[2] This chapter explores Ezekiel's complex message that announces judgment and salvation for the nations no less than for Judah itself. Our exploration will follow the literary order of the book, which is also roughly chronological, considering in turn the nations in the historical context of God's covenantal discipline of Israel (chs. 1 – 24), the nations as enemies of Yahweh and his people (chs. 25 – 32; 35; 38 – 39), and non-Israelites' sharing in a common salvation with renewed Israel (chs. 40 – 48).

The nations in the context of God's discipline of Israel (Ezek. 1 – 24)

The profile of the nations in Ezekiel 1 – 24 is quite complex, even though it includes no oracles of salvation and little eschatological material. Strikingly, God tells Ezekiel at the beginning of his ministry that foreign nations will listen to his message, whereas Israel's 'hard forehead' and 'stubborn heart' mean that it will not (3:5–7). Elsewhere, God asserts that Judah has 'rebelled against my rules . . . more than the nations, and against my statutes more than the countries all around her' (5:6–7; note also 16:46–48, 51–52). Apart from such passing comparisons with Judah, the nations in Ezekiel 1 – 24 range from being mere geographical locations to observing, contributing to and being instruments of divine punishment against Judah or other nations.

Non-Israelite nations as the stage on which Yahweh's relationship with Israel takes place

God's review of Israel's life as a nation begins at conception, as it were, with its 'origin and . . . birth' in Canaan from Amorite and Hittite parents (16:3). The historical retrospective in Ezekiel 20 begins with God's self-revelation to the Israelites in Egypt, when he 'made himself known to them' and swore to be their covenant suzerain (20:5). This entailed especially his commitment to liberate them from slavery in Egypt and bring them into the Promised Land (20:6). The negative role of Egypt as Israel's oppressor at this point in time is left aside, making Egypt, and later the wilderness (20:10–26), little more than the stage on which this episode of

[2] Strong 1995: 133.

Yahweh's relationship with his people plays out. This role is also held by Babylon, where Ezekiel was exiled in 597 BC (1:1, 3; 3:15). Once in the land, Israel's fame and beauty are seen by the nations (16:14), and this introduces the long, sad history of her departure from Yahweh in favour of foreign partners.

Although the nations to which Israel will be exiled or flee are the setting for ritually impure activities (4:13–14, where exiles will 'eat their bread unclean') and may in fact be ritually impure territory, no further negative evaluation is made of them (6:8; 11:17; 12:14–16; 20:34, 41; 22:15–16; 34:13).[3] Ezekiel himself is 'by the Chebar canal' (1:1; 10:20; etc.) when he receives the visions of God that the book records. The fact that God was a 'sanctuary' to the exiles *outside Israel* (11:16) further relativizes the negative significance of the nations as a potentially unclean place.

Non-Israelite nations not responsible for inducing Israel to sin

Ezekiel 1 – 24 typically passes over whatever role non-Israelite nations may have had in leading Israel or Judah astray through religious influence or example. Despite the likelihood that 'there is a foreign component to some, if not all, of the illicit cultic activities that Ezekiel sees' in his vision inside the Jerusalem temple in chapter 8, Yahweh consistently affirms that the house of Israel alone is responsible for its actions (8:6, 13, 14, 17; 11:12).[4] Similarly, in Ezekiel 20, God lays the blame for Israel's stubborn desire to hold on to Egyptian gods at his people's feet (20:7–9; likewise 23:3). The same holds for Israel once in the land (20:28–32). Yahweh asserts that during the monarchic period, Israel and Judah exhibited the same covenant infidelity by refusing to trust him and instead seeking security through alliances with Assyria, a relationship that proved fatal for the northern kingdom (23:5–10).[5] Following the fall of Israel, Judah's unfaithfulness worsened despite clear proof that such infidelity could not fail to kindle God's wrath. Again, God's people are held solely responsible

[3] The ritual impurity of lands outside Israel is typically connected to their practice of idolatry and worship of other gods (Josh. 22:19; Ezek. 36:18; Amos 7:17); see Block 1997: 186; Greenberg 1983: 107. Notably, the temple and the land of Israel in Ezekiel's day are also ritually impure (Ezek. 5:11; 9:7; 22:3–5; 33:26; 36:18).

[4] Crouch 2023: 279.

[5] Israel's occasional mistreatment of foreign 'sojourners' during this time should not go unnoticed (22:7, 29), especially since the same group appears in 47:22–23 (the only other use of the term is in 14:7).

for their mistaken perception of the Assyrians, then the Babylonians and finally the Egyptians as the best option for security, prosperity and well-being (23:11–21). Only in the later oracles against the nations does God level accusations against some non-Israelite states for their role in these misguided partnerships (e.g. 29:6–9).

Non-Israelite nations as the adversarial audience of Judah's judgment and salvation

Negative evaluations of the nations sometimes appear in contexts where they witness the shame of punished or exiled Israel, a role that Crouch asserts is part of '[t]he foremost role of the foreign nations in the book of Ezekiel'.[6] This role first appears when God announces judgment against 'all the house of Israel' (5:4) and then focuses on Jerusalem. Placed 'in the center of the nations, with countries all around her',[7] Jerusalem will suffer God's judgments of her unmatched 'wickedness' and 'abominations' in view of the nations (5:6–9). By inflicting these punishments, God will make his people 'an object of reproach' among the nations, 'a reproach and a taunt, a warning and a horror, to the nations all around [them]' (5:14–15).[8] The circumstances that generate such disdain include massive destruction (36:4), famine (36:30) and even cannibalism (36:13–15), as well as Judah's actions in general, whether before (16:52–53, 57; 22:4–5) or during its exile (22:16).[9] Exceptionally, the Judeans themselves are foreseen verbalizing the reasons for their shameful status to 'the nations where they go', having escaped the more severe punishments for the sins that give rise to that status (12:16).

Even though God himself brings shame on Judah, making it a genuine object of disdain or 'derision',[10] the nations seem unable to perceive this shame or reproach correctly. Yahweh assigns reproach, 'a loss of status in

[6] Crouch 2023: 284. A few exceptions exist but do not overturn the points made here. Ezek. 16:57 ('has become a laughingstock' [Block 1997: 514], without condemnation) and 28:24, 26 (of Sidon) are the only cases in which Ezekiel uses a verb meaning 'to despise' (*š-w-ṭ*) with non-Israelites as the subject and Israel as the object, underlining the nations' active role in assigning disdain apart from Yahweh's evaluation of the situation. The related noun *šʾṭ* is used to similar effect in 25:6, 15; 36:5. See Clines 2009: 443 for discussion of the verb and ibid. 453 for the noun.

[7] Wu (2016: 125) briefly summarizes some recent discussion of this phrase.

[8] The land, once desolated by divine judgment, is also seen as such by those who pass by (Ezek. 36:34). The same is true of the mountains of Israel (36:1–5).

[9] Wu 2016: 107.

[10] Ibid. 121.

the eyes of the observing other',[11] to his sinful people in a way that reflects without diffraction their guilt and corruption, whereas the nations inevitably perceive the situation differently.[12] The *Schadenfreude* or aggression of the nations, their own expression of derision or their appropriation of Yahweh's land accompany their seeing Israel's shameful condition and render them guilty. Thus, when an anonymous enemy celebrates with the words 'The ancient heights [of Israel] have become our possession' (Ezek. 36:2), after making Israel and its land 'prey and derision' and appropriating it 'with wholehearted joy and utter contempt' (36:4–5), that enemy is condemned to suffer reproach itself (36:5–7).[13] In such cases, as Crouch puts it, the nations 'mistook Israel's devastation in YHWH's hands as a sign of their own triumph; they believed that Israel could belong to them, rather than recognizing that Israel belongs only to YHWH'.[14] Despite the distortion of the nations' response to Israel's reproach due to their pride, the reproach properly understood reflects the sad reality that 'Israel's behavior does not reflect the nature of YHWH; rather, it is abhorrent to and incompatible with YHWH'.[15]

The nations are less frequently the witnesses of Israel's restoration. In these cases, non-Israelites will see God 'manifest [his] holiness' when he restores Israel (20:41; 28:25; 36:23; 38:16, 23; 39:27) or will bear witness to the radical transformation of the 'land that was desolate' into 'the garden of Eden' with flourishing crops, cities and inhabitants (36:35–36; 37:28). Most if not all of these passages are ambiguous as to whether these situations are positive for the nations.

Non-Israelite nations, especially Babylon, as God's means for punishing unfaithful Judah

With Israel's guilt a recognized fact from the book's first pages (2:3), the first role given to non-Israelite nations in Ezekiel is linked to Yahweh's decision to punish 'the house of Israel' (4:4–8). God reveals to the prophet that he

[11] Ibid.

[12] Israel's own evaluation of its honour (or shame) is often also 'quite different' from God's, as noted by Block (1997: 515).

[13] Greenberg (1997: 718) notes that only here does Ezekiel use a Hebrew term for 'gloating and contempt' (*la'ag* [36:4]), which aligns well with the attendant arrogance that drives these nations to assume control of Yahweh's land.

[14] Crouch 2023: 285. I disagree with Crouch's subsequent conclusion that this misunderstanding, primarily or by itself, required Yahweh to destroy the nations in order to correct it.

[15] Ibid.

will expel his people from the land and drive them into exile (4:13). These early announcements that unnamed nations will play a role in destroying Judah and exiling its population are followed by others (5:12; 6:8–9; 7:21, 24; etc.). Yet these portents of exile also emphasize that Yahweh is in control of these events: *he* will 'drive' his people into exile (4:13), 'scatter to all the winds' a third of his people (5:12), and 'judge' and 'punish' them for their violation of his covenant (7:3–4, 8–9; 11:9–12). It is presumably this emphasis on Yahweh's agency that explains the intriguing absence, in these contexts, of condemnation of these states for their often violent treatment of Judah. As with cases in which the nations induced Israel/Judah to sin, condemnation for violence against Israel/Judah is reserved for the oracles against the nations, where it is shown to be part of imperial ideology.

The case of Babylon is exceptional in this regard, for although it was directly responsible for Jerusalem's fall, it is never condemned in Ezekiel despite being termed 'the most ruthless of nations'.[16] Babylon is first mentioned in 12:13 as the place to which Zedekiah and the residents of Jerusalem will be exiled, although some of them will subsequently be driven elsewhere (12:15). God's sovereign orchestration of this deportation is very clear in 12:13: 'I will spread my net over him [Zedekiah], and he shall be taken in my snare. And I will bring him to Babylon'. In the parable of Ezekiel 17, Babylon's subjugation of Jerusalem, which involved deposing Jehoiachin and deporting the entire royal court, is presented in terms that are surprisingly positive. The deported king is resettled in Babylon, while Zedekiah, the newly appointed puppet king, is 'planted . . . in fertile soil' next to 'abundant waters' (17:5). The failure of Zedekiah's subsequent attempt to escape Babylon's grasp in favour of Egypt was inevitable given that his covenant with Babylon was made with Yahweh as witness (2 Chr. 36:13),[17] further underlining the legitimacy of Babylon's role from God's point of view.

Babylon's punitive role is clear even in the tragic fall of Jerusalem a decade later. An oracle announcing that Yahweh has drawn *his* sword is followed by a command to Ezekiel to sketch a map and make a signpost to guide Nebuchadnezzar and *his* sword towards Jerusalem (Ezek.

[16] Nevader 2023: 223. Greenberg (1997: 572) translates the Hebrew expression as 'most terrible of nations'; Allen (1990: 89) prefers 'the most brutal nation in the world'; Block (1998: 97) proposes 'the most ruthless of nations'. Although not a major change, 'terrifying' is probably a better translation and would further temper Ezekiel's description of the nations in this role; cf. Clines 2009: 346; Koehler and Baumgartner 2001: 888.

[17] Crouch 2023: 282.

21:18–23).[18] In response to Israel's and Judah's perpetual unfaithfulness, God announces in 23:24 that he 'will commit the judgement' of Judah's infidelity to Babylon and its allies, her former lovers having become her enemies.[19] Even though these enemies will mistreat Judah violently and with 'hatred' (23:25–26, 30, 46–47), no condemnation of Babylon is offered in this or other passages. The siege of Jerusalem is also closely connected to God's own actions of judgment and retribution against his sinful people (24:9–14), again with Babylon as his instrument.

Non-Israelite nations as God's means for punishing other nations

Although Babylon is the only nation clearly assigned a punitive role with respect to Judah, it is not alone in its related role as God's instrument for punishing other nations. The list of punishers is long: 'brutish men' will serve as Yahweh's means of destruction against Ammon (Ezek. 21:28–32), as will the 'people of the East' and 'the nations' (25:1–7). The people of the East have the same role against Moab and Seir (25:8–11). Likewise, 'many nations' and Babylon take up arms against Tyre (26:1–14; 'foreigners' in 28:1–10 may also refer to Babylon). The list of Babylon's victims continues, notably including Egypt (29:17–20; 30:20–26), a role that Babylon again shares with 'messengers' and 'foreigners' (30:9, 12). Finally, the Babylonians, described as '[f]oreigners, the most ruthless of nations', were also sent against Assyria (31:3–18).[20]

Throughout these passages, the nations' actions are intermingled with divine agency:

> They shall destroy the walls of Tyre . . . and I will scrape her soil from her
> (Ezek. 26:4)

> I will put an end to the wealth of Egypt,
> by the hand of Nebuchadnezzar
> (Ezek. 30:10)

---

[18] Block 1998: 684; Allen 1990: 26–27.

[19] The identities of Pekod, Shoa and Koa are obscure; see Block 1997: 749; Allen 1990: 50; Greenberg 1997: 481.

[20] In one instance, Israel is to be the agent of Yahweh's vengeance against Edom (25:12–14).

> I will strengthen the arms of the king of Babylon and put my sword in his hand, but I will break the arms of Pharaoh
> (Ezek. 30:24)

> I will throw my net over you
> with a host of many peoples,
> and they will haul you [Pharaoh] up in my dragnet.
> (Ezek. 32:3)

In one case, God is the only agent of punishment mentioned (against Sidon [Ezek. 28:20–24]), and God is, of course, also solely responsible for bringing nations down to Sheol (31:15–17; 32:18–32). The emphasis on God's agency and justice as the primary cause and goal, respectively, of the nations' actions accounts for their very selective presentation in these contexts. As a result, there is relatively little mention of their violence (note, however, 23:25), and no explicit moral evaluation of their actions is offered. By contrast, the oracles at the centre of Ezekiel's book, to which we now turn, present the nations in a much broader perspective and relentlessly critique their ideologies and resulting behaviours, affirming thereby that no injustice or wrong will remain unpunished.

The nations as enemies of Yahweh and his people

Most of Ezekiel's oracles dealing with foreign nations appear in chapters 25 – 32, where seven different states or empires are mentioned. Chapter 25 deals with the nations nearest to Judah (Ammon to the north, Moab to the east, Edom to the south and Philistia to the west), while chapters 26 – 28 focus almost entirely on Tyre and chapters 29 – 32 on Egypt.[21] One of the oracles' primary functions is to announce divine judgment, often realized through human means, upon those in these nations whose beliefs, values and actions are those alleged in the oracles.[22] Our focus on ideology prompts us to ask, first, what the nations do and what those actions reveal about their ideology and fundamental commitments. Second, we

[21] Renz 2002: 94–95.

[22] L. Lee (2016) has argued, as have several before her, that these oracles are also implicit condemnations of Judah; see also Renz 2002: 94.

will consider what God does in response to the nations' sinful actions and how the divine response affects both the nations and his people. The oracles against Ammon, Moab and Seir, Edom, Philistia, and Sidon are treated more briefly in light of Ezekiel's focus on Tyre and Egypt.

Ammon (Ezek. 21:28–32; 25:1–7)

Ezekiel 21:28–32, the first oracle against a foreign state in the book, asserts that even though Babylon will initially direct its forces against Jerusalem rather than Ammon (21:20–22), the latter will not escape Yahweh's judgment (Ammon was later subjugated by Babylon).[23] This oracle most likely refers to the period surrounding Jerusalem's fall, and focuses on Ammon's 'reproach' (*ḥerpâ* [21:28]) against Israel by which it sought 'to arouse an emotion of shame' in Israelites.[24] This betrays an extremely negative estimation of both Israel and Yahweh, one grounded in divination ('false visions' and 'lies' [21:29]) performed by Ammon's religious specialists. The diametric opposition of Ammon's optimism concerning its future and its assumption of Israel's negligible importance in the grand scheme of things draws attention to the epistemological dimension of the conflict that all the oracles criticize and deconstruct so that Israel might live in accord with truth.[25] In this case, the Babylonian sword that Ammon rightly sees coming against Jerusalem will not destroy God's people entirely, whereas God's judgment against Ammon *will* reduce to ruin those Ammonites who were guided by visions of security that they intended to achieve by themselves, without regard for Yahweh and his purposes. These Ammonites are the 'profane wicked' (21:25, 29) whose time of judgment at God's hands has come. Ironically, as 'gleeful spectators of God's judgment' against Judah, Ammonites will be 'struck by the very judgment which they, despite their guilt, thought they could escape'.[26] The collapse of the Ammonite state in 21:28–32 is God's definitive response to the pride and self-serving interpretation of reality offered by its diviners.

The related oracle in chapter 25 develops this critique of reproach that denigrates Yahweh and his people by exposing Ammon's satisfaction

[23] So Allen 1990: 28; Sedlmeier 2002: 307; and others. Burnett (2016: 320) notes that archaeology attests to a 'thriving economy' in Ammon throughout the exilic period and perhaps later (Neh. 2:10, 19; 13:1–2; 2 Macc. 4:26).

[24] De Blois 2021 *sub loco*.

[25] Brueggemann 1991: 15.

[26] Sedlmeier 2002: 309.

('Aha!') at seeing the Jerusalem temple profaned, the land of Israel made desolate and many Judeans exiled (25:3).[27] To this self-serving joy over Judah's suffering, 25:6 adds the even stronger charge that Ammon, personified as a single individual, rejoiced 'with all the malice within [his] heart' (my translation) against Israel and expressed this hatred with verve, clapping his hands and stamping his feet (hands and feet form a merism for the whole body).[28] These attitudes and actions are most plausibly understood in reference to Ammon's political and religious leaders, for whom Judah was a means to an end – either an erstwhile ally against the Babylonian threat or a rival whose harm is automatically to Ammon's benefit. These attitudes align well with what is known of Ammon's religious–political ideology. In one inscription, the national deity Milcom promises that he will 'surely destroy' the enemies who 'surround' his worshippers as they 'gaze in awe' at his power.[29]

Ammon's self-affirming misinterpretation of Judah's fall is an ideological reflex that is the polar opposite of God's plan to use Israel to bring blessing to the world (Gen. 12:1–3). By the same token, Ammon falls under the curse that God threatened against those who belittle him and his people (Gen. 12:3). Yahweh's judgment of Ammon will demonstrate irrefutably that his justice is unavoidable, that Milcom is unable to resist his power, and that Judah's fall is not the end of God's people or of the good he has in store for the world.

Moab and Seir (Ezek. 25:8–11)

God's condemnation of Moab shows a similar failure on its part to recognize Judah's significance: 'the house of Judah is like all the other nations' (25:8).[30] This mistaken belief, perhaps an inference from Judah's fall, failed to grasp the complexities of God's relationship with his covenant people. Such a misunderstanding of Yahweh and his people was already evident in Moab's royal ideology in the ninth century, when the Moabite king Mesha asserted in an inscription that the chief national deity Chemosh

[27] Similarly, Ps. 35:25 includes the exclamation 'Aha!' as well as mention of the 'heart's desire' in connection with the wish of the psalmist's enemies that he might die; elsewhere in Ezek. 26:2; 36:2.

[28] The Hebrew term translated here as 'malice' is unique to Ezekiel (elsewhere in 16:57; 28:24, 26; 36:6). Greenberg (1983: 435) refers to this attitude as 'malicious glee'.

[29] Aufrecht 2003: 139.

[30] The Septuagint does not include 'Seir' in 25:8, and the presence of an adjoining oracle against Edom (25:12–14) confirms that the present oracle is concerned only with Moab.

had 'delivered [him] from all kings' (including Jehoram, from whose rule Moab broke free [2 Kgs 3]) and that 'Israel has gone to ruin, it has gone to ruin for ever!'[31] In the light of God's affirmations through Ezekiel that he would preserve his people *from all twelve tribes* (16:53, 55; 37:15–28; 47:13), Mesha's ancient boast is not only premature but also at odds with Yahweh's plan. In response to Moab's proud bluster, this oracle announces that it is not God's people but rather Moab, meaning those Moabites who embrace the conglomeration of political power and religious belief that underlies such boasting, that will leave the scene of history (25:10). Tragically, as was the case with Ammon, Moab's realization of God's unique deity and holiness ('that I am Yahweh') and of Chemosh's inability to deliver the nation from him will be inseparable from the destruction of all those in Moab who resolutely oppose Yahweh and his people (25:11).

Edom (Ezek. 25:12–14; 35:1–15)

Edom, closely related to Israel by its descent from Esau, nonetheless had generally poor relations with Israel and Judah prior to the sixth century BC (Num. 20:14–21; Amos 1:11), worsened by a growing number of Edomite incursions into southern Judah in the late seventh century BC.[32] Its apparent interest in joining with Judah and other Levantine states to resist the imposition of Babylonian control was a brief exception to this pattern (Jer. 27:1–11). God describes Edom's participation in the destruction and despoiling of Jerusalem and its Judean kinsfolk in the early sixth century as unmitigated 'vengeance' (25:12; cf. Gen. 25:19–24; Obad. 11–14), although the Edomites involved constituted 'some, but hardly all, of the Edomite population.'[33] Because these actions were hateful in his eyes, God promises widespread destruction of what lives in the land ('man and beast' [Ezek. 25:13]) and the transformation of Edom's territory into 'a wasteland' (my translation).[34] This retributive vengeance (25:14, the same root as in 25:12) will exceptionally be implemented 'by the hand of my people Israel', such that the victim is the instrument of

[31] Smelik 2003: 137.

[32] Stern 2001: 293–294.

[33] Timmer 2021c: 5.

[34] Babylon established hegemony over Edom c.553 BC, during the reign of Nabonidus, although without causing widespread destruction, per Tebes 2023: 251.

God's punishment of the aggressor (the explanation of Amos 9:11–12 in Acts 15 sheds light on the fulfilment of this oracle).[35]

The related oracle in Ezekiel 35 is part of a double contrast between Edom/Seir and Judah. The judgment of Edom is followed by the restoration of Judah in Ezekiel 36, and the content of chapter 35 reuses material from a similar judgment against Judah in Ezekiel 6.[36] The first charge levelled against Edom is that of 'perpetual enmity' (35:5; also 25:15), which led it to hand over Judeans to death, and to do so with hatred and spite (35:5–6, 11–12). Edom is also condemned for its spite against God himself. Even though God was present in a special way in the temple and more generally with *his* people in *his* land (35:10), Edom 'multiplied [its] words against' him' (35:13) and, in the consummate expression of pride, asserted its intention to assume ownership of Yahweh's land (35:10). 'Edom' thus embodies absolute autonomy and self-worship – it will do as it wishes with whole populations, with no regard for human life or Yahweh's awesome deity, in order to gain territory and secure its position in the Levant. 'Autonomy and the ethic of violence are a natural fit for each other', but they are also destructive of the self and of the other.[37] As the sole oracle of salvation for non-Israelites in this section shows (29:13–16; see below), the security and peace that Edom pursued through self-authorized violence can only come as a divine gift that is humbly received through reconciliation with God.[38]

Philistia (Ezek. 25:15–17)

The series of oracles against the states nearest to Judah closes by looking westward towards the Philistines. In the same terms used of Edom, Philistia is accused of exacting 'revenge' and 'taking vengeance' with deep malice (see 25:15, as in 25:6) and the intention 'to destroy in never-ending enmity'. The objects of this virulent hatred, evident over centuries, were Judah and Israel. No human agent is identified as the means by which God will repay the Philistines in kind by destroying them with 'great

---

[35] See Timmer 2019b: 484–487.

[36] Gosse 1989.

[37] Watkin 2022: 147.

[38] Strong (2017a: 286) interprets Ezekiel 35 as a 'thoroughly theological' conquest in which Yahweh marches 'into the land for the sake of his honor'.

vengeance' and 'wrathful rebukes', thereby teaching them who he is: 'I am Yahweh' (25:16–17).[39]

Several features of this series of oracles stand out. It focuses on sins against Yahweh and Israel/Judah; puts limited emphasis on the ideologies that motivate those sinful attitudes and actions; generally applies *lex talionis* punishments; sees divine punishment as sometimes implemented through human agents (Judah or non-Israelites) and other times not; occasionally describes divine retribution as the expression of divine wrath or anger; and reveals God as the defender of his people and the judge of evil anywhere in his world. His judgments demonstrate to all that he alone is God and that they oppose or ignore him at great risk.

Tyre and the quest for dominion and divine glory (Ezek. 26:1 – 28:19)

The rest of Ezekiel's oracles against foreign 'nations' focus either on states that were particularly significant during Judah's final decades (Tyre in Ezek. 26 – 28 and Egypt in 29 – 32), or on Gog of Magog, a collective that represents all the enemies of God's people (Ezek. 38 – 39). Nevader's observation that 'more than half of the oracles' in chapters 26 – 32 'specifically address the king of each nation, not the body politic', highlights the prominence of royal ideology in this section.[40] This royal focus also reminds the reader that the link between the nations named in a particular oracle and the more abstract entity to which the oracle refers requires teasing out. Typically, these oracles focus on a carefully chosen set of political ideals and religious beliefs and the individuals or groups who adopt them in order to pursue their and their state's flourishing on their own terms. In so doing, they either ignore Yahweh or choose to actively resist his purposes.

Tyre as a totalizing commercial–materialist enterprise (Ezek. 26 – 27)

The oracles against Tyre put its energetic trading activities under the microscope, and use two levels of magnification: one focused on the city-state as a commercial entity, the other more narrowly on the king. As 'the

[39] Babylon destroyed or subjugated the Philistines in 604 BC, and the last attested conflict between Judah and the Philistines dates to the late eighth century BC (2 Kgs 18:8; cf. Ezek. 16:57).

[40] Nevader 2015b: 162.

most important of the Phoenician cities', Tyre boasted a trade network that reached to north Africa and Spain, with colonies at Carthage and Cyprus (the latter being under its 'hegemonic rule . . . at least until the end' of the eighth century BC).[41] Against this backdrop, the first oracle (26:1–14, dated to 587–586, shortly before Babylon laid siege to Tyre in 585) introduces Tyre by means of a brief citation that exposes the value system that animated its economic activity: 'Aha! . . . now that she [Jerusalem] lies in ruins I will prosper' (26:2 NIV). Whether this means that the leaders and magnates of Tyre saw in Jerusalem's fall the elimination of a commercial rival, an opportunity for finding new clients, or both, they perceived a situation that seemed to be entirely for Tyre's benefit and thus cause for celebration (26:2).[42] The city-state's glee is not open disdain or hatred for Judah, but its desire to prosper in relation to Jerusalem's fall is blatantly utilitarian: *what is economically good for Tyre is good, period.* At the same time, Tyre's hands were not unstained with respect to other nations around the ancient Mediterranean and Aegean: it 'imposed . . . terror' on all those in its orbit (26:17; note its involvement in a slave trade [27:13]).[43] This moral element comes more fully into view in the second oracle (27:1–36), as does the extent of Tyre's materialistic identity.

The bulk of chapter 27 portrays Tyre as a metaphorical commercial ship filled to overflowing with merchandise (27:3b–9, 26–36).[44] The first section is framed by Tyre's 'beauty', reflecting its dominant status as a trading power and the massive wealth it produced. It is significant that Tyre *claims this desirable status for itself*: 'I am perfect in beauty' (27:3b, 11).[45] While this might appear to be mere vanity (and it is vain), it is also the belief that Tyre was the apogee of beauty defined as international status and material wealth that – so Tyre believed – elicited the admiration and

[41] Bryce 2009: 728. For a careful analysis of Ezek. 27 in relation to Tyre's trade network, see Liverani 1991.

[42] On the earlier successful economic cooperation between monarchic Israel and Tyre, see Kuhrt 1995: 408–409.

[43] It is unlikely that Tyre's terror affected its own citizens; see Greenberg 1997: 537–538. Such 'terrorizing' behaviour (cf. Ezek. 32:23–27, 30) is characteristic of all the nations that go down to the 'pit', whether the threat they posed was military or economic in nature.

[44] The claim of Arthur (2023: 16) that this 'ship itself is a thinly disguised metaphor for the Jerusalem temple' seems implausible in the light of the many features in chs. 26 – 28 that apply to Tyre but not to Judah or Jerusalem.

[45] Willis (2012) helpfully explores beauty and glory in Ezekiel.

appreciation of those whose opinions it valued.[46] However, when beauty is mentioned elsewhere in Ezekiel, it is *God* who grants to Israel *another kind* of beauty and splendour (16:14) rooted in his sovereign love for her and reflecting, insofar as she remains his faithful covenant partner, his glory (16:15).[47] This is utterly incompatible with Tyre's self-attributed allure, which Tyre had supposedly attained by its own efforts.

The metaphorical commercial ship of state at the centre of the chapter reveals the vigour and seriousness with which Tyre pursued its beauty and fame. Premium materials, luxurious decorative touches and the most skilled human resources available produced a commercial behemoth in which all other ships were contained (27:9). The equipment of Tyre's mercenaries (so Tyre thought) contributed to its splendour (27:10) and 'made perfect' its beauty (27:11).[48] The extensive list of trading partners in 27:12–25 surveys the geographical range of Tyre's clients and the impressive variety of wares and goods that passed through the holds of its fleet, summarized as 'great wealth of every kind' (27:12, 18, including slaves [27:13]). The description culminates in 27:25 with the image of the ship 'filled and heavily laden' with this limitless cargo.

It is precisely at this most illustrious of moments that the 'east wind' (perhaps a hint at Babylon's coming siege) unexpectedly wrecks Tyre (27:26). The purportedly beautiful ship, built of the finest materials, manned by the most skilled mariners, present in every market and filled with every possible kind of cargo, will simply 'sink into the heart of the seas' and disappear (27:27). This event is significant in several ways. First, the reactions (26:16; 27:28–32a) and lament (27:32b–36) of Tyre's former trading partners portray the dismay and fear they feel when it falls. Tyre's demise causes them to lament bitterly, since it had 'satisfied many peoples' and 'enriched the kings of the earth' with its 'abundant wealth and merchandise' (26:17–18; 27:33). At the same time, they are in horror at the

---

[46] Drawing on De Blois 2021 *sub loco*. On the 'totalizing' nature of this description, see Vayntrub 2020.

[47] Willis 2012: 6, 8. Strong (2015: 188) also notes the derived nature of Jerusalem's beauty: 'For Ezekiel, Jerusalem ultimately owes its perfect beauty to the fact that it is the seat of Yahweh's throne.'

[48] Greenberg (1997: 552), Block (1998: 64–65) and Allen (1990: 86) agree that mercenaries are in view here.

double prospect of (economic) life without Tyre and Babylon's apparent intention to extend its control still further into the Levant (26:16).[49]

Second, God's response to Tyre as the parade-example of materialistic success and allure goes far beyond the termination of the city-state as a commercial empire. The divine 'I am against you' (26:3) highlights the profoundly *theological* nature of Tyre's commercial enterprise and associated values and beliefs.[50] Its intention to pursue economic dominance and material luxury as the highest goods in Yahweh's world is fundamentally opposed to Yahweh's glory, will and actions in history.[51] To demonstrate the depth of the conflict between Tyre's world view and the world as it really is, God will use 'many nations' to destroy the supposedly self-sufficient economic superpower. Tyre will be scraped from its rock into the sea (26:3–4), and its riches will be taken by others (26:5, 12).[52]

Third and finally, Yahweh declares that he will bring Tyre, understood as everyone whose values, beliefs and actions align with those attributed to Tyre in these chapters, 'down with those who go down to the pit': 'I will bring you to a dreadful end, and you shall be no more' (26:20–21). Tyre's materialism, self-glorification, oppression of some of its trading partners, and trade in slaves weigh it down like cargo in a sinking ship. As a consequence, it is brought down to the pit of divine judgment rather than entering an afterlife protected by 'apotropaic amulets, plaques, and figures . . . intended to ward off evil and to provide physical or spiritual resurrection to the deceased', as Tyre's elites would likely have hoped.[53] Babylon's thirteen-year siege and subsequent subjugation of Tyre temporarily interrupted its commerce and eventually ended its status as the premier trading partner in the Mediterranean. However, this falls short

[49] Babylon did not destroy Tyre, but apparently brought it into a vassal relationship in which Tyre continued to thrive; see Mattingly 2000b: 230; Bryce 2009: 728–729.

[50] Although Ezekiel does not mention Tyre's gods, Baal of Tyre and his consort Ashtart were believed to be primarily responsible for the city's well-being, and both included a maritime facet in their identity; see Woolmer 2017: 113.

[51] On Tyre's rise in the tenth to eighth centuries BC, see Aubet 2014. Strong's (2015: 180–190) proposal that Ezekiel condemns Tyre because it seeks to replace Jerusalem is insightful, but since Jerusalem's beauty and standing are derived from Yahweh's transcendent glory, Tyre's aspirations are ultimately self-idolatry. Allen (1990: 88) similarly observes that '[i]n opposing Babylon, Tyre stood against Yahweh, and so could not stand'. This is surely true, but Ezekiel's condemnation focuses on the *reasons for which* Tyre chose to take that stance.

[52] Chatonnet (2023: 1098) concludes that 'the city remained unconquered', apparently retaining 'its independence, and its king'.

[53] Woolmer 2017: 131–132.

of the full extent of the 'end' that God threatened against it and so suggests a progressive fulfilment focused on Tyre as it is selectively defined here.[54]

Tyre is not co-referential with the stones and mortar of the city, or with every member of its population (lack of clarity on this point has generated needless worries about the apparently unfulfilled prophecies of Ezek. 26 – 27 and Isa. 23).[55] Tyre in these oracles ultimately refers to those Tyrians, and by extension to others regardless of where and when they live, who define human flourishing in exclusively or primarily material or social terms and pursue it by such means. The near-term destruction of Tyre consists most visibly in the collapse of the city-state's economic dominance but more precisely in the undoing of *the ideology that underlay it and those who held it*. This collapse, wherever and whenever it comes about, exposes the ephemeral nature of self-ascribed beauty and the inability of those who pursue material goals by human means to achieve anything more than temporary, material dominance of the geographical, political or cultural domain they inhabit.

Tyre's king as a self-proclaimed deity whom Yahweh will eliminate (Ezek. 28)

The final oracle against Tyre is more overtly theological than the preceding ones, and focuses exclusively on Tyre's king. Unlike the two preceding chapters, the wealth of the city remains in the background, and the sin of pride is in the foreground (28:2–10). The king's pride, most clearly expressed in the image of him sitting 'in the seat of the gods', is fuelled by Tyre's self-perceived dominance (28:2), the king's unmatched (and self-attributed) 'wisdom' and 'understanding', and the wealth that the city enjoyed (28:4).[56] All this leads the king to assert his quasi-divine status (28:2, 6, 9 *bis*) as the height of his hubris.[57]

---

[54] Woolmer (2017: 46) concludes that Babylon's actions had 'a severely detrimental impact on Phoenician commercial ventures' that lasted until Persia conquered Babylon.

[55] Renz (2000) offers helpful reflections on the nature of prophecy and fulfilment.

[56] See Gordon 2010: 55.

[57] As with some of his other attributes, the king's self-ascribed 'wisdom and understanding' (note the same accusation against the king of Assyria [Isa. 10:12–13]) ape divine gifts that are most often tied to a relationship of covenant love and obedience to God, who is their source and perfect manifestation (Jer. 10:12). See, e.g., Deut. 4:6 (obedient Israel); 1 Kgs 4:29 (Solomon); Job 28:28; Ps. 111:10; Dan. 1:4 (Daniel); Isa. 11:2 (the Messiah). Exceptionally, note the wisdom of Hiram of Tyre (1 Kgs 7:14) and Bezalel and Oholiab (Exod. 31:1–11) for construction of the temple and tabernacle, respectively.

This passage presents the king as nothing less than self-idolizing. He elevates himself over all else and pursues self-preservation and self-glorification by any means, all on the assumption of his unsurpassed importance.[58] If the Tyrian king's claims to divinity are part of Tyrian royal ideology, as Nevader suggests, God's rejection of his boast simultaneously deconstructs 'the very foundation upon which' that ideology is constructed.[59] The lament in 28:11–19 further illuminates the inflated self-image of Tyre's ruler. In a complex network of allusions to other biblical texts and to the *Epic of Gilgamesh* (or perhaps other sources), Ezekiel presents the king as a sort of Adam-figure, ruling (according to the king's self-description) with wisdom and beauty in 'Eden, the garden of God' ('the holy mountain of God'), and surrounded by gems and precious metals (28:12–14).[60] Originally blameless, the king eventually sinned through violence in his commercial activities and through pride in his wisdom and beauty, and so was expelled from the garden (28:14–18a).

The reference to Eden draws the Tyrian king's soliloquies into the scope of God's creation of all things and his majestic supremacy over them – the king of Tyre included. The removal of the arrogant monarch from his constructed ideological world and his integration into the biblical creation account also ties his pride to the archetypal sin that brought death and mortality into the world.[61] The deadly mix of arrogated perfection, wisdom, beauty and status is definitively undone when Yahweh declares the king profane, expels him from the garden, imposes the death penalty upon him and ultimately destroys him in Sheol (28:16–19). Yahweh's judgment deconstructs Tyrian royal ideology by bringing its vaunted ruler down from the heights of his self-attributed superiority to the ground from which he was taken. God's sole agency in this retribution demonstrates that he alone possesses the power, glory and status that Tyre's ruler tried to grasp.

---

[58] In a contemporary Neo-Babylonian text published by W. R. Mayer, the primordial king is 'distinctively superior' to other human beings, and is given both 'the task of warfare' and 'a beautiful appearance' by the gods; see Van Seters (1989), who cites Mayer 1987.

[59] Nevader 2015b: 167.

[60] For discussion of possible extrabiblical sources or parallels for some of the images and concepts here, see Nevader 2015a, some of whose insights I follow in this discussion.

[61] Osborne (2018) also highlights pride as the king's most characteristic sin.

An oracle against Sidon (Ezek. 28:20–24)

The oracles against Phoenicia end with a short prophecy against Sidon, a city-state on the coast north of Tyre and a potential ally of Judah around the time of Ezekiel's ministry (Jer. 27:3). Although no formal charges are brought against Sidon, the fact that its destruction will prevent any 'brier' or 'thorn' from harming 'the house of Israel' implies that it had committed wrongs that were to Israel's hurt. These included the 'contempt' that elicits condemnation throughout the oracles in chapters 26 – 28 (28:24). Yahweh's punishment of Sidon, perhaps fulfilled in Nebuchadnezzar's subjugation of the city in the first half of the sixth century BC, will manifest God's glory and holiness as he punishes the enemies of his people and uses Babylon's campaigns in the Levant for his purposes.[62]

Egypt and the violent quest for domination and glory (Ezek. 29 – 32)

Egypt is the seventh and last nation mentioned in the collection of oracles concerning the nations in Ezekiel 25 – 32, and is itself the subject of seven oracles, one of which surprisingly announces Egypt's restoration after punishment (29:13–16). Unlike Tyre, which existed at a certain remove from the events in Judah's last decades, Egypt was directly involved in the political turmoil of that period, often presenting itself – and being perceived by Judah's rulers – as a source of protection against the advance of Babylon. Judah's penchant for trusting other states rather than Yahweh was so established that Ezekiel addressed it repeatedly, prophesying 'the destruction of Egypt at each moment that an alliance appears most appealing' to Judah.[63] Since five of the seven oracles in this section are addressed to or focus on the pharaoh, they highlight the importance of royal and imperial ideologies and their cosmological and theological foundations as 'the powers that propel and undergird' Egypt's aspirations and actions (29:1–16; 30:20–26; 31:1–18; 32:1–16, 17–32).[64] This funda-

---

[62] The absence of any mention of Sidon in extant cuneiform sources makes impossible any detailed reconstruction of its history between the time when an Assyrian governor was installed in the early seventh century BC and the mention of its ruler as a member of the court of Nebuchadnezzar II about a century later (most likely subsequent to its involvement in the short-lived conspiracy mentioned in Jer. 27 – 28); see Elat 1991: 29–30; Chatonnet 2023.

[63] Nevader 2015b: 177; Carvalho 2015: 201.

[64] Odell 2005: 340; I demur at her suggestion that chaos (*tĕhôm*) is in view.

mental opposition to Yahweh is particularly evident in Egypt's pride, and Yahweh's response to Egyptian imperialism focuses on this fundamental sin.

Pride as a claim of sovereignty over creation and the rejection of God's order (Ezek. 29)

Pronounced just after Hophra took the throne, the opening oracle of Ezekiel 29:1–16 most likely refers to the activity of both Hophra (r. 589–557 BC) and his predecessor Psammetichus II (595–589 BC). God describes the pharaoh with a term that can be translated as 'serpent', 'crocodile' or 'dragon' (*tannîm*, a biform of *tannîn*).[65] In the Old Testament, a 'dragon' often appears in cosmological settings (Gen. 1:21; Job 7:12; Ps. 74:13; Isa. 27:1, 51:9; etc.). When this creature represents opposition to Yahweh and his created order, as it does here, such passages typically present Yahweh as the one who vanquishes or destroys it (Pss. 74:13; 91:13; Isa. 27:1; 51:9; Ezek. 32:2–3).[66] The nature of the conflict between the pharaoh and God is sparked by the dragon's claim that 'I made [the Nile] for myself' (29:3). In ancient Egypt, this feat was first attributed to Egypt's gods but was also part of Egyptian royal ideology. The conflict here thus arises from the fact that the pharaoh claims for himself (with the assistance of Egyptian gods) *Yahweh's* exclusive creation, ownership and control of all that exists.[67] Seen in this light, the image of the pharaoh as a chaos creature is perhaps less an ironic claim that he is ill-suited to his role of maintaining social and cosmic order (*ma 'at*) than an assertion that he and imperial Egypt are ultimately incompatible with God's creational order.[68]

God's punishment of the pharaoh is a definitive response to a level of pride that manifests itself in a desire to *usurp Yahweh's control* over the cosmos he created and leads to a pattern of behaviour that runs

---

[65] Koehler and Baumgartner 2001: 1764.

[66] The adjective 'great' that modifies 'dragon' in 29:3 is almost certainly sarcastic, since Yahweh is speaking and since the dragon is fished out of the Nile without drama in 29:4.

[67] Greenberg (1997: 612) draws attention to a scarab of Thutmose III (fifteenth century BC) that reads: 'The Nile is at his service, and he opens its cavern to give life to Egypt.'

[68] The ironic interpretation is proposed in Nevader 2015b: 171. See the discussion of scriptural allusions to (primordial) chaos in Averbeck 2004. If a non-mythological sense is preferred, serpents and crocodiles carried both negative and positive connotations in ancient Egyptian religion, creating an ambiguity that Carvalho (2015: 213–214) suggests allows God to invert a positive image and so undermine the associated royal ideology.

contrary to that order. Yahweh's retribution demonstrates that as Creator, he will *maintain justice and ultimately re-establish peace* in his creation. Failure to recognize his sovereignty is thus a fatal mistake. Caught like a crocodile by Yahweh's unmatched power, thrown into the wilderness, and consumed by birds and beasts (29:4–5), the mighty beast will become a mighty feast! Moreover, the prospect that the pharaoh would not be properly buried would suggest to Egyptians that there would be catastrophic consequences for him in the afterlife.[69] The oracle in 29:17–20, from the year 571 BC, is closely related to what precedes it, and highlights God's use of Babylon to punish Egypt. The oracle limits Babylon's role to despoiling Egypt, perhaps foretelling Babylon's brief incursion into the Nile Delta in 567.[70]

Pride expressed as confidence in military power, rooted in imperial ideology (Ezek. 30; 31; 32:1–16)

Given Egypt's often illustrious past and the recent collapse of the Assyrian Empire, it is not surprising that Egypt in the early sixth century BC would have been confident in its military prowess. It is against such a background that the oracle in Ezekiel 30:1–19 widens its focus beyond the pharaoh to include the rest of Egypt and its allies (30:5–6). Two features stand out, and are presumably the reasons for which Yahweh announces Egypt's destruction: its *pride in its military power* (30:6, 18) and its *trust in its gods* ('idols' and 'images' [30:13]). Several of the cities named in 30:13–18 are likely mentioned for one or both of these reasons: Ptah 'ruled from Memphis' as its patron deity;[71] Amun's temple was at No(-Amon), that is, Thebes,[72] which was 'surrounded by a great aggregate of sacred precincts';[73] Sin/Pelusium had an important role as a defence against incursions from the north-east;[74] and Awen/On/Heliopolis was

[69] Scripture establishes a close connection between creation, renewal and righteousness; see Seifrid 2000. 'The damned were those who had failed to have the proper funerary rituals carried out', according to Szpakowska (2014: 511); similarly, Frood (2014: 488–489) notes that the mortuary cult that completed the 'funeral and ritual performances' on behalf of the dead 'ensured . . . the afterlife of the deceased'.

[70] See Perdu 2014: 147–148.

[71] Morris 2014: 208.

[72] Clarysse 2014: 277.

[73] Greenberg 1997: 625.

[74] Ibid. 625–626.

'the center of the cult of the sun god Re'.[75] More generally, Egypt had often used its military power to dominate territories beyond its borders, as it did with much of Canaan in the late second millennium BC, in order to extract financial profit and natural resources. The self-serving use of force and violence reveals the close link between such violence and the autonomy that is essential to imperialism.[76]

The same focus on self is evident in the way in which Egypt's ideology involved the gods. As noted in chapter 2 of this volume, Egypt's imperialism was believed to be directly dependent on the multifaceted involvement of Egypt's gods. Yet pride in its military might suggests that this dependence on the gods was imperfect, and did not prevent Egypt's military and political leaders from basking in the limelight of victories and glory that the gods had purportedly given them. Although the gods were to be served, their approval of the king and the army (when successful) suggests that they have been created in the image of their worshippers.[77] Egypt's gods served its purposes, and it served its gods, in a symbiotic idolatry that nourished its appetite for 'glory' and 'greatness' (31:18).

Egypt's confidence in its ability to defend itself from any threat also revealed the belief that it was peerless and permanent. God exposes the folly of this (very comforting) belief by comparing Egypt with Assyria. Assyria had ruled large parts of the ancient Near East quite successfully for centuries and inflicted several painful defeats on Egypt, including the sacking of Thebes in 663, before it fell into rapid decline and was conquered by Babylon a few decades later. Egypt, the comparison alleges, is like Assyria before its fall, congratulating itself as a metaphorical tree for possessing the self-attributed traits of 'greatness' (31:2), beauty and superlative height (31:3, 5, 7, 8, 9), and providing shade for 'all great nations' (31:6). By interpreting reality this way, however, one essential element was overlooked: it was *Yahweh's gifts* that made Egypt great. Rather than looking upward to the Creator, those who embraced Egypt's royal and imperial ideologies believed that Egypt was without rival, had achieved this status by itself and would continue to flourish indefinitely (31:8–9).[78] The last passage in which Egypt's military strength is vaunted

[75] Wilson 2014: 784.

[76] 'Autonomy and the ethic of violence are a natural fit for each other' (Watkin 2022: 147).

[77] Voltaire: 'If God made us in his image, we have certainly returned the compliment', cited in Williams 2023: 9.

[78] There are echoes of creation of varying clarity in Ezek. 31 (including the mention of the

Finally, in chapter 32, Yahweh contradicts the flawed judgments that are inherent in the pharaoh's grasping after lion-like invincibility and assigns him a quite different identity, that of a simple crocodile. The extremely limited significance of the latter, which merely muddies the waters in which it swims, gives the most diminutive sense possible to the Hebrew term *tannîm*, and reveals that the pharaoh has badly overestimated his significance and power. Egypt's ruler will be treated like a crocodile that is caught, dragged from the river, killed, and served as carrion to 'the beasts of the whole earth' (32:4). Denied burial, the pharaoh's afterlife is in extreme jeopardy according to ancient Egyptian beliefs about life after death.[82] Ironically, the king *qua* crocodile could figure as the villain in Horus's symbolic elimination of the wicked by killing crocodiles[83] or be associated with the enemies that the empire's New Kingdom military texts depicted as crocodiles.[84]

Pride expressed as overconfidence or narcissism, rooted in self-adoration (Ezek. 30:20–26; 32:17–32)

The last kind of fruits that pride produces and that account for God's condemnation of Egypt arise from disordered loves. Overconfidence is familiar to all of us, and arises when we overestimate our ability or underestimate a task or challenge. This may produce unpleasant or even harmful results (in mountain climbing, for example), yet such failings might come under moral critique only obliquely. The case of Egypt in Ezekiel 30:20–26 is quite different, however. This oracle, dated to 587 BC, was delivered just before Jerusalem's fall and after Babylon had laid siege to the city. Yahweh announces that he will complete the process of weakening the pharaoh's military power, symbolized by his arm, hand and sword, by breaking both his arms and causing the sword to fall from the ruler's hand (30:21–22). At the same time, God will strengthen Babylon and put *his* sword in Nebuchadnezzar's hand, granting him victory over Egypt (30:24–26). The pharaoh's pride produces his *failure to perceive* that earlier setbacks were providential indicators that he had overstepped his bounds, or that his attempts to deliver Jerusalem from the Babylonians ran contrary to God's stated intention to lead his people into exile. These flawed interpretations

[82] Szpakowska 2014: 511; Frood 2014: 488–489; Carvalho 2015: 217.

[83] Keel 1978: 147. Carvalho (2015: 212–214) explores other associations of the crocodile in Egyptian religion.

[84] Abo El Magd 2016: 331–333.

of reality are rooted in a refusal to recognize Yahweh's unique deity, word and actions in the world for what they are. God's power and justice will demonstrate the inevitable result of proudly living as if Yahweh can be safely ignored. Egypt's military forces will be destroyed and its people will be scattered 'throughout the countries' (30:26), effectively ending its existence as the superpower its leaders believed it to be.

The disordered loves that are inseparable from pride are even more evident in the final oracle against Egypt (32:17–32), which unpacks God's promise that he will bring Egypt down to Sheol (31:18). Rather like Tyre, the justification for Egypt's ultimate destruction involves its belief in its attractiveness to neighbouring nations because of its power and occasional supremacy (32:19). God's question draws attention to Egypt's self-fascination:

> Whom do you surpass in beauty?
> Go down and be laid to rest with the uncircumcised.
> (Ezek. 32:19)

'Consumed by extravagant self-love'[85] and blinded to its moral flaws and strategic miscalculations by its self-infatuation, Egypt's narcissism seems to have culminated in the conclusion that it had 'arrived' and could never enter a decline, much less come to an end. This unqualified self-affirmation surely smothered any self-critique, but could not protect it from Yahweh's condemnation.

God's diametrically opposed evaluation of Egypt is expressed, first, in the metaphorically 'uncircumcised' condition that places Egypt among those who reject Yahweh's claims upon them (32:19, 21).[86] It is also likely that Egypt is guilty of spreading 'terror' on earth if the same accusation against the other empires applies to it as well (32:23, 24, 25, 26, 27, 30). Be that as it may, in 32:32 the seventh and final use of 'terror' in chapter 32 sees Yahweh, not Egypt, bringing 'terror' *to Egypt* and dragging the pharaoh down to Sheol. This divine judgment, especially at the end of the final Egypt oracle, is radically more significant and definitive than anything Egypt's military may have achieved against its enemies, and removes Egypt-as-empire and its gods from the stage of history.

---

[85] Naugle 2008: 67.

[86] This is all the more cutting since Egyptian kings and priests were circumcised; Greenberg 1997: 661–666.

Pride, sin and imperialism

Behind Egypt's military activity and Tyre's commercial dominance, God's word through Ezekiel identifies pride as the cardinal sin that will justify his punishment of these states. While some forms of pride can be virtuous, such as parental pride when celebrating a child's achievements, the pride exhibited by Egypt and Tyre is the very opposite, and so is a vice.[87] Chapters 26 – 32 identify several distinct but interconnected dimensions of pride and show how it affects the beliefs of those who formulate or embrace state or royal ideology, how the ideology itself expresses pride and how the actions these states undertook demonstrated pride.

The oracles against Egypt and Tyre assert, first, that pride involves giving 'inordinate prominence' to oneself.[88] It is thus a matter of how one perceives oneself and, by necessity, the rest of reality. These states, like the others that the prophets critique, are epistemologically self-authorizing – they accept their interpretation of reality as the truth. This self-authorization at the level of perception and interpretation inevitably produces self-elevation more generally. This stage of pride's development takes different forms in these chapters: the desire to be admired (vanity), the belief that one is superior to others (conceit), or the arrogance that disregards what others think and embraces one's self-given absolute importance.[89]

As these oracles reveal, all such expressions of pride refuse to accept that as creator, God alone has the authority to attribute meaning and value to the elements of his creation. The excessive importance that a proud person or royal ideology gives to the one concerned and that person's interpretation of reality are thus terribly deformed misunderstandings that are 'not in accord with right reason'.[90] Unless corrected, this flawed understanding of self, God, others and the world will inexorably lead to the failure of one's projects and relationships and ultimately to separation from God and all that is good.

The archetypal example of pride is the primordial couple's attempted arrogation of godlikeness (Gen. 3:5), arguably the theological backdrop for Ezekiel's condemnations of imperial ideology. It reveals a number of

[87] Roberts (2009: 123) defines virtuous pride as 'generous joy in the other's flourishing'.

[88] Roberts 2009: 124.

[89] Sands 2010: 42–43.

[90] Timpe and Tognazzini 2017: 216; Wilson 2011: 621.

flawed conclusions that involve epistemological autonomy (failure to trust Yahweh's word and the suspicion that he may have withheld something good from them), self-determination (they, not God, determine what they are or can become), reliance on one's own actions to attain one's goals (eating the forbidden fruit), and more.[91] In Eden, as in Egypt and Tyre, pride in the short term produces alienation from God and others in favour of self-worship,[92] and death in the long term.[93] The same verdict of death announced in Eden is also heard concerning Egypt and Tyre, whose pride brings them or their representative ruler down to Sheol: 'In God's world ideological pride in human achievement is doomed to end in destruction.'[94]

Gog and his allies as the last enemies of Yahweh and restored Israel (Ezek. 38 – 39)

The primary figure in this passage is 'Gog, of the land of Magog', but the list of actors is drawn from across the ancient Near East. The impossibility of proposing a clear referent for either Gog or Magog, like the ambiguous nature of the coalition that comes against restored Israel, invites the reader to understand these terms as general references to a yet-unseen eschatological enemy. In Yahweh's sovereign will (38:16), this foe will come against God's restored but not fully delivered people in their land,[95] which has become 'the centre of the earth' (38:11–12), with the intention to plunder it.[96]

---

[91] Some of these thoughts are capably developed in Watkin 2022: 208–221.

[92] Other fruits of pride, often interrelated, include 'domination, arrogance, vanity, and conceit' as well as 'egotism, hyper-autonomy, grandiosity, pretentiousness, snobbery, impertinence or presumption, haughtiness, self-righteousness, selfish ambition, and self-complacency', according to Roberts 2009: 123.

[93] Here I draw on a few points made by Wilson (2011) and Provan (1999: 26), who asserts that '[w]e must reckon, at the heart of the human condition, with the worship of the self. Genesis 3 describes its inception and progress'.

[94] Allen 1990: 127.

[95] See, e.g., Block 1998: 432–436; Allen 1990: 204–205; Strine 2014: 96 (demurring at her suggestion that Gog is a deity); Galambush 2006; Lee 2017: 4. Sulzbach (2023: 482) asserts that Gog/Magog 'must somehow be a cryptic reference to Babylon'. For discussion of Gog and Magog in Rev. 19:17–21; 20:8–10, see Beale 1999: 976–982, 1022–1028.

[96] Lee's contention that Gog and its allies are 'Judah's [former] allies' (2017: 5) makes too much of incidental lexical links such as 'on that day' (2017: 4). However, Ezekiel does allow that former allies can become enemies, as the Egypt oracles show, and Lee is correct to see Gog and its allies as 'a metahistorical evil power that stands in opposition to Yahweh and the restored Israel in the eschatological era' (2017: 4). Strine (2014) similarly overemphasizes possible Babylonian elements in some elements of the description of Gog and Magog to argue that Babylon is in view. This is

God's counteroffensive against Gog and its allies will reveal to them who he is to his enemies (38:16, 23). The expression of Yahweh's anger, jealousy and 'blazing wrath' (38:18–19) against them is presented as an earthquake that affects every domain of the terrestrial creation, from the fish in the seas to the mountains, and as a sixfold judgment of pestilence, bloodshed, 'torrential rains and hailstones, fire and sulphur' (38:22). Gog will fall dead on the territory of restored Israel, and his corpse will be eaten by scavengers (39:4–5, 17–21), ending his existence with abysmal shame.

The destruction of Israel's enemies is also its final deliverance, and once the slain are buried (39:11–16) the land will once again be pure and Israel's permanent security will be ensured (cf. 28:25–26).[97] The double significance of God's actions is spelled out repeatedly in these chapters by means of the recognition formula, in which Yahweh is known either in judgment (cf. 'I am against you'; see 38:18) or in salvation (see 39:1–7, 21, 25). This pair of divine actions reveals, in ways suited to each group, who Yahweh is in relation to those who worship him faithfully once they are radically renewed (see chs. 33 – 34; 36 – 37) and to those who doggedly seek to impose their will over against his as they pursue material goals. Like Egypt in Ezekiel 32, the actions of Gog and its allies are driven by a pride that sets them against their creator, whose order they cannot endure and whose power brings justice upon them despite their resolute pursuit of unchallenged autonomy.

Salvation for some from the nations

The restoration of Israel and the final destruction of its enemies in chapters 38 – 39 lead directly into Ezekiel's extensive description of the new temple that defines the land of Israel in chapters 40 – 48. Readers of Ezekiel would be justified in tentatively concluding that in this section the nations have all been destroyed, with the exception of restored Egypt (29:13–16) – but even restored Egypt does not appear here.[98] Carly

intriguing in the light of the fact that Babylon is the only nation in Ezekiel not addressed by an oracle of judgment and serves only as the means by which Yahweh punishes various nations. However, it seems better to see Babylon as (potentially) part of the larger assemblage of nations that oppose Israel and to view Gog as their human, rather than divine, leader.

[97] Allen 1990: 204.

[98] So Sulzbach (2023: 480): 'All the neighboring nations have been effectively erased by means of the oracles against them.'

Crouch's conclusion that the nations are almost out of sight is correct as far as it goes, but a good deal should be said about non-Israelites as the recipients of Yahweh's grace and deliverance. Our consideration of the few passages that predict the salvation of non-Israelites will corroborate John T. Strong's proposal that Ezekiel teaches that the 'blessings for the foreign nations' mentioned repeatedly in the Old Testament 'would come to the nations by means of Israel'.[99]

Sodom adopted as a daughter by superlatively restored Judah (Ezek. 16:49–63)

We begin with a surprising candidate for divine blessing: Sodom. Mentioned briefly in the review of Israel's and Judah's infidelity and eventual restoration, Sodom is condemned for its pride and complacent prosperity in the face of the needs of the 'poor and needy', and its resultant destruction is summarized as 'removal' by God (see 16:49–50). Yet God goes on to announce that he 'will restore their fortunes, both the fortunes of Sodom and her daughters, and . . . Samaria and her daughters' (16:53), along with those of Judah (16:54). This unexpected development involves the adoption of the remnants of the 'older sister' (Sodom) and the younger sister (Samaria, i.e. the northern kingdom of Israel) by restored Judah, with whom Yahweh renews or makes an 'everlasting covenant' (16:60–61).[100] God's unprecedented atonement for Judah's sins (16:63)[101] means that 'New Israel is to be cleansed from everything Old Israel stood for', and the same is true of Sodom.[102] This act of adoption integrates the transformed remnants of Sodom and Samaria into the covenant community that Yahweh continues to enlarge in fulfilment of the Abrahamic covenant.

---

[99] Strong 1995: 133.

[100] The final clause of 16:61, 'and/but not from/because of/apart from your covenant' probably means that the grace that comes to Sodom and Samaria is not dependent on Jerusalem's standing; see Sedlmeier 2002: 220; Block 1997: 518. Renz (2002: 169) summarizes a wide variety of interpretative possibilities.

[101] Block (1997: 516–518) argues carefully for this, whereas Renz (2002: 167) concludes that 'from a more formal point of view, this has to be a new covenant'.

[102] Renz 2002: 172.

Egypt shares a common eschatological restoration with Judah (Ezek. 29:13–16)

The fact that Egypt can be the subject of an oracle of judgment (29:1–12) *and* an oracle of restoration (29:13–16) reminds us that it is possible for a single term ('Egypt') to refer to two distinct entities in different contexts: Egypt as Judah's self-interested and proud ally, and Egypt as humble and peaceable.[103] Despite its brevity, the description of its restoration in chapter 29 uses language that Ezekiel often uses to describe the restoration of Judah and/or Israel:[104] *gather* (11:17; 20:34, 41; 28:25; 34:13; 36:24; 37:21); *restore the fortunes of* (16:53; 39:25); *bring back to their land* (34:16; with different verbs but equivalent meaning, 20:34–35, 42; 34:13; 36:24; 37:12, 21); and '*know that I am Yahweh Elohim*' in connection with deliverance (16:62; 20:42, 44; 34:27, 30; 36:11, 38; 37:6, 13, 14; 39:22, 28). Egypt also undergoes an exile, as does Judah.

When two different things share prominent characteristics, these characteristics function as criteria of identity: shared traits that, without fusing the two entities into one, highlight what they have in common as superlatively important.[105] In Ezekiel 29, this means that restored Egypt, which is also purged of the pride that made it a threat to pre-exilic Judah, bears a very clear resemblance to restored Judah in the most important ways possible: God re-creates *both* in ways that make them suited for covenant life with him. *Once purged of pride and submitted to Yahweh*, Egypt will enjoy his favour on terms comparable to those that describe the restoration of Israel itself (cf. Ezek. 34:13, 16; 39:25). One final point deserves notice: unlike the other examples of the eschatological Israel–nations relationship in Ezekiel, Egypt is portrayed as still existing as a distinct state after its restoration rather than being integrated into Israel.

Sojourners worship God and inherit the land alongside Israelites (Ezek. 47:22–23)

A third and final passage, Ezekiel 47:22–23, draws non-Israelites into a saving relationship with God and an extremely close identification with

[103] Block (1998: 143) also assumes a transformation of 'Egypt': 'the God of Israel will reverse his judgment of Egypt and correct its causes'. Allen's (1990: 107) suggestion of 'reappraisal' attempts to explain the radical shift of position pragmatically and diachronically.

[104] For a much fuller list of terms, see Saur 2020: 162.

[105] Gibson 2001: 140–150.

his people. By way of contrast and introduction, in chapter 44 Yahweh castigates the Israelites, and especially the Levites, for previously having allowed 'foreigners, uncircumcised in heart and flesh', to access his temple, profaning it (44:7).[106] In the new, perfect paradigm that Ezekiel foresees, God declares: 'No foreigner, uncircumcised in heart and flesh, *of all the foreigners who are among the people of Israel*, shall enter my sanctuary' (44:9, emphasis added). Although there exists the abstract possibility that such 'uncircumcised' foreigners would be present, it is more salient that in this eschatological scenario, *ethnic non-Israelites* are among God's people ('of all the foreigners') and would be allowed to access the temple as his worshippers.[107]

This qualified admission of some non-Israelites (self-evidently *circumcised* 'in heart and flesh') aligns well with a parallel discussion of each tribe's inherited territory in 47:13 – 48:29.[108] The relevant passage, 47:22–23, makes several crucially important points. First, when Israel allots the land-as-inheritance per the instructions later in this divine speech, they are to allot it to 'the sojourners who reside among [them] and have had children among [them]' (47:22). This prevents short-term or temporary residents from enjoying a right that is by its very nature to be permanent. Second, the children of the sojourner are to be reckoned as 'native-born children' or landed citizens (*ʾezraḥ*). Yahweh adds that sojourners who have already settled somewhere in the land shall receive their allotment within the territory of the tribe among whom they have lived until now (47:23), further emphasizing permanence.

In this passage, the inheritance of the land of Israel functions as another criterion of identity: it recognizes that the sojourner has come from outside Israel in ethnic and geographic terms, but subordinates such differences to this settled existence, enjoyed in common with the rest of God's renewed people. In this radically new scenario, non-Israelites share with Israelites proximity to Yahweh's temple-filling presence (48:35) atop the holy mountain (43:12) and access to the life-giving river that flows from it and to the trees on its banks (47:1–12; cf. Rev. 22:2). The

[106] For a concise discussion of Israel's 'abominations' or 'detestable practices' with attention to Ezek. 8 and 23:38–40, see Kilchör 2017: 198–201.

[107] In other words, some 'sojourners' (*gērîm*) may not be proselytes, but those who are may enter the sanctuary; cf. Koehler and Baumgartner 2001: 184.

[108] Peterson (2004: 178) suggests that physical circumcision alone may be implied, but the opposing pair 'heart . . . flesh' makes this unlikely.

prominence of the land in this inclusive model for the blessing of non-Israelites highlights the Abrahamic dimension of this new reality (Gen. 14:19; Rom. 4:13; Heb. 11:10, 14–16).[109] As part of Israel's resettlement in the land after exile and the return of Yahweh's presence to the ideal temple, these non-Israelites are in the fullest sense part of the consummation of Yahweh's purposes for his restored people and his consummated creation as a whole.[110]

Summary and New Testament developments

The theme of the nations in Ezekiel runs the gamut from judgment to salvation. The limited attention that the book gives to the salvation of non-Israelites is likely due to the book's focus on the people of Israel at a critical point in their existence on the one hand, and to their centrality in redemptive history on the other. Taken together, these points align well with the Abrahamic covenant's emphasis on blessing coming to the nations through Abraham's line and with the same covenant's eschatological horizon that extends beyond the curses of the Sinai covenant (Lev. 26; Deut. 30; Ezek. 33 – 34; 36 – 37). The various subcategories that this chapter has used for the nations in the context of God's judgment of his people reflect the priority of God's agency in bringing covenant sanctions on his people and the importance for the nations of a proper understanding of the importance of Israel/Judah as the means through which God will bring salvation to them (Rom. 9 – 11).

The oracles against the nations, by contrast, identify, analyse and critique the ideologies that underlie the nations' antagonism towards Yahweh and his chosen people. As Nevader observes, those kings in Ezekiel who espouse a 'royal mythology' or ideology, all of whom usurp divine status or prerogative in one way or another, are inevitably '*bad* kings', and that includes all of them![111] Lest these oracles be mistaken for nationalism or

[109] Renz (2002: 69), who notes equal exclusivity with respect to those who do not revere Yahweh (also 218–222). This exclusivity may offend modern sensibilities; note Carley 2004: 120: 'it firmly excludes the participation of a significant part of God's creation from the crucial gifts of the restored community.' Such perspectives do not adequately reckon with the fundamental connection between God and life; note that 'the land, as Yahweh's inheritance, had been defiled by heterodox worship practices' that account for exile and judgment, per Strong 2017b: 260.

[110] Zehnder (2005: 524) offers a concise, perceptive treatment of this passage.

[111] Nevader 2015b: 177.

worse, a moment's reflection will show that Judah's beliefs and actions in the context of its covenant with Yahweh often exhibit the *same* aspiration for autonomy, self-congratulation, and security and prosperity through material, political or generically religious means – all without submitting to Yahweh in trust and confidence in the light of his grace, patience and fidelity.[112] In other words, the primordial sin of pride is evident in Judah and the nations alike, and only Yahweh is able and willing to overcome it.

In the New Testament, almost all the facets of the nations-theme that are evident in Ezekiel continue to develop, albeit often with significant changes driven by progress in revelation and the accomplishment of redemption. Keeping in mind that 'the nations' remains a term or concept that can refer to God's enemies in one context (Rev. 11:2, 9, 18; etc.) and to those who receive the gospel in another (Rev. 15:4; 21:24, 26; 22:2), a rapid survey of the roles and significance of the nations in Ezekiel shows significant continuity with the New Testament.

With an eye to the categories that guided our survey of non-Israelites in Ezekiel, the nations, first, bear a certain resemblance to the world as the context in which believers live and before whom God's saving actions are evident (stage, audience). Second, noting the difference between the Sinai covenant's category of covenant discipline and the concept of innocent suffering that figures largely in the New Testament, God sovereignly allows his enemies and the enemies of his people ('was given/permitted to . . .' [see Rev. 6:2, 4; etc.]) to harass, persecute and even kill believers as he continues to build his kingdom.[113] The nations' instrumental role as God's means for punishing other nations also appears in Revelation, as when the 'ten horns' and the beast destroy the prostitute in Revelation 17:16–17.

The great prostitute of Revelation 17 – 18 represents the culmination of the pride, self-serving and idolatrous ideology, relentless pursuit of power, unchecked materialism, and violence that characterized the nations that are the subjects of Ezekiel's oracles of judgment (Ezek. 25 – 32; 35; 38 – 39). These same ideologies are present in countless forms in the world around us, and require both vigilance to avoid them and critical engagement as we deconstruct them by means of the gospel. Just as God's explicit, personal, direct and overwhelming opposition to the nations in Ezekiel brings all of them, in the end, down to Sheol, this battle reaches

[112] In the same vein, the oracles of salvation for Judah do not foresee the salvation of all Judeans, but only a remnant. Contrast Strong 1995: 116–117.

[113] Beale 1999: 377.

its climax and final resolution near the end of Revelation.[114] The fall of the great prostitute in Revelation signals the final undoing of its ideology, which drove Rome in particular as 'a system of violent oppression, founded on conquest', that practised 'political tyranny and . . . economic exploitation' and absolutized itself.[115]

Finally, in much the same way that the salvation of the nations in Ezekiel involves their integration into Israel by adoption (Ezek. 16) or other images (Ezek. 29; 47), God's people in Revelation are drawn from 'every tribe and language and people and nation' (Rev. 5:9). The full experience of salvation, following upon the resurrection to life, is presented in ways very similar to Ezekiel's temple vision: God's presence is central, glorious and accessible; he is known and worshipped; and the renewed land or city is equivalent to the cosmos purged of sin and perfected. John's vision also surpasses that of Ezekiel in several ways: the temple is superseded by the glory of God and the light of the Lamb (Rev. 21:23), the nations reconciled to God play a much more visible role, and the beatific vision crowns their experience (22:4).

---

[114] See Hays 2023: 246.

[115] Bauckham 1993: 35–39, citations from 35, 37.

6
Hosea

The dominant theme of the book of Hosea is Israel's infidelity to Yahweh as his covenant partner. This reality is symbolized by Hosea's marriage to Gomer: 'the land commits great whoredom by forsaking [Yahweh]' (Hos. 1:2). The theme of infidelity is dynamic, however, for at its inception Israel's relationship with Yahweh was pristine (2:15). Similarly, the judgments that God will bring against his unfaithful people are both punishment (5:11–16; 9:9; 12:14; 13:7–16) and discipline (5:2; 7:12; 10:10), which demonstrate the folly of abandoning him and can prompt the repentance through which God will superlatively restore his covenant with them (2:16–23; 11:11; 14:1–8).

The prominence of this theme in Hosea means that non-Israelite nations play roles that fit within that larger optic so completely that Hosea is the only prophetic book that contains no oracles, whether of judgment or salvation, concerning the nations. Following Hosea's lead, this chapter examines the references to foreigners in the redemptive-historical framework that traces Israel's covenant relationship with Yahweh from its origins in Egypt and formalization at Sinai through its degradation and rupture in the land, leading to punishment in exile and finally to its restoration, which leads a radically transformed Israel back to the land.

Covenant beginnings: no nations, no idols

Egypt appears at the very beginning of Yahweh's history with his people.[1] Israel finds itself there as an ethnic group that God summons to himself, so that Egypt is only a point of departure. Yet Israel is able to leave Egypt

[1] The reference to 'your fathers' in Hos. 9:10 likely goes further back in Israel's history, to the patriarchs.

only because Yahweh is its God, the 'saviour' (Hos. 13:4) of the 'son' he loves and 'called' out of Egypt (11:1).[2] God's protection and guidance of his people from the very beginning were realized 'by a prophet', Moses (12:13), and the promise of restoration in Hosea 12:9b harks back to Israel's safety and satiety in the wilderness. Climactically, Yahweh attests that he 'knew' Israel in the wilderness (13:5), an image of the consummated marriage covenant into which he drew her (2:15).[3] This intimate knowledge is the high point of Yahweh's relationship with his people, both historically in the exodus and eschatologically in the second exodus (2:20; see below). As such, however, it becomes the height from which Israel all too rapidly falls into infidelity.

Covenant infidelity and rupture: the nations as lethal idols

The Israelites' fidelity to Yahweh begins to show weakness even before they leave the wilderness. Numbers 25 recounts Israel's participation in the Moabite cult of Baal-Peor at Shittim in terms of prostitution (*z-n-h*, frequently in Hosea) and 'putting oneself in yoke with' another deity (see Num. 25:3, 5). Hosea 9:10 describes the same catastrophic event as Israel consecrating herself with love to Baal of Peor rather than to Yahweh (contrast Num. 6:1–21).[4] This is a rare instance in which a non-Israelite nation and the literal sin of idolatry are interconnected, and Hosea more often presents idolatry as 'the equivalent of turning to foreign nations for assistance'.[5] Several centuries later, Israel's penchant for the nations as sources of provision and protection is tantamount to seeking fertility and help from a (quasi-)deity rather than from Yahweh. Yisca Zimran's proposal that 'Egypt . . . Assyria' forms a 'correlative pair' that expresses 'distance from God'[6] in Hosea translates those nations' geographic distance from Israel into a theological register, and is also applicable to each of these nations individually. This religious or covenantal distance is expressed in various ways in Hosea, although behind all of them lurks

[2] Dewrell (2021: 503–504, 506) helpfully summarizes Egypt's roles in Hosea as a place of origin, a 'source of assistance' or a place of exile.

[3] Barstad 2013: 95.

[4] Hwang 2021: 245; Hamborg 2023: 138.

[5] Zimran 2021: 16.

[6] Ibid. 4, 7.

the fundamental error of *wrongly perceiving* these empires as potential sources of provision or protection rather than returning to Yahweh for the real, durable blessings he offers in his covenant.[7]

Sources of protection and provision: idols

As a relatively small state in the Levant surrounded by states with their own ambitions, the nation of Israel could never take its safety for granted. Yahweh's covenant bond with Israel promised blessings, including security, as long as Israel remained faithful to him. The rapid decline of Yahweh-worship in the northern kingdom (1 Kgs 12) meant that such blessings would become increasingly rare (cf. Hos. 9:1–3).[8] But rather than taking seriously the warnings of the prophets or seeing the occasional skirmish with its neighbours as indicative of divine displeasure (5:13), Israel's kings decided to take whatever measures they thought necessary to secure the kingdom on their own terms. They therefore turned to the Egyptian Empire to the south or the more powerful Assyrian Empire to the north-west, 'hiring' them as 'lovers' (that is, illegitimate objects of its desire and hope) and allies (see 8:9–10; also 7:8–10). The protection that these arrangements procured required significant vassal payments (8:10; 10:6) that demonstrated in concrete ways the lengths to which Israel was willing to go to promote its schemes for self-preservation. The link between this form of idolatry and more literal forms reappears in such cases, since vassal payments to any foreign king, such as Sennacherib (inseparable from Ashur [10:6]), were Israel's affirmation that the foreign king and the gods who supported his reign were in fact more able or more reliable helpers than Yahweh.[9] The book's closing section proposes for Israel's repentance a prayer in which this fatally misplaced trust is corrected, and Yahweh (rather than Assyria or Egypt) is recognized as the *only* one who can save Israel (14:3). In general, however, spiritual blindness prevented Israel from recognizing that its natural resources were Yahweh's gracious gifts rather than the result of Israel's worship of Canaanite fertility gods

[7] Fischer 2012: 102.

[8] Note, however, the occasional intervention of divine mercy, e.g. 2 Kgs 14:25–27.

[9] Hwang (2021: 254) recognizes the link between Sennacherib and the national deity Ashur, as does Aster (2017: 103); contrast the arguments of Garrett (1997: 154). Goldingay (2021b: 22) observes more generally that 'political alliances . . . would involve shared religious rites implying recognition' of other nations' gods.

(2:5–13), another instance of affiliation with non-Israelites involving literal idolatry.[10]

Enemies: lethal idols

The connection between sin and death is foundational to biblical theology (Gen. 2:17; Rom. 6:23).[11] Since sinful human hearts habitually interpret good as evil and evil as good, what sinners pursue as good invariably turns out to be to their harm. Such is the case with Israel in Hosea. Thinking to yoke itself with foreign partners, Israel unwittingly made a covenant with death. In some cases the issue is presented as one of mistaken perception: what Israel sees as an ally is in fact a dangerously opportunistic and pragmatic state or empire that will use Israel for its own ends, ultimately destroying it. This is clearly the case with Assyria, of which Israel was a vassal for much of the eighth century BC but which progressively destroyed the northern kingdom over several decades as their relationship frayed. This failure to perceive correctly is also evident in the juxtaposition of 'strangers' who would devour any crop Israel produces (Hos. 8:7) with Israel being treated like a 'useless vessel' by the nations, including its erstwhile suzerain, Assyria (8:8–9; cf. 11:5).[12] The same holds for Egypt, which will 'gather' and 'bury' Israel (9:6). This outcome is particularly ironic in this case since Memphis, 'where the pharaohs of the Delta resided' and 'the Egyptian kings who were contemporary with Jeroboam II were active', was also the site of an immense necropolis.[13] In all these cases, Israel's lovers turn out to be ironically involved in her death, and in the case of Egypt the lover would have ample room to bury its spurned partner.

Covenant discipline: nations as witnesses or masters

Israel's exile in 722 BC was both the inevitable consequence of her infidelity to Yahweh (Hos. 8:11–14) and the result of Assyrian imperialism.

[10] Garrett 1997: 84; Hwang 2021: 105.

[11] Vlachos 2004. O'Donovan (1994: 14) speaks of the first sin as 'Adam's decision to die'.

[12] Dearman (2010: 228) suggests that the evaluation of the metaphorical vessel is Hosea's; Hwang (2021: 219–220) sees it as the nations' opinion, and thus as dehumanizing, and the opinion of Stuart (1987: 134) is similar.

[13] Barstad 2013: 98; on the necropolis at Thebes, see Pischikova 2014.

The latter receives no attention whatsoever in Hosea, however, and Assyria's conquest of the northern kingdom is simply described as Yahweh's discipline of his people (10:10, where the Assyrians are referred to as 'nations'). In that scenario, other former lovers witness Israel being shamed on the international scene (2:10; Egypt in 7:16).

A glimmer of hope appears in the prediction that Israel's exile will involve not only the dissolution of its political system but also the abandonment of the 'ephod' and 'household gods' (Hos. 3:4).[14] However, the idea of the exile as an 'anti-exodus' that returns Israel to slavery in a foreign state is more prominent (8:13 [Egypt]; 9:3, 6 [Egypt and Assyria]).[15] Israel's exile is also presented as a constant wandering among the nations (9:17), or more concretely as coming under Assyrian rule after repeatedly rejecting Yahweh's rule (11:5). The dissociation of Yahweh from his people under the Sinai covenant reaches its most extreme form in Hosea 1:9, in his statement to Israel (and, by extension, Judah [cf. 1:11]): 'You are not my people, and I am not your God.'

Covenant restoration: no nations, no idols

Contrasting sharply with the undoing of Yahweh's relationship with Israel due to the latter's infidelity, Hosea's preferred image for Israel's restoration is a second exodus, which will be preceded by a radical change of heart on Israel's part (Hos. 3:5; 5:15). Notably, this profound transformation of Israel is far more than a geographical return from exile (11:11). Israel's eschatological flourishing (note the 'latter days' in 3:5; frequently elsewhere, e.g. Num. 24:14; Deut. 4:30; Isa. 2:2) includes all twelve tribes, a massively multiplied population and the commitment to follow one Davidic king (1:10–11; cf. 3:5), something the northern kingdom of Israel had never done. The most fundamental transformation occurs at the level of the Israelites' relationship with Yahweh. The removal of the word 'Baal' from the mouths of Yahweh's people symbolizes the purification of their

[14] Hwang (2021: 129–132) sees 3:4 as an implicit announcement of exile, as does Stuart (1987: 67). Hos. 3:4 is not a summary of religious reform, since sacrifice and the ephod are legitimate whereas the pillar and household gods are not, per Stuart 1987: 67.

[15] This casts doubt on the claim of Ueberschaer (2023) that the earliest form of the book knew nothing of the exodus or deliverance from slavery. Contrast the less sceptical arguments of Hwang (2016).

hearts (2:16–17; cf. Zeph. 3:9); a new covenant that includes all of creation will bring Israel the peace and security it had fruitlessly sought elsewhere (Hos. 2:18); and Yahweh's love and faithfulness to his renewed covenant partner will be grounded in (and produce in her) the righteousness, justice, steadfast love, trust, mercy and faithfulness that render the relationship unbreakable (2:19–20; note also Israel's reverence for Yahweh in 3:5). Finally, this transformational and reconciling relationship is one of personal knowledge that binds Israel to Yahweh as his people, and Yahweh to Israel as its God (2:20–23; cf. 14:3).[16] Since the nations in Israel's experience have brought only violence and the occasion for temptation to substitute their partnership for God's blessing and protection, they do not appear in descriptions of renewed Israel's life with Yahweh (11:11; 14:3).

Summary and New Testament developments

The nations in Hosea are secondary characters and prove to be almost transparent. Although the nations are used by Israel in its infidelity, they are never identified as its source, nor is any ideology attributed to them. Instead, the emphasis is on *Israel's* ideology of material satisfaction, which leads her to join herself to whatever power or partner gives her the things she wants. The nations in Hosea are thus presented in terms of what Israel perceives them to be: sources of protection, lovers, trading partners – basically, her 'gods' who will supply what she needs and ensure her safety. Even in their most negative role, serving as Yahweh's means of punishing his people, their imperial motives are left entirely aside so that Israel's infidelity and its consequences predominate. Happily, in Yahweh's gracious purposes there is salvation beyond judgment, and the benefits of Israel's renewal spill over to the benefit of the non-Israelite nations (Gen. 12:3; Exod. 19:5–6). Several significant salvific connections between the nations and the renewal of Israel deserve attention and lead us to consider Hosea's reception in the New Testament.

The eschatological renewal of Israel has as its foundation Yahweh's spiritually transformative intervention. Among other things, this means that ethnic non-Israelites can be part of renewed Israel because its most fundamental identity is spiritual rather than ethnic. For example, the

[16] Irvine 2021: 404.

incalculable multiplication of 'the children of Israel' of Hosea 1:10, which harks back to 'the promise to Abraham and Jacob that God would multiply their descendants beyond number' (cf. Gen. 15:5; 16:10; 32:12), may be alluded to in the description of God's people of all times and places in Revelation 7:9.[17] More clearly, the Genesis passages alluded to in Hosea 1:10 are used by several New Testament authors in relation to the salvation of Gentiles (Rom. 4:18; Heb. 11:12; Rev. 12:4), confirming that the referent of Hosea 1:10 should not be limited to national Israel. Similarly, the image of renewed Israel as a tree that blossoms, takes root and sends out *new shoots* (Hos. 14:6–7) conveys the meaning that these new shoots were not indigenous to Israel itself (analogous to the trunk–branch metaphor) by using the plural 'they' to refer to those coming to dwell under the shadow of the singular tree (14:7).[18]

Second, Paul's interpretation of Hosea 1:10, 2:23 in Romans 9:26–29 discerns 'the pattern of salvation that is found in Israel's past and has been repeated in the present' in 'the calling of a people from among both Jews and Gentiles'.[19] The substitution of the verb 'call' (Rom. 9:25) for 'say' in Hosea 1:10b underlines the creative power of God's word of salvation to 'a new people', while Romans 9:26 shows that the promise of Israel's return to the land has a 'broadened, eschatological compass'.[20] On this understanding, God's eschatological calling of Israel, which has effectively become 'a Gentile nation' through its second exile, is one with his calling of Gentiles. 'As he did with Israel in the past, so now God calls those who were not his people, both Jews and Gentiles.'[21] Peter (1 Pet. 2:9–10) interprets Hosea 2 to the same effect, bolstered by the application of Exodus 19:5–6 to believers.[22] Since God 'disowned' the northern kingdom due to its persistent covenant infidelity, 'all those who have entered into the new covenant by the mercy of God in Jesus Christ were in fact "Gentiles" in

[17] Beale and McDonough 2007: 1108; Beale 1999: 426–427.

[18] Garrett 1997: 274–275; similarly, Stuart 1987: 216; Andersen and Freedman 1980: 647. The emendation of the third-person 'his shadow' to the first person, as in the ESV ('my shadow'), is unwarranted, as noted by Gelston (2010: 73*).

[19] Seifrid 2007: 647.

[20] Ibid. 648. The observation of Garrett (2023a: 338) that Hosea sometimes links 'an eschatological work of God to some corresponding event in Israel's history' would make Paul's hermeneutic here a continuation of Hosea's. In this connection, it is notable that a 'mixed multitude' of non-Israelites left Egypt with the Israelites (Exod. 12:38).

[21] Seifrid 2007: 648.

[22] Carson 2007: 1030–1032.

need of mercy', and Hosea's prophecy applies to Jew and Gentile alike.[23] In a similar way, the New Testament ties the children of the living God to the redefinition of God's people 'according to one's response to Jesus himself' (Luke 12:32; Acts 15:22, 36).[24] This wholehearted trust in and allegiance to God is also evident in the anticipation that the repentant people of Israel will reject the nations as protectors and providers (cf. Assyria and Egypt's horses [Hos. 14:3], suggestively paralleled with physical idols) and 'feel and taste that the Lord is for [their] delight' as his love and grace progressively transform them in his image (2 Cor. 3:17–18).[25]

[23] Ibid. 1032.

[24] Pao and Schnabel 2007: 298.

[25] Vos 1994: 21, 24.

7
Joel

Most likely set in the post-exilic era following the rebuilding of the temple (1:9, 13, 14), the book of Joel addresses the Judean exiles who returned to Judah (now the Persian province of Yehud) but found themselves faced with agricultural disaster and the possibility of worse at the hands of their enemies. Even with Jerusalem and its temple rebuilt, their situation was far from the superlative restoration promised by earlier prophets (3:1), due in part to sins that had prompted covenant discipline in the form of a locust plague and the accompanying agricultural shortages. In this very lacklustre situation, Joel calls his audience to repent and restates God's promises that he will restore and multiply his people even in the face of the nations' concerted efforts to assert themselves against him and those who belong to him.

Non-Israelites are also included in God's plans for salvation, not only for judgment, in the Day of Yahweh (1:11; 2:2, 11, 30; 3:14).[1] God's promise to pour out his Spirit on all flesh flows out of the restoration of his people and culminates in God's protection, presence and salvation being given to all who call on his name, Israelite and non-Israelite alike. To capture the various roles of non-Israelites in Joel, we will consider them in the past, present and future perspectives through which the book traces the progress and culmination of Yahweh's global judgment and salvation.

The nations in the past and present: foes, threats, antagonists

Joel presents the 'nations', referred to in various ways, as having a history with Israel that is consistently negative. Since Joel's brief message is not comprehensive, the fact that it does not mention examples of

[1] Rendtorff 2000: 78–80.

non-Israelites' good behaviour (for example, the hospitality of some Egyptians during a portion of Israel's sojourn there [Deut. 23:7]), or even faith in Yahweh and integration into Israel (Josh. 6:25), is not a denial that non-Israelites occasionally enjoyed a harmonious relationship with Israelites. Still, the picture that Joel paints is true to the generally adversarial nature of the nations' relations with Israel and Judah to this point, nowhere more so than in the destruction of Israel by Assyria and of Judah by Babylon.

It is within this overall perspective that Egypt and Edom are mentioned in Joel 3:19 as having enacted lethal violence against 'the people of Judah'. Further, and probably more recently, several city-states on the eastern Mediterranean coast have come to possess some of the spoils of the Jerusalem temple (3:4–5) and have even sold Judeans as slaves (3:6). More generally, the assertion that 'all the nations' (Assyria and Babylon are primarily in view) have 'scattered' *Yahweh's* heritage and people and divided *his* land (3:2) is a reminder that both the people and what had been their homeland ultimately belong to Yahweh. This underscores the theological significance of these nations' aggression and constitutes the primary ground for their punishment in the future (3:7–8, 9–21).[2] Similarly, the military threat that loomed against the Jews in Yehud presumes a negative evaluation of God and his people among the 'nations' and 'peoples' involved that created antipathy or indifference towards both (2:17, 19, 26, 27).

The most vivid representation of non-Israelites as a clear and present danger to Joel's audience appears in Joel 2:1–17. Although a number of interpreters understand this imagery as depicting a literal plague of locusts, it seems more likely that a foreign invader is in view.[3] Locusts rarely came into the Levant from the north, and the threat itself is unprecedented (2:2) even when compared to the locust plague that had already affected the returned exiles. More significantly, the north is often the direction from which the prophets foresee the coming of a dangerous enemy, whether against Israel/Judah or other states, and this force is

[2] For careful discussion of divine retribution in Joel 3:4–8, see Thomas 2021.

[3] Arguments against a literal interpretation may predominate at present; see Barker 2020: 75–77; Romerowski 1989: 36–43; Assis 2013; Barton 2001. Crenshaw (1995: 129–130), Garrett (1997: 355–357) and Snoek (2023) are among those who favour a literal army. The use of literal locusts in the covenant curses preserved in the Sefire Inscriptions may strengthen the case for seeing literal locusts in Joel 2; see Scott 2023.

consistently presented as one composed of human beings.[4] Two other considerations are notable. First, the phrase in 2:17 sometimes translated as 'a byword among the nations' (so ESV, NAU and others) is better understood as denoting subjugation, 'to rule over them' (*limšāl-bām*).[5] Second, the phrase 'has done great things' (2:20, 21) is probably sarcastic with respect to the northerner, since its intentions were never realized, and probably captures its 'self-aggrandizement', something that cannot be attributed to locusts.[6] This boast is undone by Yahweh's intervention in which he incontrovertibly will do 'great things' against this enemy (2:21) in delivering his people from that threat.

Not all non-Israelite groups are so clearly opposed to God's people or dismissive of his involvement in their affairs, however. Persia constitutes the sole example in the book of a non-Israelite group prior to the Day of Yahweh that is not in conflict with God and his people. Admittedly, the empire remains intriguingly in the background, but it had granted the Judean exiles permission to return to Judah and provided significant financial support for the efforts to rebuild the temple and the city of Jerusalem. The ambiguity of its role with regard to Judah, which included both its generally beneficent posture towards the exiles and its firm commitment to its imperial project, may explain why it is not brought into the foreground in Joel (Haggai, Zechariah and Malachi treat Persia in similarly ambivalent or ambiguous ways).

The nations in the future: life through the Spirit or death through judgment

God's gracious response to the community's repentance following the locust plague and its assumed plea for mercy (Joel 2:17) when confronted with destruction at the hands of an anonymous enemy (2:1–11) entails far more than restoration of the 'grain, wine, and oil' lost to the locusts and the elimination of the threat posed by 'the northerner' (2:18–27). The promised restoration quickly develops beyond a return to the status quo to include the land's superlative fertility and the people's permanent

[4] Timmer 2015: 33. Among many references, see Isa. 14:31; 41:25; Jer. 1:13–15; 51:48; Ezek. 23:24; 26:7; 38 – 39; also Dan. 11.

[5] See Snoek 2023: 15–17; Timmer 2015: 32.

[6] Barker (2020: 122), who notes the use of the same root in Ps. 35:26–27 and the common image of foreign nations boasting of their superiority over Yahweh and his people.

security and unprecedented knowledge of God as deliverer (2:21–24). Yahweh's gifts will be so abundant that Israel 'shall never again be put to shame' (2:26). In terms of one's relation to and experience of God, these gifts will include his presence among his people in ways not yet seen. Israel, for its part, will know with unparalleled certainty and joy that Yahweh is its God and that no other claimant to deity is worthy of its trust and submission.[7] This radical transformation is connected to the outpouring of God's Spirit in 2:28–32, which expands and deepens the restoration of God's people.

Salvation for those who call on Yahweh, Israelite and non-Israelite alike

The frequent connection between Yahweh's Spirit and the creation or maintenance of life (Gen. 1:2; 2:7; Ps. 104:30; Isa. 32:15; Ezek. 37:14) suggests that the 'afterwards' of 2:28 is logical as much as it is sequential.[8] As a harbinger of the Day of Yahweh (2:30–31), God's pouring out of his Spirit will produce radical developments in two spheres: his revelation to his people (2:28–29) and a response of 'calling on' his name among those whom *he* calls (see 2:32; cf. Rom. 10:10–14). Unless modified contextually (e.g. Isa. 66:16; Jer. 25:31), 'all flesh' is normally a comprehensive phrase that refers to all human beings (Gen. 6:12) or to all living things (Gen. 6:13, 17, 19; 9:17; etc.).[9] Here (Joel 2:28), context makes it reasonable to restrict the scope of the expression to those whom it affects – namely, all those to whom Yahweh reveals himself and who call on his name. More restrictive uses in earlier prophetic books (Isa. 44:3; Ezek. 37:1–14; 39:29; Zech. 12:10) underline the covenantal nature of this eschatological event and connect it to other elements of God's renewal of his people.

The Israel-focused renewal that Joel announces is thus crucially important for the pouring out of Yahweh's Spirit on an *ethnically unrestricted* group that includes Israelites (2:28–29) and others with no link to Israel. They are united exclusively by the definitive act of calling on Yahweh's name.[10] This is particularly striking because this is perhaps the only text in the Old Testament that explicitly connects the Spirit of God directly

[7] VanGemeren 2005: 389–390.

[8] See the discussion in Barker 2020: 135, 137. On the Spirit's role in creation, see Hubbard 2011.

[9] Moore 2011: 250; similarly, Barton 2001: 96; Paul 2012: 624.

[10] Fischer 2012: 106. Hamborg (2023: 238) argues that 'all flesh' is restricted to Israelites.

with God's saving work among non-Israelites (note Moses' wish for the same within Israel in Num. 11:29).[11] The Spirit's radical *transformation* of non-Israelites makes them trust in Yahweh, accept his will, and live in peace with his people rather than pursuing violence against them and denigrating God and his people as they had done in the past. It also establishes a remarkable criterion of identity between Israelites and non-Israelites (see Isa. 32:15–20; 44:3; 59:21) that is a key factor in recognizing the eschatological expansion of the people of God, beginning at Pentecost, to include non-Jews in the New Testament era (Acts 10:47; 15:8; 19:6).[12] In Joel, the inclusive scope of the Spirit's work thus creates a group composed of Israelites and non-Israelites identified by their reception of Yahweh's Spirit, their experience of a new stage of divine self-revelation through prophecy and similar phenomena, and their calling on Yahweh's name for salvation.[13] This group contrasts as sharply as possible with 'the nations' in Joel 3, with the exception of ethnicity, which is inconsequential.

Destruction for those who militate against Yahweh and his people

Following the creation of an international group defined by its allegiance to Yahweh and reception of his Spirit in Joel 2:28–32, it is logical to understand 'all the nations' (3:2) as those who have *not* called on Yahweh's name and do *not* seek deliverance from the Day of Yahweh in Mount Zion and Jerusalem.[14] They remain Yahweh's enemies, as their subsequent actions demonstrate. It is stunning that these obdurate enemies of their creator and judge would accept his challenge to ready their weapons and meet him in battle (3:9–11), but this is simply another example of the pride, misinterpretation of reality and pursuit of autonomy evident throughout the oracles against the nations. The only moral attribute predicated of this group here is 'great evil' (3:13), which, while accurate with respect to their past offences (3:2–6), is equally suitable to their decision to challenge Yahweh's universal rule and condemnation of them. The outcome of God's retribution against his enemies is presaged in the command to

[11] Possible exceptions include Isa. 59:21, where 'them' may well refer to Israelites and non-Israelites who fear Yahweh; cf. Koole 2001: 211–212.

[12] Angers 2018: 300–301; Köstenberger and O'Brien 2001: 134–135.

[13] The argument here is developed further in Timmer 2015: 34–35.

[14] Roth 2005: 74–75.

an unidentified group to tread the winepress of divine judgment that will destroy them (3:13).

A renewed earth with Jerusalem at its centre

Our discussion thus far has shown that the outcomes of the Day of Yahweh (3:14) are both negative and positive. Negatively, the destruction of Yahweh's enemies means that Jerusalem, like the rest of the world, is no longer home to 'strangers' (3:17). Far from indicating xenophobia, the sense of this term here (*zārîm*) involves the strangers' incompatibility with God's presence and people in the eschatological Jerusalem, now made holy by Yahweh and co-referential with his presence (3:21). Contrariwise, Yahweh is the 'refuge' of his Spirit-bearing people who trust him for salvation (3:16).[15] Quite unlike the death by desiccation of Egypt and Edom as punishment for their lethal violence against Yahweh's people (3:19), the radically renewed land of Judah will be overflowing with sweet wine, milk and fresh water (3:18; cf. Isa. 32:15–20). The life-giving presence of Yahweh among his multinational people is reinforced by the image of a fountain that begins within the temple itself, where God alone dwells, and irrigates territory outside the city and presumably throughout Judah, in keeping with the holistic scope of 3:18 (cf. the river from the temple in Ezek. 47:1–12). Like other prophets, Joel presents superlatively restored and transformed Jerusalem as a world of inextinguishable life in God's presence against a backdrop of arid, lifeless space that has been emptied by the destruction of his enemies.

Summary and New Testament developments

The theme of the non-Israelite nations in Joel is closely tied to that of God's people and is equally dynamic. Beginning with their past and present antipathy towards Israel/Judah, that simple theme is then split into two, with the nations either receiving Yahweh's Spirit and becoming his followers or recklessly taking up God's challenge to meet him in battle, a decision that brings with it the gravest possible consequences (3:14). The prominence of God's covenant commitments to Israel/Judah runs

[15] Barton (2001: 108) suggests that 3:17 and other passages in Joel 3 include 'xenophobia'.

through the book, so that the nations are drawn into the salvation that God brings through, and first grants to, his historic covenant people.[16]

This redemptive-historical sequence and expansion (Israel, then the nations) is central to the New Testament.[17] The outpouring of the Spirit by the ascended Christ (Acts 2:32) upon Jews from across the Mediterranean world at Pentecost constitutes the first stage of fulfilment of the prophecy in Joel 2:28–32. The apostles and those with them at Pentecost 'are the nucleus of a restored and reconstituted Israel' that takes up 'the task of the Isaianic Servant' in bringing the gospel to the ends of the earth (Acts 13:47).[18] As Duane Garrett notes, however, Acts 2 includes far more than the expansion of the Spirit's work to Gentiles as recounted throughout much of Acts, and extends to the end of the age.[19]

The Day of Yahweh also includes the judgment of the nations (Joel 3:1–15). That passage is taken up in the book of Revelation to describe the harvest-for-judgment of the wicked, collected with a sickle and crushed in the winepress of God's wrath (Rev. 14:17–20; cf. Joel 3:13).[20] Revelation 14:20 locates this judgment 'outside the city' of Jerusalem, in much the same way that restored Zion, as the locus of God's presence, contrasts with the Valley of Jehoshaphat and the destruction of his enemies earlier in Joel 3.[21] The river that flows from the new temple is very similar to that in Ezekiel 47, and shows that life is to be found exclusively in Yahweh's presence as his called, repentant, acquitted and holy people, the 'new, Spirit- and glory-filled dwelling place of God'.[22]

[16] For a thorough study of Joel's connections to other parts of the canon, see Strazicich 2007.

[17] See Goldsworthy 2023.

[18] Köstenberger and O'Brien 2001: 132.

[19] Garrett 2023b: 392–393.

[20] Bauckham 1993: 95. Joel 3 is the only text that includes 'the images of harvest and treading the winepress together', according to Beale 1999: 775.

[21] Dow 2010: 191; Ladd 1972: 201–202.

[22] Johnson 2023: 336. Fischer (2012: 108) appropriately connects God's eschatological renewal and expansion of his people in Joel to the 'gracious and compassionate' divine character revealed in those terms in Exod. 34:6 and mentioned in Joel 2:13.

8
Amos

Despite its focus on the northern kingdom of Israel, the book of Amos reveals a horizon that is international and ultimately global. At the very beginning of the book, after the effects on Israel of Yahweh's initial roar from Zion are summarized (1:2), their significance for the surrounding nations is explored in detail (1:3 – 2:3) before the focus shifts back to Israel. Similarly, the final sections of the book connect the purification and restoration of Israel with the fate of a 'remnant' of non-Israelite states (9:12), announcing that God will bring his transforming, perfecting rule to the nations through his people and especially through the Davidic Messiah.

Secondary roles: witnesses, comparisons and instruments of God's covenant discipline

We begin our survey of the nations in Amos with secondary roles that are mentioned only in passing. In Amos 3:9–10, Yahweh commands an unidentified group to summon Egypt and the Philistine city-state of Ashdod to stand on the mountains around Samaria so that they might witness the disorder, oppression, 'violence' and 'robbery' that characterize Israel's capital city. Ashdod's and Egypt's role, and the damning evaluation of Samaria's business-as-usual attitude that is capped off by the affirmation that it does not 'know how to do right', presuppose that these non-Israelite states, although hardly boasting impeccable moral records, are in a position to recognize Israel's injustice and sin for what it is.[1]

[1] Timmer 2022a: 122.

At a crucial turning point in the book, this sort of comparison is cast in the most powerful form possible (9:7). The people of Israel, whom Yahweh has known in a unique way by freeing them from slavery in Egypt (3:1–2), are put on par with Cushites, whose non-elect status and location in one of the farthest corners of the world as ancient Israel knew it symbolize the fracture of God's covenant bond with sinful Israel.[2] Stunningly, Yahweh relativizes the exodus, the very birth of the nation of Israel, by asserting that he has similarly directed the relocation of the Philistines and the Arameans (i.e. Syrians). The comparison in 6:2 is less dramatic but points in the same direction: Israel is neither better nor more powerful than other cities and states whose 'wings were clipped' by an enemy, most likely Hazael of Damascus.[3]

In each of these passages, the nations' roles of witness and negative comparison lead to the third role, in which some of them will be the means by which Yahweh punishes the largely unfaithful northern kingdom (3:11; 6:7; 9:8–10; also 5:27, which refers to Assyria).[4] With one exception, the nations that fulfil this role remain anonymous, and no mention or criticism is made of their ideology, violence or motives. As a result, the emphasis falls on *God's* punishment of his people through an unremarkable instrument.

Past offences and imminent punishment

There is almost certainly a strategy of surprise behind the placement of the six oracles against the nations in Amos 1:3 – 2:3 prior to the seventh against Judah (2:4–5) and the final, emphatic oracle against Israel that begins in 2:6. More importantly, the oracles against six non-Israelite states around Israel/Judah demonstrate that God's justice is not limited to his people's offences against the Sinai covenant in particular, but will reach the guilty regardless of nationality or ethnicity.

All of the offences mentioned in 1:3 – 2:3 consist of the violent misuse of power: the excessive, brutal violence of the Arameans (Damascus) that reduced Gilead to ruin (1:3–5); the kidnapping by the city-state of Gaza of an entire people group that it then sold to Edom, presumably as slaves

[2] Ibid. 236.

[3] See Maier 2004; Younger 2016: 592.

[4] 'Largely' captures the extent and power of evil in Samaria rather than serving as a generalization, since those condemned in Israel were a small, elite minority.

(1:6–8), an offence also alleged against Tyre (1:9–10); Edom's merciless violence against Israel/Judah (1:11–12); heinous Ammonite violence against Israelite women in particular in order to gain territory (1:13–15);[5] and Moab's burning of the bones of the king of Edom, apparently in the belief that it would deny him a (peaceful) afterlife (2:1–3).[6] Three of these oracles make clear that the violence was inflicted upon Israelites (1:3, 11, 13), and the Gaza and Tyre oracles may refer to the same. With respect to Gaza, the Philistines shared a border only with Judah and Israel; with respect to Tyre, Hiram of Tyre had made an alliance with Solomon his 'brother' (1 Kgs 9:13). In any case, the oracle against Moab leaves no doubt that Yahweh does not punish only those sins which are committed against his covenant people.

The theological nature of the sins of the nations is also evident from the Hebrew term that appears in the introduction to all of these oracles: *peša'*. Usually translated 'transgressions' but better rendered as 'rebellion', it underscores the fact that these actions are first of all *rebellion against God*. Although these nations were not privy to the detailed revelation of Yahweh's will that was part of the Sinai covenant, God holds them responsible for their innate (if corrupted) knowledge of his deity and will (Rom. 1:18–21). This knowledge, of which the prohibition against murder was only a small part (Gen. 9:5–6), made them sufficiently aware of 'the reality and ultimacy of the living God in human affairs'[7] for their violent mistreatment of their neighbours to be a rejection of God's holistic claim upon them and authority over them.

Notably, in every case the focus of divine punishment against these nations focuses on either royal rulers ('the house of N') or military infrastructure (strongholds, fortresses, gate bars, and so on). The reason for this focus is not hard to understand: the sins that are condemned here require planning, military force, and the impetus and support of political leaders. This means that these condemnations are not brought against the entire population to which the proper nouns used would normally refer. Although the population at large sometimes suffers as a result of offences committed by a group within it, as in the exile of Aram/Damascus (1:5), there is no explicit divine condemnation of those not directly tied to these

[5] Cogan 1983; Dubovsky 2009.

[6] Wazana (2013: 487, 495–496) understands the act as consisting only of tomb desecration.

[7] Baugus 2022: 56.

states' political–military apparatus. Furthermore, God's use of Assyria to subjugate Aram several decades later does not eliminate Assyria's moral responsibility or its 'messiness' with respect to Yahweh's verdict against Aram's leaders here.[8] Divine justice discriminates between the innocent and the guilty outside Israel as well as within it, a point that will become increasingly significant as Amos's book moves towards its eschatological conclusion.

The remnant of Israel and the remnant of the nations

Although the majority of the book of Amos presents the prophet's condemnations of Israel (2:6, 11; 3:1; etc.), not all Israelites are guilty of the sins mentioned throughout the book. On the contrary, many of these offences can only be perpetrated by those who have some kind of superiority – physical, economic or social – over *Israelites* whom they abuse, exploit or dominate (2:6–8, 12; 3:10; 5:10–12; 8:4–6). This domineering minority is consistently distinguished from its victims, who are referred to as the 'righteous' (2:6; 5:12), 'poor' (2:7; 4:1; 5:11; 8:4) or 'needy' (2:6; 4:1; 5:12; 8:4, 6).[9] This distinction runs parallel to others, including those who 'seek [Yahweh] and live' (5:6) over against those who refuse to do so and are thus in danger of his judgment (5:16–17, 18–20). The gradual introduction of the theme of the remnant articulates the same inner-Israel distinction (3:12; 4:11; 5:3, 14–15; 6:9).[10]

Non-Israelites return to centre stage only after the faithful Israelite remnant has been definitively distinguished from the rest of Israel as described in 9:8–10 (note the less nuanced description of the total destruction of Israelite sinners in 9:1–4). In this radical divine judgment, Yahweh removes 'all the sinners of [his] people' from 'the house of Jacob' while preserving those who are faithful to him.[11] This intervention occurs alongside another that superlatively restores the Davidic monarchy. Although Judah became Israel's vassal during the reign of Jeroboam II (2 Kgs 14:13–19; 2 Chr. 25:27), Amos's prediction in chapter 9 goes far

---

[8] For further discussion of theodicy in such cases, see Stump 2010; Carroll R. 2015.

[9] King 2021: 109–114.

[10] See Carroll R. 2020: 326–327.

[11] Goldingay 2021b: 345–346.

beyond Judah's regained independence and relatively secure existence under kings such as Hezekiah and Josiah.

In the brief oracle of 9:11–12, God announces that restored Israel (the first verb in 9:12 is plural), purified of all sinners and under the care and guidance of a king whose allegiance to Yahweh protects and promotes theirs (2 Sam. 7; Ps. 72), will 'possess the remnant of Edom and [of] all the nations over whom my name is called' (my translation).[12] The verb 'possess' echoes Israel's initial entry into Canaan under Joshua (Deut. 7:1; Josh. 1:11; 23:9), but the identification of the non-Israelites who will come under the Davidic king's rule as those over whom Yahweh's name has been called makes clear that another type of rule is being exercised here.[13] Apart from this text, every other instance in the Old Testament in which God's name is called over a group (with this or a similar phrase) refers to God's covenant relationship with Israel, which was initiated by his gracious deliverance of them (Exod. 19:1–6), not his conquest of them (see Deut. 28:9–10; 2 Chr. 7:14; Isa. 64:19; Jer. 14:9; Dan. 9:19).

As radical as this idea might seem at first glance, the inclusion of many non-Israelites in God's eschatological people is simply the counterpart of the purification of Israel summarized in 9:8–10. The nation of Israel had wandered so far from God that his patience had run out (note the fivefold depiction of covenant discipline in 4:6–11 and the refrain 'yet you did not return to me'; cf. Lev. 26). As a result, Yahweh brings judgment on those Israelites who refuse his grace and truth much as he brought judgment against the nations around Israel. These twin movements of judgment and deliverance usher in the unparalleled expansion of Yahweh's reign through his chosen king, and this includes the integration into his renewed people of non-Israelites who belong to him in the same way that faithful Israelites do. The non-Israelites' ethnic distinctiveness is not erased, although their territories are now part of the eschatological king's radically expanded realm. This expanded 'land' (9:15) will know only peace and abundance as Israelites and non-Israelites alike live in uninterrupted fellowship with Yahweh, whose blessings are the culmination of the Abrahamic (Gen. 17:1–21), Sinai (Lev. 26:5) and Davidic covenants (Ps. 72).

---

[12] See Timmer 2019b.

[13] Sæbø 1978; Braulik 1997.

Summary and New Testament developments

The non-Israelite nations in Amos bear a clear resemblance to Israel. This similarity is initially negative, in that both the nations (1:3 – 2:3) and Israel (2:4 – 9:6) are guilty of a variety of sins and so stand exposed to divine punishment. Yet God's mercy preserves a remnant of both, and the remnants are brought together under an ideal Davidic dynasty after God removes sin and sinners from among his people. The identification of the non-Israelite remnant as consisting of those over whom Yahweh has called his name shows that they share the same standing as citizens of his perfected kingdom as the Israelite remnant.[14] Planted in a land that has been expanded to include nations far and near, God's eschatological people will enjoy his beneficent rule and abundant blessings without end (9:13–15).

Despite the brevity of Amos's vision of the inclusion of non-Israelites in renewed Israel, Amos 9:11–12 played a major role in explaining the redemptive-historical changes that accompanied the gospel's spread among non-Jews in the first decades of the church's existence.[15] Notably, the Jerusalem council understood that the integration of non-Israelites into God's purified and restored people foretold in Amos 9 and sealed by the gift of the Holy Spirit (Acts 10:44–48; 11) did not necessitate their circumcision or adoption of other identity markers tied to earlier covenants. The rebuilding of the Davidic 'house' in Amos 9 most likely refers to the messianic king (2 Sam. 7; Luke 1:32–33; Acts 2:33–35), and the transnational expansion of his kingdom is nothing other than the progress of the gospel (Acts 13:47; 28).[16] The agricultural abundance in which 'wine would flow freely' (see Amos 9:14) also hints at the consummation of that kingdom in the new heavens and the new earth (Isa. 25:6; Matt. 26:29; Mark 14:25; John 2:1–11).[17]

---

[14] Timmer 2024a: 58.

[15] Peterson (1998: 531) argues that the entire second half of the book of Acts is 'a commentary on Amos 9:11–12 (LXX)'.

[16] For reflection on the implications of this passage for practical theology, see Buckwalter 1998; Timmer 2017.

[17] Köstenberger 2007: 431.

9
Obadiah

The fact that Obadiah follows Amos in Bibles that adopt the Hebrew ordering of the Minor Prophets makes the contrast between Amos and Obadiah rather jarring at first sight. Whereas Amos 9 announces that 'the remnant of Edom' and other nations will become part of the people over whom God's messianic king rules, Obadiah might be thought to exclude such a scenario.[1] However, closer attention to the way in which Obadiah characterizes Edom reveals that Amos's 'remnant of Edom' is quite different from Obadiah's 'Edom'. However, even though Obadiah foretells that when God establishes his kingdom in the Day of Yahweh, all those who fit the description of Edom as he describes it will fall under God's judgment, he announces the salvation of all who, ethnically Edomite or not, humbly seek refuge on Mount Zion (Obad. 17).

Edom (Obad. 1–14)

Edom is characterized from three interrelated angles in the short oracles that make up most of the book (vv. 2–4, 5–9, 10–14). In the first, Edom is *proud*, and so will be humbled. More specifically, Edom's pride has 'deceived' it into imagining that its geographic elevation and relative inaccessibility guaranteed its impregnability, such that it trusted 'in topography rather than' in Yahweh's protection (see v. 3).[2] Its fall will take place at Yahweh's behest, but the nations involved undertake the task willingly – and surely for their own purposes (v. 1). After its fall, Edom

[1] For a capable discussion of the book's composition, see Assis 2014. There is evidence of an Edomite presence in southern Judah between the eighth and sixth centuries BC ('semi-nomadic groups, including Edomites') that advanced northward towards the end of this period (Anderson 2022: 381–382).

[2] Ben Zvi 1996: 250. Ferries (2022: 485) perceives in Obad. 3–4 an 'aspiration toward divinity, fueled by hubris'.

will be 'small among the nations' (v. 2; cf. Egypt in Ezek. 29:15). In this and the next oracle, other nations, most notably Babylon, serve God's punitive purposes.[3]

The rhetorical questions with which the next oracle begins ('If . . . ') imply that unlike thieves who take only what they think is most valuable or harvesters who leave some grapes behind, Edom's non-Israelite enemies will leave nothing (vv. 5–6). Here, too, Edom's fall is tied to its *pride and resultant naivety* (despite thinking itself wise [v. 8]). As elsewhere in the prophetic books, the defining feature of pride is a self-congratulatory but distorted interpretation of reality, and Edom's pride has allowed it to be deceived by those closest to it. Edom's hubris prevented it from detecting the stratagems of its erstwhile allies who surreptitiously plotted its fall (v. 7), and Edom will pay dearly for it (vv. 8–9).

The now-familiar link between pride or autonomy and violence makes the focus of the third oracle unsurprising (vv. 10–14): 'the violence done to your brother Jacob' (v. 10).[4] Here the love, compassion and fidelity normally entailed by the ties of kinship that bound the descendants of Esau and Jacob together are not merely absent, but replaced by a shocking lack of compassion. In addition to standing by while 'strangers' and 'foreigners' pillaged Jerusalem (v. 11), Edom acted towards its relative as if it were 'one of' the foreign nations (v. 11) by gloating and rejoicing in Judah's fall, entering Jerusalem and joining in its looting, and even killing or remitting to its other enemies the escapees it captured (vv. 12–14). The sentence for such behaviour is twofold: shame and destruction (v. 10).

As comprehensive as this condemnation of Edom is, one must not overlook its very clearly defined referent. 'Edom' is not the entire Edomite population – unless, that is, every man, woman and child fits the description of Edom presented in these oracles: characterized by a pride that produces an inflated sense of security and a naivety that blinds one to danger, and driven to extreme violence by hatred and a desire for self-advancement at the cost of others' lives.[5] Similar complexity in terms of what 'Edom' refers to is evident in Jeremiah's oracle against Edom, and reappears at the end of Obadiah as well.[6] By the same token, this ref-

[3] On Babylon's anonymity in Obadiah, see Hagedorn 2012: 323–324.

[4] On this link, see Watkin 2022: 147.

[5] Mason (2000: 591) understands Edom in this context as 'a symbol . . . of certain sinful human characteristics'.

[6] Noted by Haney (2007: 85).

erent includes, by extension, persons of any ethnicity whose pride drives them to interpret reality in ways that allow them to pursue their goals and 'good' by whatever means they choose.

'All the nations', including 'Edom' (Obad. 15–21)

Obadiah 15 connects Edom's threatened punishment (which is not eschatological) to the Day of Yahweh, which will usher in a radically new state of affairs.[7] Addressed to Edom, verse 15 promises proportional retribution for its wrongs, and connects its further punishment to Yahweh's judgment of 'all the nations', whose Edom-like opposition to God is presupposed by the divine judgment announced in verse 16. This judgment will end the very existence of these hardened enemies of God, and is complemented by the permanent dispossession of their territory (vv. 19–20; cf. Deut. 2:4–5). Both these features echo the expulsion and destruction of the people groups inhabiting Canaan in the second half of the second millennium BC (Gen. 15:16; Lev. 18:24–25; Deut. 18:12). Conversely, Mount Zion will be 'holy' and will offer protection from divine wrath (vv. 16–17), implying that the sins of its inhabitants have been definitively dealt with and their opposition to God replaced by submission, obedience and love.[8] In Obadiah's vision of the eschatological future, the full destruction of the 'house of Esau', understood *as all those Edomites who actively oppose Yahweh and his people*, coincides with the reunification of Judah and Israel (v. 18) and the expansion of the land beyond almost all biblical descriptions of its limits (except Gen. 15:18; Exod. 23:31; and similar statements).[9] This superlative restoration of God's kingdom, which takes place without the mention of a Davidic king, culminates in a kingdom which belongs exclusively to Yahweh (v. 21).[10]

---

[7] Peterson 1992.

[8] Timmer 2021c: 22.

[9] Block's proposal (2013: 102) that Edom/Esau here is 'representative for all the nations' understood as God's opponent receives support from Obad. 15–16.

[10] The 'saviours' of Obad. 21 are subordinate to Yahweh and may carry over the category of judges from the period that followed Israel's initial (and partial) possession of the land; cf. Block 2013: 102; Phillips 2022: 62; Timmer 2021c: 28.

Summary and New Testament developments

The prominence of 'possession' in the reallocation of territory described in the closing verses of Obadiah and the expanded limits of the land are key elements in the book's presentation of a new conquest, a reunited and perfectly faithful Israel, and 'an "ideal" land of Israel'.[11] If the (military) dispossession of Israel's land were to be taken literally, one might be inclined to interpret these statements of complete destruction as hyperbolic ancient Near Eastern conquest accounts.[12] However, such an approach neglects Obadiah's very focused and selective characterization of Edom as composed *exclusively* of those whose pride, foolishness and hatred of God's people drove them to acts of violence against his people. Any historical fulfilment, therefore, would by its very nature be imprecise, imperfect and incomplete. Indeed, one looks in vain for such a fulfilment before, during or after the sixth century BC.[13] The subjugation of Edom by Babylon around 552 is the closest thing to fulfilment, but it falls far short of what Obadiah announces due to its purely military and political nature and the absence of any retribution focused on those Edomites who are targeted by Obadiah's oracles.[14]

When the Day of Yahweh came more fully into view with the incarnation and earthly ministry of Jesus Christ, the Jews and Gentiles who make up the 'Israel of God' (Gal. 6:16) began to make disciples of all nations on the model of Isaiah's suffering Servant (Matt. 28:18–20; Acts 13:47). Not only are political, national and compulsory elements absent from canonical accounts of the fulfilment of prophecy through Christ and the earliest generations of believers, but also Jesus himself made very clear that such means are incompatible with the nature of his kingdom in this age (John 18:35–37; Acts 1:6–8; at his return, Christ's almighty power will destroy 'every rule and every authority and power' and 'put all his enemies

[11] Ben Zvi 1996: 227.

[12] See Younger 1990; Hoffmeier 2003b.

[13] Hassler (2016) argues well that no clear, complete fulfilment of Obadiah is evident in history and that numerous biblical passages point towards its eschatological fulfilment, although his conclusion that eschatological fulfilment will involve a *national* Edom differs from the interpretation proposed here.

[14] Babylon's subjugation of Edom did not cause widespread destruction according to Tebes (2023: 251).

under his feet' [1 Cor. 15:24–25]). The risen Christ, as the final Davidic king granted all authority, extends his rule over his global kingdom through the preaching of the gospel,[15] transcending the relatively limited depiction of the territory of restored Israel in Obadiah.[16] As Bruce Waltke puts it, the New Testament (and Rom. 11 in particular) 'teaches the restoration of Israel to the kingdom, not of the kingdom to Israel'.[17] With respect to prophecy in particular, the symbolic nature of much prophetic language thus needs to be appreciated for what it is.[18] In the same vein, the fulfilment of these prophecies begun in the New Testament with Jesus as 'the new Israel' sets the course for New Testament biblical theology.[19] The faith of Abraham is supranational (Rom. 4:18; Gal. 3:8) and aligns God's promises of salvation and judgment with believers and unbelievers, respectively, with no regard for ethnicity or nationality. Similarly, the final judgment is the unique prerogative of the risen and ascended Christ (Rev. 11:18; 19:11–16). Until then, the fulfilment of Obadiah's prophecy is being realized by the risen Christ who extends his rule by his Spirit and through the gospel.

[15] Dempster 2003: 233.

[16] Martin 2023: 447, who contends that 'the land promised to Abraham and his offspring [is] to be finally fulfilled in the (physical) new creation as a result of the person and work of Christ'.

[17] Waltke 2007: 206.

[18] Ibid.

[19] Dempster 2003: 232.

10
Jonah

The book of Jonah is the only prophetic book that records the deliverance of a guilty non-Israelite group from threatened divine judgment during the same prophet's ministry. This possibility is clearly set out in Jeremiah 18:7–8 ('if that nation, concerning which I have spoken, turns from its evil, I will relent'), but its realization in the history of Neo-Assyria, a recurrent menace to the well-being and even existence of Israel and Judah over three centuries, is surprising, to say the least. And that is the point of the book of Jonah! This chapter explores this unusual book with an eye to its equally unusual cast of non-Israelite characters: sailors who apparently begin with only vague and casual knowledge of the God of Israel, and Assyrians who for the most part are not directly involved in the imperial corps and take an unknown prophet at his word.

The non-Israelite sailors

Rather ironically, the conversion of the sailors whom Jonah meets in the course of his attempt to flee from Yahweh's presence is sparked by the prophet's own desire to *prevent* the manifestation of God's mercy to another non-Israelite group, the residents of Nineveh (4:2). God's interruption of Jonah's attempt to flee by means of a severe storm brings about the extreme circumstances in which the characterization of the sailors begins in earnest. The narrator introduces them in ways that contrast them with Jonah, and gradually traces a clear shift from their original polytheism to a new identity defined by a holistic commitment to Yahweh. Their fear of death in the circumstances is quite understandable, as is their turning to their gods for help (1:5). Their prayers (Jonah apparently does not pray while above the waves) demonstrate their belief that certain gods had some measure of control over the sea. Whether they prayed to a storm deity to relent, or to a god who could exercise control over the sea to intervene against the storm deity responsible for their current plight, their prayers went unanswered, proving that those deities were either unable or unwilling to help.[1] They also took extreme measures to save the lives of those aboard by jettisoning the ship's cargo. By contrast, Jonah is so soundly asleep that it is impossible for him to feel fear, pray, or otherwise do what he can to avoid the death of all onboard.[2] The captain rouses him from his slumbers, but even once he is awake the narrative implies that he remained almost totally inert.

Despite their polytheism, the narrator shows the sailors to be more attuned to the theological dimension of their precarious situation than Jonah. Their lot-casting reveals that Jonah is responsible for the arrival of the storm, but his response to their questions is far from an admission of guilt: he first signals his Hebrew ethnicity, then asserts that he fears Yahweh, 'the God of heaven, who made the sea and the dry land' (1:9). This information, which the narrator includes as direct speech, suggests that Jonah's ethnicity is quite important, although we are not told why. The veracity of Jonah's claim that he reveres Yahweh remains suspect, since the narrator never attributes it to him, and the prophet's actions suggest the opposite. Only an earlier remark (not recorded) divulged the reckless nature of his flight (1:10), and the sailors assume that such sins must be punished. They also seem to understand that it is not possible to flee from Yahweh the Creator, whose power is already evident in the storm that is buffeting their ship.[3] The narrator draws attention to the crew's appreciation of the seriousness of Jonah's sin by noting that they went from being 'afraid' (1:5) to being 'exceedingly afraid' (1:10), while Jonah's emotional state is unknown.

Jonah's unprecedented suggestion that he be thrown overboard should be understood as a self-imposed death sentence, albeit one that the non-Israelite sailors immediately reject.[4] Only after vainly attempting yet again to save his life do they abandon that course of action. Having understood that Yahweh alone has control over the sea and over their lives, they address their prayer to him, asking that he not hold them accountable

[1] See, for example, the worship of Baal at Ugarit, described in Levine and de Tarragon 1993; on storm gods across the ancient Near East, see Ayali-Darshan 2020.

[2] Jonah's deep sleep (*rādam*) most likely refers to a sleep that prevents one from perceiving or doing what is important and urgent; cf. Prov. 10:5; 19:15; Isa. 29:10.

[3] Bosma (2013) discusses the possible polemical import of the echo of Ps. 95:5 in this context.

[4] For an alternative view, see Phillips 2022: 110–111.

for murder given the circumstances and what they assume is a legitimate death sentence against Jonah (1:14). The wording of their petition alludes to Psalm 115:3 or 135:6 (or both) and recognizes Yahweh's incomparable sovereignty (Pss 115:2, 4–8; 135:5, 15–18) and unlimited power to save (Pss 115:1, 9–18; 135:7–14). When the storm suddenly ended, they 'feared [Yahweh] exceedingly' and in due time 'offered a sacrifice to [Yahweh] and made vows' (1:16). These actions signal that their spiritual transformation is complete, and likely allude to Psalm 50:14 for the paired actions of offering sacrifices and making vows that distinguish between the faithful and the 'wicked' (Ps. 50:16) *within Israel*.[5]

Recognizing that whereas the narrator's statements are always reliable, those of literary characters may not be, the contrasts outlined in Table 1 contribute to a radically positive portrayal of the formerly polytheistic sailors. In short, the non-Israelite crew not only abandon their gods but also demonstrate a holistic conversion to and reverence for the God of Israel. The allusions to other parts of the Old Testament induct them into very exclusive company – and all this before Jonah even arrives in Nineveh! The point of this narrative can be put very simply: not all

Table 1 Contrasts between the sailors and Jonah

The sailors	*Jonah*
Are aware of the danger in which they find themselves	Is insouciant and asleep
Do what they can to preserve human life (jettison cargo, row towards land, pray to their gods)	Remains inactive and offers no help
Fear when they learn of Jonah's sin against Yahweh	Never confesses his sin
Do all they can to avoid being complicit in what may be a wrongful death	Proposes his own death
Abandon their gods and demonstrate profound reverence for Yahweh	Never confesses his sin, denies by his attempt to flee his profession that God is sovereign over land and sea, attempts to abort his mission by assisted suicide

[5] Timmer 2023a: 405; note also the combination of these actions in Isa. 19:21 as a partial description of spiritually transformed Egyptians.

Israelites fear Yahweh, and it is possible – even prior to the 'last days' in which the biblical prophets foresee such change on a large scale – for non-Israelites to turn to Yahweh.

Nineveh

Background: Neo-Assyrian imperialism

The point that non-Israelites can turn to Yahweh is also made in the book's second half, this time with Nineveh in the non-Israelite category. To put it mildly, Nineveh, especially insofar as it represents Neo-Assyria, is far less promising than the formerly pagan sailors. Still, although the religious change of Nineveh's citizens is less clear-cut, it is met with divine grace, compassion, patience and fidelity (4:2).

Here it is helpful to review some of the relevant features of Neo-Assyrian imperialism, surveyed in chapter 2, as the background that informed Jonah's quite uncharitable (but understandable) attitude towards Assyria. By the early eighth century BC, Assyrian imperialism had already been felt intermittently in Israel – and was more frequently evident beyond its borders – for the better part of a century. Assyria's imperial mission was to bring about on earth, typically through violent conflict, the same kind of order that Ashur was credited with achieving in the Neo-Assyrian version of the *Enūma Elish* cosmology.[6] The Assyrian king, with various gods at his side, was to lead his forces in battle, subduing any people group or political entity that came within their reach. Since this ongoing, violent, exploitative, self-focused enterprise was the will of the gods, and therefore was believed to be good and necessary, the often gruesome violence of Assyria's armed forces was justified and praiseworthy in the eyes of its political and military leaders.[7]

The self-evident incompatibility of this ideology with the biblical world view sheds light on the numerous grounds that lay behind God's determination that the time to address Assyria's 'evil' had come (1:2). But, as Jonah realized to his profound chagrin, the call to go to Nineveh created the possibility that Yahweh might show grace to a group that was in flagrant rebellion against him and presumably was involved to some degree

[6] Crouch 2009: 27; Frahm 2010: 8.

[7] For a comprehensive overview of Neo-Assyrian imperialism, see Liverani 2017.

in the empire's usurpation of divine prerogative, heinous treatment of other human beings, and self-entitled use of whatever natural and human resources came to hand. How far can Yahweh's grace reach?

Foreground: non-Israelites' repentance, Yahweh's compassion and deliverance

The author's account of Nineveh's response to Jonah's message (whatever its duration) begins with the citizens. First, they 'believed in God', meaning they accepted the truth of Jonah's message, and repented (3:10).[8] This change in behaviour, spelled out in the order issued by the city's ruler to the population to turn from its 'evil' way and violence (3:7–8), was accompanied by widespread fasting and the wearing of garments of mourning by the city's residents.[9] The 'king' led by example in this regard even as he recognized that Nineveh's repentance could not constrain grace, which is always a gracious gift (3:9). God, seeing this repentance, relented, and the city was spared.

Familiarity with the story should not prevent us from hearing clearly the incredible tone of Jonah's livid reaction to this divine mercy and grace. Whereas God himself described the large-scale and sustained violence, exploitation and multifaceted idolatry that Nineveh represented as 'evil' (1:2), Jonah experienced *God's* patience and compassion towards Nineveh as 'extremely evil' (4:1, my translation)! Whatever Jonah's theological reasoning in 4:2, the fact that this is the only passage in the Old Testament that invokes the glorious description of Yahweh's character in Exodus 34:6–7 to explain God's treatment of non-Israelites reminds us of the book's main theme. God's covenant with Israel does not prohibit him from exercising the same grace and compassion towards non-Israelites. Indeed, Israel had broken, just before the events of Exodus 34, the very covenant that obliged Israel to represent Yahweh and his gracious, saving character to the world (Exod. 19:4–6). The same point is reiterated in Yahweh's closing rebuke to Jonah after the prophet reacted to the withering of a large plant that had grown over him and given him shelter (Jon. 4:6–8). If Jonah could be 'troubled' (*ḥûs* [4:10, my translation]) about the plant, in which he had

[8] Fuller discussion of Nineveh's repentance can be found in Timmer 2011: 100–111.

[9] Schaumberger (1934) documents several examples of rituals of mourning or repentance from the Neo-Assyrian period, including one that involves the person's 'cattle, sheep, and donkeys' (133, my translation). Further examples from the Persian and Hellenistic periods are noted in Timmer 2022a: 323–324. Goldingay (2021b: 398) thinks that the decree could be hyperbolic or literal.

invested no effort and which was short-lived, was not Yahweh justified in having compassion (*ḥûs* [4:11]) on Nineveh, the value of whose numerous human inhabitants (not to mention its animals), with no detailed knowledge of God and his will, vastly outweighed that of the plant?[10]

Summary and New Testament developments

The responses of both the sailors and the Ninevites cast Jonah in a very unfavourable light. But the main point of the book is not to expose the prophet to ridicule and condemnation, although the narrator seems to find each of these appropriate.[11] The book of Jonah strongly emphasizes the glorious truth that God's grace is absolutely free and sovereign, and that as a result no one is beyond the reach of his saving goodness – not even Assyrians! The narrative is focused on Yahweh's inexplicable grace and his commitment to bring grace and mercy to non-Israelites even when his designated Israelite spokesman fails miserably.

As we have seen in a few other cases, the imperialism of the non-Israelite state (in this case, Assyria) remains in the background, most likely because it is well known yet irrelevant in the light of Yahweh's free grace.[12] What is foregrounded instead is the prophet's antipathy towards the spread of God's grace beyond Israel's borders and, above all, the glorious fact that God's grace cannot be constrained or limited. The book is thus a strong caution against a religious parochialism that would seek to limit divine favour to one's own group and, in that case, take it for granted.

The New Testament draws on the story of Jonah in ways that confirm the interpretative approach taken above.[13] Rather than castigating Jonah, the evangelists simply affirm that Jesus is 'greater than' Jonah and that his preaching merits a correspondingly greater or fuller reception (Matt. 12:41). Similarly, Jonah's reckless decision to end his life rather than make possible Nineveh's repentance is subsumed under the 'sign' (Matt. 12:39–40; Luke 11:29–30) of Jonah's emergence from the near-equivalent of the

[10] The different senses of the same verb (on which see Koehler and Baumgartner 2001: 298) are required by their respective objects here.

[11] Sternberg (1987: 102) concludes that Jonah 'would not listen' to God's command because of 'arrogance'.

[12] Thelle 2021: 191.

[13] Some of what follows is drawn from Timmer 2023a.

underworld (cf. Jon. 2). Benjamin Gladd is correct, however, to perceive in Jesus' calm trust in divine providence (Mark 4:35–41) a state of heart that contrasts sharply with Jonah's insouciance or indifference following his direct disobedience of a divine commission.[14] An even stronger note of discontinuity is sounded by the contrast between Jonah, the only prophet in the entire Old Testament to be sent to a non-Israelite audience who nonetheless found grace towards them to be intolerable, and the mission of Israel in the Old Testament that finally blossoms in the New.[15] In the latter case, following the failure of many first-century Jews to respond to the gospel, the apostles turned to the Gentiles. Convinced that this was the mission of Christ himself as Isaiah's Servant (Acts 13:47) and having tasted God's grace themselves, the apostles demonstrated a commitment to preaching the gospel that was as profound as Jonah's aversion to seeing Assyrians spared judgment (1 Cor. 9:16). Like Yahweh's history with Israel, Christ's compassion for sinners calls readers of Jonah, by means of a striking negative example, to love and imitate the God whose grace and compassion to them in Christ will for ever exceed their grasp:

> We are to love what God is and what God has done; we are to direct our lives toward him as our goal, and to make him our supreme delight and joy . . . to echo in what we say and what we do that great Yes which God speaks in his Son.[16]

---

[14] Gladd 2021: 138.

[15] See Timmer 2011: 30–42 and Riecker 2016 for complementary definitions and overviews of mission in the OT.

[16] Webster 2015: 185.

11
Micah

The roles of the nations in Micah are almost inseparable from those of Israel/Judah, underlining the importance of Israelites and non-Israelites alike in redemptive history. From the inclusion of non-Israelites in the 'peoples' who hear Yahweh's condemnation of the world (Mic. 1:2) to Assyria's role as the one who will devastate much of Judah and deport many citizens of the northern kingdom of Israel (1:10–16) and the nations' eschatological submission and obedience to Yahweh's teaching, different non-Israelite groups are – in equally different ways – an integral part of Micah's message.

The nations in negative roles in non-eschatological settings

Micah's first oracle (1:2–9) is addressed to a global audience ('O earth, and all that is in it') that includes 'you peoples, all of you' (1:2). The mix of imagery that depicts God's descent to judge the world (1:3–4; cf. Nah. 1:2–5, 8) sets all that follows against the backdrop of God's eschatological judgment.[1] However, the focus on the sins of Israel and Judah in the condemnation that follows (1:4–7), and the imminent arrival of Assyria before the gates of Jerusalem later in the chapter, make the late eighth century BC the nearest horizon of much of Micah's message.[2] In that context, Achzib (if it was indeed independent of Israel/Judah at that time) is the only non-eschatological example of a harmonious relationship between Judah and a non-Israelite state, apparently making common cause against Assyria.[3]

---

[1] Collins 2009.

[2] Aster 2017: 110–111.

[3] Timmer (2015: 95) notes that Sennacherib mentions Achzib alongside other non-Israelite

An adversarial role for the nations during the time of Micah's ministry is much more common. Examples include the Assyrian 'conqueror' (1:15), whose destruction of many Judean towns prefigures the nation's fall and exile (1:16; Babylon is named in 4:10 as the site of Judah's exile) and the destruction of the Jerusalem temple (3:12). Unsurprisingly, Micah portrays the nations around Judah as committed to the worship of gods other than Yahweh (4:5).[4]

Non-Israelites in negative roles in eschatological settings

The prediction of Judah's exile and of the destruction of Jerusalem and its temple in 3:9–12 marks a turning point in Micah's book. From that point onward, the nations appear in settings that can be described as eschatological since they are quite discontinuous with respect to the preceding stage of redemptive history. In that context, Micah presents the nations as having one of two roles: as faithful worshippers of Yahweh (4:1–4) or as those who do not 'obey' him (5:15) and fall under his judgment to an unprecedented degree.

In negative roles, meaning those that involve adversarial attitudes or actions towards Yahweh and his people, the nations are consistently the objects of condemnation and judgment. Although Babylon's brutal violence against Judah a century after Micah is barely hinted at in 4:10, the imperial gaze of 'many nations' that focuses on Zion in 4:11 is telling: 'Let her be defiled, and let our eyes gaze upon Zion.'[5] The first clause expresses the nations' wish that Daughter Zion would be polluted or defiled, with violent, heinous or sexual overtones.[6] Since this desire is expressed by military powers that are intent on Zion's harm, the violence

---

entities and separately from Judah in his account of his siege of Jerusalem in 701 BC. Gath was likely under Judean control from about the middle of the eighth century until it fell to Assyria around 711 (Zukerman and Shai 2006: 732), so its relationship with Judah might also be described as peaceful or harmonious.

[4] The 'we' there is Judah's faithful remnant, represented by Micah; note also the 'we' of the obedient nations in the eschatological setting of 4:1–4. I accept Renaud's argument (1987: 87) that each 'now' in 4:9 – 5:1 introduces more or less sequential stages in Jerusalem's fall, from suffering (4:9) to the threat posed by the nations (4:11) and the siege of the city and humiliation of its 'judge'.

[5] For a careful consideration of this gaze, see Smith-Christopher 2015: 157–159.

[6] See Averbeck 1997; Goldingay 2021b: 462. For pollution of the land of Israel through murder, see Num. 35:33; Ps. 106:38; for pollution through rampant sin, Isa. 24:5; for pollution of the land through sexual sin, see Jer. 3:1, 2, 9. It is difficult to understand 'godlessness' in non-Israelite

that transforms an intact city into ruins seems most likely here. This violence manifests these states' desire for control, acquisition of material wealth or territory, and glory. Yet, thanks to Yahweh's mercy, the aggression of 'many nations' against Judah that runs through 4:9 – 5:1 does not spell the end of God's people. In due time, Daughter Zion, representing the remnant, will 'arise and thresh' her enemies, with their material wealth being consecrated to Yahweh as the Divine Warrior (4:13; the same verb is used of the spoils of Jericho [Josh. 6 – 7]).[7]

In a more developed eschatological context that follows the exile and return of God's people (5:3) and is centred on the rule of the long-anticipated messianic king (5:2–4), Assyria and the Assyrian (5:5–6) return as an *eschatological* opponent. Since Assyria in 5:6 appears after Judah's return from exile, the proper noun does not refer to the empire, which fell to the Babylonians at the close of the seventh century BC. Similarly, the reference to 'the land of Nimrod' refers to Babylon (cf. Gen. 10:8–10), which also fell before the various returns of Judean exiles to their ancestral territory in the late sixth century BC. The terms 'Assyria' and 'Babylon' thus symbolize threats posed by 'the enemies of God' more generally.[8]

The symbolic role of these fallen empires presupposes the transhistorical nature of the opposition to God and his purposes that often characterized these empires and others after them. At the heart of the theological nature of these empires' ideologies, sketched in chapter 2 of this volume, is the conflict between their gods and the god(s) of the nations against which they take up arms. Significantly, Micah 5:1–6 presents this perennial enemy against the backdrop of God's already established but not yet consummated global kingdom, with a Davidic ruler empowered by Yahweh to bring 'peace' (*šālôm*) by vanquishing his adversaries (5:5–6) but also by *reconciling* non-Israelites (7:16–17)

remarks against Zion, but note Yahweh's use of the word 'godless' when describing Judah in Isa. 10:6; 33:14.

[7] Dobbs-Allsopp (2009: 130) proposes that the referent of 'Daughter (of) Zion' is often 'a leading – or even *the* leading – citizen of Zion'; Floyd (2008: 502) thinks it refers to 'the women of Jerusalem' as they represent the general population in relation to 'rejoicing and lamentation'; and Dearman (2009) thinks it refers to 'YHWH's (adopted) daughter' (157) or 'spouse' (158), and more generally as representing 'metaphorically female profiles for the people of YHWH' (159). Smith-Christopher (2015: 160–162) proposes that Mic. 4:13 'represents a view other than Micah's own: a promise of Judean nationalist strength, against which Micah is preaching' on the basis of several parallels with the words of Micaiah ben Imlah's opponent in 1 Kgs 22:11. Against this view, the content of Mic. 4:13 is essentially identical to other oracles of salvation in Micah that involve renewed Israel's defeat of its enemies (e.g. 5:5–6).

[8] Dempster 2017: 140.

and Israelites alike to God (7:18–20). The conflict is thus between an immanent ideology achieved by violence that yielded material goods and human glory and the nascent kingdom of God whose ruler will shepherd his international subjects with a transcendent, transformative power that promotes the 'majesty' of Yahweh's name.

The nations' ill-fated attempts to harm God's people are more than a miscalculation – they reveal a failure to understand the nature of Yahweh's kingdom, the limits of these groups' own power, and what is truly good. Such aggression against God's people and king is a classic manifestation of human pride raising its autonomous fist against the only one who can deliver it from such self-destructive sin. The same adversarial posture on the part of the nations is assumed in 5:8, where the remnant, by means that are not spelled out, defeats those among whom it lives *and who seek its harm* (other nations among whom the remnant lives clearly respond to it quite differently; see below on 5:7). The final point in the trajectory of conflict between God's people and his and their enemies appears at the end of the book's second section, where Yahweh asserts: 'I will vindicate myself in anger and wrath against the nations which have not listened' (5:15).[9] This judgment most likely marks the end of the age in which the remnant lives among the nations.

Non-Israelites in positive roles in eschatological settings

In sharp contrast to the *negative* role of the nations in Micah 5:6, 8, which presumes an unwillingness to respond to the remnant's witness (cf. 4:2) and the just, gracious rule of its messianic king, 5:7 reveals that the remnant's existence after the Messiah's appearance can affect other non-Israelites nations *positively*, in the same way that dew nourishes, preserves and brings life to vegetation.[10] Compared to the opposite response in 5:8, these non-Israelites find in the remnant a source of good and are able to benefit from it so that they flourish. Recognizing that the remnant is 'liberated, empowered, and defended by YHWH', these non-Israelites'

---

[9] As translated in Timmer 2021c: 101.

[10] Dew is regularly positive (and never negative) in its literal and metaphorical uses in the OT (Gen. 27:28, 39; Deut. 32:2; 33:13–14, 28; 2 Sam. 1:21; Ps. 133:3; Hos. 14:5; Hag. 1:10; Zech. 8:12), and the lion–dew contrast in Prov. 19:12 confirms that the two images naturally form a contrast.

response necessarily involves a clear recognition of Yahweh's uniqueness as creator, king and saviour.[11] The remnant's positive role constitutes a striking fulfilment of the promise to Abraham in Genesis 12:3 that his descendants would be a conduit of blessing for 'all the families of the earth' (see esp. Gen. 27:28; Deut. 32:2; 33:28; Isa. 26:19; note also the comparison of the Davidic king with rainfall in Ps. 72:6, and of Yahweh with dew [Hos. 14:5]).

The well-known passage in Micah 4, shared with Isaiah 2, shows in more detail how faithful Israelites bring good to the nations. This eschatological scenario, set in 'the latter days' (4:1), involves the superlative elevation of Yahweh's temple above every other mountain.[12] This symbolizes the fuller revelation of God's unique deity and glory across the world (cf. 5:4), in response to which 'peoples shall flow to' the eschatological temple.[13] The dissemination of Yahweh's word and *tôrâ* from Jerusalem (4:2) also signals a new era in which the people of God go to the nations rather than attracting them (often passively), the typical pattern during the Old Testament period.[14]

The account of these non-Israelites' reception of Yahweh's word is given added force by being presented as direct speech. These people encourage one another to 'go up' to Yahweh's mountain and temple, and identify the God whose word they are already obeying as 'the God of Jacob' (4:2). Moreover, their intention is to learn 'his ways' so as to 'walk in his paths', activities that underline both Yahweh's agency as their teacher and the radical transformation that his supernatural word brings about. Significantly, this criterion of identity is shared with the faithful Israelites in 4:5.

No less amazing is the effect that God's transforming word has on these non-Israelites' relation to others (4:3). The judging or adjudicating of their conflicts, and the rebuke or reproof that comes with it, produce radically new attitudes and actions among these groups. In contrast to their formerly violent pursuit of their interests at the expense of those around them, their efforts are now directed towards peaceful coexistence

[11] Timmer 2015: 100.

[12] For robust arguments in favour of the strongly eschatological nature of this phrase, see Dempster 2018.

[13] The NT uses temple-language to speak of the Messiah, the people of God, and the new heavens and new earth.

[14] Timmer 2011: 32–37.

under Yahweh's authority, protection and blessing, much like the remnant in 5:4–5. In addition to the other criteria of identity that demonstrate that these non-Israelites adopt Israel's faith and submit to 'the God of Jacob', their idyllic existence as described in 4:4 echoes Israel's halcyon days under Solomon (1 Kgs 4:25). Likewise, these non-Israelites share in the blessings that were promised to obedient Israel under the Sinai covenant (Lev. 26:6) and attributed to restored, reunified Israel elsewhere in prophecy (Isa. 11:11–13; Jer. 30:10; 46:27; Ezek. 34:28; 39:26; Zeph. 3:13).

Demonstrating the close link between Israel and the nations who are blessed through it, Micah 7 presents several complementary perspectives on the response of some non-Israelites to Jerusalem's eschatological restoration (7:11–13) and the renewal of God's people as the culmination of a second exodus (7:14–17). The first passage announces to repentant, restored and vindicated Israel (the feminine singular grammar justifies identifying the addressee as the remnant or Daughter Zion[15]) that God plans to radically increase her population. Daughter Zion is commanded to build her walls and extend her boundaries in order to accommodate a massive influx of new residents, namely, new members of the collective that is Daughter Zion. Here, as in 4:1–4, the nations come *peacefully* to Zion from all directions. Assyria and Egypt, formerly dangerous empires, now submit to Yahweh and *join his people.*[16] The phrase 'from sea to sea and from mountain to mountain' (7:12) highlights the global extent of this exodus/*eisodos* movement which, according to Micah 4, is driven by Yahweh's omnipotent word. The contrast in 7:13 between Zion and the rest of the world, which is desolated by the punishment of the sins of those who did *not* come to Zion, underscores the ideal and exclusive nature of perfected life in Zion.

The last passage that mentions non-Israelites focuses on the process by which God's *enemies* are reconciled to him. It begins with a prayer for the restoration of God's people, presented in terms of peaceful life in the land. The prayer is met with a positive response in which God affirms that he will bring about a deliverance that rivals (or exceeds) the first exodus (7:14–15; cf. 2:12–13) and that demonstrates his supreme power to 'the nations' (7:16). Seeing God's amazing deeds on behalf of his people, 'nations' (such as Rahab) abandon trust in their ability to

[15] Dempster (2017: 183) and others make the same identification.

[16] The claim of Kessler (2021: 468) that '[t]he nations do not become Israel' is probably somewhat overstated.

defend themselves against God's justice. In place of their self-sufficiency and assumed dominance, 'dread' and 'fear' (7:17) are evidence of positive internal transformations no less significant than those described in Micah 4:2–3.[17] Israel's second exodus, which marks the end of the exile and includes its settled existence in the land, is thus radically more beneficial for the nations than the entry under Joshua. Even more positively, Israelites and non-Israelites share fundamental criteria of identity that establish their shared identity as worshippers of Yahweh even as they retain other secondary distinctions.

Summary and New Testament developments

Non-Israelite nations figure prominently in Micah's message, and their various identities and characteristics mean that they appear in very different roles. Like Judah, they are exposed to the danger of divine justice because of their sins. Like Judah's remnant (Daughter Zion), some non-Israelites will be so radically transformed by God that they will submit to him, abandon the ideologies that defined them until then and orient their lives in accord with his will. In these positive scenarios, Judah's remnant plays a role, bringing Yahweh's word to them (Mic. 4:2) and having a radically positive dew-like effect on many (5:7). Less frequently, the remnant participates in Yahweh's judgment of his enemies (4:13).

Recognizing the organic continuity between Judah's remnant and the first generation of Christians, the redemptive-historical developments just mentioned carry over to the early church. Jesus Christ, born in Bethlehem, not only arises as the 'ruler who will shepherd my people Israel' (Matt. 2:6; cf. 2 Sam. 5:2) but also accomplishes the full expiation of sin in fulfilment of the covenant with Abraham (7:19; cf. Luke 1:54–55).[18] That same covenant entails the integration of non-Israelites into the New Testament people of God, without any need to adopt Jewish practices (Acts 15). The apostles first of all, and all Christians in general, are called to participate in Christ's commission to bring the gospel to the ends of the earth (Matt. 28; 1 Pet. 2:9; 3:15). They can do so being confident that God

[17] For arguments in favour of understanding the last line of 7:17 as equivalent to 'revering Yahweh', see Kessler 1999: 308–309; Timmer 2021c: 223; contrast Phillips 2022: 349–350.

[18] Dempster 2023: 527, 528.

will continue to augment Zion's population (Mic. 4:3–4; 7:11–12) even if, as with the remnant in Micah 5, they are 'to one a fragrance from death to death, to the other a fragrance from life to life' (2 Cor. 2:16). Through the same gospel, God transforms his enemies into his worshippers (Rom. 5:6–10; Eph. 2:1–10; Titus 3:3–7; cf. Mic. 4:13), bringing 'peace' (Rom. 5:1; cf. Mic. 4:1–4; 5:5).

12
Nahum

The nations-theme is at the heart of the seventh-century BC book of Nahum. More precisely, condemnation of one nation, Assyria, predominates throughout most of the book. Yet Nahum is hardly a screed against Assyrians, for several reasons. First, the opening poem in 1:2–8 makes no clear reference to Assyria at all. On the contrary, it portrays a global theophany in which judgment threatens God's 'enemies' without any ethnic, national or similar specificity. With this passage's distinction between those who seek refuge in Yahweh (1:7) and those who remain his enemies (1:8) setting the stage for what follows, the rest of the book can hardly propose an ethnically or nationally focused condemnation of Assyria. And this indeed is the case; the precision with which Nahum limits his presentation of Assyria to those who participate in and direct its imperial project is a second argument against understanding its condemnations as ethnically or nationally focused. Appropriately enough, this same complexity is evident in the book's presentation of Judah, such that the main portion of the book (1:9 – 3:19) retains the supra-ethnic perspective of the introductory poem even as it zooms in on geopolitical events in and around Judah in the second half of the seventh century BC.

Global, individual, definitive judgment and salvation of humanity (Nah. 1:2–8)

The first passage in which non-Israelites are present in Nahum is, intriguingly, one in which they are not identified as such.[1] The opening poem (1:2–8) presents a global, definitive judgment in which the nature of one's relationship with God is the *only* way in which individuals are identified,

[1] It is not clear whether the feminine singular suffix on the Hebrew term translated 'her/its place' or 'the adversaries' (Nah. 1:8 ESV, following LXX) refers to Assyria.

and the only basis on which they will be either definitively punished or delivered from that punishment. Since this judgment is connected to individuals solely on the basis of their relationship with Yahweh, it threatens 'all who dwell' on earth (1:5) – Assyrians, Judeans and everyone else.

The passage begins by announcing that God is 'jealous' (1:2) for his own glory, which is infringed upon by humans whenever they live in ways that fail to recognize his absolute claim upon them as their creator.[2] This passage presumes that such rebellion is universal, and so stresses repeatedly (including three affirmations that God is one who 'avenges') that Yahweh's wrath is about to break out against his 'adversaries' and 'enemies', whom, as such, he holds guilty (1:3). The only interruption to the steady litany of terms related to judgment and punishment appears in an echo of Exodus 34:6–7 in Nahum 1:3a, which affirms that God's wrath is not out of control or premature but does not clearly introduce the possibility of deliverance.[3]

Nahum drives home the unmatched significance of this eschatological event for every human being by posing a seemingly rhetorical question:

> Who can stand before his indignation?
>   Who can endure the heat of his anger?
> (Nah. 1:6)

Happily, the last two verses of the poem reveal that there are *two* possible outcomes of this judgment, each of which is paired with a defining characteristic of the respective group. First, those who 'take refuge in him' (1:7) will find that God offers protection against the punishment threatened against their sin, implying that he will grant the justice and pardon they lack. The Hebrew text puts Yahweh's goodness at the beginning of the sentence to emphasize his grace and compassion even to the rebellious (cf. Exod. 33:19; Ps. 68:18).[4] Yet, like an 'overflowing flood' and a relentless pursuer, he will 'make a complete end' of 'his enemies' (1:8).[5] The outcome of God's final intervention in human affairs is thus twofold: salvation and judgment. Those who submit to Yahweh and trust in him

---

[2] Peels 1997.

[3] Timmer 2020a: 79.

[4] Buth 1999: 106.

[5] These elements, the massive destruction that God's descent to earth produces in 1:4–5, and other features in the passage justify seeing it as eschatological per Arnold 2008.

receive perfect justice, life and glorification, while those who continue to struggle against 'the ordered relation to God in which alone the creature can [truly] be' tragically separate themselves from life and goodness.[6]

In addition to being inseparable from the universal perspective of the rest of the passage, the connection of definitive judgment or deliverance to individuals clearly distinguishes the horizon of this passage from the penultimate or limited punishments and deliverance that appear in the rest of the book. Nonetheless, it is possible to see a typological relationship between the fall of Assyria and the final judgment of God's enemies on the basis of the book's twofold structure and the animus towards Yahweh that is bound up with the empire's ideology.

Selective, limited judgment of Assyria (Nah. 1:9 – 3:19)

What is 'Assyria' in Nahum?

Although at first glance the rest of the book of Nahum seems to focus on Assyria as an apparently homogeneous nation (cf. 1:1; 2:8; 3:7, 18), Nahum's condemnations and taunts hardly mention any Assyrians other than the king, the army and those directly tied to the empire's diplomatic and economic apparatus. This focus on imperial personnel is complemented by a consistent emphasis on prominent features of the ideology behind the empire's project of dominating the known world with the help of its gods. These two perspectives work together to produce an image of 'Assyria' that includes only a small fraction of its population rather than every person residing in Assyrian territory. This subset of the Assyrian population, along with its ideology and the false gods believed to ensure its success, is the 'Assyria' that God promises to destroy in Nahum.

Nahum's selective depiction of Assyria is quite accurate, whether evaluated on the terms of the culture of the Assyrian elite or of Judah's interaction with the empire. As shown earlier in this volume, Assyria's cultic personnel, royal scholars, prophets, and above all the monarch himself, were committed to promulgating and reinforcing a royal ideology in which the king was to realize on earth the gods' will for Assyria's

[6] Webster 2003: 84; the bracketed term is added for clarity.

global dominion.[7] Like Nahum, these sources identify a select few, typically the king and the army, as the agents responsible for bringing this imperial vision to reality. Similarly, Assyria was known to Judah exclusively in military and geopolitical roles, which notably included its conquest of the northern kingdom of Israel in 722 BC and Judah's narrow escape from Sennacherib following his destructive campaign that ended in front of Jerusalem in 701 BC.

Yahweh versus Assyria: God as supremely important

A prominent feature of the world view promoted by Assyria's imperial ideology is captured in God's terse statement in Nahum 1:9 that Nineveh has plotted against Yahweh. Assyrian aggression against Judah involves intentional opposition to Yahweh for at least two reasons. First, the Judeans are God's covenant people and he is their God, so harming them or subordinating them (unless in careful performance of its role as an instrument of covenant punishment; cf. Isa. 10) is a rejection of God's express purposes for his people and his sovereignty over them and Assyria alike. Second, Neo-Assyrian imperial ideology overtly portrays the empire's conflict with other states as theological in nature, something the speech of the Assyrian Rabshakeh recognizes in various ways (2 Kgs 18 – 19; Isa. 36 – 37). The direct nature of the conflict between God and Assyria is evident throughout the book of Nahum, and its oracles emphatically reject Assyria's attempts to usurp God's role and nullify his purposes for Judah and for the world. In the next few sections we will consider several passages in which this conflict is presented and deconstructed.

Rejection of the monarch as the personification of empire and omnipotent defender and provider

We begin with a survey of several passages in which the Assyrian monarch is singled out for critique and condemnation. In Nahum 1:14, Yahweh dismisses the ruler's legacy, divine empowerment and unparalleled status in blunt, absolute terms. While Ashurbanipal (669–627 BC) was not literally the last king of the Sargonid dynasty, the dissolution of

[7] Liverani 2017. On some of the less well-known figures, see Radner 2011.

the empire was well under way by the time of his death. This rapid decline was provoked by the final, and ultimately successful, rebellion of the restive province of Babylon (652–648), after which both Ashurbanipal's administration and the empire's grasp on its peripheral regions grew weaker, ultimately leaving a crumbling empire to his successors.[8] God's promise to do away with the gods believed to underwrite and enable Assyria's military dominance strikes at the very heart of the Assyrian imperial project. Although it was common for the victor to relocate a conquered population's cult statues to temples in the victor's land as a sign of those gods' support of the conqueror, it was extremely rare for these statues to be destroyed.[9] Without their gods, king and empire alike would be almost powerless, while Yahweh's supremacy over all other claimants to deity would be undeniable. Finally, the king himself is slated for burial as one who is simply insignificant, a blunt rejection of the grandiose claims he and every other Neo-Assyrian monarch made concerning themselves. In sum, Nahum 1:14 is a rejection of the king as the personification of the Assyrian imperial project. The incipient collapse of the empire, the demonstration that its gods were powerless to sustain it, and the king's inability to prevent this decline spell the end of Assyria as empire: the king, his gods and the religious–political belief structure in which they were situated.

Yahweh counters the military aspect of the Assyrian monarch's role no less aggressively in 2:11–13. Assyrian royal ideology sometimes portrayed the king in terms of a lion who protected his people from the forces of chaos, most clearly present in the unruly regions outside the empire's control.[10] For example, one of Esarhaddon's royal inscriptions recounts that in his conquest of Egypt he sought the help of the gods and then '[raged like] a lion, put on ([his]) coat of mail' and attacked his enemy.[11] The use of the lion-metaphor here accentuates the killing and consumption of prey, which is taken in such quantities that the lion's caves and dens are full of 'prey' and 'torn flesh' (Nah. 2:12). In addition to conveying the power and appetite of the lion and his pride, the metaphor reveals how the empire creates a difference of value between itself and its enemies that legitimizes its violent consumption of them as a natural, even necessary,

[8] Kuhrt 1995: 589.

[9] Holloway 2001: 118–122.

[10] Liverani 2017: 57–58.

[11] Leichty 2011: 53.

facet of its existence. In effect, the empire dehumanizes its victims as part of its ideology.[12]

This attitude and the violence it spawns militate against the value of (some) human beings as created in the image of God and corrupt the use of power in pursuit of self-advancement and self-glorification.[13] Yahweh emphatically asserts that he is 'against' the monarch in this role, and commits to destroying the means by which the empire has pursued its vicious goals. Notably, God's judgment will destroy both military and diplomatic personnel, since both have participated in the empire's violent mission. While this participation is self-evident on the part of the armed forces ('chariots' and 'young lions' [2:13]), the messengers or envoys negotiated and formalized treaties and 'capitulation documents' on behalf of the empire that gave concrete form to its imperialism.[14]

Deconstruction of Nineveh's impregnability and splendour

Nahum also presents Assyria under the guise of one of its leading cities, Nineveh, which became its capital in 705 BC. Nineveh was home to a third-millennium temple to Ishtar, goddess of love and war,[15] and its ziggurat was 'the pride of Nineveh'.[16] Around the beginning of the seventh century BC, Sennacherib undertook extensive building campaigns intended to make Nineveh 'a city whose size and splendor would astonish the civilized world',[17] including the construction of Sennacherib's palace 'without a rival', the digging of a canal to bring water from the River Khosr (some 10 miles [16 km] from Nineveh) and the building of a massive exterior defensive wall around the city.[18] The ideological significance of these projects was multifaceted.[19] Some city gates bore names such as 'May the Vice-Regent of the God Aššur Endure' and 'The God Erra is the One

[12] Zehnder 2005: 64–66.

[13] 'Ideological polarization of indigenous order over and against enemy chaos is germane to our understanding of Assyrian foreign affairs' (Crouch 2009: 21).

[14] Berlejung 2006: 335. There may have been an official of this sort in Jerusalem at some point; see Morrow 2013: 55.

[15] Gut, Reade and Boehmer 2001: 74–75; Abusch 1999: 452.

[16] Reade 2005: 384. In this section I draw occasionally on Timmer 2020a: 125–138.

[17] Reade 1978: 50.

[18] Ibid. 64.

[19] Karlsson (2022: 265) notes that such projects were intended 'to impress the deities and posterity but also to awe the contemporary general population'.

Who Cuts Down Enemies',[20] while the renovation of temples for Sin, Ningal, Shamash, Aya and Ishtar of Nineveh promoted the uninterrupted continuation of these gods' goodwill.[21] The annals of Sennacherib that recount some of these projects are prefaced by a lengthy introduction that shows the mythological, cosmological and ideological roots of Nineveh's significance:

> Nineveh, the exalted cult center, the city . . . in which all of the rituals for god and goddesses are present; the enduring foundation (and) eternal base whose plan had been designed by the stars . . . of the firmament and whose arrangement was made manifest since time immemorial . . . in which since time immemorial earlier kings, my ancestors, before me exercised dominion . . . they received an income unsurpassed in amount, the tribute of the rulers of the four quarters (of the world).[22]

The ancient origins, contemporary splendour and religious significance of Sennacherib's Nineveh gave it a (very realistic) aura of impregnability, defended by a massive wall without and its gods within. However, despite its splendour and vitality, as shown by its magnificent gardens, it was a city built with slave labour and blood, financed by the payments of vassal states and the spoils of wars undertaken for the fame of the empire. The vision of Nineveh's fall in Nahum 2 steadily dismantles the chimera of the city's impregnability, moving from the impressiveness of the approaching foe to the dishevelled defenders (2:5), the spoiling of Ishtar's temple (2:7), and the flight and panic of its defenders (2:9, 10). The impotence of Ishtar, who in Assyrian royal and prophetic texts regularly intervenes to destroy the king's enemies, is a clear denial of her deity. The external beauty and splendour of the city are also subjected to incisive critique in Nahum 3:1–4, which reveals the bloody price paid by the empire's victims for the continuation of its imperial mission. A series of taunts later in Nahum 3 criticizes the false security that Nineveh's inhabitants derived from its defences (3:8–11), asserts that the fortresses scattered throughout the empire would fall (3:12–15a) and foretells that despite their sizable

---

[20] Grayson and Novotny 2012: 18.

[21] Ibid. 21.

[22] Ibid. 53.

numbers, Assyria's merchants, princes and palace personnel would be scattered to the winds (3:15b–17).

This series of critiques announces sweeping condemnations of Assyria that focus exclusively on its military, royal and economic personnel and actions. Taking Nineveh as representing the empire, Nahum denies that the gods who purportedly stand ready to protect it will be able to defend it when Yahweh's punishment falls. This theological critique entails the city's vulnerability, which the prophet also portrays in vivid images that show it to be weak and ready to fall despite appearances and regardless of its illustrious past. The fall of the empire also sees its leaders disappear from the stage, essentially decapitating the nation and leaving the rest of the population as sheep without shepherds (3:18). Most significantly, Nineveh's fall will vindicate Yahweh as the only God worthy of the title, the sole sovereign over history, and the judge whose justice cannot be thwarted or ignored with impunity. Not only Judah but also all the nations that had suffered under Assyria's excesses (and which the book does not condemn) would breathe a sigh of relief and even celebrate when it would finally fall at the very end of the seventh century BC (1:15; 3:19).[23]

What of the others?

Nahum's focus throughout most of the book (1:9 – 3:19) on a small sector of the Assyrian population, and on a subset of their sins that was tied directly to imperialism, limits his condemnations of 'Assyria' to that group. This is confirmed by the *survival* of individuals who are without any clear link to the empire (2:10; 3:18). What is the status of this larger group, made up of the majority of Assyrians, who are without any clear involvement in the legitimation, propagation or realization of the empire's violent, self-justifying, autonomous pursuit of power, wealth and stability on its terms?

One could argue that the fall of Assyria, which inevitably brought hardship, suffering or death to some of the population, indicates that they had a part (however small) in Assyria's imperial mission and to that degree were culpable. As tidy as that proposal seems from the perspective of theodicy, it is better to preserve Nahum's clear distinction between

[23] The siege, spoiling and destruction of the city are described in Babylonian Chronicle 3, in Grayson 2000: 94. The city of Harran fell in 610 or 609 BC, and Egypt, which had come to Assyria's aid, was decisively defeated at the battle of Carchemish in 605.

the guilty and the rest. On this view, it is enough to explain the messiness of the fall of Assyria, and the pain and suffering endured by those not involved in its imperialism, as the inevitable concomitant of human involvement as a means of divine punishment.[24] The consistency with which the Old Testament condemns the violence, arrogance and self-serving nature of the nations that God uses to punish Israel and Judah favours the conclusion that 'human agents (especially empires) simply cannot be instrumental in the application of divine justice without adding various objectionable elements to its realization'.[25]

This leaves the majority of Assyrians in the book of Nahum in a liminal place, neither condemned nor exonerated, neither opposing Judah nor turning to its God for refuge (1:7). The situation is the same for those Judeans who, until the time of Nahum's ministry, were under divine punishment for unstated sinful behaviours (1:12). Since Nahum identifies 'Judah' as 'made up of those Judeans who accept the validity of God's disciplinary punishment of their nation and recognize that his deliverance of them is due to his grace and his faithfulness to his promises'[26] (1:13, 15; 2:2), that group is certainly not identical to the Judean population as a whole. The rest of the Old Testament makes clear that most Judeans were not so aligned with the purposes and will of God. They too, therefore, are in a liminal position as far as Nahum is concerned, neither discounting God's intervention on Judah's behalf nor turning to him in faith and repentance. Their on-the-fence status can only be clarified on the terms of the definitive judgment and salvation that are announced in 1:2–8, which remain future. The fact that both some Judeans and some Assyrians are left in limbo, as it were, demonstrates the finesse with which Nahum treats the theme of the nations, and quite fittingly leaves its resolution for a later point in redemptive history when spiritual–relational realities are the sole and infallible criteria.

[24] Via 2007: 21.

[25] Timmer 2021a: 166–167. While there can be 'multiple kinds of participation by the wider population' (so Carroll R. 2015: 124) in the misdeeds of the empire and its elite, I am less convinced now of my suggestion that this is the case with the general Assyrian population. See Timmer 2021a: 170 for arguments in favour of 'graded retribution', in which heavier punishments fall on those who practise imperialism and lighter ones on those who merely benefit from it.

[26] Timmer 2024f: 76.

Summary and New Testament developments

The theme of the nations in Nahum deals almost exclusively with Assyria, and more specifically with Assyria's king, military and imperial personnel as those engaged in realizing or supporting its imperial mission of 'warfare, kingship, order'.[27] In direct contradiction of the emperor's claims and the empire's far-reaching ideology, Yahweh asserts that the monarch is mortal and relatively impotent. By the same token, the gods purportedly committed to Assyria's programme of conquest and consolidation are themselves powerless to oppose God's plans for Judah and the world at large. Indeed, by dismantling this empire and so disproving the foundational elements of its ideology in historical reality, Yahweh demonstrates to the nations that he alone is God. His deliverance of Judah from Assyria's clutches similarly demonstrates to them his grace, patience and covenant fidelity despite their sin.

Nahum's prediction of a divine theophany in 1:2–8 is radically different. Its eschatological nature jumps to the end of the nations-theme, as it were, by looking ahead to the final judgment in which ethnicity and political affiliation play no role whatsoever, and indeed are not even mentioned. Yet Revelation's use of Babylon as a cipher for all organized human opposition to God and his people reveals that the spectre of Assyria-as-empire has not left the stage of history – it is simply present in new garb.[28]

The same passage, finally, sheds light on how the idealized Judah that appears briefly in Nahum can incorporate those Judeans and Assyrians who do not figure prominently in Nahum. Yahweh is the only God, the only source of deliverance from the punishment that looms over every sinful individual. Just as Israelite ethnicity is no guarantee that one is truly a child of Abraham, so non-Israelite ethnicity is no barrier to being grafted graciously into God's people.[29]

The two main sections of Nahum flow into the New Testament in different ways. The opening theophany remains unfulfilled as the final judgment of all human beings and the restoration of all things (1 Cor. 1:8; 5:5; 1 Thess. 5:2; 2 Pet. 3:10). The rest of Nahum contributes to the

[27] Crouch 2009: 27.

[28] Timmer 2023b: 559–560.

[29] Firth 2019: 177; see Rom. 11:17.

New Testament's use of 'Babylon' as a symbol for Rome and all collectives, political or otherwise, that employ 'violence, pride, idolatry, divination, and economic power' to advance their self-glorifying projects.[30] Much like Nahum's nuanced definition of Nineveh and Assyria, God's judgment of Babylon will bring down 'the systems – political, economic and religious – which oppose God and his righteousness'.[31] The celebrations that attended the collapse of Assyria (Nah. 3:19) find their fulfilment in the jubilation of the heavenly multitude over the destruction of Babylon (Rev. 19:1–5), and the restoration of the majesty of 'Jacob' (Nah. 2:2) culminates in the consummation of Yahweh's relationship with his people, drawn 'from every tribe and language and people and nation' (Rev. 5:9). This is symbolized by the marriage supper of the Lamb (Rev. 19:6–10) and realized in the admission of God's people to the new Jerusalem, from which all that is sinful is excluded and in which there is perfect security and joy in God's presence (Rev. 21:8, 22–27).

[30] Timmer 2024f: 88.

[31] Bauckham 1993: 89.

13 Habakkuk

In a world where small- and large-scale armed conflicts seem to appear continuously, the immediate relevance of Habakkuk's message is self-evident. Its intersection with the theme of the non-Israelite nations has an edge, however. Rather than simply condemning Babylon-as-empire (which it does with verve), Habakkuk's accompanying condemnation of unjust individuals in Judah shows that both groups manifest, to different degrees, the same fundamental sins.[1] This makes the nations a subversive theme in Habakkuk, one that condemns the misuse of power, the headlong pursuit of autonomy, and the attempt to claim divine prerogatives by individuals or collectives, whether in Judah, Babylon or elsewhere.

Much like the book of Nahum, Habakkuk falls into two sections. Chapters 1 – 2 limit their scope to Judah and Babylon near the end of the sixth century BC, while chapter 3 (apart from the opening and closing verses) shifts its focus to a global, eschatological horizon. Like Nahum's opening poem, the poem in Habakkuk 3 does not mention any particular political entity in its description of Yahweh's definitive battle against evil. Our survey of the nations in Habakkuk will take up these two parts separately, while recognizing their theological interrelation as well as their potent practical implications.

Babylon as God's instrument for punishing sinful Judah

The book of Habakkuk is not, in the first place, concerned with the nations. The prophet is severely perturbed by sin and violence in Judah, which are so widespread that the norms of Israel's covenant with Yahweh seem to have disappeared completely from Judean society (1:4). Furthermore, this

[1] Timmer 2015: 148.

problem has gone on too long (so the prophet believes), making it appear as if God is complicit in, or at least indifferent to, the domination of the righteous by the wicked (1:2–4). It is in this already challenging situation that the nations make – from Habakkuk's initial point of view – a most unwelcome appearance. God knew, of course, that the prophet would respond in disbelief to his announcement that he would use Babylon to discipline his wayward people (1:5–6). It is not the idea that foreign nations might serve as the instrument for divine punishment of Judah's covenant infidelity that troubles Habakkuk, for this was announced in the very Torah to which he makes reference in 1:4 (see Lev. 26:14–39; Deut. 28:15–68). Rather, it was the prophet's assumption that Judah was 'more righteous' than 'wicked' Babylon (1:13) that caused his disbelief and chagrin.

Babylon as God's enemy

Interestingly, God's description of Babylon in 1:6–11 is no less negative with regard to the empire's sinful nature than are Habakkuk's critiques of its utilitarian violence (1:15), idolatry (1:16) and insatiable appetite for more (1:17). It is also significant that both God and the prophet present Babylon as consisting essentially of its armed forces and emperor (the latter in the masculine singular 'he' in 1:15–17) rather than as a single homogeneous group that includes all the empire's citizens. This focused use of 'Babylon' to refer to those who propagate and enact the empire's imperial ideology runs through most of the first two chapters, and provides the basis for seeing Babylon-as-empire as typological of those who oppose God throughout redemptive history.[2] A closer look at these descriptions of Babylon will shed light on the beliefs and practices that elicit God's condemnation.

Babylon in the dialogue of Habakkuk 1

The ways in which God and his prophet depict Babylon in chapter 1 not only are accurate with respect to Babylon but also ably capture the main lines of ancient Near Eastern imperialism in general.[3] To begin with what the forces of empire do, they accumulate material property ('dwellings

[2] Bauckham 1993: 144–164; Bauckham 2011.

[3] See Larsen 1979; Morris and Scheidel 2009.

not their own' [1:6]) and wealth, taking territory, infrastructure and natural resources at will. Exercising lethal violence, they also capture and enslave whole populations (1:9) to serve as military conscripts, forced labour for imperial building projects, and so on. The massive influx of wealth also allows Babylon-as-empire, that is, the elite and not the entire population, to live in luxury, build temples for its gods and strategically invest the spoils of war in local economies (1:16).[4] An inscription of Nebuchadnezzar lists, with care and flair, a variety of spoils and their use:

> Gold, silver, exceedingly valuable gemstones, thick cedars, heavy tribute, expensive presents, the produce of all countries, goods from all inhabited regions, before Marduk the great lord, the god who created me, and Nabû his lofty heir who loves my kingship, I transported and brought into Esagil and Ezida.[5]

The finality (portrayed by the verb 'swallows up' [1:13]) and uninterrupted nature of the imperial project leads Habakkuk to portray Babylon, quite fittingly, in terms of a fisherman who ceaselessly catches human beings like fish (1:15–17). This metaphor captures the godlike aspirations to control territory and people worldwide, and highlights the dehumanizing or demeaning approach of the empire to those presently outside it. Such a view of the 'other' is part of a set of beliefs and attitudes that constitute the empire's ideology. Additional elements include the ritual celebration of Babylon's victories (1:16), the self-affirmation and self-justification that come with a project purportedly authorized and empowered by the gods (1:7, 16), and proud disdain for any who would oppose the empire's irresistible will (1:10).

The ultimate goals of Babylon's programme of conquest are also indebted to its imperialism. Babylon pursues its imperial project with the aim of subjugating the world in fulfilment of the king's divine commission. In his coronation ceremony, Nabopolassar affirmed his role (most likely addressing the god Bel, i.e. 'the lord' Marduk): 'With the standard I shall constantly conquer [*your*] enemies, I shall place [*your*] throne in Babylon', and the participants exclaimed: 'O lord, O king, may you live forever! [May you conquer] the land of [your] enemies! May the king of

[4] Levavi 2020: 75.

[5] Cited in Vanderhooft 1999: 46.

the gods, Marduk, rejoice in you!'[6] The linkage between the king, the gods and the imperial mission comes to clear expression in Nebuchadnezzar's inscription on the Etemenanki ziggurat in Babylon:

> The widespread people whom Marduk, my lord, entrusted to me, whose shepherdship the hero Šamaš gave me, the totality of countries, the whole of all inhabited regions, from the Upper Sea to the Lower Sea, remote countries, the peoples of the widespread inhabited regions, kings of distant mountain regions and faraway islands in the Upper and Lower Sea – whose lead ropes Marduk, my lord, placed into my hands in order to pull his chariot pole – I conscripted . . . for the building of Etemenaki I imposed the work-basket upon them.[7]

Strikingly, this frank recognition of the enslavement of conquered peoples sits side by side, in the corpus of royal inscriptions generally and in this inscription in particular (where subjugation is described as 'shepherdship'), with the rosy picture of Nebuchadnezzar causing 'people everywhere to thrive'.[8] This subjugation was essentially political and did not involve the imposition of Babylonian religion on conquered peoples,[9] reinforcing the impression that the imperial project ultimately served not the glory of the gods involved but an imperial ideology in which human glory, the acquisition of material wealth, and the pursuit of security and stability in an immanent framework are uppermost. This impression is strengthened by the fact that explicit, negative moral evaluations are immediately tied to the (self-)idolatrous nature ('guilty' [1:11, 16]) and violent exercise (treacherous, 'evil', 'wicked' [1:13]) of Babylon's imperialism.[10]

Babylon's imperialism and idolatry will be punished (Hab. 2)

The emphasis on the moral condemnation of Babylon-as-empire grows stronger in Habakkuk 2, where it is based on a careful analysis of the

[6] Grayson 1975: 85.

[7] Vanderhooft 1999: 36–37, who observes that 'the stock phrases of imperial hegemony imply the fiction of world domination' (39).

[8] Vanderhooft 2003: 250.

[9] Oded 1995: 209.

[10] Fischer (2012: 123) sees this as a key transition in the theme of divine justice in the book.

actions, attitudes and aims that characterize Babylon's imperialism and those who pursue its realization. Developing the fundamental contrast between the one who is 'puffed up' and pursues success and security on his or her own terms and the one who believes Yahweh's word and is righteous (2:4–5), a series of woe oracles in 2:6–20 focuses on Babylon as the parade example of proud self-sufficiency. Each oracle identifies and condemns an aspect of Babylon's imperial activities and the dispositions that motivate them, announcing a corresponding punishment for each.

The first oracle, in 2:6–8, exposes the inevitably violent and destructive nature of the empire's taking by force of people, material wealth and resources outside its borders. Quite suitably, the woe is put in the mouths of Babylon's victims (2:6), who will eventually participate in its retribution. Indeed, payback is literally present in the condemnation, since the speaker refers to the things Babylon has taken as massive debts for which payment will one day be demanded rather than something rightfully acquired (2:6–7). The last verse of the oracle connects this acquisition with widespread bloodshed, ecological damage, and the destruction of cities and their populations, wrongs that are developed in the following oracles.

The link between the spoils of war and the literal and figurative construction of the empire is the focus of the second woe oracle (2:9–11). The ideal of security is uppermost in the fitting metaphor of a nest built out of reach of any threat, but that metaphor gives way to one of a house (or palace) whose stones and beams are composed of those whom the empire subjugates (2:11).[11] Their testimony will condemn Babylon, since its rapacious actions have 'forfeited [its] life' (2:10). This outcome reveals in the clearest way possible the immanent, impermanent and self-destructive nature of this ideology and those who practise it, whether empires or individuals. This is all the more striking since Nebuchadnezzar lauded his palaces as objects 'of wonder for all of the people'.[12] The third woe underlines this last point by asserting that the buildings, victories, and tasks performed by the various people groups that Babylon enslaved and wearied are only 'fire' and 'nothing' (2:13). The transitory nature of the

[11] Vanderhooft (1999: 162) suggests that 'palace' may refer specifically to 'Nebuchadnezzar's palatial building projects' and contrasts the condemnatory cries of Babylon's victims here with the usual praise 'to the patron deity or deities' that concludes Babylonian royal building inscriptions.

[12] Karlsson (2022) surveys the use of the phrase for a variety of royal building projects in Assyria and Babylonia.

empire, despite Nebuchadnezzar's hope that his name would be remembered and his 'statutes' and 'decrees' preserved, is in the sharpest possible contrast to God's kingdom, which will completely fill the earth with the knowledge of his glory (2:14) and sweep away whatever opposes it.[13]

The fourth woe (2:15–17) reveals Babylon's malign, calculated exploitation of its commercial partners, especially those whom it subjugated or from whom it forced concessions. J. J. M. Roberts describes with suitable directness how oppressive exaction or outright political conquest, 'after rendering the conquered peoples helpless, systematically strips away their dignity and honor for the conqueror's own selfish, shameful, and insatiable gratification'.[14] This violence is presented in an understated way in some of Nebuchadnezzar's annals:

> Upon his [Marduk's] august trust, he repeatedly escorted me in remote lands, distant mountains . . . and I slew the unsubmissive. I captured the enemy . . . the evil one and the wicked one I drove away from the people.[15]

Similarly violent taking of what one wants from a defenceless or subdued victim is evident in the 'violence' that Babylon brings to Lebanon (2:17). Vanderhooft observes that the ideological significance of the Babylonian king's 'heroic conquest of Lebanon', including its cedars, is 'precisely that such conquest demonstrates the king's imperial achievement'.[16] In one of his inscriptions, Nebuchadnezzar describes his exploitation of Lebanon's forest in terms that underscore the ease with which he pursued this task and the glory he derived from it:

> What no former king had done (I achieved): I cut through steep mountains, I split rocks, opened passages and (thus) I constructed a straight road for the (transport of the) cedars. I made the Arahtu flo[at] (down) and carry to Marduk, my king, mighty cedars, high and strong, of precious beauty and of excellent dark quality, the abundant yield of Lebanon, as (if they be) reed stalks (carried by)

---

[13] Oppenheim 1969: 307.

[14] Roberts 1991: 124.

[15] Wallenfels 2008: 290.

[16] Vanderhooft 1999: 153.

> the river . . . I ere[cted there] a stela (showing) me (as) everlasting king (of this region).[17]

Habakkuk's final woe (2:18–20) focuses on idolatry, arguably the heart of the imperial project when viewed from God's perspective. In contrast to the inert, inanimate idols and the false gods who share the traits of the statues that represent them, Yahweh alone – and not the Babylonian monarch – is an omnipotent king and to be revered as such.[18]

Vanderhooft's summary of this section of Habakkuk merits citation in full:

> At least three central ideas of the Babylonian imperial creed are expressly condemned: the idea that the king rules by divine fiat; that the one-way flow of material wealth and captives into Babylonia results from the recognition of Babylon's greatness by subject peoples; and that the king honors his deities through building programs. The Babylonian ideas are undermined in Habakkuk's assessment: the king is actually a blasphemous fool; he is a looter who violently dislocates populations without regard for their well-being; and he is the author of building projects that he thinks please his gods but which only emphasize his corruption.[19]

The Divine Warrior's present–future battle against the wicked (Hab. 3)

Despite the strong focus on Babylon-as-empire in Habakkuk 1 – 2, the condemnations in those chapters carefully focus divine judgment on those who propagate and pursue the realization of the empire's ideology. Those who are simply ethnically Babylonian, or live within the empire, are thus ostensibly free of the guilt that attaches to the empire as such. This careful identification of those targeted by God's judgment is all the more evident in the vision of Habakkuk 3 (esp. 3:3–15), from which Babylon is entirely absent. Much like the poem in Nahum 1:2–8, this section

[17] Oppenheim 1969: 307.

[18] Renz (2021: 329) observes that the imperative 'hush' that begins the last line of 2:20 (ESV: 'keep silence') introduces theophanies in Zeph. 1:7 and Zech. 2:13, and the same is likely the case here.

[19] Vanderhooft 1999: 163.

mentions no political entity and identifies the two groups that constitute the binary world it concerns as either the 'wicked' (3:13, with reference to 'nations' in 3:12) whom God will destroy, or his 'people' and 'anointed' who, logic requires the reader to conclude, are not wicked but righteous (cf. 2:4) and will be delivered (3:12–13).[20]

In much the same way that the 'Babylon' condemned in Habakkuk 1 – 2 is characterized by autonomy, idolatry and self-serving violence, the nations that God 'tramples down' here (see 3:15) are those who meet him in combat, as it were, armed for war (3:14). This same 'wicked' enemy will be definitively destroyed (3:13) as part of Yahweh's global, final combat against the forces of evil already confronted in preliminary fashion in the exodus (Hab. 3:10; cf. Exod. 14:22; 15:10–16; 19:16–18), Israel's entry into Canaan (3:11; cf. Josh. 10:12–14), and other settings (Judg. 5:20; Isa. 25:8; etc.). Although the Babylonian Empire will not escape divine punishment, it is far from exhausting the scope of this oracle.[21] On the other side of the fray stand those whom Yahweh saves by means of his intervention. They are his people and his anointed, the latter being a reference to a Davidic king. Notably, neither the people nor the king bring about their own deliverance – God alone conquers his and their enemies. The outcome of this battle sees all of God's enemies, represented by the sea and the waters and including all whom he identifies as 'wicked' rather than righteous, vanquished and rendered harmless.[22]

Summary and New Testament developments

Our brief exploration of the book of Habakkuk shows that the prophet uses the term 'nations' (and the related concept) in two contrasting ways. The first, in chapters 1 – 2, places nations other than Babylon, including but not limited to Judah, in the role of the empire's victims. Neither sin nor innocence is predicated of the nations in this role, whereas Babylon's imperialism is definitely culpable and makes it ripe for judgment. The shift to an eschatological perspective in the vision of Habakkuk 3 places

[20] As noted by Renz (2021: 373, note aa), this group includes the prophet, who speaks in the first-person singular here as a representative of the righteous in Judah, as he does in Hab. 1.

[21] Renz 2021: 388.

[22] Van Bekkum 2017.

the 'nations' in the role formerly held by Babylon-as-empire. Indeed, Babylon can be seen as presaging or anticipating these nations, since they come out to wage war against the faithful in Judah and ultimately against God himself. This reveals the fundamentally anti-God orientation that characterizes them and simultaneously seals their fate. Far from being an anti-Babylonian screed that attacks those who are not ethnic Israelites, Habakkuk recognizes that there are a significant number of 'wicked' persons within Judah, and that such persons – regardless of ethnicity – are guilty of rejecting God's claims and self-revelation in history.

The authors of the New Testament draw on Habakkuk only rarely, but the few times it is cited its contribution is significant.[23] In Romans 1:17, Paul renders Habakkuk 2:4 as 'The one who is righteous by faith will live'[24] and uses it to demonstrate the instrumentality of faith as the means by which human beings can receive God's righteousness. This citation draws on the immediate and larger contexts of Habakkuk 2, and so is inseparable from God's saving and judging work that will bring his righteous kingdom to reality, not least in those who trust in him to deliver them from sin in and around them. As a result, 'the righteousness of the one who believes has its basis in the promise of salvation'.[25] Paul uses the same text in Galatians 3:11 to deny that one can be justified by works.

Habakkuk is one of a few prophets who focus extensively on Babylon, and his analysis of its imperial exploitation, idolatry, materialism and violence makes it quite likely that Habakkuk has contributed to John's presentation of Rome in terms of Babylon. G. K. Beale and Sean McDonough, for example, see Habakkuk 2:15–16 as plausibly underlying the 'oppressive measures' attributed to Babylon in Revelation 14:8.[26] Even the final sortie of Satan and his hordes aimed at the destruction of the saints and the 'beloved city' (Rev. 20:9) is cast in terms drawn from Babylon's imminent invasion of Judah in Hab. 1:6 (LXX).[27] The New Testament's reception of Habakkuk in soteriological and eschatological contexts testifies to the organic connections that its message has with

[23] Here I draw on Timmer 2024f: 164–167.

[24] Moo 1996: 63.

[25] Seifrid 2007: 610.

[26] Beale and McDonough 2007: 1132.

[27] Ibid. 1149. Note also the elements of worldwide judgment from Hab. 3:6–11 in Rev. 6:12–14 (ibid. 1104) and the silence that precedes it in Hab. 2:20 and Rev. 8:1 (ibid. 1110), as well as the wounding of the beast from the sea in Rev. 13:3, which roughly parallels Hab. 3:8–15 (ibid. 1128).

the ongoing work of God in these last days, and should help foster and sustain the faith of God's people as they wait for all things to be put under Christ's feet, including all that Babylon represents in Habakkuk and Revelation.

14 Zephaniah

The book of Zephaniah provides a remarkably broad redemptive-historical perspective for its small size. Its opening chapter presents the world of the seventh century BC against the backdrop of an originally pristine creation now disfigured and corrupted by sin, and makes God's elect people (specifically Judah) its first focus. In keeping with God's plan to bring blessing to all of humanity through his chosen people, the nations are presented in relation to Israel/Judah, predominantly as their adversaries but also (although almost always in eschatological settings) as including those who will worship Yahweh alongside or even as part of God's renewed people. In Zephaniah 3 this radically new state of affairs culminates in the worship of God by his perfected people in a Jerusalem that is completely transformed by God's presence following the completion of his two-sided work of judgment and salvation. In this chapter we will focus on the different roles and identities of non-Israelites in this boldly coloured wide-angle depiction of God's redemptive plan as it intersects Judah in the late seventh century BC.

The world as part of a supra-ethnic whole to be judged (Zeph. 1:2–3, 14–18; 3:8)

In much the same way as Nahum, Zephaniah begins with a supra-ethnic perspective on the world as it is: sinful and under condemnation. In 1:2–3, the perspective is global ('the earth' [1:2]), no distinctions are made within the generic category of humankind (*ʾādām*), and the reason given for the impending divine judgment is the divine standard of righteousness that condemns the wicked (1:3).[1] Although this universal

[1] Renz (2021: 461) surveys the text-critical issues behind the translation of 'wicked'.

optic reappears in the final section of the book (3:8–20), its immediate significance is to remind the reader of the common nature of humanity under sin, apart from and prior to any secondary distinction between Israel and the nations (cf. Gen. 1 – 11).[2] The judgment announced against worldwide sin, cast in terms that surpass even the flood, is eschatological and apparently absolute. Only gradually does it become clear that this judgment will not result in the destruction of every human being. This is hinted at, with respect to Judah, by an implicit distinction between the guilty and others, then with respect to the nations, some of whom will worship Yahweh while others cling to their autonomy and so fall under judgment.

Some Judeans and some among the nations will be judged (Zeph. 1:4–13; 2:4–10, 12–15)

The rest of Zephaniah 1 is a detailed and far-ranging critique and condemnation of sin and sinners within Judah that gradually blends into the Day of Yahweh at the end of the chapter. There are incidental connections to non-Israelites in the foreign gods (1:4–5) and foreign clothing worn by some Judean officials (1:8), but the prophet attributes Judah's sins entirely to its waywardness rather than to the corrupting influence of its neighbours. The subsequent call to repentance in 2:1–3 ends with another ominous reference to the Day of Yahweh, and that introduces the first mention of non-Israelites as such in 2:4–15.

Leaving aside for the moment the distant coastlands (*'iyyîm* [2:11]) whose occupants God will radically transform, Zephaniah 2:4–15 encompasses the entire non-Israelite world by mentioning a group or nation located in each of the four cardinal directions. Taking Judah as the centre point, Zephaniah mentions the Philistines to the west (2:4–7), Moab and Ammon to the east (2:8–9), Cush to the south (2:12) and Assyria to the north (2:13–15). The conflicts that had regularly flared up between these nations and Judah (Cush excepted) make being Judah's adversary one prominent role of these nations that reflects the more general truth that these states acted as if Yahweh did not exist.

[2] Nogalski (2013) explores the contributions of Gen. 1 – 11 to this passage.

After their arrival in the Levant around 1200 BC as part of the Sea Peoples, the Philistines had a relationship to Israel that was often adversarial until Israel's early monarchy established a balance of power of sorts.[3] Although no particular offence is alleged against the Philistines in Zephaniah, we can fairly infer that some Philistines occasionally militated against Israelites in significant ways (Amos 1:6–8) during the divided monarchy as well. Despite this ambiguity, this oracle shows that God will punish the sins of those who seek to harm his people, and he will do so in connection with the purification and restoration of his people. Once restored, the remnant of Israel will possess formerly Philistine territory and enjoy security and ample provision as God's flock (2:7). Notably, the judgment of the Philistines (more precisely, of those whose antipathy towards God and his people persists) runs roughly parallel to the judgment of Judah, from which a remnant emerges in the context of judgment (1:4–13) by means of repentance (2:1–3).

The case against Moab and Ammon is clearer, and again involves the close bond between Yahweh and his people. To taunt and revile Judah (God's people [2:8]) is to impugn God's honour as well. Moab and Ammon disregard God's deeds on behalf of Israel/Judah and his self-revelation to them, and boastfully assert themselves as supreme (2:10). A striking example of this self-centred ideology is preserved in an inscription authored by Mesha, a ninth-century king of Moab. In it, he praises the deity Chemosh for delivering him 'from all kings' and 'all my enemies', including Israel, which he mistakenly asserts 'has gone to ruin for ever!'[4] While the fate of the Philistines in the previous oracle is difficult to discern, Moab and Ammon will be subjugated to the remnant of God's people, who will be purified and renewed as in 2:4–7. As we will see, however, the reference to Moab and Ammon in 2:11 ('them') reveals that some of that group will come to worship Yahweh (cf. Zeph. 3:20; Isa. 14:2; Rom. 11:18).

The passing mention of the Cushites in Zephaniah 2:12 most likely refers to their recent fall to Assyria when Esarhaddon subjugated Egypt in 663 BC, and may also have in view earlier Egyptian activity in the Levant that showed a disregard for Israel/Judah and Yahweh.[5] Be that as it may,

---

[3] Ehrlich 2016; Shai 2011.

[4] Smelik 2003: 137.

[5] Egypt under Cushite rule intervened only sporadically in the Levant; see Naunton 2014: 124–127.

the sin of self-exaltation is predominant in the oracle against Assyria that closes this section. The personified empire's soliloquy, 'I am, and there is no one else' (2:15), is cast in terms very similar to Isaiah 47:8, 10, where consummately proud and self-assured Babylon insists on its unique supremacy even in the face of Yahweh's announcement of its doom.[6] The absolute nature of the destruction threatened against Assyria (2:13) is emphasized by presenting both the disappearance of Nineveh's inhabitants and their replacement by a variety of wild animals. Compared to the subjugation of Moab and Ammon, some of whom will be integrated into God's renewed people, and to the ambiguous fate of the Philistines in 2:4–7, the blatant self-deification of Assyria evokes the most severe consequences that leave no trace of the empire as such.

Taken as a whole, Zephaniah 2:4–10, 12–15 announces judgment against all non-Israelite nations, but that judgment is sometimes definitive and other times attenuated by the survival or outright salvation of some of those concerned (see below). The way in which each group is characterized, and whether or not there is a change in that characterization, as 2:11 shows is sometimes the case, is determinative for the fate(s) of each group. In the largest possible perspective, the varied fates of the nations in this section reflect the two outcomes anticipated in Genesis 12:3, with some being blessed as they trust and follow the God of Abraham, and others falling under the curse that is the inevitable consequence of unrepentant rebellion against him and aggression against his people.

Some among the nations will be saved (Zeph. 2:11; 3:9, 14–20)

As we noted briefly in the previous section, Zephaniah 2:11 is both quite different from, and yet connected to, the surrounding oracles of judgment. Its very presence confirms that judgment is not the only or last word God speaks concerning the nations. Quite the contrary! This verse offers a potent affirmation of Yahweh's intention to save non-Israelites, including those as geographically remote and unknown as the distant isles (cf. Gen. 10:5, which uses the same term to identify the areas to which Japheth's descendants were dispersed). It is difficult to overstate the theological conflict at the heart of this verse. Yahweh will be 'awesome' (ESV)

[6] Irsigler 2002: 310.

or 'fearsome' against these nations by 'making lean' or 'destroying' every one of their gods![7]

But this is only the destructive dimension of God's saving intervention. The other dimension is radically positive, and results in all the coastlands of the nations bowing down to and worshipping Yahweh. This is nothing less than the complete transformation of those who formerly worshipped false gods into worshippers of Yahweh! Moreover, they offer him acceptable worship where they presently are rather than in Jerusalem, hinting either at a decentralized cult or the expansion of God's presence worldwide (cf. Zeph. 3:15, 17). In either case, 2:11 leaves no doubt that God will graciously enable many non-Israelites to abandon their gods and become his faithful worshippers.

The spiritual transformation of non-Israelites that 2:11 depicts in terms of worship is described from another angle in 3:9. Following a final condemnation of Judah in 3:1–7 and the transitional announcement of global judgment in 3:8 (cf. 1:2–3), 3:9 is surprising for at least two reasons: no judgment is mentioned, and the following descriptions of deliverance through spiritual renewal mention non-Israelites first before the passage moves on to consider Israelites. Most important, however, is the spiritual transformation that 3:9 describes. Yahweh will purify the speech (literally 'give a pure lip') of an unidentified group of non-Israelites with the result that they will call upon Yahweh's name and serve him in unison.

It is difficult to imagine a more complete transformation. The purification of this group's speech reflects a change that reaches the heart (Prov. 15:7; Isa. 6:5; Hos. 14:2; Matt. 15:18), and so indicates an entirely new orientation and behaviour.[8] First and foremost, these non-Israelites call on Yahweh, a standard expression of trust and dependence that recognizes his unique deity and readiness to hear the prayers of those who petition him (cf. Joel 2:32). Second, in the light of the violence that so often characterized international relations in the ancient Near East, it is striking that these peoples (the plural requires that we see at least different ethnicities if not different nationalities as well) share a commitment to serving God that predominates over every other affiliation or identifying feature. In summary, God's gracious, unsolicited salvation turns bellicose,

[7] 'Making lean' is suggested by Clines (2009: 418), and 'destroying' by Bosman (1997: 1087).

[8] Irsigler 2002: 374.

self-interested, idolatrous people into a diverse but profoundly unified group that serves him exclusively and harmoniously.

A very similar transformation, now with respect to Israelites, is described in 3:10–13.[9] Against the backdrop of a return from exile (3:10), the end result of this restoration is presented first: their worship of Yahweh, presumably at his temple. The following verses reveal the transformation that lies behind this worship. All who are proud are removed from this group (3:11), and God's renewed people are characterized by a spiritual humility and dependence that produces trust in his mercy (3:12). The radical nature of this spiritual transformation is most evident in the negative statements that 'they shall do no injustice and speak no lies' (3:13). As with the non-Israelites in 3:9, the purification of the Israelite remnant also centres on profound changes in speech and action, such that both are flawless. This similarity invites the conclusion that purified speech, and the transformed heart from which it flows, is a criterion of identity that unites as one group Yahweh's Israelite and non-Israelite worshippers. This unity relativizes all other differences without effacing them, so that God's eschatological people are indeed one but drawn from 'every tribe and language and people and nation' (Rev. 5:9).

As amazing as the transformation of sinners into worshippers of Yahweh is, Zephaniah's presentation of God's saving work goes even further, expanding to attain the same scope as the cosmic judgment seen in the book's opening verses. The last section of Zephaniah (3:14–20) reveals that the renewed people of God, both Israelite and non-Israelite, will experience the greatest possible joy and security as the fruit of God's justification of them and presence among them (3:14–17). Here the distinction between Israelites and non-Israelites is almost invisible, apart from God's final words to the renewed Israelites that seem to be addressed to them at the time of their renewal, that is, at the same time referred to in 3:10–13: 'at that time . . . when I restore your fortunes' (3:19–20). Non-Israelites appear in this context as 'all the peoples of the earth' who recognize and applaud renewed Israel's importance (3:20). In contrast to non-Israelites who do not recognize God or his people and so taunt and revile them (for example, the Moabites and Ammonites in 2:8–9), these non-Israelites readily recognize the glory and importance of God's people,

[9] For discussion of whether those in 3:10 are Israelites or not, see Timmer 2015: 162–164; Gärtner 2012.

with whom they share the deepest, strongest possible bond that unites them in worship of God. 'This combination of justification, sinlessness, and uninhibited divine presence represents the culmination of the salvation of God's people, who are with him on his holy mountain . . . never again to be threatened by sin from within or enemies from without.'[10]

Summary and New Testament developments

Zephaniah presents non-Israelites in much the same way that the canon as a whole does – first as part of a single, unified humanity, then as distinct from God's chosen people (and often in conflict with them), and finally as integrated in large numbers into renewed Israel to compose a unified group drawn from across the world that is defined by its reconciliation with and worship of God. The redemptive-historical trajectory that the book traces from creation and fall, through God's relationship with Israel, and to its eschatological renewal and consummation very naturally finds its continuation in the New Testament.[11]

In response to the global and intractable problem of sin that dominates much of the book of Zephaniah, the New Testament presents a complex but complete solution. The sins of God's people are atoned for once and for all in the sacrificial death of Jesus Christ (Rom. 5:1; Heb. 10:12–14), while the sins of those who refuse to come to him to find life will be punished at his return (Rev. 21:8). The nature of God's work of salvation in individuals, partially sketched by Zephaniah's focus on what one worships (2:11) and what one thinks and says (3:9), is significantly developed by its connection with the work of the Holy Spirit, who unites believers to Christ (John 14:23, 28; 15:4–5; Eph. 5:32; Col. 1:26–27) and gradually conforms them to his image (2 Cor. 3:18; 1 Thess. 1:6). The new-creation dimension of salvation also clarifies the relationship between the flood imagery in Zephaniah 1 and the snapshots of salvation that follow later in the book: 'the resurrected and glorified Christ, the Adam of the Spirit, now creates life of a new order, life like his own through the power of the

[10] Timmer 2024b: 12.

[11] Timmer (2024f: 229–231) and DeRouchie (2023: 889–890) note these and other specific and general connections between Zephaniah and the NT.

Spirit: *eschatological* life' (see 1 Cor. 3:16).[12] Finally, like the canon itself, Zephaniah's eschatological vision ends with God's justified (3:14), sinless, multi-ethnic people gathered as one on the eschatological Mount Zion (Heb. 12:22–24; Rev. 21:1–2), with their saviour and king 'in [their] midst' (Zeph. 3:15; cf. Rev. 21:3) and evil for ever banished (Rev. 21:27).

[12] Ferguson 1996: 252, emphasis original.

15
Haggai

Haggai's prophetic ministry, at least as recorded in Scripture, is limited to several forceful speeches to his compatriots who had returned from exile shortly after the fall of Babylon to Persia. Dated to the second half of the year 520 BC, the prophet's addresses focus largely on the rebuilding of the temple, which had begun in 538 but faltered badly thereafter. Several of the dating formulae (1:1; 2:10) serve as indirect reminders that God's people had become subjects of Persia following its conquest of the Babylonian empire in 539. However, Haggai never mentions the Persian Empire as such, nor does he refer to the empire's generally positive role with regard to the project of rebuilding the temple. Persia is presumably spared the kind of critique levelled against Assyria and Babylon because it never undertook military action against Israelites and because it provided material support and official legitimation to the Jews who returned to rebuild Jerusalem and the temple. Yet Yahweh's word concerning the nations as announced by Haggai certainly does not ignore Persia. Rather, it is simply one of the 'nations' that Yahweh will soon shake (2:7, the first passage that deals with the nations) and ultimately destroy (2:22) as he brings glory to his temple (2:7) and establishes his worldwide kingdom (2:21–23).[1] This indirect relativization of Persia carries significant theological freight since it hints at a contrast between Persian royal ideology, including its vaunted collection of the wealth of the nations it dominated, and Yahweh's universal authority and unsurpassed glory.[2]

[1] Following the suggestion of O'Kennedy (2014: 530). Rogland (2017) argues carefully that the phrase in 2:6 often translated 'Yet once more, in a little while' should be read as a verbless clause, 'One more thing is a small matter', and is a greater-to-lesser argument to the effect that since Yahweh brought his people out of Egypt, he is surely able to bring about the temple's completion and glorification through their participation.

[2] Noted by Foster (2020: 34–38); similarly, Ben Zvi 2014: 158.

The transformative shaking of the nations and Yahweh's temple (Hag. 2:1–9)

Like the first oracle in Haggai 1, the oracle in Haggai 2:1–9 is intended to motivate the returnees to persevere in the task of rebuilding the temple.[3] God's speech begins with the lacklustre condition of the still incomplete Second Temple when compared to Solomon's temple (2:3). Its unimpressive nature ought not to discourage them, however, for three reasons. God is with them by his Spirit, as he has promised in his covenant (2:4–5; cf. Exod. 29:45–46; Lev. 26:12; Deut. 6:15; Ezek. 48:35); he will 'shake' the entire creation with a focus on 'all nations' so that their treasures come to Jerusalem; and he will 'fill this house with glory' (2:6–7). As a result of this last action in particular, the first temple's glory will be surpassed by that of the second, even though the latter was physically smaller, and there Yahweh will grant holistic well-being (*šālôm* [2:9]).

The nature of the 'shaking' here is not as negative as is sometimes thought, and is clearly different from that mentioned in 2:20–23.[4] In the light of the radical nature of the superlative glorification of the Second Temple that God promises, it should probably be understood as eschatological, and it indubitably has a remarkable effect on the nations. John Kessler observes that when Yahweh shakes (*r-ʿ-š*) the earth or nations, he typically does so in response to their aggression against Jerusalem, but through that intervention brings about their submission to him and worship of him.[5] There is no hint of military opposition against Yehud here, unlike the military language in 2:20–23. Thus, God's 'greatness and might' are evident in the shaking of the 'impersonal' heavens and earth, and his shaking of 'all nations' in 2:7 produces 'trembling' and 'fear' among them without any clear indications of destruction.[6] Further, if we recall that Persia under Cyrus and Darius had already committed its first round of financial and material support to the rebuilding of the temple (Ezra 1:4, 6, 7–8; 5:13–17; 6:8–10; later, Ezra 7:15–23), and give due weight to the international scope of the phrase 'all nations', the shaking of

[3] Foster 2020: 36.

[4] Contrast Tiemeyer 2017: 5–6.

[5] Kessler 1987: 165.

[6] Ibid. 162.

the nations in 2:7 and the wealth that would come to the temple cannot refer to Persian contributions to the reconstruction of the Jerusalem temple.[7] Moreover, the revelation of Yahweh's overwhelming glory will transform the nations into his worshippers. These considerations favour viewing the nations' contributions to Yahweh's temple which symbolizes his rule (2:7) as literal or metaphorical vassal payments that reflect their recognition of his unmatched importance and supremacy and their consequent submission to him.[8]

Keeping in mind that Haggai does not draw attention to or contest Persian hegemony, the brief glance into the future that this oracle affords is still profoundly subversive of human structures of power, particularly those as developed, widespread and theologically articulated as Persia's. The Cyrus Cylinder, which lies behind the summary in Ezra 1 of Cyrus's permission to the Judean exiles to return home, makes clear the extent of Persia's claims less than two decades before Haggai's oracles:

> I, Cyrus, king of the universe, mighty king, king of Babylon, king of Sumer and Akkad, king of the four quarters . . . eternal seed of kingship, whose reign was loved by Bel and Nabu and whose kingship they wanted to please their hearts . . . Marduk, the great lord, rejoiced at my [good] deeds. Me, Cyrus, the king . . . he blessed mercifully . . . [At his] great [command] all the kings, who sit on thrones, from all parts of the world, from the Upper Sea to the Lower Sea, who dwell [in distant regions], all the kings of Amurru, who dwell in tents, brought their heavy tribute to me and kissed my feet in Babylon . . . The lands in their totality I caused to dwell in a peaceful abode.[9]

In addition to textual sources, Persian rulers left extensive iconographic evidence of Persian royal ideology. For example, the bas-reliefs at Persepolis leading to the Apadana audience hall flank two massive staircases and are approximately 50 metres in length.[10] Depicting twenty-three different groups bringing tribute to Darius, they portray very impressively 'the grandeur of royal power, the greatness of the empire, and the majesty

[7] Timmer 2015: 172.

[8] Meyers and Meyers 1987: 53; Petterson 2015: 69.

[9] Kuhrt 2007: 72–73.

[10] Curtis 2005: 34.

of the royal religion'.[11] The audience hall itself could accommodate 10,000 guests 'at ground level alone',[12] and the doorjambs of the many entries in the palace complex were decorated with images of 'the king or "Persian hero figure" fighting a bull, a lion, or a griffin; the king with the crown prince or attendants . . . or subject peoples supporting the enthroned king under a canopy'.[13]

These examples of Persian imperial ideology, drawn from one of many such sites, leave no doubt that Yahweh's claims to supremacy and his promise to establish his Davidic king over all nations (2:22) are diametrically opposed to the project of Cyrus and the gods he invoked, which claimed universal rule and authority, received tribute from across the world, and sought to establish and maintain widespread peace, thus creating an ideal world.[14] As shown in chapter 2 of this volume, however, these two kingdoms are radically different in nature, since recognition of Yahweh's absolute otherness with respect to creation fundamentally reconfigures the nature and status of human beings, the contexts in which they can relate harmoniously to God and others, and much more. Conflict between these two world views and their adherents is thus inevitable. Although the first shaking that Haggai describes invites individuals regardless of nationality into Yahweh's kingdom, the second (2:20–23) will fully and finally realize God's rule over even his most self-obsessed, recalcitrant opponents.

The destructive shaking of the nations and Yahweh's kingdom (Hag. 2:20–23)

The oracle examined above shows that worship of Yahweh is not restricted to Israelites but is possible for anyone, anywhere (cf. Joel 2:32). That perspective contrasts sharply with the characterization of the nations in the book's final oracle. There they are portrayed as already in combat with Yahweh, who will soon destroy them (Hag. 2:21–22). The violent nature of the conflict – better, of Yahweh's victory – is emphasized in numerous ways. God's 'greatness and might' are evident as he shakes the created

[11] Dandamaev and Lukonin 2004: 243, cited in Chan 2017: 174.

[12] Curtis and Razmjou 2005: 54.

[13] Curtis 2005: 34.

[14] Wiesehöfer 2009: 88–89.

order,[15] and his shaking of the 'throne of kingdoms' and 'kingdoms of the nations' (v. 22) is explained in terms of him 'overthrowing' (*h-p-k*; cf. Gen. 19:25), 'destroying' and 'bringing down' those enemies.[16] Yahweh's opponents are also involved in one another's downfall, 'every one by the sword of his brother' (2:22).[17] The verb 'overthrow' in 2:22 is particularly significant in the light of its use in Genesis 19:21, 25, 29 (Sodom and Gomorrah, also echoed in Deut. 29:23; Jer. 49:18; 50:40; Amos 4:11).[18] Similarly, the references to horses and their riders echo Yahweh's victory over Egypt at the Reed Sea (Exod. 15:1, 21; cf. Ps. 76:6). The connections with Exodus 15 also suggest that a second exodus – more precisely, the completion of Israel's return from exile – will be fully realized when Yahweh intervenes against his enemies and for the salvation of his people.[19]

The final element of this oracle develops the second-exodus theme by introducing the Davidic ruler who will serve Yahweh as vice-regent of his people (2:23; cf. Jer. 22:24–30; 23:5–8, which also mentions a second exodus). God's people, composed of Israelites and non-Israelites who recognize his unique claim on them as their creator, trust in his justice and mercy, and know Yahweh's presence through his Spirit (Hag. 2:5). 'The climax of the book . . . focuses on the eschatological expectation that YHWH will restore the Davidic kingdom or dynasty' through which Yahweh will rule over a world purged of sin and characterized by profound peace.[20]

Summary and New Testament developments

Kenneth Ristau suggests that Haggai 'promotes a carefully considered, pragmatic, and clearly provisional approach to imperial authority, which

---

[15] Kessler 1987: 162.

[16] Foster (2020: 45) suggests that this 'throne' is Persia, which is plausible as long as that event is seen as a small, partial fulfilment of this prophecy; Jacobs (2017: 120) adds Egypt, Greece, 'and any emerging powers', which would still constitute only a partial, near-term fulfilment.

[17] Petterson (2015: 84) notes that such self-inflicted destruction is also prominent in Judg. 7:22; Ezek. 38:21; Zech. 14:13. Wolff (1988: 103) observes that fratricide is 'one of the main themes of the Behistun inscriptions'.

[18] O'Kennedy 2014: 531.

[19] Foster 2020: 35.

[20] O'Kennedy 2014: 538. Timmer (2015: 175) observes that '[t]he nations of Hag 2:6–7 seem to remain in their historical territories' even as Yahweh's temple at Jerusalem is central to the new creation.

emphasizes Yahweh's primary, if not exclusive role, as patron of the temple, the community, and the Judean leadership'.[21] This captures many of the features of the material dealing with the nations survey above, but does not take account of the emphatically *global* nature of Yahweh's rule that culminates in definitive and final salvation and judgment. The status quo is not going to remain in place, and whatever beneficence Persia showed and whatever magnificence it enjoyed, that empire will crumble along with the rest of the present order when Yahweh comes to defeat his enemies and fill his temple with glory, bringing perfect peace through his Davidic king.

The New Testament develops each of these themes in strikingly Christological ways. The second temple ('this house' [Hag. 2:7, 9]), completed within a few years of Haggai's ministry, surpassed the glory of the first only by virtue of hosting the temporary presence of God incarnate (Matt. 21:14–15; Luke 2:49), who was himself the superlative fulfilment of God's promise to be present among his people (John 1:14).[22] Both the First and Second Temples were completely surpassed and superseded by the appearance of God in Jesus Christ (Mark 14:58; John 2:19), and the riches of the nations that come to Christ-as-temple are those who are united to him by faith and offer themselves to him as sacrifices of thanksgiving (Rom. 12:1).[23] Indeed, as those who are united to Christ and to one another by the Spirit, believers are themselves 'temples' of God in the Spirit (1 Cor. 6:19–20) and part of the eschatological temple of which Christ is the cornerstone (1 Cor. 3:16–17; 2 Cor. 6.16; Eph. 2:20–22; 1 Pet. 2:4–8).[24] As Dominique Angers notes, 'It is impossible to imagine a community closer to God, or a community in which the members are closer to one another', than this spiritual temple.[25] This is especially true when viewed in terms of the relationship of non-Israelites to the temple:

> The Old Testament announced simply that at the end of time, non-Jews would come to the Jerusalem temple to worship Yahweh

[21] Ristau 2016: 121.

[22] Verhoef (1987: 109) notes, following Ridderbos, that 'more proselytes' came to the Second Temple than to the first.

[23] Petterson (2015: 71) helpfully summarizes the import of Hag. 2:1–9 as a dramatic 'transformation' of the Second Temple.

[24] McKelvey 2000: 808–810.

[25] Angers 2021: 145 (my translation).

> alongside Jews . . . Paul indicates here [in Eph. 2:20–22] the surprising and glorious way that this prophecy has been realized. The reality surpasses the expectation. Not only do Jews and non-Jews *go to the temple together* but . . . reconciled by the blood of Christ, together they form the true temple![26]

The shaking of the nations that Haggai foresaw began at Christ's first coming and will be consummated at his return. The book of Acts and the epistles bear witness to God's gracious power at work among the nations, who give their material wealth (2 Cor. 8:3–5; 9:5), their praise (Heb. 13:15; Jas 5:13) and themselves to God (Rom. 12:1; Eph. 1:12; Phil. 1:9–11) in response to his saving mercy. The final eschatological shaking also has a negative or punitive side, from which God is the only protection (Heb. 12:29). The 'removal' of all that is temporal, imperfect and evil brings with it the establishment of the only 'kingdom that cannot be shaken' (Heb. 12:28–29). In that kingdom, as Haggai's theological landscape anticipates, Christ and God as the temple (Rev. 21:3, 22) are its glory (21:23), the nations and their glory enter it (21:24, 26), and the unending reign of the triune God marks the end point of the second exodus of God's eschatological people and the full realization of the new creation (Exod. 15:17–18; Rev. 21:1; 22:1, 3).

[26] Ibid. 145–146 (my translation).

16
Zechariah

The book of Zechariah is complex in many ways, including its treatment of non-Israelites. Different nations, at different times, pursue their designs while Yahweh's people languish (1:15), will be plundered by God's restored people (2:9), are the eschatological repository of wickedness (5:5–11) and become impassioned worshippers of Yahweh (8:22–23). This chapter attempts to maintain the productive relationship between unity and diversity that animates biblical-theological reflection by examining passages that unite key elements of Zechariah's message (judgment, Israel's restoration, and the salvation or judgment of non-Israelites) in various ways. To that end, the sections that follow identify several different paradigms in which God's purification and renewal of his people are connected to similar actions involving non-Israelites. Although each paradigm is distinct, they complement one another and have in common crucially important distinctions within Israel and among the nations that reflect either submission to or rejection of Yahweh. Recognizing that Israelite prophecy typically leaves the relative chronology of the stages of God's future work rather vague, this chapter is content to leave unspecified, when clarity is not possible, the chronology of the various events that Zechariah foresees occurring between the beginning of God's superlative restoration of Israel and its consummation in the New Jerusalem.[1]

Judgment of nations, restoration of Jerusalem, integration of non-Israelites (Zech. 1:7 – 2:13; 6:1–8; 8:20–23)

Zechariah's first vision report (1:7–17, dated to 520 BC) takes as its starting point the partially restored condition of Judah and Jerusalem. Yahweh's

[1] See the wise remarks of Wolters (2014: 454) to this effect.

ardent concern for the restoration of his people marks the end of his anger against them (1:12–13) and is contrasted with the inertness of the nations, who exceeded their divine mandate as the instrument of God's punishment of his people. The nations have wrongly assumed that all is well, and Yahweh is extremely angry that in these circumstances they remain insouciant and 'at ease', as if Yahweh and his people were pawns on their geopolitical chessboard (1:15).

Judgment and destruction of the enemies of God's people

The prominent mention of God's anger against the geopolitical enemies of his people (1:15) is immediately followed by a vision of the defeat or destruction of the four 'horns that have scattered Judah, Israel, and Jerusalem' (1:19) by the four craftsmen in the second vision report (1:18–21).[2] In the eighth and final oracle report (6:1–8), which complements the first, the nations' self-contentment will be definitively ended by God's punishment and destruction of them (1:21; 2:9) and superseded by the permanent 'rest' of Yahweh's Spirit (6:8) in the very location that had formerly been the centre of the nations' power (cf. 2:6, 7; 5:11).

The restoration of Jerusalem/Zion

The third vision report (2:1–5) foresees the radical expansion of Jerusalem, whose population will far exceed the city's capacity (2:4). This apparent problem is in reality an indication of massive redemptive-historical progress, both in the multiplication of God's people and in Yahweh being a wall around his people and 'the glory in her midst' (2:5). This oracle essentially sees partially rebuilt Jerusalem with its incomplete temple and spiritually tepid population changed into a city defined by Yahweh's presence and populated by those who are reconciled with him, both Israelites and non-Israelites.

The integration of foreigners into restored Israel as *Yahweh's people*

Throughout Zechariah, the fates of the nations are inseparable from the nature of their interaction with Yahweh and his people. It is thus quite

[2] While historical referents are certainly plausible (Assyria, Babylon, Persia and Greece are most likely), the symbolic nature of the vision makes it equally plausible to see the 'four' as representing generic enemies on all sides; cf. Boda 2016: 160.

natural for them to appear in the middle of the following vision report (2:6–13). Reprising the theme of the earlier visions, 2:8–9 announces that Yahweh will render powerless ('shake [his] hand over') Judah's former enemies. Yet in the same context, Yahweh states: 'Many nations shall join themselves to [Yahweh] in that day, and shall be my people' (2:11). In this remarkable sequence, a *new* subgroup or remnant of non-Israelites is formed, as 'many nations' join themselves to Yahweh in an exclusive, holistic way.[3] Even more unexpected is Yahweh's authoritative declaration that these non-Israelites are 'my people'. This phrase is used of Israel very frequently in the Old Testament (see Zech. 8:8; Lev. 26:12; Deut. 4:20; etc.), but only here and in a few other places (e.g. Isa. 19:25) is the title applied to foreigners.[4] This expression leaves no doubt as to the spiritual identity of restored Israel/Judah and the full integration of non-Israelites *in that group*.

A similar trajectory is evident in the oracle announcing future worship of Yahweh by non-Israelites at Jerusalem (8:20–23). This passage is an outcome of Zion's superlative restoration (8:1–20), which involves God's presence among the remnant of his people (8:3), their faithfulness to him and consequent flourishing (8:4–5), a perfected covenant relationship (8:8) and divine blessing (8:13).[5] As a response to this glorious act of salvation on Israel's behalf, the 'peoples' and 'inhabitants of many cities' (undoubtedly non-Israelites) stream to Jerusalem in a multinational pilgrimage (8:20–23).[6] In fact, it is more than a mere pilgrimage if that is understood in simply geographic terms. Described as 'seeking Yahweh of Hosts' and 'entreating his favour' (see 8:22), these non-Israelites recognize God as worthy of exclusive worship and total submission. Their positive response to Israel's radical renewal is also in sharp contrast to their earlier antipathy. The proportions in the image of 'ten men from the nations of every tongue' petitioning a single Jew to accompany him to Jerusalem (8:23) make clear that a 'vast number' of individuals from among the

[3] Kellermann 1995: 476. For other uses with non-Israelites, see Isa. 14:1; 56:3, 6 (with strong covenantal elements); for use with Israelites, see Jer. 50:5, with 'covenant'.

[4] Timmer (2024a: 50) proposes that this action presupposes election; cf. Isa. 56:3, 6.

[5] In the light of the identical syntax of 'you were an object of cursing' in 8:13a, 8:13b states that restored Israel will be an 'object of blessing', as Boda (2016: 498) notes. Meyers and Meyers (1987: 424) and Petterson (2015: 208) see here an allusion to Gen. 12:3.

[6] The presence of a 'Jew' (8:23) en route to Jerusalem is one point in favour of seeing 8:20–21 as referring to non-Israelites. For other arguments in favour of seeing all the actors in 8:20–23 as non-Israelites, see Boda 2016: 512.

nations will be added to restored Israel's population as fellow worshippers of Yahweh.[7] This image develops in a dramatic way the idea that 'many nations' will become worshippers of Yahweh (2:11), and closes Zechariah 1 – 8 on a truly glorious note.[8]

Judgment, transformation and integration of foreigners (Zech. 9:1–17)

The sudden switch from salvation for non-Israelites in 8:20–23 to an oracle against Israel's enemies in the Levant in 9:1–6 reminds the reader that the same grammatical terms, whether proper nouns or not, can refer to different groups depending on their context. Indeed, in this very section a group of non-Israelites that is desolated and humbled will nonetheless become a 'remnant' for Yahweh (9:7), demonstrating that *the same term* can shift its referent *within a single passage*. Chapter 9 also juxtaposes the arrival of renewed Zion's king and the establishment of his kingdom through peace with God's use of his people to vanquish his and their foes.

Retribution against God's enemies among the nations

The unusual statement in Zechariah 9:1 that Yahweh has his eye 'on mankind and on all the tribes of Israel' hints at the close but complex relation between the two groups in this chapter, frequently summarized in the universal–particular distinction.[9] The reference to the nation-states of Tyre and Sidon includes concise grounds for their punishment. These two cities, both of which were well-established centres of trade and commerce, are presented in 9:2 as being 'very wise' (that is, in their own eyes; cf. Ezek. 28). Tyre's extensive fortifications and advantageous location just off the Phoenician coast enabled it to resist a thirteen-year siege by Babylon (585–572 BC), and its economic success outshone that of Sidon for a time.[10] Its excessive accumulation of wealth implies that Tyre had given inordinate importance to material riches in dependence on its

---

[7] Petterson 2015: 210. Meyers and Meyers (1987: 441) note the tone of importunity and submission entailed by the act of grasping the hem of another's garment.

[8] Tiemeyer 2017: 9.

[9] See Levenson 1996.

[10] Elat 1991.

economic *savoir faire*, a critique developed at length in Ezekiel 27. Its fall will demonstrate the foolishness of its self-reliance and the ephemeral nature of its riches.

Integration of some non-Israelites into renewed Israel *as Israelites*

The fall of Tyre (and presumably of Sidon as well) will inspire fear among the cities that formerly constituted the Philistine pentapolis but which figure in surprising ways in the following prophecy 'of the future restoration of the Davidic empire'.[11] It seems that they too are weakened (or worse) by events that the text only hints at, not least because of their pride (9:6). But their downfall is not God's final word: Yahweh will transform some of these same adversaries in radical ways. Zechariah's sketch of how this takes place is painted in bold colours, with Yahweh removing all obstacles to these non-Israelites becoming his people. The process begins at a most unpromising point: in Philistia (with its anti-Israel connotations) and, just as unpromisingly, with 'one of illegitimate birth' (9:6, my translation).[12] Moreover, this outsider, who is normally inadmissible in Israel's worship (Deut. 23:1–8), currently eats meat or sacrifices containing blood (Zech. 9:7), a practice prohibited not only for Israel but for all humanity (Gen. 9:6)!

None of these characteristics or the spiritual deadness that some of them reveal put the members of this group beyond the reach of Yahweh's purifying and transforming power. The removal of the 'abominations' from their teeth (9:7) is permanent, and reflects a radical change of behaviour and of belief that makes them part of Yahweh's restored people. The transformation of Philistines and others (the ethnic origins of those who settle in Ashdod in Zech. 9:6 is unknown) produces a *new* 'remnant for our God' from among the nations that will – despite initially being as different from Israel as possible – 'be like a clan in Judah, and . . . like the Jebusites' (9:7)! These non-Israelites are made Israelites in the fullest sense and in a remarkable manner, and that by the direct action of God himself.

[11] Petterson 2015: 220. This may reflect David's neutralization of the Philistine threat for an unspecified time (2 Sam 8:1); no further conflicts with Philistines are reported in the OT until Hezekiah's reign (Tsumura 2019: 152), but complete peace seems unlikely (cf. Amos 1:6–8).

[12] Hebrew *mamzēr* refers to a 'non-Judean' (Clines 2009: 225) or person of mixed descent (Koehler and Baumgartner 2001: 595). The presence of such persons among those whom Yahweh transforms into his remnant supersedes the cultic regulation of Deut. 23:2 much as Isa. 56:1–8 does.

Henceforth they *belong to Yahweh*,[13] who watches over them from his temple-city (Zech. 9:8; cf. 2:5).

Transformation or judgment of non-Israelites

The rest of Zechariah 9 pursues a similar division of the non-Israelite world. On the one hand, the messianic king eliminates weapons of war from Israel and speaks 'peace to the nations' (9:10), transforming God's enemies into subjects.[14] This unilateral, non-violent pacification of *some of* the nations creates a global kingdom characterized by 'righteousness' and 'salvation' (9:9).[15] On the other hand, 9:14–17 depicts Yahweh using his restored people as his weapons against Greece in terms that echo the first exodus (9:13–14). The snapshot of a moment of the battle in 9:13 captures the judgment–salvation pair that summarizes the kingdom's double aspect. Greece, representing a distant and fearsome opponent, is fully committed to its effort to repulse God's rule, and God's use of Zion's sons as his sword is a relatively rare case in which 'God's people are an integral part of his action as divine warrior, an instrument in his hands'.[16]

Judgment *and* deliverance of Jerusalem *and* the nations, integration of foreigners (Zech. 14:1–21)

Zechariah's final chapter presents a third perspective on the twofold relationship between Yahweh and the non-Israelite nations that complements the two examined above. The chapter can be divided into two halves (14:1–11, 12–21), each of which moves from an initial conflict between the nations and Jerusalem, through Yahweh's intervention that definitively ends the conflict, to a new, permanent and ideal situation for the remnants of Israel and of the nations.[17] The integration of non-Israelites into the eschatological community that worships Yahweh is limited to the second half of the chapter (14:16–19). The content of Zechariah 12:1–9

[13] Petterson 2015: 220; Boda 2016: 554–555.

[14] See Timmer 2015: 187–188.

[15] Fischer 2012: 131.

[16] Wolters 2014: 288.

[17] The remnant here may or may not include those who are exiled, but does not include those who are 'cut off'; cf. 13:8–9; see ibid. 455; Boda 2016: 751–752; Meyers and Meyers 1993: 415–417.

aligns well with chapter 14, at least in its main lines, and a few points of correspondence are noted below.[18]

Judgment of God's people (punishment) and their enemies (deliverance)

As was the case with Jerusalem's first exile (Zech. 1), the plans of the nations to do as they wish with God's people ultimately serve Yahweh's purposes despite the implementation of those plans by sinful human actors. Like the exile of Judah at the hands of Babylon, this attack on Jerusalem is also punitive, and half of its population will be exiled and 'cut off' from the city (14:2). But this is not the end: Yahweh himself will fight 'against those nations' (14:3; similarly, 12:4, 8–9) and God's victory leads to the establishment of his undisputed reign 'over all the earth' (14:9), with his name alone being recognized and worshipped (cf. 12:3).[19]

The negative presentation of non-Israelites continues in the second half of Zechariah 14, according to which a divine plague will strike the 'peoples' that waged war on Jerusalem and against Yahweh (14:12; cf. 12:3). Following their confusion and self-destruction, they will be despoiled in fulfilment of 14:1, and Jerusalem's spoil will be returned to her (14:13–15).

Restoration of Jerusalem and integration of non-Israelites *as worshippers of Yahweh*

From the violence described in Zechariah 14, Jerusalem emerges quite suddenly in a completely different condition. Radically restored, fully inhabited, perfectly secure, and elevated above its surroundings (cf. Isa. 2; Mic. 4), it has become a perpetual source of fresh water that will bring life as far as the Dead Sea and the Mediterranean (cf. Joel 3). Jerusalem also becomes the destination for non-Israelites who had waged war against it but survived Yahweh's intervention on its behalf. Rather than pursuing further aggression in pursuit of their self-serving goals, these *spiritually transformed* nations will celebrate the feast of Booths as an expression of their worship of Yahweh, 'the King, [Yahweh] of Hosts' (14:16), who

---

[18] For fuller discussion of the nations in 12:1–9, see Timmer 2015: 188–189.

[19] Boda 2016: 767. It seems less likely that, as Tiemeyer proposes (2017: 9), Yahweh's kingship in 14:9 does not include the subjection of the survivors, but 14:16–18 encourages caution on this question.

has brought about an eschatological exodus that liberated them to serve him.[20]

The chronological challenges mentioned earlier are particularly evident in 14:17–18, since Yahweh's apparently complete victory over evil (14:12–15; also 14:9; 12:4–6, 9) seems to coexist with the possibility that some survivors would *not* celebrate him as their saviour or worship him as their God (14:17–18). It is possible that this refusal to recognize Yahweh as King is merely hypothetical, in which case the world's Yahwistic worship centred on Jerusalem is a fully eschatological scenario, as in 14:9. Alternatively, if the refusal of some to worship Yahweh is a real possibility, the threat of drought and plague (14:17–18) would seem likely to lead ineluctably to their destruction, ushering in a fully eschatological state of affairs. The first option (opposition as a hypothetical possibility) is perhaps more likely given Jerusalem's absolute holiness and the temple's inviolate purity with respect to 'Canaanite' presence (14:21, ESV footnote), a reference to those unsuited for worship of Yahweh in his temple (cf. Isa. 52:1; Joel 3:17; Nah. 1:15).[21]

Summary and New Testament developments

André Lacocque's summary of Zechariah 14 serves well as a synthesis of the redemptive-historical dynamics that drive the developments seen in the theme of the nations throughout the book:

> The conflict, instead of being between Israel and the nations, is now between good and evil . . . [T]he historical circumstances demand a distinction, within the people [of Israel], between those who are the faithful remnant . . . and those who are to be exiled, as the sheep of chapter 11 were to be slaughtered. In parallel with this, the nations are not uniformly all under judgment and destined for destruction.[22]

[20] Wolters (2014: 469) sees possible ideological significance in the similar dates for the feast of Booths and the Persian New Year festival.

[21] For the alternative view, see Boda 2016: 778–781. Webb (2004: 182) argues that 'Canaanite' 'is almost certainly metaphorical for "idolater" here', with reference to Zech. 13:2 and Israel's history in Canaan more generally. This option also seems favoured by several images of a second exodus, e.g. 9:1–6; 10:11; 14:1. See further Meyers and Meyers 1993: 489–492.

[22] Lacocque 1981: 199 (my translation).

The full establishment of God's kingdom involves the large-scale integration of non-Israelites alongside the faithful Israelite remnant, and both enjoy the same access to God's superlative presence (2:5, 11). Indeed, all the major redemptive-historical advances, including the arrival of the messianic king (9:9–10), the full removal of sin and its consequences from God's restored people (5:5–11), the supernatural multiplication of their number (10:10) and perfect peace (9:10), will be shared in equal measure by all of Yahweh's newly multiplied people.

Most of these themes are taken up by New Testament authors, who understand them in relation to Christ's work of redemption that began with his incarnation and will be completed upon his return. The authors celebrate the full inclusion of the nations in renewed Israel. Christ's blood is 'poured out for many' (Mark 14:24; cf. Zech. 12:10; 13:7; John 19:37), including the Roman centurion (Mark 15:39).[23] As the Messiah, Christ rules over all things (1 Cor. 15:27; Eph. 1:20–22) and brings peace (Luke 1:79)[24] through the gospel, notably to Gentiles (John 14:27; Acts 10:36, where the 'good news of peace through Jesus Christ (he is Lord of all)' aligns well with Zech. 9:10).[25] The prodigious expansion of the gospel in Acts, beginning with Jews (Acts 2:41; 4:4) and extending to Gentiles (Acts 11:24; 14:21; 17:12; etc.), has a worldwide trajectory from the very beginning (Col. 1:6). Finally, as every book of the New Testament attests, '[e]nemies remain, both outside . . . and within' the church, and the church's struggle is not yet won, but the outcome is sure.[26] With that certitude in mind, the church's primary vocation remains 'to call on all people to recognize the triune God . . . as the one true King over all the earth' in fulfilment of Zechariah's vision.[27]

[23] Hill 2023: 884–885; Timmer 2023c; see further Duguid 2000: 260.

[24] Köstenberger 2007: 472.

[25] Ibid. 490–491; Cole 2023: 781.

[26] Duguid 2000: 259.

[27] Petterson 2018: 728.

17
Malachi

Although Malachi's message is focused on the community composed of those who had returned from exile to their former homeland, Israel's role as the agent for God's purposes in the world means that the nations are never completely out of view. Indeed, Malachi's strong emphasis on the purification of God's people and the emergence of a faithful remnant reveals that ethnicity is not the basis on which God dispenses grace and favour. That fundamental truth also shines through in God's assertion that many non-Israelites will come to know and revere him as he extends his kingdom far beyond the boundaries of Yehud.

Some non-Israelites as God's opponents: Edom (Mal. 1:2–5)

God's dispute with Israel in Malachi begins with a foundational feature of redemptive history: God has loved Israel (1:2). The kind of love referred to here is not an emotion, but a profound commitment that is inseparable from God's election of Jacob and that contrasts with his non-election of Esau (Gen. 25:23).[1] This election is rooted in the earlier covenant with Abraham and eventually takes form in the covenant with Israel that is inaugurated at Sinai. The post-exilic community's doubt that they are still the object of Yahweh's love reflects their difficulty in reconciling their status as God's covenant people with hardships or misunderstandings, and even leads them to think otherwise. That being said, their identity as God's elect people is not exhaustively defined with reference to their ties to Jacob, as shown by Malachi's later condemnations and insistence on

[1] Kaminsky (2007: 107–110) has advanced discussion of election in the HB/OT by introducing 'non-elect' as a neutral category between elect and anti-elect. The 'pro-elect' category proposed by Billing (2013: 39–40) clarifies the identity of non-Israelites who 'aid in and further' God's purposes.

radical repentance as necessary to receive the blessings promised in God's covenants with Abraham and Israel.

As the counterpart of his electing, covenantal love for Israel, God's 'hatred' for Esau designates his non-election of Esau, not his definitive rejection of him (see 1:3).[2] However, when it comes to Edom in Malachi's day, referred to as Esau's 'hill country' and 'heritage', things are different.[3] Due to Edom's adversarial behaviour against Israel (Amos 1:11–12; Obadiah; etc.), God has already punished the people (*ʿam*) of Edom (1:3), probably a reference to Babylon's subjugation of Edom in about 552 BC.[4] Some Edomites' stubborn commitment to their autonomy is evident in the pairing of their recognition that Yahweh had 'shattered' Edom and their resolution to 'rebuild the ruins', that is, to attempt to nullify Yahweh's condemnation of them (1:4). By presenting Edom's intentions verbatim, as it were, Malachi makes its self-determination and self-vindication central to its identity, while revealing that its ideology rejects God's sovereign punishment of it.

This characterization of Edom, which spans centuries and is justified on theological and historical grounds alike, implies that its commitment to its ideology is essentially static and unchanging. Consequently, God will undo whatever this 'Edom' undertakes and make the 'wicked' (*rišʿâ* [1:4]) territory the object of his perpetual anger. It is important to recognize that this negative moral evaluation is not levelled against Edom's population as a whole, but against those Edomites who ignore Israel's chosen status and refuse to recognize Yahweh's absolute supremacy, including his commitment to bless the nations *through* Israel (cf. 3:12). God's promise to destroy Edom *defined in these terms* is thus his promise to destroy those who threaten his people and reject him as the 'great King' (1:14) to whose beneficent rule they should submit. The exclamation in 1:5, 'Great is [Yahweh] beyond the border of Israel!', probably means that '[t]he exercise of God's sovereign action against Edom is a portent of what YHWH will do among the nations generally',[5] with the same focused definition of the nations as those who are committed to opposing Yahweh's

[2] This point is carefully argued by Bergey (2021). The theme of election in Malachi is examined by Timmer (2024a: 59–60).

[3] Wielenga (2022: 6) refers to Edom's participation in Jerusalem's destruction as 'the point of no return'.

[4] See Tebes 2023.

[5] Goswell 2013: 628.

claims upon them. Happily, God's action against those who obstinately resist his claims upon them hardly excludes the possibility that he would show grace to non-Israelites.

Some non-Israelites as God's worshippers (Mal. 1:11, 14)

If taken in isolation from the rest of Malachi, God's harsh words against Edom's flagrant rejection of his plans and people might be taken as self-congratulatory Israelite propaganda. Such a misconception is prevented by the following six disputations, which constitute the majority of the book of Malachi. And, surely not by chance, the first disputation (1:6 – 2:9) presents scathing critiques of Israel as a whole and of its priesthood in particular. These denunciations contrast what Israel *should be* as Yahweh's covenant 'son' and servant with what it is (by and large) at present: a son who does not honour his father, a servant who does not fear his master, and priests who 'despise' Yahweh's name, that is, all that he has shown himself to be, especially in relation to Israel (1:6).

These dispositions, like the beliefs regarding oneself and Yahweh that underlie them, strike at the heart of the covenant relationship that gave Israel its special status in the first place. This point is made in the most emphatic way by the fact that worship of Yahweh at his temple, with its massive theological significance and detailed prescriptions of proper procedure, is so corrupt that God wishes it would end (1:10)!

Ideal worshippers of God

It is at this critical point in God's covenantal critique of Israel that a group of non-Israelites – radically different from the Edom of 1:2–5 and from the Israelites referred to in 1:6–10 – is introduced in 1:11.[6] In contrast to the priests who despise Yahweh's name, there will be 'among the nations' those who know and affirm that Yahweh's name is 'great' and offer 'pure' offerings (contrast the polluted sacrifices in 1:7, 12, and the rejected

[6] Tiemeyer (2017: 12) notes that 'among the nations' (1:11) could conceivably refer to Israelites outside the land, but that would undermine the intense critique of the Israelite people that is the focus of the second disputation in relation to the divine name (so Kessler 2011: 150) and would validate cultic worship by Jews apart from the temple, something Malachi does not contemplate (contrast 3:4). Further, the other use of *gôyîm* (3:12) presents a similar contrast between Israel (in the land) and non-Israelites (outside the land).

offerings in 1:10).[7] This future reality is described in 1:14 in terms that unambiguously entail these non-Israelites' wholehearted commitment to Yahweh as their God: 'my name will be feared among the nations' as the 'great King'. This further sharpens the contrast with many Israelites in Malachi's society, as does God's statement that this worship will not take place at the Jerusalem temple but 'in every place' where such non-Israelite worshippers are found (1:11)![8] No indication is given of how Yahweh's word will come to these non-Israelites, but their recognition of his name ('Yahweh of Hosts') is one of several factors that suggest that they do not enter this relationship apart from his people.[9]

An identity that overlaps with that of Israel's repentant, restored remnant (Mal. 3:16–18)

Taken in isolation from its context, Malachi 1:6 – 2:9 might be misconstrued as a blanket condemnation of Israelites, much as 1:2–5 might seem to be a rejection of all non-Israelites or a vindication of all Israelites. But Malachi's presentation of both groups is nuanced, and he makes distinctions *within* the larger groups of Israelites and non-Israelites alike. Nowhere does Malachi make a distinction within post-exilic Israel more clearly than in the final disputation (3:13 – 4:3).[10] The same themes seen earlier reappear here, as some Israelites question the value of serving Yahweh (3:14) and pronounce blessings on the arrogant, believing that those who do evil (*riš'â*) 'not only prosper' but also defy God's holiness and justice with impunity (3:15; also 2:17). This unfaithful subgroup within Israel is contrasted with its faithful counterpart, namely, those Israelites who fear Yahweh and hold his name in high regard (3:16). Faithful Israelites thus share a fundamental criterion of identity with the non-Israelites described in 1:11, 14, where Yahweh's name is the object of worship and reverence four times.[11]

Near the end of the final disputation, Yahweh makes this contrast within Israel absolute by *redefining Israel* in terms of its remnant: 'They

---

[7] For arguments in favour of understanding acceptable worship of Yahweh by non-Israelites here as not yet a reality in Malachi's day, see Timmer 2015: 210–214.

[8] Fischer (2012: 134) notes the prominence of Yahweh's name and fame throughout Malachi.

[9] Timmer 2024a: 61.

[10] Snyman (2015: 162) notes that this 'disputation' nonetheless has several unique features. On inner-Israel/Judah distinctions in the OT, see Ben Zvi 1995; Apóstolo 2006.

[11] Scalise 1998: 572–573.

shall be mine' (3:17). Yahweh's epoch-making declaration that only *those Israelites who fear him* will be his people when he intervenes eschatologically draws on the terms he used of Israel long ago at Sinai: they will be his 'treasured possession' (*sĕgullâ* [3:17; Exod. 19:5]), and will be spared as a son who will serve Yahweh (Exod. 4:22; etc.).[12] This distinction within a single group of Israelites is even cast in terms of the distinction between the righteous and the wicked, between those who serve Yahweh and those who do not (3:18). This introduces a very negative criterion of identity between Edom and such Israelites, with both being 'wicked' (*riš ʿâ* [1:4]; those who do *riš ʿâ*, i.e. 'evildoers' [3:15]; the *rāšāʿ*, 'wicked' [3:18]).

Transcending the Israelite–non-Israelite distinction in the Day of Yahweh (Mal. 4:1–3)

Malachi's description of the coming eschatological 'day' described in 4:1–3 makes no use whatsoever of ethnic or national identity. Yahweh establishes a binary contrast between the 'arrogant' (4:1, used of some Israelites in 3:15) and 'evildoers' (*riš ʿâ* [4:1; also in 3:15]) on the one hand, and those who 'fear [his] name' on the other (4:2). The former will be definitively destroyed (4:1, a process in which Yahweh's eschatological people play an ambiguous role [4:3]), whereas the latter, already righteous in one sense, will experience God's saving righteousness to a superlative degree as the 'sun of righteousness' rises and heals them (4:2).

Table 2 presents the various inner-group distinctions that God makes in Malachi, with the various participants underlined to highlight how these distinctions run through Israel and the nations alike rather than treating them as homogeneous groups ('moderate antonymy' underlines the few cases in which a sharp contrast is not present; 'implicit' elements are inferred when no contrasting element is explicitly present).

In all of this, even with the emphasis on Yahweh's temple and worldwide worship of him, Persia remains in the background. The title 'great king' and other features that appear occasionally in Malachi may constitute a subtle polemic against Persia, as Erica Ehrenberg notes:

> Royal Achaemenid titles such as: great king, king of kings, king of all countries, king of the world, king in this great earth far and wide,

[12] Jacobs 2017: 316. Wielenga (2022) helpfully explores the relation of Malachi's eschatology to other elements of early Israel.

Table 2 Contrasting descriptions that distinguish between and within Israelites and non-Israelites in Malachi

Negative	*Positive*
Hated by Yahweh (covenantal): Esau (1:2)	Loved by Yahweh (covenantal): Jacob (1:2)
'Wicked' territory: Edomites (1:4)	Land of 'delight': repentant Israel (3:12) (*moderate antonymy*)
Object of Yahweh's perpetual anger: Edomites (1:4)	Land of 'delight': repentant Israel (3:12) (*moderate antonymy*)
Despise Yahweh's name: some Israelite priests (1:6)	Yahweh's name is or will be great or esteemed: by some 'among the nations' (1:11 [x2]); by Levi (in the past [2:5]); by some Israelites (3:16)
Offer polluted or unacceptable offerings or sacrifices: some Israelites and Israelite priests (1:7, 8)	Present pure offerings: some 'among the nations' (1:11); purified Israelite priests (3:3–4)
Do not fear Yahweh's name: some Israelites (3:5)	Fear Yahweh's name: some 'among the nations' (1:14); some Israelites (3:16 [x2])
Wicked: some Israelites (3:18)	Righteous: some Israelites (3:18); those healed by the 'sun of righteousness' (i.e. those who fear Yahweh's name [4:2])
Evildoers: some Israelites (3:15); generic (4:1)	(*implicit obedience to Yahweh*)
Arrogant: some Israelites (3:15); generic (4:1)	(*implicit humility*)
(*implicit non-belonging*)	Belonging or election, treasured possession: Yahweh's people ('mine'); some Israelites (3:17)

> king of the multitude, and king of countries containing all kinds of men, emphasize the enormity of the realm.[13]

Himbaza's observation that Darius I (522–486 BC) introduced the title 'king of the peoples' is also notable in the light of Malachi's focus on the 'nations'.[14] However, Edom is the only clear example of a political entity

[13] Ehrenberg 2008: 104.

[14] Himbaza 2012: 361–362.

whose leaders direct their polity's resources and energies in ways that counter Yahweh's plans and word – that is, as an implemented ideology.

Summary and New Testament developments

Despite its small size, the book of Malachi presents a nuanced perspective on non-Israelites. Edom is singled out in the first disputation, where it figures in God's argument that his chosen people still benefit from their status as his people, and it is condemned because of its resolute opposition to Yahweh and his purposes in the world and through Israel/Judah. By contrast, Persia remains almost entirely in the background, with only a passing mention or two giving evidence of the imperial context in which Malachi ministered (note the 'governor' in 1:8). Although the only empire to which Malachi might refer is thus almost entirely ignored, at least as a specific subject, Persia is nonetheless part of the 'nations' among whom Yahweh will be recognized and exclusively worshipped in the future.[15] Although Malachi's eschatology is less indebted to geopolitical categories than that of Haggai and Zechariah, it is not for that reason less insistent on Yahweh's unique status as God or the certainty that his rule will ultimately produce a world without sin in which those who know and revere him will flourish.

The most prominent features of Malachi's treatment of the nations, including God's ongoing opposition to those who resist his purposes through his people as did Edom, continue in the New Testament. Unlike many of the other prophetic books, the non-Israelite nations do not pose a threat to Israelites in Malachi. Rather, apathy and scepticism threaten to alienate God from those among his people who lose sight of the fact that one's well-being is uniquely dependent on a relationship in which one receives God's grace and responds with love, obedience and gratitude (Deut. 6:5).

The positive criteria of identity that Malachi uses to describe those who receive God's salvation are crystallized as repentance and faith in Christ in the New Testament. Several examples of this faith on the part of non-Israelites appear even in the Gospels, and include the magi,

[15] Timmer (2015: 211–114) presents arguments for seeing the nations' worship as monotheistic and focused on Yahweh.

Roman centurions, the Syro-Phoenician woman, and others. Just before his ascension, Christ's solemn commission to the apostles in Matthew 28 puts at the very centre of the church's vocation the evangelistic project by which the non-Israelites whom Malachi foresaw turning to the Lord will hear of him. Closely connected to that mission, the prominence of the 'name' of Jesus Christ in the book of Acts (Acts 2:38 and throughout the book) is the culmination of Malachi's emphasis on Yahweh's name, a point made by several passages in Acts that assert a fundamental identity between Yahweh and Jesus Christ (note Joel 2:32 and Acts 2:21, 36; Acts 4:7–12; Phil. 2:9 most likely refers to Yahweh conferring on Jesus Christ 'his own name . . . in its most sublime sense . . . the personal name of the God of Israel, that is, Yahweh').[16] Finally, Jesus himself inaugurates the Day of Yahweh, which entails the proclamation of the gospel to all nations (Mark 13:10) and culminates in the final and irrevocable distinction between sheep and goats on the basis of knowing or not knowing God (Matt. 24 – 25; Mark 13), confirming the significance of applying Malachi's criterion of identity.

[16] O'Brien 1991: 238; Bauckham 2007.

18
The nations, contemporary ideologies and the gospel

Our survey of the writing prophets' messages concerning non-Israelites has carried us across most of the ancient Near East and across more than a millennium of its history. Our primary optic has been determined by the prophets' careful focus on key elements of the ideologies that legitimated and motivated the behaviours of the nations that God condemned in their pronouncements. Using imperialism as a lens, we saw that the ideologies that these states developed, maintained and enacted were built upon cosmogonic, ontological, theological, anthropological, ethical and teleological beliefs. Yahweh, speaking through his prophets, critiques and condemns these ideologies and their implementation. Furthermore, he announces in their stead the coming of a radically different, global kingdom. The nature and function of this kingdom reflect very different beliefs centred on Yahweh as creator and his works of judgment and salvation as the only means by which justice, peace and the perfection of creation can be attained.

To begin with the salvific dimension of their messages, the prophets present the integration of non-Israelites into God's renewed people in many different ways: becoming members of the Davidic Messiah's kingdom (Amos 9), being adopted by restored Judah and entering Yahweh's eternal covenant with her (Ezek. 16), being changed by Yahweh into his worshippers (Zech. 9), coming to superlatively exalted Jerusalem to learn God's ways (Isa. 2), seeking refuge in Yahweh (Nah. 1), and seeing one's false gods evaporate before Yahweh's majesty and worshipping him instead (Zeph. 2). Sometimes these non-Israelites worship God where they are (that is, not in Israel or at Jerusalem), as in Malachi 1 and Isaiah 19, while in other cases they settle in the renewed land (Ezek. 47) or in a superlatively transformed Jerusalem (frequently in Isaiah; Joel 3; Mic.

7), or travel to Jerusalem periodically to celebrate festivals (Zech. 14). Despite the impressive variety of these descriptions, the non-Israelites who figure in them have in common the fundamental criterion of identity that defines the people of God regardless of ethnicity or any other subordinate difference: they have abandoned their gods and ideologies and the lifestyle tied to them and have entrusted themselves to Yahweh as *their* God. Their new life in covenant with Yahweh is holistically oriented towards him, guided by his word, and characterized by humility, righteous speech and action, and trust in his mercy and protection. The prophets unanimously affirm that these converts are full members of the renewed people of God.[1]

Turning to the prophetic critique of the nations, our exploration of the oracles *against* the nations has shown that these oracles are predominately focused not on the homogeneous, empirically defined political entity that 'nation' designates in normal discourse, but on a subset of a political entity's population that is defined by their support and enactment of a particular ideology. This distinction between the nation in the usual sense of the word and those responsible for supporting and enacting its ideology allowed the prophets to present damning critiques of the 'nation' as an ideological construct but also to announce that others within the same political entity would be savingly transformed by God's grace and integrated into renewed Israel. This inner-group distinction among non-Israelite nations was frequently juxtaposed with the prophets' parallel condemnation of much of Israel or Judah and the restriction of their promises of salvation to a remnant that was defined by its turning to God, repentance from sin and pursuit of righteous behaviour.

This chapter explores how to apply the prophets' oracles, and their ideological focus in particular, to some aspects of contemporary Western culture. It does so first by critiquing a sampling of contemporary ideologies along the lines sketched by the prophets and then by considering how the gospel presents a radically superior analysis of, and solution to, the fundamental problems that afflict human beings. While it is relatively simple to understand why the gospel 'promised beforehand through his prophets' (Rom. 1:2) applies to the contemporary world, the relevance of their critiques of ancient imperial ideology requires some explanation.

Applying the prophets' critique of *ancient* ideologies to *contemporary*

[1] See the helpful discussion in Beale and Gladd 2014: 186–197.

realities is possible for the same reasons that, with few exceptions, the oracles do not condemn the totality of the nation that is named but only a subgroup that embraces and implements an ideology condemned and rejected by God. Because these condemnations consistently focus on ideology rather than historically bounded features such as ethnicity, the oracles' relevance is not limited to the manifestation of that ideology *within a particular nation*, that is, within an ethnically or nationally defined group.[2] This point receives further support from the consistency of the prophets' critiques of nations small and large across the geographic and historical tapestry of the ancient Near East and from the significant commonalities between the royal and imperial ideologies of these states.

In short, those who embrace these ideologies are 'dispersed in time and space', to borrow the description of a key theme in Augustine's *City of God*, and so can be found in the world of the twenty-first century no less than in the ancient Near East – indeed, wherever and whenever human beings exhibit the 'destructive attachment' to a world view and way of life in which the triune God is not fundamental and love for him is not the primary human orientation.[3] Incidentally, Augustine's approach in his *City of God* is similar to the one sketched below, although he developed it with much greater sophistication. After proposing an alternative definition of 'people' as 'the association of a multitude of rational beings united by a common agreement on the objects of their love', Augustine explains on that basis that

> what I have said about the Roman people and the Roman commonwealth I must be understood to have said and felt about those of the Athenians and of any other Greeks, or of that former Babylon of the Assyrians, when they exercised imperial rule, whether on a small or a large scale, in their commonwealths – and indeed about any other nation whatsoever.[4]

Applying the prophets' critiques of ideology and related world views in contemporary contexts is also possible because, despite their diverse

[2] Kim (2020: 71) argues that prophetic condemnations of the nations show a tendency to shift from 'concrete historical referents' to more abstract, universal referents that apply 'to different audiences across generations and geography'.

[3] Weithman 2001: 236. Ciftci (2018: 20) identifies the focus of this 'destructive attachment' as Augustine's city of man.

[4] Augustine 2003: 890–891 (19.24).

manifestations, the ideologies implemented by ancient Egypt, Assyria and other states *have a number of key features in common with modern ones*. They usurp countless divine prerogatives, especially the determination of the *meaning* of the cosmos and what it contains;[5] they limit themselves to a view of reality that is essentially *material* and without genuine transcendence; they pursue especially material *security* within that immanent framework by exercising *power* (often violently), thus promoting their supposed *mastery* of those domains of the world around them that they take to be most important;[6] and all this is driven by a profound *hubris* that manifests a commitment to self-definition, self-sufficiency, self-perfection and self-glorification. This is not to imply that 'circumstantial factors' do not give a particular cast to modern ideologies, so that their realization looks rather different, for example, from Tyre's pursuit of economic dominance, a Babylonian ruler's narcissistic self-aggrandizement, or Assyria's imperial swagger and violence.[7] Nonetheless, the same sinful loves and the actions they lead to manifest themselves in ways that are familiar from the prophetic books.

A final point of correspondence between ancient and contemporary ideologies is the way in which they motivate concrete actions that flow from the idolatrous reductions or perversions of truth underlying them. Functioning as a lens through which one sees the world, ideologies serve 'not to render reality transparent, but to motivate people to do or not do certain things'.[8] Since ideology makes human glory, material wealth, power and other created things *supreme*, its self-authorized 'attribution of meaning' to things that *God* has created and given meaning to is idolatrous at its root.[9] In the present as in the past, therefore, ideologies feed the desire for, and facilitate the headlong pursuit of, mastery over some part or sphere of creation in order to satisfy the quest for godless self-sufficiency and autonomy.

This chapter traces the path for moving from prophetic critique of the nations and their ideologies to critique of contemporary ideologies and their supporting world views and the alternative proposed by the gospel,

[5] O'Donovan 2014: 108.

[6] Smith (2004: 106) asserts that 'the plane of immanence can only be a realm of essential violence'.

[7] Minich 2023: 41.

[8] Sypnowich 2019.

[9] O'Donovan 2014: 108.

and does so in three steps. First, it briefly reviews the main features of the imperial ideologies summarized in chapter 2 and explored in later chapters. It then sketches a few of the most important forms that these fundamental commitments, beliefs and values have taken in the last several centuries and their relation to widespread contemporary ideologies, particularly in the West. Finally, in contrast to the chimeric utopias offered by contemporary ideologies and world views, we will reflect on how the significance of the prophetic message of salvation presents an ideology-transcending world view and way of life that are radically more permanent, far more hopeful and infinitely more life-giving than the idols held out by modern ideologies as objects of faith, hope and love.[10]

The main elements of ancient imperial ideologies

The ideologies of the nations *failed to interpret reality properly* because they ignored Yahweh's existence and his self-revelation in creation, discounted the unparalleled significance of his covenant bond with his people and affirmed that their gods – despite being part of the universe rather than transcending it – were collectively in charge of history.[11] The gods' choice of the monarch, tied to the primordial formation and violent ordering of the world by means of various founding myths, established him as the gods' vice-regent and therefore as responsible for implementing on earth an order that reflected their own tenuous supremacy in the divine realm.

This gave rise to a national or imperial mission in which submission to the king and suitable participation in the nation or empire were essential to human flourishing. Those who refused to become subjects of the empire were seen as rebelling against this divine–human order, demonstrating their culpable foolishness (and, often, lesser value) by pursuing life outside it. As a result, the violence that was essential to the progress of the imperial mission was justified and regularly celebrated by

[10] As Smith asserts, 'Embedded in every liturgy is an implicit worldview' (2009: 25); even more suitably for a discussion of ideologies that are dependent on and also produce idolatry, he asserts the link between 'worship and worldview' (2009: 39) and the 'sedimentation' of Christian doctrine in 'a kind of noncognitive "understanding"' (2009: 69). Naugle (2002: 329) concludes that a world view 'is responsible in the main for the shape of a variety of life-determining human practices'.

[11] Fate or chance was prominent in some ancient Egyptian thought; see Assmann 2003: 239–240; Bricker 2001.

its perpetrators. If the groups in question chose to submit, however, the conqueror could also be their saviour, as the empire's actions transformed them and the formerly untamed regions in which they lived. To this end, states exerted propagandistic, diplomatic and economic pressure (and violence if necessary) to integrate the 'other' into itself and extend its dominion. The fully established empire, supposedly free of internal dissension and safe from all external threats, was presented as the earthly dimension of the cosmos brought to quasi-perfection (although never fully purged of the violence inherent in it or the evil provoking it).

Some contemporary expressions of ideology

Despite the vast chronological distance that separates the non-Israelite empires and states whose ideologies the prophets condemn from the twenty-first-century West, a number of contemporary ideologies bear striking similarities to elements of these much older, primarily political ideologies. (The same is true of the prophets' critiques of Israel and Judah, of course, but they are not the focus of this volume.) This section briefly surveys a small number of prominent contemporary ideologies and vehicles for them, identifying some of the ways in which they are vulnerable to the same kind of critiques found in the prophets' oracles. Until this point, I have used 'ideology' to refer to a network of interconnected beliefs that are intended to legitimate and motivate participation in a state or empire and its self-assigned role or mission in the world. In the present chapter, the term is applied to both political *and non-political* expressions of world views that are intended to legitimate and promote participation in social, cultural, political or technical projects that pursue some promised good for those who participate.[12] As the brevity of these examples implies, they are intended to prompt reflection and further exploration of them – and many others not mentioned here – rather than to provide substantive description, analysis and critique.[13] The literature in the footnotes points

[12] This definition underscores the *motivated action* that an ideology drives; the comparable 'love and practice' pair is evident in the 'cultural liturgies' described by Smith (2009: 23).

[13] For other modern idols and related ideologies, see Provan 1999.

readers towards material that will help them take up this crucially important task.[14]

A good case can be made for seeing the elimination of transcendence (and ultimately of God) as the defining characteristic of modern thought.[15] To begin with cosmology, human origins are typically located within an entirely material cosmos whose origins are unknown and of which all things are part. This entails or assumes the non-existence of God or of any other genuinely transcendent entity.[16] Although modernity forces human nature into the same immanent framework, the reach of human knowledge makes it possible (so it is believed) for humanity to exert control and even attain mastery over much of this world, if not beyond it.[17] Although there is no single epistemology associated with modernity, many modern epistemologies are essentially unanimous in their affirmation that adequate if not perfect knowledge can be gained from sense perception, reason or other human means.[18] Their postmodern counterparts typically shy away from such certitudes and favour the belief that 'reality is relative, indeterminate, and participatory' in such a way that objective knowledge is impossible.[19]

In almost all permutations of both modernism and postmodernism, divine revelation is neither necessary nor possible, and no divine grace is required to correct innate human weakness or the malfunctioning of the human faculties. Rather, it is believed that the human person can legitimately distinguish between good and evil (or, just as likely, reject that distinction as meaningless), identify goals towards which one should move (or deny that such goals exist), and choose and implement the most suitable means for attaining them. All of this, at least on more optimistic

---

[14] Watkin 2022 is a trenchant, far-ranging and accessible example. Note also Milbank, Pickstock and Ward 1999; Trueman 2020.

[15] Pfau (2016: 739) concludes that 'Kant attempts nothing less than to dissolve the 2,000-year-old theological distinction between a transcendent/divine and a finite/human plateau of reality into a single, continuous, and anthropomorphic domain'. For a survey of recent interpretations of the nature and origin of modernity, see Minich 2023: 11–66.

[16] Green (2004) observes that atheism was foundational to Nietzsche's thought.

[17] Christian Wolff (1679–1754) held that '[h]uman reason is capable of knowing all possible things as God knows them' (Tseng 2020: 22). Several decades ago, Zubrin (1996) anticipated that colonizing Mars would promote 'a new branch of civilization' and 'interplanetary commerce' through which '[p]eople create wealth' and in which people *are* 'wealth and power'.

[18] Examples include, respectively, John Locke's empiricism, Descartes's rationalism, and Kant's synthesis of empiricism and rationalism.

[19] Rasmussen 2017: 31.

accounts, sets humanity on a course for continual, cumulative development and self-improvement that may eventually lead to perfection, whether omniscience, immortality or simply global peace. Salvation, in other words, is often thought to be within humanity's reach, and no external aid is required to attain it.

Various combinations of some or all of these convictions produce a wide array of ideologies that share many fundamental elements with one another and with the imperial ideologies that figure prominently in the Old Testament prophetic books. The following sections identify some of the more striking ways in which they contribute to beliefs about the human being, the material world, the goals that one can legitimately pursue and the means for attaining them in the twenty-first century.

The human being

We begin, appropriately enough, with the human being, characteristically placed at the centre of modern thought. The person is almost universally believed to be without serious flaws, without any significant dependence on something external to itself for identity and purpose, and capable of significant development towards increasingly good or even ideal existence. This chain of secular humanistic elements is captured in magnificent fashion by Immanuel Kant's condescending imperative to the unenlightened person to have the courage to use his or her self-determination rather than accept and follow another's guidance.[20] This autonomy lies very near the heart of modernity, and authorizes the human being to determine what is good and how it is to be pursued.

As a first example, recent decades have witnessed a massive increase in the malleability of the human being. Consider the belief that biological sex and gender are unrelated. This belief, which resembles Gnosticism's spite for the body in preference for the soul, allows individuals to determine their gender without respect to their physical, biological sex, making a fundamental marker of their identity rather like a switch that can be thrown in one direction or the other at will.[21] Surgical and hormonal modification of the person often follows, extending the malleability of the individual from the mental sphere to the physical, ironically

[20] Kant 1991: 54.

[21] Favale 2022; Pearcey 2018: 35–36.

acknowledging the inescapable reality and significance of the physical while according to 'psychological feelings . . . an authority denied to the body'.[22]

Some of the visions for the integration of artificial intelligence (AI) with the human being propose equally radical 'improvements' that assume our ability to beneficially transform human beings in other ways. The idea itself is hardly new: Francis Bacon announced in his *Novum Organum* (1620) that 'the task and purpose of human power' is 'to generate and superinduce a new nature or new natures, upon a given body'.[23] Even though 'body' in this context is not limited to the human body, and Bacon's work is peppered with allusions to Scripture and 'true religion', his project unambiguously promotes human attempts 'to renew and enlarge the power and empire of mankind in general over the universe'.[24] In Bacon's judgment, humanity's 'innumerable' miseries stemmed 'not from human sin, but from the "ignorance of things"' and how they work, and he held out the hope that science's achievement of immortality would be the final step in reversing the effects of the fall.[25]

The prodigious pace of technological development in the twenty-first century has made even the most ambitious goals, such as omniscience or immortality, seem plausible to some.[26] The ideological nature of much thinking along these lines is evident in its intertwining of anthropology, cosmology and teleology:

> Reality is understood [by science] in value-neutral and materialistic terms while the distinctiveness of human existence is our capacity to exercise power (freedom) in the creation of values, values specified through law, art, morality, economics, and the like, in an open future. What is basic to this ontology insofar as it is concerned with values we ought to seek is then power itself. Only through access to power do agents or communities of agents endow their world with meaning, only through the exercise of power, the capacity to change

[22] Trueman 2024: 25; see also Anderson 2019: 93–116; Favale 2022: 117–119.

[23] Bacon 1902 (1620): 108 (book II, aphorism 1). I owe this and the following reference to Faulkner 2003: 213.

[24] Bacon 1902 (1620): 105 (book I, aphorism 129).

[25] Innes 2019: 12. Trueman (2024: 25) notes that whereas death was once 'a sacred mystery . . . now we mobilize social and technological forces to deny it'.

[26] Barba-Kay 2023: 216.

> the world for human purposes, is the distinctiveness of human life to be found. This technological age is merely the working out and institutionalization of this moral ontology.[27]

Although implanting chips in the human brain may – for now – seem relatively extreme, the idea of improving oneself by technological means takes many forms, some of which are so common as to seem banal.[28] In his far-ranging examination of the 'formation' of human beings by the digital world and devices they use, Antón Barba-Kay proposes that technology allows us to pursue in new and captivating ways the ideal of personal perfection: 'to re-create my better self'. Attempts to reach this goal range from the presentation of a curated, idealized version of oneself – and interaction with those of others – on social media to investing AI 'with a sort of personality' that presents us with 'the shape of our own intentions and of the social world quantified, aggregated, projected into digital form, and thereby rendered authoritative'.[29]

Thomas Pfau raises similar concerns regarding the 'simulation of cognitive and emotive processes by means of complex algorithmic processes'.[30] With a nod to Augustine and Pascal, Pfau characterizes the human activity of knowing as always dependent on the Creator's gifts and grace, and thus thick with moral and metaphysical significance. Unlike the outputs produced by AI, human thought and knowledge 'cannot be reduced to a strictly computational procedure'.[31] Further, thinking involves appraising 'the truth value of our propositions not just relative to their object but also vis-à-vis an antecedent greater good that can neither be posited by our will nor arise, as it were by default, from the fluctuations of thought'.[32] In short, our thoughts are not AI's thoughts, but are ontologically different.[33]

These concerns are not those of Luddites or anti-technology troglodytes. Pfau, for example, recognizes that 'the salutary and the menacing

[27] Schweiker 1995: 214, cited in Schroeder 2001: 23.

[28] Winkler (2024) notes that this line has been crossed without much ado.

[29] Barba-Kay 2023: 214, 237.

[30] Pfau 2023: 7.

[31] Ibid. 12.

[32] Ibid.

[33] Ibid.

aspects of new technologies are inextricably intertwined'.[34] Rather, critical reflection on technology asserts the importance of developing and using it fittingly, that is, in ways that recognize and preserve the origin of all that exists in God's creative act, the God-given nature of human beings, the relational nature of knowledge, the recognition that sin is the ultimate source of human ills and suffering, and so on.[35] Insofar as technologies or their use contribute to 'a much larger historical project of securing total dominion over nature that, at last, finds itself confronted with the final frontier',[36] namely our own nature, or shift 'the goal of scientific advance . . . from a humanist to a post-humanist one',[37] they bear the marks and the hubris of ideologies that are committed to self-perfection or the substitution of immanent reality for 'what Christians expect from the transcendent power of God'.[38] In such cases, they are all the more vulnerable to critique.

The material world

The technological dimension discussed in the previous section is inseparable from the participation of the material world in our understanding of reality and in the formulation of ideologies. But the ideological significance of the material world is hardly limited to technology. For example, capitalism, aided and abetted by the inveterate human penchant for material possessions and 'free-market economic globalization', has proven immensely successful at creating a consumer-driven economy.[39] A century ago, the 1929 US 'Report of the Committee on Recent Economic Changes of the President's Conference on Unemployment' tied the greater 'consuming power of the American people' to 'the expansibility of human

[34] Ibid. 7.

[35] See, on the last three issues mentioned, Pfau 2016; Meek 2011; Bauckham 2007, respectively. Bauckham (2007: 312) notes that despite the quasi-eschatological role afforded by modernity to the ideal of progress, it can offer 'no redemption of the past and no hope for the dead'. Of creation, Gunton (1997: 155) argues that '[i]f we cease to see the world as God's creation, we shall treat it not as a project in which we are invited to share but as an absolute possession to be exploited as we will'.

[36] Pfau 2023: 16.

[37] Bauckham 2007: 314.

[38] Ibid. Scruton (1998), cited in Dooley 2009: 7, warns that 'the hubris which leads us to believe that science has the answer to all our questions, that we are nothing but dying animals and that the meaning of life is merely self-affirmation . . . contains already the punishment of those who succumb to it'.

[39] Bauckham 2007: 314. For a helpful survey of Radical Orthodoxy's critique of capitalism as usually practised, see McMuller 2014.

wants and desires' and perceived an 'almost insatiable appetite for goods and services'.[40] Coincidentally, one year earlier, Edward L. Bernays had published a monograph in which he analysed the power of advertising and public relations to shape the behaviour of the public.[41] His observations are striking as much for their prescience as for their perception of the ideological nature and function of such discourses across a wide range of cultural spheres:

> The conscious and intelligent manipulation of the organized habits and opinions of the masses is an important element in democratic society. Those who manipulate this unseen mechanism of society constitute an invisible government which is the true ruling power of our country.[42]

Seven decades later, Harvey Cox published an essay entitled 'The Market as God: Living in the New Dispensation'.[43] Therein he contends that the 'Market', which until roughly 1800 'had operated within a plethora of other institutions that restrained it' by functioning as alternative 'centers of value and meaning', had essentially taken over the dominance, importance and power formerly accorded to God.[44] With bitter irony, Cox asserts that the market is able to 'convert creation into commodities', desacralizing it in the process: land, the human body and even human life itself can be assigned a monetary value.[45] Paradoxically, the opposite transformation is also evident when material things are marketed as vehicles (sometimes literally) of satisfaction and meaningfulness, a message reinforced by the market's 'First Commandment': 'There is never enough.'[46] These omnipresent discourses present material goods as a source of 'meaning and identity', and their presentation is rendered

---

[40] Committee on Recent Economic Changes of the President's Conference on Unemployment 1929: xv, <www.nber.org/system/files/chapters/c4950/c4950.pdf> (accessed 31 October 2024). I owe this reference to Higgs 2021.

[41] Bernays 1928.

[42] Ibid. 9.

[43] Cox 1999: 20.

[44] Ibid.

[45] Birnie 2022.

[46] Cox 1999: 23.

effective by an ideology of 'immaterialist materialism' that assigns transcendent significance to them.[47] They are thus immensely powerful:

> The unleashing of desire for consumptive purposes is near the center of our present cultural story. The turn toward consumption both follows and precipitates the turn to the subject in the wider culture, and it is entirely vulnerable to a peculiar idolatry of possession.[48]

Politics

Last but surely not least, a discussion of ideology in the twenty-first century cannot bypass the realm of politics.[49] Since the following examples are drawn from the West in the twilight of modernity, we will focus on political liberalism, which has ideological significance itself and forms the backdrop for other political paradigms that developed within it or against it.[50]

Patrick J. Deneen summarizes the liberal project as the pursuit of a 'supreme and complete freedom through the liberation of the individual from particular places, relationships, memberships, and even identities – unless they have been chosen, are worn lightly, and can be revised or abandoned at will'.[51] In contrast to earlier political theory in which 'virtue and self-rule' were the primary means for constraining 'the impulse to and assertions of tyranny' and thus ensuring liberty, liberalism proposed a new paradigm based on a very different anthropology and morality. In Deneen's account, this paradigm consists of three elements. First, the harnessing of human 'pride, selfishness, greed, and the quest for glory' for pragmatic political purposes.[52] Second, the belief that the supplanting of 'religious belief and practice' by an 'individualistic rationality' rooted

---

[47] Watkin (2022: 360), who refers to this phenomenon as 'excarnational polytheism' rather than an ideology (361). For an overview of insightful and provocative critiques of many forms of capitalism, see Smith 2004: 247–254; McMuller 2014. Note also the contention of Herring (2023) that if 'governed by a sound anthropology and an ethic grounded in natural law', capitalism 'remains the best method humans have developed for elevating themselves from poverty into freedom of choice and action'.

[48] Lints 2006: 223.

[49] For a wide-ranging overview, see Heywood 2012.

[50] Freeden and Stears (2013: 329) see liberalism as 'a political theory, as an ideology and as a set of moral injunctions for human interaction'.

[51] Deneen 2018: 16.

[52] Ibid. 25.

in universal, rational human nature would extirpate conflicts ignited by differences in inherently irrational religious beliefs, while 'the legal prohibitions and sanctions of a centralized political state' would establish the necessary limits to freedom.[53] Finally, the hope that progressive domination of nature through knowledge, coupled with its use for the betterment of humanity, would produce 'an expanding and potentially limitless human capacity to control circumstance and effect human desires upon the world'.[54] In this way, as Bauckham puts it, modernity replaced the 'transcendence of God "above"' with a false 'transcendence of the future "ahead"' that was to be realized by 'science, technology, and education'.[55]

The paradigm of political liberalism thus begins with a world that is disconnected from anything transcendent (except, notably, the presumed universality of a particular kind of rational human nature). The human being is an actor who can be used to produce stability and multiform progress, notably through 'the expansion of profit and of economic growth'.[56] No redemption or reconciliation with the Creator or with other people is necessary for 'full scale individual flourishing'.[57] As a result, any morality or ethics is purely utilitarian, and the 'greatest good' is the anticipated – but very fragile – balance between the state's maintenance of social order (by lethal force, if necessary) and the flourishing of sinful human beings in competition with one another for immanent social and material goods. Despite its real and imagined successes, Deneen contends that liberalism is threatened by the very features that define it: 'the corrosive social and civic effects of self-interest', various ecological and biological harms brought about by human efforts to control nature, and the 'loosening of social bonds in nearly every aspect of life'.[58]

There are, of course, many alternative political paradigms whose proponents argue that they are better suited to creating and preserving

[53] Ibid. 25–26; similarly, Freeden and Stears (2013: 331) note early liberalism's 'claim to universal status as the inevitable outcome of the reason with which individuals were endowed in the state of nature'.

[54] Deneen 2018: 26.

[55] Bauckham 2007: 312.

[56] Freeden and Stears 2013: 332; there they also observe that '[t]he ideological rendering of such market freedoms also often depended on the quest for a scientific foundation, embodying the sense that any objective observer analysing the sources of prosperity in a modernizing world would be drawn to the need for a stable and energetic market economy'.

[57] Ibid. (334), describing the liberal thought of John Stuart Mill.

[58] Deneen 2018: 29–30. King (1999) advances similar criticisms.

peaceful societies, access to adequate material resources and the well-being of the greatest number than the dominant forms of liberalism. Insofar as these political paradigms or structures pursue these goods without elevating one or more elements of the created order as ultimate, they (like liberalism) have the potential to aid a state that adopts them in the pursuit of justice, equity and peace.[59] However, because of the secular nature of the state in the West and its foundational commitment to human autonomy, political systems that modify or depart from liberalism inevitably manifest weaknesses and flaws, many of which are no less serious than those just noted of liberalism.

The few examples to be mentioned here illustrate two weaknesses that should decisively dampen any far-reaching hope attached to them: the political sphere cannot *supply the deepest needs of human beings*, nor can it *correct our deepest flaws*. This is so for the simple reason that these political alternatives remain locked in an immanent framework from which God as creator, redeemer and consummator is excluded.[60] For example, socialism as an ideology tends 'to distrust individual freedom or other alternative communities' because it idolizes 'the economic class'.[61] As a result, its recognition of 'the claims of individuals and communities . . . to a fair share of the economic resources of a given body politic' tends to 'assimilate all legitimate forms of ownership into a single monolithic form'.[62] As another example, ideological nationalism, whether focused on the state to which one owes ultimate allegiance (the civic variety) or the supposedly homogeneous people who are its citizens (the ethnic variety), sees the nation so defined as freeing or protecting the group 'from the rule of others outside its self-defined boundaries'.[63] However, civic nationalism accords such importance to the state that it uses its communications, education and other means to 'solidify national unity', and its more extreme forms tend towards a fascism in which loyalty to the state

[59] Koyzis 2013: 260–261, 265–266.

[60] The quite different approach of Christian Reconstructionism is nonetheless mistaken, I believe, in its vision of Christianizing the state or using the state to promote Christianity. Gribben (2021: 146) captures the difficulty well: 'As their most prominent spokesmen recognize, the efforts of conservative evangelicals to find political solutions to what they might otherwise regard as spiritual problems have not succeeded, and genuine social change can only be achieved as a consequence of individual regeneration. The experience of history suggests that all efforts tending toward the perfection of human society will eventually fail.'

[61] Koyzis 2013: 31, 38.

[62] Ibid. 261.

[63] Ibid. 108–113, 106.

is 'the highest loyalty a person can have'.[64] Similarly, ethnic nationalism is prone to promoting 'a double standard of justice' or value that favours 'the members of the titular ethnic group over those of other ethnic groups'.[65] In either case, nationalism cannot accommodate 'a variety of communities with different structures and with overlapping claims on the person's loyalties' due to its pursuit of a fully homogenized state or nation.[66]

As a final example, consider imperialism and decolonization. It is helpful to treat these ideologies together since the latter is defined in terms of the former, and because both ironically share key ideological elements. Imperialism, as we have seen throughout this volume, involves the intentional, ideologically driven project of subjugating as much of the world as is necessary for the attainment of the empire's goals.[67] In modern contexts it has been used to Christianize societies, appropriate natural resources, enlarge the scope of state sovereignty, or achieve some combination of these and other goals, notably self-glorification.[68] The imperial project characteristically assumes the inferior value of the population to be colonized or controlled, the moral integrity of the empire's project and the permissibility of whatever means are necessary to bring it about. Decolonization essentially inverts this paradigm, with the added justification of retribution or self-protection.[69] It too adopts violence as necessary, in contrast to lesser ideological responses of hybridity or subaltern existence, as the path towards self-realization and an ordered world.[70] Both imperialism and decolonization, whatever ostensible justifications might attend them, accord superlative importance to the political self, view the 'other' as morally inferior, define the good in immanent terms, and employ violence without hesitation in order to attain or recapture that good. Both ideologies fail to recognize that the ability to define what is good and the power to achieve it are fundamentally divine

---

[64] Ibid. 114. Bowie (2003: 114) contends that in the nineteenth century, 'the need for self-transcendence via devotion to something higher, which had been focused on God, move[d] its focus onto the collective in the form of the nation'.

[65] Koyzis 2013: 115.

[66] Ibid. 116. For evaluations of the current situation in the United States, note Alberta 2023 and Gribben 2021.

[67] Slightly modifying the definition of ancient Near Eastern imperialism in Liverani 2017: 1.

[68] For a survey, see Getz and Streets-Salter 2011.

[69] For a historical survey, see Sivanandan 2004.

[70] This point is made clearly by Peter (2023).

prerogatives and that God alone can deliver individuals from the loss of what is truly good.[71]

Koyzis's proposal for wise evaluation of political options and suitable participation in them captures nicely the discernment that Christians must exercise in this arena. He asserts that the 'distorted nature' of ideologies

> should indicate to Christians from the outset why Christians cannot simply join with one or more of these ideologies and champion their agendas . . . If an ideology is based on a deification of something within God's good creation, then Christians above all should be in a position to discern correctly the difference between idolatry and a more modest estimation of the things being idolized.[72]

In other words, Christian involvement in politics must shun any utopianism that relativizes the gospel and the church. Conversely, Christian hope, enjoyed 'already' in new life in Christ and the new creation ushered in by his resurrection, must look resolutely towards the 'new heavens and a new earth in which righteousness dwells' (2 Pet. 3:13).[73]

> Anything that conflates the political endeavors of this age with the renewal of God's justice in the age to come is . . . not Christian. Complacent theologizing that baptizes the status quo conflates today's politics with God's judgment and must be rejected; calls for revolution to usher in a utopia of 'social justice' do so as well and must likewise be rejected.[74]

Ideology and individuals

Our discussion so far has focused largely on collective manifestations of ideology. Although these collectives are made up of human beings who

[71] O'Donovan (1995: 146–147) argues that the exercise of dominion in society is 'inherently ambiguous' and is typically driven by an 'overweening love for glory'. The history of the earthly city, he concludes, 'turns out to be a demonic history', and '[w]hat appears to be civilisational progress is, in fact, on the moral and spiritual level, self-defeating'.

[72] Koyzis 2013: 189; Storrar (1996: 4) also argues that states 'can lay no claim to any ultimate human loyalty'.

[73] Trueman 2023: 34.

[74] Ibid.

are organized or connected in some way (culturally, nationally and so on), their ideology is conjointly constructed and promulgated by *individuals*.[75] Indeed, all ideologies have their beginning in the rebellious minds and hearts of sinful human beings. Since it is at the individual level that ideologies are rooted, it is also at that level that they can be challenged and corrected or undone. As argued in the previous section, large-scale ideological undertakings, conflictual or not, political or not, *cannot* change the human heart or restore what sin has lost.

As we have seen, prophetic oracles that focus on the imperialism of the empires around ancient Israel and Judah, although dealing with collectives, assign guilt specifically to those *individuals* who promote those projects of domination and self-deification. Their condemnations reflect Scripture's consistent claim that sinful behaviour at any level of collectivity has its roots in the sinful individual.[76] Just as the prophetic critiques of various rulers put pride at the top of the list and show that it is inseparable from idolatry, so the rest of the canon identifies human pride and the desire for unfettered autonomy as the first sin and the root of all other sins. Pride is the classic form of idolatry, and when transformed into a course of action, pride and idolatry give birth to ideology.[77]

One further point should be made. If *idolatry* can be described as the expression of disordered desires and loves or a 'way of relating' to them, *ideology* formulates a way of seeing the world that corresponds to those disordered loves.[78] That is, 'an ideology *flows out of* the (idolatrous) religious commitment of a person or community'.[79] Pride is thus inseparable from both idolatry and ideology. It is the consummate expression of idolatry, and the commitment to self-superiority that defines pride is also the essence of a personal ideology that allows one to authoritatively interpret one's world. Thus, *whether expressed individually or collectively*, the kind of ideology that the prophets – and the canon as a whole – condemn is one that

[75] This point is made powerfully by Dooley (2023).

[76] Trueman (2023: 30) argues that '[w]e are idolaters because we want to be. We are not hapless tools of a system that dominates our individual agency and thus absolves us of any responsibility.'

[77] Reno (2006: 166) argues that 'Augustine's phenomenology of sin grounded in self-love is consistent with and enriches the predominant biblical worry about idolatry'.

[78] Watkin 2022: 311. For an excellent treatment of disordered loves, see Naugle 2008.

[79] Koyzis 2013: 27; similarly, O'Donovan 1994: 82; Gunton 2005: 105.

in thought and practice keeps us attached to the Earthly City, i.e. to a nihilistic vision of society and nature reducible to the competitive self-assertions of individuals' mutually-antagonistic wills, according to which 'meaningful action is successful action . . . meaning is power . . . and any discourse of justice is illusory'.[80]

Salvation as God-given, gracious, non-ideological restoration

The outline of this earthly 'city' is easily discerned in the words of the prophets. They announced salvation in a world in which both Israel and the nations had rebelled against God, separating themselves from him and pursuing self-defined goods without him and ultimately in opposition to him. Previous sections of this chapter have argued that despite the many differences between the ancient Near East and the (Western) world in the twenty-first century, sinful human beings continue their quest for autonomy, happiness and security on the same bases and with the same outcomes. Here we will turn to explore the unique character of salvation as it relates to ideology and the sins of pride and idolatry that lie at its root.

Three traits of the Christian doctrine of salvation are especially noteworthy in this context. First, God's saving intervention in the lives of human beings involves their *holistic transformation* and restoration at every level, beginning with spiritual renewal expressed in repentance and faith in Jesus Christ and culminating in eternal life in the new heavens and new earth. This salvation radically relativizes the goods that can be obtained or attained in any political context or paradigm. Second, since *God* is the sole agent of salvation in all its dimensions, a biblically faithful view of God, the world and the human being avoids the imbalance inherent in all ideologies by refusing to elevate an element of the created order as the highest good or as the means of attaining that good. Third, the mere fact that salvation is accomplished and is offered freely by God to those who are at that very moment his enemies highlights the *redemptive* focus of the prophets that should also characterize all Christian critique of culture.[81]

[80] Ciftci 2018: 23, citing Williams 2005: 1.

[81] Trueman 2023: 30; Watkin 2022.

Over against the self-enclosed, secular, directionless universe that all sinners naturally espouse, and whatever world view they employ to do so, Scripture reveals to us a cosmos that is created by God for his glory and for the flourishing of his image-bearers, who live in joyful conformity to his beneficent will. The Christian doctrine of creation includes the very important entailment of participation, meaning that there is 'no region of thought or practice, nor any realm of nature or culture, which could claim to be autonomous or independent of the divine.'[82] As a result, all things have meaning only because God has created them so – meaning cannot be assigned by human will or fiat.[83] More specifically, the cosmos as created by God was originally 'very good' and without sin or conflict, such that moral order and righteousness are 'ontologically basic' to it.[84] Consequently, the sinful exercise of autonomy by Adam and Eve (and, antecedently, by those angels who rebelled [Jude 6]) was an intrusion, a flagrant violation of the world's 'intrinsic moral shape.'[85] Astonishingly, even the heinous rebellion of those created in God's image was met not with his immediate and unmitigated judgment but with inexplicable grace (Gen. 3:15). In the light of the essential commonalities between individual sin and its collective expression in ideologies, O'Donovan's description of deliverance from misplaced faith in political ideologies holds true for the nature and effects of the work of salvation as a whole, which he presents in terms of biblical wisdom understood as knowledge of God above all: 'Repentance at the beginning of knowledge and the vision of God at the end are the conditions on which we may be protected from the force of [political] eros,' which 'focuses our aspiration to wisdom upon worldly structures that are necessarily imperfectible.'[86]

The relationship between God and fallen image-bearers that salvation restores is diametrically opposed to the pride and self-determination that mark the imperial ideologies examined in this volume. Scripture declares that the human person's very existence is the result of God's unconstrained, wonderfully generous creative act; human beings are

[82] Ciftci 2018: 21.

[83] As te Velde (2007: 79) puts it, 'No finite thing is simply finite, existing *in se* [in itself – DCT], but is something that appears as a finite expression . . . of the infinite perfection of being in which it participates.'

[84] Ciftci 2018: 21.

[85] Trueman 2023: 31.

[86] O'Donovan 2014: 109–110.

given their unique essence by virtue of being created in God's image; and God is central in his ineffable transcendence and in his astonishing condescension and immanence. A person who is brought from being dead in sin to being alive in Christ by the Spirit is henceforth committed to the repentant rejection of pride and self-sufficiency in favour of life in the realm of grace, where thankful reception of the multifaceted blessings of salvation is (and increasingly becomes) natural. This realm is not just any realm, but the kingdom of God in which he alone is sovereign and exalted:

> The kingdom that Christ announces is then truly a power-regime; the power of divine weakness that has triumphed over worldly strength, the power of 'the age to come' interrupting, upsetting, and in the end finally unseating the powers of 'this present evil age'.[87]

In the present context, it is important to underline the spiritual rather than political nature of Christ's kingdom as well as the spiritual nature of whatever ideology is raised up against it, as Michael Horton reminds us:

> That 'we struggle not against flesh and blood, but against principalities, and powers in spiritual places' is ominously illustrated in Nietzsche's boast: 'We immoralists are today the strongest power: the other great powers need us – we construe the world in our image.'[88]

Scripture's new-creation imagery, used of aspects of salvation both individual (2 Cor. 5:17; Gal. 6:15) and cosmic (Rom. 8:18–23; Eph. 1:9–10), likewise emphasizes the spiritual rather than political nature of God's people and the Lord's exclusive agency in establishing his kingdom through the reign of the ascended Christ by the Spirit.

Reading, preaching and hearing the oracles concerning the 'nations'

The prophets spoke and wrote in order to address both their contemporaries and the generations that would follow, including believers in the

[87] Horton 2002: 199, citing Nietzsche 1967: 71.

[88] Ibid.

twenty-first century (1 Pet. 1:10–12). While all orthodox Christians affirm that Scripture is authored by God and given for our learning, correction and edification, it is not stretching the imagination to suppose that the prophets' oracles concerning the nations are not among the texts most frequently used in Christian preaching. Insofar as that broad generalization captures current trends, this book, and this chapter in particular, are intended to encourage Christians in all walks of life to explore, share and apply the rich theology of these texts to themselves and their world.

Preachers, like all other readers of Scripture, can benefit in many ways from the prophetic books and the nations-focused oracles that figure prominently in them. First and foremost, in the light of their nature as the living Word of God, which both tears down and brings new life (2 Cor. 10:1), this two-sided role of dismantling what is false and wrong and revealing and pressing home the truth and goodness of God, as fully revealed in the gospel, is intimately connected to the prophets' twin emphases of judgment and salvation. 'God's Word addresses sinful creatures, and enters into conflict with them . . . God's Word outbids falsehood and issues an empowering summons to reason.'[89] More generally, the prophetic oracles are organically connected to the gospel and to the salvation of sinners that God accomplishes through it. As God renews a person's heart, mind and will, a new understanding of oneself, of God and of the world leads to radically new behaviour flowing from equally new motives and loves (Rom. 12:1–2; 2 Cor. 5:17).[90] The oracles' focus on pride, misplaced trust and disordered loves makes them very suitable tools for exposing the sinful commitments and dispositions that afflict human hearts.

Similarly, the focus on ideologies that is central to the prophets' oracles invites readers of every stripe to use them as lenses, revealing ideologies, world views, beliefs and loves that are essentially identical to those critiqued and condemned by the prophets, even if presented in very different dress. For the same reason, the salvation that the prophets announce is consummately relevant as well, since it shows how the grace of God, gloriously free of human control, deconstructs ideologies and all that underlies them and establishes a new reality from which human power, dominion, glory and artifice are excluded. In other words, the oracles against the

[89] Webster 2014: 20, 22.

[90] These changes are discussed in more detail in Timmer 2024f: 239–246.

nations are prime material for cultural apologetics or, in another key, biblical-critical theory.[91] Finally, the prophets' pronouncements concerning the nations are ultimately applicable to individuals of any ethnicity or nationality, just as prophetic addresses to ancient Israel and Judah retain their relevance for contemporary hearers by virtue of the fundamental distinction between those who revere God and those who do not.

The messages of the prophets, not least their oracles concerning the nations, are like a prism that reflects every colour of the light of the gospel. They present clearly the many ways in which human rebellion expresses itself; they encourage and foster solid hope in God's gracious promise to progressively renew our minds, reshape our disordered loves and purify our motives; and they foresee with surprising if imperfect clarity that Christ will reign until the Father 'has put all his enemies under his feet' (1 Cor. 15:25; cf. Isa. 42:4; Jer. 23:5–6; Amos 9:11–12; Mic. 5:4; Zech. 9:10). Being convinced, I hope, that these enemies are not to be identified simplistically with discrete, empirical political entities or nations, we should find salutary Oliver O'Donovan's identification of the gospel as the antidote to all kinds of 'false imaginations of the world' (ideologies included):

> The Gospel offers a central and normative focus of joy, the resurrection of Christ, which becomes a torch to illumine the goods of the world, a vantage point from which we can explore, discover, and appreciate all other objects of joy. And when false imaginations of the world are overcome from this vantage point, the world that God made is made new for us, and offers itself to new adventures of love and knowledge.[92]

Living between Christ's resurrection and his return, it is fitting to close this volume with a prayer that follows John Calvin's lecture on Malachi 1:10–13:

> Almighty God . . . grant us grace so that we might maintain true purity, that we might strive to serve you wholeheartedly and sincerely, that thus we might do what pleases you; also, that we might invoke and so magnify your name that it will be known for

[91] With a nod to the work of Tim Keller and Christopher Watkin, respectively.

[92] O'Donovan 2014: 112.

certain that you have accomplished in us what you testified by your prophets in the past: namely, that your name would be triumphant and celebrated by all, as it has been manifested to us in the person of him who is your only Son, our Savior. Amen.[93]

[93] Calvin 1563: 579.

Bibliography

Abernethy, A. (2016), *The Book of Isaiah and God's Kingdom: A Thematic-Theological Approach*, NSBT 40, London: Apollos; Downers Grove: InterVarsity Press.

Abo El Magd, A. (2016), 'Dehumanization of the "Other": Animal Metaphors of Defeated Enemies in the New Kingdom Military Texts', *JARCE* 52: 329–341.

Abusch, T. (1999), 'Ishtar', in K. van der Toorn, B. Becking and P. W. van der Horst (eds.), *Dictionary of Deities and Demons*, 2nd edn, Leiden: Brill, 452–453.

Aland, B. et al. (1994) (eds.), *The Greek New Testament*, 4th edn, Stuttgart: Deutsche Bibelgesellschaft.

Alberta, T. (2023), *The Kingdom, the Power, and the Glory: American Evangelicals in an Age of Extremism*, New York: HarperCollins.

Allen, J. P. (1988), *Genesis in Egypt: The Philosophy of Ancient Egyptian Creation Accounts*, New Haven: Yale Egyptological Seminar.

—— (2003), 'From the "Memphite Theology" (1.15)', *COS* 1:21–23.

Allen, L. C. (1990), *Ezekiel 20–48*, WBC 29, Dallas: Word.

—— (2008), *Jeremiah: A Commentary*, OTL, Louisville: Westminster John Knox.

Amesz, J. G. (2004), 'A God of Vengeance? Comparing YHWH's Dealings with Judah and Babylon in the Book of Jeremiah', in M. Kessler (ed.), *Reading the Book of Jeremiah*, Winona Lake: Eisenbrauns, 99–116.

Andersen, F. I., and D. N. Freedman (1980), *Hosea: A New Translation with Introduction and Commentary*, AB 24, Garden City: Doubleday.

Anderson, B. (2022), 'Edom's (Dis)Possession', *CBQ* 84.3: 365–384.

Anderson, R. T. (2019), *When Harry Became Sally: Responding to the Transgender Moment*, New York: Encounter.

Angers, D. (2018), *L' "Aujourd'hui" en Luc-Actes, chez Paul et en Hébreux: Itinéraires et associations d'un motif deutéronomique*, BZAW 215, Berlin: De Gruyter.

—— (2021), *Éphésiens*, Parle-moi maintenant, Marpent: BLF Éditions.

Apóstolo, S. S. S. (2006), 'On the Elusiveness and Malleability of "Israel"', *JHebS* 6: art. 7.

Arnold, B. T. (2000), 'Babylon', in T. D. Alexander and B. S. Rosner (eds.), *New Dictionary of Biblical Theology*, Leicester: Inter-Varsity Press; Downers Grove: InterVarsity Press, 393–394.

—— (2004), *Who Were the Babylonians?*, SBLABS 10, Atlanta: Society of Biblical Literature.

—— (2008), 'Old Testament Eschatology and the Rise of Apocalypticism', in J. L. Walls (ed.), *The Oxford Handbook of Eschatology*, Oxford: Oxford University Press, 23–29.

Arthur, D. (2023), 'Satire and Subversion in the Oracles of Ezekiel', *VT* 20: 1–25.

Aspray, B. (2021), '"A Throne Will Be Established in Steadfast Love": Welcoming Refugees and the Davidic Kingdom in Isaiah 16:1–5', *Open Theology* 7, <https://doi.org/10.1515/opth-2020-0169>.

Assis, E. (2013), *The Book of Joel: A Prophet between Calamity and Hope*, LHBOTS 581, London: T&T Clark.

—— (2014), 'Structure, Redaction and Significance in the Prophecy of Obadiah', *JSOT* 39.2: 209–221.

Assmann, J. (2003), *The Mind of Egypt: History and Meaning in the Time of the Pharaohs*, tr. A. Jenkins, Cambridge: Harvard University Press.

Aster, S. Z. (2017), 'Treaty and Prophecy: A Survey of Biblical Reactions to Neo-Assyrian Political Thought', in S. Z. Aster and A. Faust (eds.), *The Southern Levant under Assyrian Domination*, Winona Lake: Eisenbrauns, 89–118.

Aubet, M. E. (2014), 'Phoenicia during the Iron Age II Period', in A. E. Killebrew and M. Steiner (eds.), *The Oxford Handbook of the Archaeology of the Levant c. 8000–332 BCE*, Oxford: Oxford University Press, 706–716.

Aufrecht, W. E. (2003), 'The Amman Citadel Inscription (2.24)', *COS* 2:139.

Augustine (2003), *Concerning the City of God against the Pagans*, tr. H. Bettenson, Penguin Classics, London: Penguin.

Averbeck, R. E. (1997), 'חנף', *NIDOTTE* 2:206–209.

—— (2004), 'Ancient Near Eastern Mythography as It Relates to Historiography in the Hebrew Bible: Genesis 3 and the Cosmic Battle', in J. K. Hoffmeier and A. R. Millard (eds.), *The Future of Biblical Archaeology: Reassessing Methodologies and Assumptions*, Grand Rapids: Eerdmans, 328–356.

Ayali-Darshan, N. (2020), *The Storm-God and the Sea: The Origin, Versions, and Diffusion of a Myth throughout the Ancient Near East*, tr. L. Keren, ORA 37, Tübingen: Mohr Siebeck.

Bacon, F. (1902), *Novum Organum*, ed. J. Devey, New York: P. F. Collier & Son.

Barba-Kay, A. (2023), *A Web of Our Own Making: The Nature of Digital Formation*, Cambridge: Cambridge University Press.

Barker, J. (2020), *Joel*, ZECOT, Grand Rapids: Zondervan Academic.

Barstad, H. (2013), 'Hosea and the Assyrians', in R. P. Gordon and H. M. Barstad (eds.), *'Thus Says Ishtar of Arbella': Prophecy in Israel, Assyria, and Egypt in the Neo-Assyrian Period*, Winona Lake: Eisenbrauns, 91–110.

Bartholomew, C. G. (2022), *The Old Testament and God: Old Testament Origins and the Question of God*, London: SPCK; Grand Rapids: Baker Academic.

Barton, J. (2001), *Joel and Obadiah*, OTL, Louisville: Westminster John Knox.

Bauckham, R. (1993), *The Theology of the Book of Revelation*, NTT, Cambridge: Cambridge University Press.

—— (2007), 'Eschatology', in J. Webster, K. Tanner and I. Torrance (eds.), *The Oxford Handbook of Systematic Theology*, Oxford: Oxford University Press, 306–322.

—— (2011), 'Babylon (New Testament)', in *EBR*, 3:269–273.

Baugus, B. P. (2022), *The Roots of Reformed Moral Theology*, Grand Rapids: Reformation Heritage.

Beale, G. K. (1999), *The Book of Revelation*, NIGTC, Grand Rapids: Eerdmans.

Beale, G. K., and D. A. Carson (eds.) (2007), *Commentary on the New Testament Use of the Old Testament*, Grand Rapids: Baker Academic; Nottingham: Apollos.

Beale, G. K., and B. L. Gladd (2014), *Hidden but Now Revealed: A Biblical Theology of Mystery*, Nottingham: Inter-Varsity Press.

Beale, G. K., and S. M. McDonough (2007), 'Revelation', in G. K. Beale and D. A. Carson (eds.), *Commentary on the New Testament Use of the Old Testament*, Grand Rapids: Baker Academic; Nottingham: Apollos, 1081–1161.

Beaulieu, P.-A. (2003), 'Nabopolassar's Restoration of Imgur-Enlil, the Inner Defensive Wall of Babylon (2.121)', *COS* 2:307–308.

—— (2011), 'Yahwistic Names in Light of Late Babylonian Onomastics', in O. Lipschitz, G. N. Knoppers and M. Oeming (eds.), *Judah and the Judeans in the Achaemenid Period: Negotiating Identity in an International Context*, Winona Lake: Eisenbrauns, 245–266.

Ben Zvi, E. (1992), *A Historical-Critical Study of the Book of Zephaniah*, BZAW 198, Berlin: De Gruyter.

—— (1993), 'Understanding the Message of the Tripartite Prophetic Books', *ResQ* 35: 93–100.

—— (1995), 'Inclusion in and Exclusion from Israel as Conveyed by the Use of the Term "Israel" in Post-Monarchic Biblical Texts', in S. Holloway and L. Handy (eds.), *The Pitcher Is Broken: Memorial Essays for Gösta W. Ahlström*, JSOTSup 190, Sheffield: Sheffield Academic, 95–149.

—— (1996), *A Historical-Critical Study of the Book of Obadiah*, BZAW 242, Berlin: De Gruyter, 1996.

—— (2014), 'The Yehudite Collection of Prophetic Books and Imperial Contexts: Some Observations', in A. Lenzi and J. Stökl (eds.), *Divination, Politics, and Ancient Near Eastern Empires*, ANEM 7, Atlanta: Society of Biblical Literature, 145–169.

Ben Zvi, E., and J. D. Nogalski (2009), *Two Sides of a Coin: Juxtaposing Views on Interpreting the Book of the Twelve / the Twelve Prophetic Books*, ed. T. Römer, Analecta Gorgiana 201, Piscataway: Gorgias.

Bergey, R. L. (2021), '*How* Did God Hate Esau (Malachi 1:2–3)?' *Unio cum Christo* 7: 33–49.

Berlejung, A. (2006), 'Erinnerungen an Assyrien in Nahum 2,4–3,19', in R. Lux and E.-J. Waschke (eds.), *Die unwiderstehliche Wahrheit: Studien zur alttestamentlichen Prophetie; Festschrift für Arndt Meinhold*, ABG 23, Leipzig: Evangelische Verlagsanstalt, 323–356.

Bernays, E. L. (1928), *Propaganda*, New York: Horace Liveright.

Bestock, L. (2018), *Violence and Power in Ancient Egypt: Image and Idolatry before the New Kingdom*, London: Routledge.

Beuken, W. A. M. (2003), *Jesaja 1–12*, tr. U. Berges, HTKAT, Freiburg: Herder.

—— (2007), *Jesaja 13–27*, tr. A. Spans, HTKAT, Freiburg: Herder.

—— (2010), *Jesaja 28–39*, tr. A. Spans, HTKAT, Freiburg: Herder.

—— (2015), 'Isaiah 24–27: Spacing a Prophetic Vision', in M. C. A. Korpel and L. L. Grabbe (eds.), *Open-Mindedness in the Bible and Beyond: A Volume of Studies in Honour of Bob Becking*, LHBOTS 616, London: Bloomsbury T&T Clark, 45–55.

Biddle, M. E. (2021), 'Jeremiah: Content and Structure', in L. Stulman and E. Silver (eds.), *The Oxford Handbook of Jeremiah*, Oxford: Oxford University Press, 235–251.

Billing, R. (2013), *'Israel Served the Lord': The Book of Joshua as Paradoxical Portrait of Faithful Israel*, Notre Dame: Notre Dame University Press.

Birnie, E. (2022), 'What Should Be Exchanged for a Human Life? Cost-Benefit and COVID-19', *Journal of Markets & Morality* 25.2: 161–185.

Blocher, H. (2002), 'Glorious Zion, Our Mother: Readings in Isaiah (Conspectus, or Abridged)', *EuroJTh* 11.1: 5–14.

Block, D. I. (1997), *The Book of Ezekiel: Chapters 1–24*, NICOT, Grand Rapids: Eerdmans.

—— (1998), *The Book of Ezekiel: Chapters 25–48*, NICOT, Grand Rapids: Eerdmans.

—— (2013), *Obadiah: The Kingship Belongs to YHWH*, ZECOT, Grand Rapids: Zondervan.

Block, D. I., and R. L. Schultz (2015), *Bind Up the Testimony: Explorations in the Genesis of the Book of Isaiah*, Peabody: Hendrickson.

Bock, D. (2012), *A Theology of Luke and Acts: God's Promised Program Realized for All Nations*, Grand Rapids: Zondervan.

Boda, M. (2016), *The Book of Zechariah*, NICOT, Grand Rapids: Eerdmans.

Bosma, C. J. (2013), 'Jonah 1:9 – An Example of Elenctic Testimony', *CTJ* 48: 65–90.

Bosman, H. L. (1997), 'רזה', *NIDOTTE* 3:1087–1088.

Bowie, A. (2003), *Introduction to German Philosophy: From Kant to Habermas*, Cambridge: Polity.

Braulik, G. (1997), 'Die Völkervernichtung und die Rückkehr Israels ins Verheissungsland: Hermeneutische Bemerkungen zum Buch Deuteronomium', in M. Vervenne and J. Lust (eds.), *Deuteronomy and Deuteronomic Literature*, BETL 133, Leuven: Leuven University Press, 3–38.

Briant, P. (2002), *From Cyrus to Alexander: A History of the Persian Empire*, tr. P. T. Daniels, Winona Lake: Eisenbrauns.

Bricker, D. P. (2001), 'Innocent Suffering in Egypt', *TynBul* 52: 83–100.

Brosius, M. (2023), 'The Persian Empire: Perspectives on Culture and Society', in K. Radner et al. (eds.), *The Oxford History of the Ancient Near East, vol. 5: The Age of Persia*, Oxford: Oxford University Press, 949–1013.

Brueggemann, W. (1991), 'At the Mercy of Babylon: A Subversive Rereading of the Empire', *JBL* 110: 3–22.

—— (1997), *Theology of the Old Testament: Testimony, Dispute, Advocacy*, Minneapolis: Fortress.

Bryce, T. (2009), *The Routledge Handbook of the Peoples and Places of Ancient Western Asia: The Near East from the Early Bronze Age to the Fall of the Persian Empire*, London: Routledge.

Buckwalter, D. (1998), 'The Divine Saviour', in I. H. Marshall and D. Peterson (eds.), *Witness to the Gospel: The Theology of Acts*, Grand Rapids: Eerdmans, 107–123.

Bürki, M. (2013), 'City of Pride, City of Glory: The Opposition of Two Cities in Isaiah 24–27', in J. T. Hibbard and H. C. P. Kim (eds.), *Formation and Intertextuality in Isaiah 24–27*, AIL 17, Atlanta: Society of Biblical Literature, 49–60.

Burnett, J. S. (2016), 'Transjordan: The Ammonites, Moabites, and Edomites', in B. T. Arnold and B. A. Strawn (eds.), *The World around the Old Testament: The People and Places of the Ancient Near East*, Grand Rapids: Baker Academic, 309–350.

Buth, R. (1999), 'Word Order in the Verbless Clause', in C. L. Miller (ed.), *The Verbless Clause in Biblical Hebrew: Linguistic Approaches*, LSAWS 1, Winona Lake: Eisenbrauns, 79–108.

Calvin, John (1563), *Leçons et exposition familières de Jean Calvin sur les douze petis prophètes, asçavoir, Hosée, Joel, Amos, Abdias, Jonas, Michée, Habacuc, Sophonias, Aggée, Zacharie, Malachie*, Lyon: Sebastien Honorati.

Carley, K. (2004), 'From Harshness to Hope: The Implications for Earth of Hierarchy in Ezekiel', in S. L. Cook and C. L. Patton (eds.), *Ezekiel's Hierarchical World: Wrestling with a Tiered Reality*, SBLSymS 31, Leiden: Brill, 109–125.

Carroll R., M. D. (2015), '"I Will Send Fire": Reflections on the Violence of God in Amos', in M. D. Carroll R. and J. B. Wilgus (eds.), *Wrestling with the Violence of God: Soundings in the Old Testament*, BBRSup 10, Winona Lake: Eisenbrauns, 113–132.

—— (2020), *The Book of Amos*, NICOT, Grand Rapids: Eerdmans.

Carson, D. A. (2007), 'I Peter', in G. K. Beale and D. A. Carson (eds.), *Commentary on the New Testament Use of the Old Testament*, Grand Rapids: Baker Academic; Nottingham: Apollos, 1015–1045.

Carvalho, C. (2015), 'A Serpent in the Nile: Egypt in the Book of Ezekiel', in A. Mein et al. (eds.), *Concerning the Nations: Essays on the Oracles against the Nations in Isaiah, Jeremiah and Ezekiel*, LHBOTS 612, London: T&T Clark, 195–220.

Chan, M. J. (2017), *The Wealth of Nations: A Tradition-Historical Study*, FAT 2.93, Tübingen: Mohr Siebeck.

Chatonnet, F. B. (2023), 'The Iron Age States on the Phoenician Coast', in K. Radner et al. (eds.), *The Oxford History of the Ancient Near East, vol. 4: The Age of Assyria*, Oxford: Oxford University Press, 1027–1114.

Childs, B. S. (2001), *Isaiah*, OTL, Louisville: Westminster John Knox.

Ciftci, M. (2018), 'Saint Augustine and the Theological Critique of Ideology', *NBf* 99.1079: 20–29.

Claassens, L. J. M. (2019), 'Going Home? Exiles, Inciles and Refugees in the Book of Jeremiah', *HTS* 75.3: 1–6.

Clarysse, W. (2014), 'Egyptian Temples and Priests: Graeco-Roman', in A. B. Lloyd (ed.), *A Companion to Ancient Egypt*, Chichester: Blackwell, 274–290.

Clines, D. J. A. (ed.) (2009), *The Concise Dictionary of Classical Hebrew*, Sheffield: Sheffield Phoenix.

Cogan, M. (1983), '"Ripping Open Pregnant Women" in Light of an Assyrian Analogue', *JAOS* 103: 755–757.

—— (2003), 'Cyrus Cylinder (2.214)', *COS* 2:314–316.

Cole, G. A. (2023), 'Shalom', in G. K. Beale et al. (eds.), *Dictionary of the New Testament Use of the Old Testament*, Grand Rapids: Baker Academic, 779–783.

Collins, J. J. (2009), 'The Beginning of the End of the World in the Hebrew Bible', in J. J. Ahn and S. L. Cook (eds.), *Thus Says the Lord: Essays on the Former and Latter Prophets in Honor of Robert R. Wilson*, London: Bloomsbury, 137–155.

Collins, J. J., and A. Y. Collins (1993), *Daniel: A Commentary on the Book of Daniel*, Hermeneia, Minneapolis: Fortress.

Committee on Recent Economic Changes of the President's Conference on Unemployment (1929), *Recent Economic Changes in the United States*, 2 vols., n.p.: National Bureau of Economic Research, <www.nber.org/system/files/chapters/c4950/c4950.pdf> (accessed 31 October 2014).

Couey, J. B. (2015), 'Evoking and Evading: The Poetic Presentation of the Moabite Catastrophe in Isaiah 15–16', in E. K. Holt, H. C. P. Kim and A. Mein (eds.), *Concerning the Nations: Essays on the Oracles against the Nations in Isaiah, Jeremiah, and Ezekiel*, LHBOTS 612, London: Bloomsbury T&T Clark, 19–31.

Cox, G. (2013), 'The "Hymn" of Amos: An Ancient Flood Narrative', *JSOT* 38: 81–108.

Cox, H. (1999), 'The Market as God: Living in the New Dispensation', *The Atlantic* 283.3: 18–23.

Craigie, P. C., P. H. Kelley and J. F. Drinkard Jr (1991), *Jeremiah 1–25*, WBC, Dallas: Word.

Crenshaw, J. L. (1995), *Joel: A New Translation with Introduction and Commentary*, AB 24, New York: Doubleday.

Crouch, C. L. (2009), *War and Ethics in the Ancient Near East: Military Violence in Light of Cosmology and History*, BZAW 407, Berlin: De Gruyter.

—— (2011), 'Ezekiel's Oracles against the Nations in Light of a Royal Ideology of Warfare', *JBL* 130.3: 473–492.

—— (2023), 'Ezekiel and the Foreign Nations', in C. Carvalho (ed.), *The Oxford Handbook on Ezekiel*, Oxford: Oxford University Press, 278–294.

Curtis, J. (2005), 'The Archaeology of the Achaemenid Period', in J. Curtis and N. Tallis (eds.), *Forgotten Empire: The World of Ancient Persia*, London: British Museum Press, 30–49.

Curtis, J., and S. Razmjou (2005), 'The Palace', in J. Curtis and N. Tallis (eds.), *Forgotten Empire: The World of Ancient Persia*, London: British Museum Press, 50–103.

Dalley, S. (2021), *The City of Babylon: A History, c. 2000 BC–AD 116*, Cambridge: Cambridge University Press.

Dandamaev, M. A., and V. G. Lukonin (2004), *The Culture and Social Institutions of Ancient Iran*, Cambridge: Cambridge University Press.

David, R. (2007), 'Ancient Egypt', in J. R. Hinnells (ed.), *Penguin Handbook of Ancient Religions*, London: Penguin, 46–104.

Davidson, S. V. (2021), 'Geographies of Otherness: Otherness in Territorial Organization in the Oracles against the Nations', in S. V. Davidson and D. C. Timmer (eds.), *Prophetic Otherness: Constructions of Otherness in Prophetic Literature*, LHBOTS 687, London: T&T Clark, 192–207.

De Blois, R. (2021), 'Semantic Dictionary of Biblical Hebrew', <https://semanticdictionary.org/semdic.php?databaseType=SDBH&language=en> (accessed 30 March 2024).

Dearman, J. A. (2009), 'Daughter Zion and Her Place in God's Household', *HBT* 31: 144–159.

—— (2010), *Hosea*, NICOT, Grand Rapids: Eerdmans.

Dekker, J. (2021), 'Salvation for Israel and the Nations: Disputing the

Interpretation of Isaiah 25:6–8 as an Announcement of Doom', *BBR* 31.2: 154–166.

Delorme, J.-P. (2019), 'The Āl-Yāhrūdu Texts (ca. 572–477 BCE): A New Window into the Life of the Judean Exilic Community of Babylonia', in L. J. Greenspoon (ed.), *Next Year in Jerusalem: Exile and Return in Jewish History*, SJC 30, West Lafayette: Purdue University Press, 71–98.

Dempster, S. G. (2003), *Dominion and Dynasty: A Theology of the Hebrew Bible*, NSBT 15, Leicester: Apollos; Downers Grove: InterVarsity Press.

—— (2017), *Micah*, THOTC, Grand Rapids: Eerdmans.

—— (2018), '"At the End of the Days" (באחרית הימים) – An Eschatological Technical Term? The Intersection of Context, Linguistics and Theology', in E. C. Jones (ed.), *The Unfolding of Your Words Gives Light: Essays on Biblical Hebrew in Honor of George L. Klein*, Winona Lake: Eisenbrauns, 118–141.

—— (2023), 'Micah, Book of', in G. K. Beale et al. (eds.), *Dictionary of the New Testament Use of the Old Testament*, Grand Rapids: Baker Academic, 526–529.

Deneen, P. J. (2018), *Why Liberalism Failed*, New Haven: Yale University Press.

DeRouchie, J. S. (2023), 'Zephaniah, Book of', in G. K. Beale et al. (eds.), *Dictionary of the New Testament Use of the Old Testament*, Grand Rapids: Baker Academic, 886–890.

Desmond, W. (2013), 'The Metaphysics of Modernity', in N. Adams, G. Pattison and G. Ward (eds.), *The Oxford Handbook of Theology and Modern European Thought*, Oxford: Oxford University Press, 543–563.

Dewrell, H. D. (2021), 'Depictions of Egypt in the Book of Hosea and Their Implications for Dating the Book', *VT* 71: 503–530.

Dobbs-Allsopp, F. W. (2009), 'Daughter Zion', in J. J. Ahn and S. L. Cook (eds.), *Thus Says the Lord: Essays on the Former and Latter Prophets in Honor of Robert R. Wilson*, London: Bloomsbury, 125–134.

Dooley, M. (2009), *Roger Scruton: The Philosopher on Dover Beach: An Intellectual Biography*, London: Continuum.

—— (2023), 'The Religion of Antichrist', *European Conservative* 28: 127–130.

Dow, L. K. F. (2010), *Images of Zion: Biblical Antecedents for the New Jerusalem*, NTM 26, Sheffield: Sheffield Phoenix.

Doxey, D. M. (2002), 'Sobek', in D. J. Redford (ed.), *The Ancient Gods Speak: A Guide to Egyptian Religion*, Oxford: Oxford University Press, 336–337.

Dubovsky, P. (2009), 'Ripping Open Pregnant Arab Women: Reliefs in Room L of Ashurbanipal's North Palace', *Or* 78: 394–419.

Duguid, I. (2000), 'Zechariah', in T. D. Alexander and B. S. Rosner (eds.), *New Dictionary of Biblical Theology*, Leicester: Inter-Varsity Press; Downers Grove: InterVarsity Press, 257–260.

Eck, J. (2021), 'Metamorphoses of a Tyrant: Isaiah 14:4b–21 Read in Its Wider Context', in J. Stromberg and J. T. Hibbard (eds.), *The History of Isaiah*, FAT 150, Tübingen: Mohr Siebeck, 407–429.

Ehrenberg, E. (2008), 'Dieu et mon droit: Kingship in Late Babylonian and Early Persian Times', in N. Brisch (ed.), *Religion and Power: Divine Kingship in the Ancient World and Beyond*, OIS 4, Chicago: Oriental Institute of the University of Chicago, 103–131.

Ehrlich, C. S. (2016), 'Philistia and the Philistines', in B. T. Arnold and B. A. Strawn (eds.), *The World around the Old Testament: The People and Places of the Ancient Near East*, Grand Rapids: Baker Academic, 353–377.

Elat, M. (1991), 'Phoenician Overland Trade within the Mesopotamian Empires', in M. Cogan and I. Eph'al (eds.), *Ah, Assyria . . . Studies in Assyrian History and Ancient Near Eastern Historiography Presented to Hayim Tadmor*, Jerusalem: Magnes, 21–35.

Faulkner, R. K. (2003), 'Francis Bacon, *New Organon* (1620): The Politics and Philosophy of Experimental Science', in J. J. E. Gracia, G. M. Reichberg and B. N. Schumacher (eds.), *The Classics of Western Philosophy: A Reader's Guide*, Oxford: Blackwell, 210–216.

Favale, A. (2022), *The Genesis of Gender: A Christian Theory*, San Francisco: Ignatius.

Ferguson, S. (1996), *The Holy Spirit*, CCT, Leicester: Inter-Varsity Press.

Ferries, R. A. R. (2022), 'Edom and Babylon: Archetypal Enemies of God and His People; A Comparative Analysis of Obadiah and Isaiah 13:2–14:23', *OTE* 35.3: 475–495.

Firth, D. G. (2019), *Including the Stranger: Foreigners in the Former Prophets*, NSBT 50, London: Apollos; Downers Grove: InterVarsity Press.

Fischer, G. (2012), *Theologien des Alten Testaments*, NSKAT 31, Stuttgart: Katholisches Bibelwerk.

Fischer, I. (1995), *Tora für Israel – Tora für die Völker: Das Konzept des Jesajabuches*, SBS 164, Stuttgart: Katholisches Bibelwerk.

Floyd, M. H. (2008), 'Welcome Back, Daughter of Zion!' *CBQ* 70: 484–504.

Foster, B. R. (2003), 'Epic of Creation (1.111)', *COS* 1:390–402.

—— (2005), *Before the Muses: An Anthology of Akkadian Literature*, 3rd edn, Bethesda: CDL Press.

—— (2012), 'Enuma Elish as a Work of Literature', *CSMS Journal* 7: 19–23.

Foster, R. L. (2020), *The Theology of the Books of Haggai and Zechariah*, OTT, Cambridge: Cambridge University Press.

Frahm, E. (2010), 'Counter-Texts, Commentaries, and Adaptations: Politically Motivated Responses to the Babylonian Epic of Creation in Mesopotamia, the Biblical World, and Elsewhere', *Orient* 45: 3–33.

Franke, C. A. (1996), 'Reversals of Fortune in the Ancient Near East: A Study of the Babylon Oracles in the Book of Isaiah', in R. F. Melugin and M. A. Sweeney (eds.), *New Visions of Isaiah*, JSOTSup 214, Sheffield: Sheffield Academic, 104–123.

Freeden, M., and M. Stears (2013), 'Liberalism', in M. Freeden and M. Stears (eds.), *The Oxford Handbook of Political Ideologies*, Oxford: Oxford University Press, 329–347.

Frood, E. (2014), 'Social Structures and Daily Life: Pharaonic', in A. B. Lloyd (ed.), *A Companion to Ancient Egypt*, Chichester: Blackwell, 469–490.

Galambush, J. (2006), 'Necessary Enemies: Nebuchadnezzar, YHWH, and Gog in Ezekiel 38–39', in B. E. Kelle and M. B. Moore (eds.), *Israel's Prophets and Israel's Past: Essays on the Relationship of Prophetic Texts and Israelite History in Honor of John H. Hayes*, LHBOTS 446, New York: T&T Clark, 254–267.

Galter, H. D. (2007), 'Looking down the Tigris: The Interrelations between Assyria and Babylonia', in G. Leick (ed.), *The Babylonian World*, London: Routledge, 527–540.

García, J. C. M. (2021), 'Egypt, Old to New Kingdom (2686–1069 BCE)', in P. F. Bang (ed.), *The Oxford World History of Empire, vol. 2: The History of Empires*, Oxford: Oxford University Press, 13–42.

Garrett, D. (1997), *Hosea, Joel*, NAC 19A, Nashville: Broadman & Holman.

—— (2023a), 'Hosea, Book of', in G. K. Beale et al. (eds.), *Dictionary of the New Testament Use of the Old Testament*, Grand Rapids: Baker Academic, 336–341.

—— (2023b), 'Joel, Book of', in G. K. Beale et al. (eds.), *Dictionary of the New Testament Use of the Old Testament*, Grand Rapids: Baker Academic, 390–393.

Gärtner, J. (2012), 'Jerusalem – City of God for Israel and the Nations in

Zeph 3:8, 9–10, 11–13', in R. Albertz, J. D. Nogalski and J. Wöhrle (eds.), *Perspectives on the Formation of the Book of the Twelve: Methodological Foundations – Redactional Processes – Historical Insights*, BZAW 433, Berlin: De Gruyter, 269–283.

Gelston, A. (2010), *The Twelve Minor Prophets*, BHQ 13, Stuttgart: Deutsche Bibelgesellschaft.

George, A. R. (2016), 'Die Kosmogonie des alten Mesopotamien', in *Anfang und Ende: Vormoderne Szenarien von Weltentstehung und Weltuntergang*, Darmstadt: Philipp von Zabern, 7–25, 140–142.

Getz, T. R., and H. Streets-Salter (2011), *Modern Imperialism and Colonialism: A Global Perspective*, Boston: Prentice Hall.

Geyer, J. B. (2004), 'Ezekiel 31 and the Cosmic Tree', in *Mythology and Lament: Studies in the Oracles about the Nations*, SOTSMS, Burlington: Ashgate, 57–74.

Gibson, A. (2001), *Biblical Semantic Logic: A Preliminary Analysis*, 2nd edn, The Biblical Seminar 75, Sheffield: Sheffield Academic.

Gladd, B. L. (2021), *Handbook on the Gospels*, Grand Rapids: Baker Academic.

—— (2023), 'Mystery', in G. K. Beale et al. (eds.), *Dictionary of the New Testament Use of the Old Testament*, Grand Rapids: Baker Academic, 551–555.

Goldingay, J. (2021a), *The Book of Jeremiah*, NICOT, Grand Rapids: Eerdmans.

—— (2021b), *Hosea-Micah*, BCOTPB, Grand Rapids: Baker Academic.

Goldingay, J., and D. Payne (2006), *Isaiah 40–55*, 2 vols., London: T&T Clark.

Goldsworthy, G. (2000), *Preaching the Whole Bible as Christian Scripture: The Application of Biblical Theology to Expository Preaching*, Grand Rapids: Eerdmans.

—— (2006), *Gospel-Centered Hermeneutics: Foundations and Principles of Evangelical Biblical Interpretation*, Downers Grove: IVP Academic.

—— (2023), 'Israel and the Church, The Story of', in G. K. Beale et al. (eds.), *Dictionary of the New Testament Use of the Old Testament*, Grand Rapids: Baker Academic, 356–361.

Gordon, R. P. (2010), 'The Gods Must Die: A Theme in Isaiah and Beyond', in M. van der Meer et al. (eds.), *Isaiah in Context: Studies in Honour of Arie van der Kooij on the Occasion of His Sixty-Fifth Birthday*, VTSup 138, Leiden: Brill, 45–61.

Gosse, B. (1989), 'Ézéchiel 35–36, 1–15 et Ézéchiel 6: La Désolation de la montagne de Séir et le renouveau des montagnes d'Israël', *RB* 96: 511–517.

Goswell, G. (2013), 'The Eschatology of Malachi after Zechariah 14', *JBL* 132: 625–638.

—— (2014), 'Isaiah 16: A Forgotten Chapter in the History of Messianism', *SJOT* 28.1: 91–103.

Graybill, R. (2021), 'The Jeremian Oracles against the Nations', in L. Stulman and S. Edward (eds.), *The Oxford Handbook of Jeremiah*, Oxford: Oxford University Press, 387–404.

Grayson, A. K. (1975), *Babylonian Historical-Literary Texts*, TSTS 3, Toronto: University of Toronto Press.

—— (2000), *Assyrian and Babylonian Chronicles*, Winona Lake: Eisenbrauns.

Grayson, A. K., and J. Novotny (2012), *The Royal Inscriptions of Sennacherib, King of Assyria (704–681 BC), Part 1*, RINAP 3:1, Winona Lake: Eisenbrauns.

Green, G. (2004), 'Modernity', in G. Jones (ed.), *The Blackwell Companion to Modern Theology*, Oxford: Blackwell, 162–179.

Greenberg, M. (1983), *Ezekiel 1–20*, AYB 22A, New Haven: Yale University Press.

—— (1997), *Ezekiel 21–38*, AYB 22B, New Haven: Yale University Press.

Greenwood, K. (2006), 'Tiglath-Pileser I's Subjugation of the Nairi Lands', in M. Chavalas (ed.), *The Ancient Near East: Historical Sources in Translation*, Oxford: Blackwell, 157–160.

Gribben, C. (2021), *Survival and Resistance in Evangelical America: Christian Reconstructionism in the Pacific Northwest*, Oxford: Oxford University Press.

Griffiths, J. G. (2002), 'Myths (Solar Cycle)', in D. J. Redford (ed.), *The Ancient Gods Speak: A Guide to Egyptian Religion*, Oxford: Oxford University Press, 255–261.

Gunton, C. (1997), 'The Doctrine of Creation', in C. Gunton (ed.), *The Cambridge Companion to Christian Doctrine*, Cambridge: Cambridge University Press, 141–157.

—— (2005), 'In the Image and Likeness of God', in *Christ and Creation*, Eugene: Wipf & Stock, 99–116.

Gut, R., J. Reade and R. M. Boehmer (2001), 'Ninive: Das späte 3. Jahrtausend v. Chr.', in J.-W. Meyer, M. Novák and A. Pruß (eds.), *Beiträge zur Vorderasiatischen Archäologie: FS Winfried Orthmann*, Frankfurt am Main: Johann Wolfgang Goethe-Universität Archäologisches Institut, 74–129.

Hagedorn, A. (2012), 'Diaspora or No Diaspora? Some Remarks on the Role of Egypt and Babylon in the Book of the Twelve', in R. Albertz, J. D. Nogalski and J. Wöhrle (eds.), *Perspectives on the Formation of the Book of the Twelve: Methodological Foundations – Redactional Processes – Historical Insights*, BZAW 433, Berlin: De Gruyter, 319–336.

Hagelia, H. (2001), *Coram Deo: Spirituality in the Book of Isaiah, with Particular Attention to Faith in Yahweh*, CBOTS 49, Stockholm: Almqvist & Wiksell.

Hamborg, G. R. (2023), *Hosea, Joel, and Amos*, NCBC, Cambridge: Cambridge University Press.

Hamilton Jr, J. K. (2014), *With the Clouds of Heaven: The Book of Daniel in Biblical Theology*, NSBT 32, Nottingham: Apollos; Downers Grove: InterVarsity Press.

Haney, L. (2007), 'YHWH, the God of Israel . . . and of Edom? The Relationships in the Oracle to Edom in Jeremiah 49:7–22', in J. Goldingay (ed.), *Uprooting and Planting: Essays on Jeremiah for Leslie Allen*, London: T&T Clark, 78–115.

Harrison, R. K. (1973), *Jeremiah and Lamentations: An Introduction and Commentary*, TOTC 21, Leicester: Inter-Varsity Press.

Harvey, B. (2000), 'Anti-Postmodernism', in A. K. M. Adam (ed.), *Handbook of Postmodern Interpretation*, St Louis: Chalice, 1–7.

Hasel, G. F., and M. G. Hasel (2015), 'The Unique Cosmology of Genesis 1', in G. A. Klingbeil (ed.), *The Genesis Creation Account and Its Reverberations in the Old Testament*, Berrien Springs: Andrews University Press, 9–29.

Hassler, M. (2016), 'The Setting of Obadiah: When Does the Oracle Concerning Edom Transpire?' *JETS* 59.2: 241–254.

Hauser, S. R. (2017), 'Post-Imperial Assyria', in E. Frahm (ed.), *A Companion to Assyria*, Hoboken: Wiley Blackwell, 229–246.

Hayes, E. R. (2009), 'Of Branches, Pots and Figs: Jeremiah's Visions from a Cognitive Perspective', in H. M. Barstad and R. G. Kratz (eds.), *Prophecy in the Book of Jeremiah*, Berlin: De Gruyter, 89–102.

Hays, J. D. (2023), 'Ezekiel, Book of', in G. K. Beale et al. (eds.), *Dictionary of the New Testament Use of the Old Testament*, Grand Rapids: Baker Academic, 241–246.

Herring, J. (2023), 'Biblical Critical Theory and Other Errors', *Religion*

& Liberty Online, 19 January, <https://rlo.acton.org/archives/124161-biblical-critical-theory-and-other-errors.html> (accessed 26 January 2024).

Heywood, A. (2012), *Political Ideologies: An Introduction*, 5th edn, New York: Palgrave Macmillan.

Hibbard, J. T. (2015), 'Isaiah 19:18: A Textual Variant in Light of the Temple of Onias in Egypt', in E. K. Holt, H. C. P. Kim and A. Mein (eds.), *Concerning the Nations: Essays on the Oracles against the Nations in Isaiah, Jeremiah, and Ezekiel*, LHBOTS 612, London: Bloomsbury T&T Clark, 32–52.

Higgs, K. (2021), 'A Brief History of Consumer Culture', *The MIT Press Reader*, 11 January, <https://thereader.mitpress.mit.edu/a-brief-history-of-consumer-culture> (accessed 27 January 2024).

Hill, A. E. (2023), 'Zechariah, Book of', in G. K. Beale et al. (eds.), *Dictionary of the New Testament Use of the Old Testament*, Grand Rapids: Baker Academic, 880–885.

Hill, J. (1999), *Friend or Foe? The Figure of Babylon in the Book of Jeremiah MT*, BibInt 40, Leiden: Brill.

—— (2004), '"Your Exile Will Be Long": The Book of Jeremiah and the Unended Exile', in M. Kessler (ed.), *Reading the Book of Jeremiah: A Search for Coherence*, Winona Lake: Eisenbrauns.

Himbaza, I. (2012), '"*YHWH Seba'ot* devient le grand roi": Une interprétation de Ml 1,6–14 à la lumière du contexte perse', *VT* 62: 357–368.

Hintze, A. (2014), 'Monotheism the Zoroastrian Way', *JRAS* 24.2: 225–249.

Hoffmeier, J. K. (1997), *Israel in Egypt: The Evidence for the Authenticity of the Exodus Tradition*, Oxford: Oxford University Press.

—— (2003a), 'The Gebel Barkal Stela (2.2B)', *COS* 2:14–18.

—— (2003b), 'Understanding Hebrew and Egyptian Military Texts: A Contextual Approach', *COS* 3:xxi–xxvii.

Holladay, W. L. (1999), 'Text, Structure, and Irony in the Poem of the Fall of the Tyrant, Isaiah 14', *CBQ* 61.4: 633–645.

Hollis, S. T. (2009), 'Egyptian Literature', in Carl S. Ehrlich (ed.), *From an Antique Land: An Introduction to Ancient Near Eastern Literature*, Lanham: Rowman & Littlefield, 77–136.

Holloway, S. (2001), *Aššur Is King! Aššur Is King! Religion in the Exercise of Power in the Neo-Assyrian Empire*, CHANE 10, Leiden: Brill.

Horton, M. S. (2002), *Covenant and Eschatology: The Divine Drama*, Louisville: Westminster John Knox.

Hubbard Jr, R. L. (2011), 'The Spirit and Creation', in D. G. Firth and P. D. Wegner (eds.), *Presence, Power, and Promise: The Role of the Spirit of God in the Old Testament*, Downers Grove: InterVarsity Press, 71–91.

Hwang, J. (2013), 'The Missio Dei as an Integrative Motif in the Book of Jeremiah', *BBR* 23.4: 481–508.

—— (2016), '"I Am Yahweh Your God from the Land of Egypt": Hosea's Use of the Exodus Traditions', in J. K. Hoffmeier, A. R. Millard and G. A. Rendsburg (eds.), *'Did I Not Bring Israel Out of Egypt?' Biblical, Archaeological, and Egyptological Perspectives on the Exodus Narratives*, Winona Lake: Eisenbrauns, 243–253.

—— (2021), *Hosea*, ZECOT, Grand Rapids: Zondervan Academic.

Innes, D. C. (2019), *Francis Bacon*, Great Thinkers, Phillipsburg: P&R.

Irsigler, H. (2002), *Zefanja*, HTKAT, Freiburg: Herder.

Irvine, S. A. (2021), 'Hosea', in J. M. O'Brien (ed.), *The Oxford Handbook of the Minor Prophets*, Oxford: Oxford University Press, 399–410.

Israelit-Groll, S. (1998), 'The Egyptian Background to Isaiah 19.18', in M. Lubetski, C. Gottlieg and S. Keller (eds.), *Boundaries of the Ancient Near Eastern World*, LHBOTS 273, London: Bloomsbury T&T Clark, 300–303.

Jacobs, M. (2017), *The Books of Haggai and Malachi*, NICOT, Grand Rapids: Eerdmans.

Janák, J., and F. Coppens (2017), 'The Near and Distant King: Two Oppositions in the Concept of Divine Authority of the Egyptian King', in T. A. Bács and H. Beinlich (eds.), *Constructing Authority: 8th Symposium on Egyptian Royal Ideology*, Königtum, Staat und Gesellschaft 4.5, Wiesbaden: Harrassowitz, 131–144.

Johnson, D. E. (2023), 'Holy Spirit, Eschatological Role of', in G. K. Beale et al. (eds.), *Dictionary of the New Testament Use of the Old Testament*, Grand Rapids: Baker Academic, 331–336.

Kähler, S. (2021), 'Who Is Who in Babylonia? Identity and Belonging in the Prayer for the Babylonian City (Jer 29:7)', *TZ* 77.2: 102–119.

Kaminsky, J. S. (2007), *Yet I Loved Jacob: Reclaiming the Biblical Concept of Election*, Nashville: Abingdon.

Kant, I. (1991), 'An Answer to the Question "What Is Enlightenment?"', in H. Reiss (ed.), *Kant: Political Writings*, Cambridge: Cambridge University Press, 54–60.

Karlsson, M. (2022), '"An Object of Wonder for All the People": Ideology and Propaganda in the Neo-Assyrian and Neo-Babylonian Empires', in

L. Portuese and L. Pallavidini (eds.), *Near Eastern Weltanschauungen in Contact and in Contrast: Rethinking the Terms Ideology and Propaganda*, Münster: Zaphon, 245–269.

Keel, O. (1978), *The Symbolism of the Biblical World: Ancient Near Eastern Iconography and the Book of Psalms*, tr. T. J. Hallett, Winona Lake: Eisenbrauns.

Kellermann, D. (1995), 'לוה', *TDOT* 7:475–476.

Keown, G. L., P. J. Scalise and T. G. Smothers (1995), *Jeremiah 26–52*, WBC 27, Dallas: Word.

Kessler, J. (1987), 'The Shaking of the Nations: An Eschatological View', *JETS* 30: 159–166.

Kessler, M. (2004), 'The Scaffolding of the Book of Jeremiah', in M. Kessler (ed.), *Reading the Book of Jeremiah: A Search for Coherence*, Winona Lake: Eisenbrauns, 57–66.

Kessler, R. (1999), *Micha*, HTKAT, Freiburg: Herder.

—— (2011), *Maleachi*, HTKAT, Freiburg: Herder.

—— (2021), 'Micah', in J. M. O'Brien (ed.), *The Oxford Handbook of the Minor Prophets*, Oxford: Oxford University Press, 461–472.

Kilchör, B. (2017), 'The Meaning of Ezekiel 44,6–14 in Light of Ezekiel 1–39', *Bib* 98.2: 191–207.

Kim, H. C. P. (2020), 'The Oracles against the Nations', in L.-S. Tiemeyer (ed.), *The Oxford Handbook on Isaiah*, Oxford: Oxford University Press, 59–78.

King, A. M. (2021), *Social Identity and the Book of Amos*, LHBOTS 706, London: T&T Clark.

King, D. (1999), *In the Name of Liberalism: Illiberal Social Policy in the USA and Britain*, Oxford: Oxford University Press.

Klink III, E. W., and D. Lockett (2012), *Understanding Biblical Theology: A Comparison of Theory and Practice*, Grand Rapids: Zondervan.

Koehler, L., and W. Baumgartner (2001), *The Hebrew and Aramaic Lexicon of the Old Testament*, study edn, 2 vols., Leiden: Brill.

Koet, B. J. (2005), 'Isaiah in Luke-Acts', in S. Moyise and M. J. J. Menken (eds.), *Isaiah in the New Testament*, London: T&T Clark, 79–100.

Kohler, S. R. (1879), *Architecture, Sculpture, and the Industrial Arts among the Nations of Antiquity: A Series of Illustrations Arranged Chronologically, and Forming an Atlas, to Be Used in Connection with Any Work on the History of Art*, authorized American edn, Boston: L. Prang and Company, series I, plate 1, figure 1, posted publicly for all uses as a work in the public domain at <www.flickr.com/photos/psulib-scollections/5833058665> (accessed 29 March 2024).

Koole, J. L. (1997), *Isaiah III, vol. 1: Isaiah 40–48*, tr. A. P. Runia, HCOT, Kampen: Kok Pharos.

—— (2001), *Isaiah III, vol. 3: Isaiah 56–66*, tr. A. P. Runia, HCOT, Kampen: Kok Pharos.

Köstenberger, A. J. (2007), 'John', in G. K. Beale and D. A. Carson (eds.), *Commentary on the New Testament Use of the Old Testament*, Grand Rapids: Baker Academic; Nottingham: Apollos, 415–512.

Köstenberger, A. J., and P. T. O'Brien (2001), *Salvation to the Ends of the Earth: A Biblical Theology of Mission*, NSBT 11, Leicester: Apollos; Downers Grove: InterVarsity Press.

Koyzis, D. (2013), *Political Visions and Illusions: A Survey and Christian Critique of Contemporary Ideologies*, Downers Grove: IVP Academic.

Kramer, S. N. (tr.) (1969), 'A Sumerian Lamentation', in *ANET*, 455–463.

Kuhrt, A. (1995), *The Ancient Near East c. 3000–330 BC*, Routledge History of the Ancient World, 2 vols., London: Routledge.

—— (2001), 'The Achaemenid Persian Empire (c. 550–c. 330 BCE): Continuities, Adaptations, Transformations', in S. Alcock, T. D'Altroy, K. Morrison and C. Sinopoli (eds.), *Empires: Perspectives from Archaeology and History*, Cambridge: Cambridge University Press, 93–123.

—— (2007), *The Persian Empire: A Corpus of Sources from the Achaemenid Empire*, London: Routledge.

Lacocque, A. (1981), 'II Zacharie', *Aggée, Zacharie, Malachie*, Commentaire de L'Ancien Testament 11c, Neuchâtel: Delachaux & Niestlé, 127–216.

Ladd, G. E. (1972), *A Commentary on the Revelation of John*, Grand Rapids: Eerdmans.

Landy, F. (2021), 'Language and Silence in Isaiah's Oracles against the Nations', in S. V. Davidson and D. C. Timmer (eds.), *Prophetic Otherness: Constructions of Otherness in Prophetic Literature*, LHBOTS 687, London: T&T Clark, 105–125.

Larsen, M. T. (ed.) (1979), *Power and Propaganda: A Symposium on Ancient Empires*, Copenhagen: Akademisk Forlag.

Lee, L. (2016), *Mapping Judah's Fate in Ezekiel's Oracles against the Nations*, ANEM 15, Atlanta: Society of Biblical Literature.

—— (2017), 'The Enemies Within: Gog of Magog in Ezekiel 38–39', *HTS* 73.3: 1–7.

Lee, P. Y. (2016), 'Jeremiah', in M. V. Van Pelt (ed.), *A Biblical-Theological Introduction to the Old Testament: The Gospel Promised*, Wheaton: Crossway, 277–303.

Leichty, E. (2011), *The Royal Inscriptions of Esarhaddon, King of Assyria (680–669 BC)*, RINAP 4, Winona Lake: Eisenbrauns.

Leprohon, R. J. (2006), 'Royal Ideology and State Administration in Pharaonic Egypt', *CANE*, 273–287.

Lesko, L. H. (1991), 'Ancient Egyptian Cosmogonies and Cosmology', in B. E. Shafer (ed.), *Religion in Ancient Egypt: Gods, Myths, and Personal Practice*, Ithaca: Cornell University Press, 88–122.

Lessing, R. (2003), 'Satire in Isaiah's Tyre Oracle', *JSOT* 28.1: 89–112.

Letham, R. (2019), *Systematic Theology*, Wheaton: Crossway.

Levavi, Y. (2020), 'The Neo-Babylonian Empire: The Imperial Periphery as Seen from the Centre', *JANEH* 7: 59–84.

Levenson, J. D. (1996), 'The Universal Horizon of Biblical Particularism', in M. Brett (ed.), *Ethnicity and the Bible*, BibInt 19, Leiden: Brill, 143–169.

Levine, B. A., and J.-M. de Tarragon (1993), 'The King Proclaims the Day: Ugaritic Rites for the Vintage', *RB* 100: 76–115.

Lichtheim, M. (2003), 'The Victory Stela of King Piye (Piankhy) (2.7)', *COS* 2:42–51.

—— (2006), *Ancient Egyptian Literature, vol. 1: The Old and Middle Kingdoms*, Berkeley: University of California Press.

Lincoln, B. (2008), 'The Role of Religion in Achaemenian Imperialism', in N. Brisch (ed.), *Religion and Power: Divine Kingship in the Ancient World and Beyond*, OIS 4, Chicago: Oriental Institute of the University of Chicago, 221–241.

—— (2013), 'Religion, Empire, and the Spectre of Orientalism: A Recent Controversy in Achaemenid Studies', *JNES* 72.2: 253–265.

Lints, R. (2006), 'Imaging and Idolatry: The Sociality of Personhood in the Canon', in R. Lints, M. S. Horton and M. R. Talbot (eds.), *Personal Identity in Theological Perspective*, Grand Rapids: Eerdmans, 204–225.

Liverani, M. (1991), 'The Trade Network of Tyre According to Ezek 27', in M. Cogan and I. Eph'al (eds.), *Ah, Assyria . . . Studies in Assyrian History and Ancient Near Eastern Historiography Presented to Hayim Tadmor*, Jerusalem: Magnes, 65–79.

—— (2017), *Assyria: The Imperial Mission*, tr. A. Trameri and J. Valk, Winona Lake: Eisenbrauns.

Lloyd, A. B. (2014), 'Chronology', in A. B. Lloyd (ed.), *A Companion to Ancient Egypt*, Chichester: Blackwell, xxxvii–xlviii.

Lundbom, J. R. (2004), *Jeremiah 37–52: A New Translation with Introduction and Commentary*, AB 21C, New York: Doubleday.

Luther, M. (1974), *Luther's Works, vol. 19: Lectures on the Minor Prophets II: Jonah, Habakkuk*, ed. H. C. Oswald, St Louis: Concordia.

McConville, J. G. (2023), *Isaiah*, BCOTPB, Grand Rapids: Baker Academic.

Machinist, P. (2016), '"Ah, Assyria . . ." (Isaiah 10:5ff.): Isaiah's Assyrian Polemic Revisited', in G. Bartoloni and M. G. Biga (eds.), *Not Only History: Proceedings of the Conference in Honor of Mario Liverani Held in Sapienza-Università di Roma, Dipartimento di Scienze dell'Antichità, 20–21 April 2009*, Winona Lake: Eisenbrauns, 183–217.

McKelvey, R. J. (2000), 'Temple', in T. D. Alexander and B. S. Rosner (eds.), *New Dictionary of Biblical Theology*, Leicester: Inter-Varsity Press; Downers Grove: InterVarsity Press, 806–811.

McMuller, S. (2014), 'Radical Orthodox Economics', *Christian Scholar's Review* 43: 343–364.

McNicol, A. J. (2011), *The Conversion of the Nations in Revelation*, LNTS 438, London: T&T Clark.

Maier, A. M. (2004), 'The Historical Background and Dating of Amos VI 2: An Archaeological Perspective from Tell Eṣ-Ṣâfi/Gath', *VT* 54: 319–334.

Martin, O. (2023), 'Land', in G. K. Beale et al. (eds.), *Dictionary of the New Testament Use of the Old Testament*, Grand Rapids: Baker Academic, 445–449.

Mason, R. (2000), 'Obadiah', in J. Barton and I. Muddiman (eds.), *The Oxford Bible Commentary*, Oxford: Oxford University Press, 590–592.

Mathews, K. (1996), *Genesis 1–11:26*, NAC, Nashville: Broadman & Holman.

Mathewson, D. (2005), 'Isaiah in Revelation', in S. Moyise and M. J. J. Menken (eds.), *Isaiah in the New Testament*, London: T&T Clark, 190–210.

Mattingly, G. L. (2000a), 'Children', in *DANE*, 72–73.

—— (2000b), 'Phoenicia', in *DANE*, 229–230.

Mayer, W. R. (1987), 'Ein Mythos von der Erschaffung des Menschen und des Königs', *Or* 56: 55–68.

Mazurel, J. W. (2004), 'Citations from the Book of Jeremiah in the New

Testament', in M. Kessler (ed.), *Reading the Book of Jeremiah: A Search for Coherence*, Winona Lake: Eisenbrauns, 181–190.

Meek, E. L. (2011), *Loving to Know: Introducing Covenant Epistemology*, Eugene: Cascade.

Melville, S. C. (2006), 'Apology and Egyptian Campaigns', in M. Chavalas (ed.), *The Ancient Near East: Historical Sources in Translation*, Oxford: Blackwell, 363–365.

Meyers, C. L., and E. M. Meyers (1987), *Haggai, Zechariah 1–8*, AB 25B, New York: Doubleday.

—— (1993), *Haggai, Zechariah 9–14*, AB 25C, New York: Doubleday.

Milbank, J., C. Pickstock and G. Ward (1999), *Radical Orthodoxy: A New Theology*, New York: Routledge.

Millard, A. (2000), 'Creation Legends and Cosmogonies', in *DANE*, 81–82.

—— (2012), 'From Woe to Weal: Completing a Pattern in the Bible and the Ancient Near East', in I. Provan and M. J. Boda (eds.), *Let Us Go Up to Zion: Essays in Honour of H. G. M. Williamson on the Occasion of His Sixty-Fifth Birthday*, VTSup 153, Leiden: Brill.

Minich, J. (2023), *Bulwarks of Unbelief: Atheism and Divine Absence in a Secular Age*, Bellingham: Lexham Academic.

Moo, D. J. (1996), *Romans*, NICNT, Grand Rapids: Eerdmans.

Moore, E. (2011), 'Joel's Promise of the Spirit', in D. G. Firth and P. D. Wegner (eds.), *Presence, Power, and Promise: The Role of the Spirit of God in the Old Testament*, Nottingham: Apollos, 245–256.

Morgan, C. (2006), 'The Construction of a New Capital', in M. Chavalas (ed.), *The Ancient Near East: Historical Sources in Translation*, Oxford: Blackwell, 153–156.

Morris, E. F. (2014), 'The Pharaoh and Pharaonic Office', in A. B. Lloyd (ed.), *A Companion to Ancient Egypt*, Chichester: Blackwell, 201–217.

Morris, I., and W. Scheidel (eds.) (2009), *The Dynamics of Ancient Empires: State Power from Assyria to Byzantium*, Oxford: Oxford University Press.

Morrow, W. (2013), 'Were There Neo-Assyrian Influences in Manasseh's Temple? Comparative Evidence from Tel-Miqne/Ekron', *CBQ* 75: 53–73.

Naugle, D. K. (2002), *Worldview: The History of a Concept*, Grand Rapids: Eerdmans.

—— (2008), *Reordered Love, Reordered Lives: Learning the Deep Meaning of Happiness*, Grand Rapids: Eerdmans.

Naunton, C. (2014), 'Libyans and Nubians', in A. B. Lloyd (ed.), *A Companion to Ancient Egypt*, Chichester: Blackwell, 120–139.

Nevader, M. (2015a), 'On Reading Ezekiel by the Rivers of Babylon', *Die Welt des Orients* 45.1: 99–110.

—— (2015b), 'YHWH and the Kings of Middle Earth: Royal Polemic in Ezekiel's Oracles against the Nations', in E. K. Holt, H. C. P. Kim and A. Mein (eds.), *Concerning the Nations: Essays on the Oracles against the Nations in Isaiah, Jeremiah, and Ezekiel*, LHBOTS 612, London: Bloomsbury T&T Clark, 161–178.

—— (2023), 'Ezekiel and Politics', in C. Carvalho (ed.), *The Oxford Handbook on Ezekiel*, Oxford: Oxford University Press, 218–236.

Nguyen, K. L. (2021), 'Cyrus: A Righteousness', in J. Stromberg and J. T. Hibbard (eds.), *The History of Isaiah*, FAT 150, Tübingen: Mohr Siebeck, 475–492.

Nietzsche, F. (1967), *The Will to Power*, tr. W. Kaufmann and R. J. Hollingdale, New York: Random House.

Noegel, S. B. (2007), 'Dismemberment, Creation, and Ritual: Images of Divine Violence in the Ancient Near East', in J. K. Wellman Jr (ed.), *Belief and Bloodshed: Religion and Violence across Time and Tradition*, Lanham: Rowman & Littlefield, 13–27.

Nogalski, J. D. (1993a), *Literary Precursors to the Book of the Twelve*, BZAW 217, Berlin: De Gruyter.

—— (1993b), *Redactional Processes in the Book of the Twelve*, BZAW 218, Berlin: De Gruyter.

—— (2013), 'Zephaniah's Use of Genesis 1–11', *HBAI* 2: 351–372.

O'Brien, P. T. (1991), *The Epistle to the Philippians: A Commentary on the Greek Text*, NIGTC, Grand Rapids: Eerdmans.

Oded, B. (1995), 'Observations on the Israelite/Judean Exiles in Mesopotamia during the Eighth–Sixth Centuries BCE', in K. van Lerberghe and S. Anton (eds.), *Immigration and Emigration within the Ancient Near East*, OLA, Leuven: Peeters, 205–212.

Odell, M. S. (2005), *Ezekiel*, SHBC, Macon: Smyth & Helwys.

O'Donovan, O. (1994), *Resurrection and Moral Order: An Outline for Evangelical Ethics*, 2nd edn, Grand Rapids: Eerdmans.

—— (1995), 'Augustine's *City of God* XIX and Western Political Thought', in D. F. Donnelly (ed.), *The City of God: A Collection of Critical Essays*, New York: Peter Lang, 135–150.

—— (2014), *Ethics as Theology, vol. 2: Finding and Seeking*, Grand Rapids: Eerdmans.

Oehler, G. F. (1883), *Theology of the Old Testament*, tr. and ed. G. E. Day, New York: Funk & Wagnalls.

O'Kennedy, D. F. (2014), 'Haggai 2:20–23: Call to Rebellion or Eschatological Expectation?' *OTE* 27.2: 520–540.

Oppenheim, A. L. (tr.) (1969), 'Babylonian and Assyrian Historical Texts', *ANET*, 265–317.

Ortlund Jr, R. C. (1996), *Whoredom: God's Unfaithful Wife in Biblical Theology*, NSBT 2, Leicester: Apollos; Grand Rapids: Eerdmans.

Osborne, W. R. (2018), 'Wisdom Gets "Tyred" in the Book of Ezekiel', in M. J. Boda et al. (eds.), *Riddles and Revelations: Explorations into the Relationship between Wisdom and Prophecy in the Hebrew Bible*, LHBOTS 634, London: T&T Clark, 108–123.

Oswalt, J. (1986), *The Book of Isaiah: Chapters 1–39*, NICOT, Grand Rapids: Eerdmans.

—— (1996), 'Judgment and Hope: The Full-Orbed Gospel', *TrinJ* NS 17: 191–202.

—— (1997), 'Righteousness in Isaiah: A Study of the Function of Chapters 56–66 in the Present Structure of the Book', in C. C. Broyles and C. A. Evans (eds.), *Writing and Reading the Scroll of Isaiah: Studies of an Interpretive Tradition*, 2 vols., VTSup 70, Leiden: Brill, 1:177–192.

—— (1998), *The Book of Isaiah: Chapters 40–66*, NICOT, Grand Rapids: Eerdmans.

—— (2006), 'The Nations in Isaiah: Friend or Foe, Servant or Partner', *BBR* 16: 41–51.

—— (2023), 'Isaiah, Book of', in G. K. Beale et al. (eds.), *Dictionary of the New Testament Use of the Old Testament*, Grand Rapids: Baker Academic, 351–356.

Pannkuk, J. (2021), *King of Kings: God and the Foreign Emperor in the Hebrew Bible*, Waco: Baylor University Press.

Pao, D. W., and E. J. Schnabel (2007), 'Luke', in G. K. Beale and D. A. Carson (eds.), *Commentary on the New Testament Use of the Old Testament*, Grand Rapids: Baker Academic; Nottingham: Apollos, 251–414.

Paul, S. M. (2012), *Isaiah 40–66: Translation and Commentary*, ECC, Grand Rapids: Eerdmans.

Pearcey, N. R. (2018), *Love Thy Body: Answering Hard Questions about Life and Sexuality*, Grand Rapids: Baker.

Peels, H. G. L. (1997), 'קנא', *NIDOTTE* 3:937–940.

—— (2007), '"You Shall Certainly Drink!" The Place and Significance of the Oracles against the Nations in the Book of Jeremiah', *EuroJTh* 16.2: 81–91.

Perdu, O. (2014), 'Saites and Persians (664–332)', in A. B. Lloyd (ed.), *A Companion to Ancient Egypt*, Chichester: Blackwell, 140–158.

Peter, S. (2023), 'Fanon's Seduction of the Left', *First Things*, 13 October.

Peterson, D. L. (1992), 'Eschatology (OT)', *ABD* 2:575–579.

—— (1998), 'Luke's Theological Enterprise', in I. H. Marshall and D. Peterson (eds.), *Witness to the Gospel: The Theology of Acts*, Grand Rapids: Eerdmans, 521–544.

—— (2004), 'Creation and Hierarchy in Ezekiel: Methodological Perspectives and Theological Prospects', in S. L. Cook and C. L. Patton (eds.), *Ezekiel's Hierarchical World: Wrestling with a Tiered Reality*, SBLSymS 31, Leiden: Brill, 169–178.

Petterson, A. R. (2015), *Haggai, Zechariah and Malachi*, AOTC 25, Nottingham: Apollos; Downers Grove: InterVarsity Press.

—— (2018), 'Zechariah', in I. M. Duguid, J. M. Hamilton Jr and J. Sklar (eds.), *ESV Expository Commentary*, Wheaton: Crossway, 7:629–728.

Pfau, T. (2016), 'Religion', in P. Hamilton (ed.), *The Oxford Handbook of European Romanticism*, Oxford: Oxford University Press, 730–751.

—— (2023), '*Grandeur et misère de l'homme*: AI and/or Human Flourishing', unpublished paper, <www.academia.edu/112367821/_Grandeur_et_Mis%C3%A8re_de_l_homme_AI_and_or_Human_Flourishing> (accessed 27 January 2024).

Phillips, E. A. (2022), *Obadiah, Jonah and Micah*, AOTC, London: Apollos.

Piotrowski, N. G. (2023), 'Exodus, The', in G. K. Beale et al. (eds.), *Dictionary of the New Testament Use of the Old Testament*, Grand Rapids: Baker Academic, 235–241.

Pischikova, E. (2014), *Tombs of the South Asasif Necropolis: Thebes, Karakhamun (TT 223), and Karabasken (TT 391) in the Twenty-Fifth Dynasty*, Cairo: American University in Cairo Press.

Plant, R. J. R. (2008), *Good Figs, Bad Figs: Judicial Differentiation in the Book of Jeremiah*, LHBOTS 483, New York: T&T Clark.

Pongratz-Leisten, B. (2012), 'Creation and Cosmogony (Mesopotamia)', *EBR* 5:963–966.

Porter, S. E. (2016), *Sacred Tradition in the New Testament: Tracing Old Testament Themes in the Gospels and Epistles*, Grand Rapids: Baker Academic.

Provan, I. (1999), 'To Highlight All Our Idols: Worshipping God in Nietzsche's World', *ExAud* 15: 19–38.

Raabe, P. R. (1995), 'Why Prophetic Oracles against the Nations?' in A. Beck, A. Bartlett, C. Franke and P. Raabe (eds.), *Fortunate the Eyes That See: Essays in Honor of David Noel Freedman in Celebration of His Seventieth Birthday*, Grand Rapids: Eerdmans, 236–257.

—— (2013), 'Christ and the Nations: Israel's Gentile Oracles', *Concordia Journal*, Winter: 25–33.

—— (2018), 'What Is Israel's God Up To among the Nations? Jeremiah 46, 48, and 49', in J. R. Lundbom, C. A. Evans and B. A. Anderson (eds.), *The Book of Jeremiah: Composition, Reception, and Interpretation*, VTSup 178, Leiden: Brill, 230–252.

Radner, K. (2011), 'Royal Decision-Making: Kings, Magnates, and Scholars', in K. Radner and E. Robson (eds.), *The Oxford Handbook of Cuneiform Culture*, Oxford: Oxford University Press, 358–379.

Rasmussen, J. (2017), 'The Transformation of Metaphysics', in J. Rasmussen, J. Wolfe and J. Zachhuber (eds.), *The Oxford Handbook of Nineteenth-Century Christian Thought*, Oxford: Oxford University Press, 11–34.

Reade, J. (1978), 'Studies in Assyrian Geography, Part 1: Sennacherib and the Waters of Nineveh', *Revue d'assyriologie et d'archéologie orientale* 72: 47–72.

—— (2005), 'The Ishtar Temple at Nineveh', *Iraq* 67: 347–390.

Redford, D. B. (1992), *Egypt, Canaan, and Israel in Ancient Times*, Princeton: Princeton University Press.

—— (2002), *The Ancient Gods Speak: A Guide to Egyptian Religion*, Oxford: Oxford University Press.

Renaud, B. (1987), *Michée, Sophonie, Nahum*, SB, Paris: J. Gabalda et Cie.

Rendtorff, R. (2000), 'How to Read the Book of the Twelve as a Theological Unity', in J. D. Nogalski and M. A. Sweeney (eds.), *Reading and Hearing the Book of the Twelve*, SBLSymS 15, Atlanta: Scholars Press, 75–87.

Reno, R. R. (2006), 'Pride and Idolatry', *Int* 60: 166–180.

Renz, T. (2000), 'Proclaiming the Future: History and Theology in Prophecies against Tyre', *TynBul* 51.1: 17–58.

—— (2002), *The Rhetorical Function of the Book of Ezekiel*, VTSup 76, Leiden: Brill.

—— (2021), *The Books of Nahum, Habakkuk, and Zephaniah*, NICOT, Grand Rapids: Eerdmans.

Richelle, M. (2012), 'L'Affluence des nations à Jérusalem en vue du salut', in A. Nisus (ed.), *L'Amour de la sagesse: Hommage à Henri Blocher*, Charols: Excelsis, 103–119.

Ricoeur, P. (1967), *The Symbolism of Evil*, tr. E. Buchanan, Boston: Beacon.

Riecker, S. (2016), 'Mission in the Hebrew Bible Revisited: Four Theological Trails instead of One Defining Concept', *Missiology* 44: 324–339.

Ristau, K. A. (2016), *Reconstructing Jerusalem: Persian-Period Prophetic Perspectives*, Winona Lake: Eisenbrauns.

Roberts, J. J. M. (1991), *Nahum, Habakkuk, Zephaniah*, OTL, Louisville: Westminster John Knox.

Roberts, R. C. (2009), 'The Vice of Pride', *Faith and Philosophy* 26.2: 119–133.

Robertson, O. P. (2004), *The Christ of the Prophets*, Phillipsburg: P&R.

Rogland, M. (2017), 'A "Cryptic Phrase" in Haggai 2:6', *JBL* 136: 585–592.

Romerowski, S. (1989), *Les Livres de Joël et d'Abdias*, CEB, Vaux-sur-Seine: Édifac.

Rosner, B. S. (1998), 'The Progress of the Word', in I. H. Marshall and D. Peterson (eds.), *Witness to the Gospel: The Theology of Acts*, Grand Rapids: Eerdmans, 215–233.

—— (2000), 'Biblical Theology', in T. D. Alexander and B. S. Rosner (eds.), *New Dictionary of Biblical Theology*, Leicester: Inter-Varsity Press; Downers Grove: InterVarsity Press, 3–11.

Rossi, B., D. S. Irudayaraj and G. Hens-Piazza (eds.) (2023), *Unity in the Book of Isaiah*, LHBOTS 732, London: T&T Clark.

Roth, M. (2005), *Israel und die Völker im Zwölfprophetenbuch: Eine Untersuchung zu den Büchern Joel, Jona, Micha und Nahum*, FRLANT 210, Göttingen: Vandenhoeck & Ruprecht.

Sæbø, M. (1978), 'Vom Grossreich zum Weltreich: Erwägungen zu Pss. lxxii 8, lxxxix 26; Sach. Ix 10b', *VT* 28: 83–91.

Sals, U. (2014), '"Babylon" Forever, or How to Divinize What You Want to Damn', in D. V. Edelman and E. Ben Zvi (eds.), *Memory and the City in Ancient Israel*, Winona Lake: Eisenbrauns, 293–308.

Sands, P. (2010), 'The Deadly Sin of Pride', *Faith and Community Ministries: Empowering through Faith* 23.4: 40–49.

Sandy, D. B. (2002), *Plowshares and Pruning Hooks: Rethinking the Language of Biblical Prophecy and Apocalyptic*, Downers Grove: InterVarsity Press.

Saur, M. (2020), 'Vom Untergang Ägyptens: Ez 29–32 im Kontext des Ezechielbuches', in J. C. Gertz et al. (eds.), *Das Buch Ezechiel: Komposition, Redaktion und Rezeption*, Berlin: De Gruyter, 151–174.

Scalise, P. J. (1998), 'Malachi 3:13 – 4:3: A Book of Remembrance for God-Fearers', *RevExp* 95: 571–581.

Schart, A. (2012), 'Twelve, Book of the: History of Interpretation', in M. J. Boda and J. G. McConville (eds.), *Dictionary of the Old Testament: Prophets*, Downers Grove: IVP Academic, 806–817.

Schaumberger, J. B. (1934), 'Das Bussedikt des Königs von Ninive bei Jonas 3, 7. 8 in keilschriftlicher Beleuchtung', *Miscellanae Biblica* 2: 123–134.

Scheidel, W. (2013), 'Studying the State', in P. F. Bang and W. Scheidel (eds.), *The Oxford Handbook of the State in the Ancient Near East*, Oxford: Oxford University Press, 5–57.

Schmid, K., and O. H. Steck (2001), 'Restoration in the Prophetic Literature', in J. Scott (ed.), *Restoration: Old Testament, Jewish, and Christian Perspectives*, SJSJ 72, Leiden: Brill, 41–81.

Schnittjer, G. E. (2021), *Old Testament Use of Old Testament: A Book-by-Book Guide*, Grand Rapids: Zondervan Academic.

Schroeder, C. O. (2001), *History, Justice, and the Agency of God*, BibInt 52, Leiden: Brill.

Schuele, A. (2014), 'Build Up, Pass Through: Isaiah 57:14–62:12 as the Core Composition of Third Isaiah in the Book of Isaiah', in R. J. Bautch and J. T. Hibbard (eds.), *The Book of Isaiah: Enduring Questions Answered Anew; Essays Honoring Joseph Blenkinsopp and His Contribution to the Study of Isaiah*, Grand Rapids: Eerdmans, 83–110.

Schulmeister, I. (2012), 'Signale von "Grenzkonstruktion und die Grenzdestruktion" in Dtn 23,2–9 und Jes 56,1–8', in G. Baumann et al. (eds.), *Zugänge zum Fremden: Methodisch-hermeneutische Perspektiven zu einem biblischen Thema*, LPhThB 25, Frankfurt am Main: Peter Lang, 31–51.

Schultz, R. (2005), 'Isaiah, Book of', in K. J. Vanhoozer (ed.), *Dictionary for Theological Interpretation of the Bible*, Grand Rapids: Baker Academic, 336–344.

—— (2009), 'Nationalism and Universalism in Isaiah', in D. G. Firth and H. G. M. Williamson (eds.), *Interpreting Isaiah: Issues and Approaches*, Downers Grove: IVP Academic, 122–144.

Schweiker, W. (1995), 'Power and the Agency of God', *ThTo* 52: 204–224.

Scolnic, B. (2023), 'Let My Outcasts, Moab, Find Asylum in You:

Compassion for Fugitives from Disaster in Isaiah 15–16', *JBQ* 51: 97–107.

Scott, K. (2023), 'Time and the Locust Plagues in the Book of Joel and the Sefire Inscriptions', *CBQ* 85: 19–35.

Scruton, R. (1998), *Philosopher on Dover Beach: Essays*, South Bend: St Augustine's Press.

Scurlock, J. A. (2022), 'Assyria and Babylon in the Oracles against the Nations Tradition: The Death of a King', *JAOS* 140: 395–413.

Sedlmeier, F. (2002), *Das Buch Ezechiel: Kapitel 1–24*, NSKAT 21.1, Stuttgart: Katholisches Bibelwerk.

Seifrid, M. A. (2000), 'Righteousness, Justice, and Justification', in T. D. Alexander and B. S. Rosner (eds.), *New Dictionary of Biblical Theology*, Leicester: Inter-Varsity Press; Downers Grove: InterVarsity Press, 740–745.

—— (2007), 'Romans', in G. K. Beale and D. A. Carson (eds.), *Commentary on the New Testament Use of the Old Testament*, Grand Rapids: Baker Academic; Nottingham: Apollos, 607–694.

Shai, I. (2011), 'Philistia and the Philistines in the Iron Age IIA', *ZDPV* 127: 119–134.

Sharp, C. J. (2015), 'Embodying Moab: The Figuring of Moab in Jeremiah 48 as Reinscription of the Judean Body', in E. K. Holt, H. C. P. Kim and A. Mein (eds.), *Concerning the Nations: Essays on the Oracles against the Nations in Isaiah, Jeremiah, and Ezekiel*, LHBOTS 612, London: Bloomsbury T&T Clark, 95–108.

Shead, A. G. (2000), 'The New Covenant and Pauline Hermeneutics', in P. Bolt and M. Thompson (eds.), *The Gospel to the Nations: Perspectives on Paul's Mission*, Downers Grove: InterVarsity Press, 33–49.

—— (2013), *A Mouth Full of Fire: The Word of God in the Words of Jeremiah*, NSBT 29, Nottingham: Apollos; Downers Grove: InterVarsity Press.

—— (2023), 'Jeremiah, Book of', in G. K. Beale et al. (eds.), *Dictionary of the New Testament Use of the Old Testament*, Grand Rapids: Baker Academic, 366–372.

Shupak, N. (2003), 'The Prophecies of Neferti (1.45)', *COS* 1:106–110.

Silverman, D. P. (1991), 'Divinity and Deities in Ancient Egypt', in B. E. Shafer (ed.), *Religion in Ancient Egypt: Gods, Myth, and Personal Practice*, Ithaca: Cornell University Press, 7–87.

Sivanandan, T. (2004), 'Anticolonialism, National Liberation, and Postcolonial State Formation', in N. Lazarus (ed.), *The Cambridge*

Companion to Postcolonial Literary Studies, Cambridge: Cambridge University Press, 41–65.

Smelik, K. D. (2003), 'The Inscription of King Mesha (2.23)', *COS* 2:137–138.

—— (2014), 'My Servant Nebuchadnezzar: The Use of the Epithet "My Servant" for the Babylonian King Nebuchadnezzar in the Book of Jeremiah', *VT* 64: 109–134.

Smith, J. K. A. (2004), *Introducing Radical Orthodoxy: Mapping a Post-Secular Theology*, Grand Rapids: Baker Academic.

—— (2009), *Desiring the Kingdom: Worship, Worldview, and Cultural Formation*, Grand Rapids: Baker Academic.

Smith-Christopher, D. L. (2015), *Micah*, OTL, Louisville: Westminster John Knox.

Smothers, T. G. (1988), 'A Lawsuit against the Nations: Reflections on the Oracles against the Nations in Jeremiah', *RevExp* 85.3: 545–554.

—— (1996), 'Isaiah 15–16', in J. Watts and P. House (eds.), *Forming Prophetic Literature: Essays on Isaiah and the Twelve in Honor of John D. W. Watts*, London: Bloomsbury, 70–84.

Snoek, D. (2023), 'Joel 2:17 and the Calamities of Joel 1:2–2:11', *JHebS* 23: art. 3, 1–23.

Snyman, S. D. (Fanie) (2015), *Malachi*, HCOT, Leuven: Peeters.

Soza, J. R. (2000), 'Jeremiah', in T. D. Alexander and B. S. Rosner (eds.), *New Dictionary of Biblical Theology*, Leicester: Inter-Varsity Press; Downers Grove: InterVarsity Press, 223–227.

Spencer, N. (2014), 'Priests and Temples: Pharaonic', in A. B. Lloyd (ed.), *A Companion to Ancient Egypt*, Chichester: Blackwell, 255–273.

Stern, E. (2001), *Archaeology of the Land of the Bible, vol. 2: The Assyrian, Babylonian and Persian Periods (732–332 B.C.E.)*, ABRL, New York: Doubleday.

Sternberg, M. (1987), *The Poetics of Biblical Narrative: Ideological Literature and the Drama of Reading*, Bloomington: Indiana University Press.

Storrar, W. (1996), '"Vertigo" or "Imago"? Nations in the Divine Economy', *Them* 21:3, 4–9.

Strawn, B. A. (2005), *What Is Stronger Than a Lion? Leonine Image and Metaphor in the Hebrew Bible and the Ancient Near East*, OBO, Göttingen: Vandenhoeck & Ruprecht.

Strazicich, J. (2007), *Joel's Use of Scripture and Scripture's Use of Joel*, BibInt 82, Leiden: Brill.

Strine, C. A. (2014), 'Chaoskampf against Empire: YHWH's Battle against Gog (Ezekiel 38–39) as Resistance Literature', in A. Lenzi and J. Stökl (eds.), *Divination, Politics, and Ancient Near Eastern Empires*, ANEM 7, Atlanta: Society of Biblical Literature, 87–108.

Stromberg, J., and J. T. Hibbard (eds.) (2021), *The History of Isaiah*, FAT 150, Tübingen: Mohr Siebeck.

Strong, J. T. (1995), 'Ezekiel's Use of the Recognition Formula in His Oracles against the Nations', *PRSt* 22.2: 115–133.

—— (2015), 'In Defense of the Great King: Ezekiel's Oracles against Tyre', in E. K. Holt, H. C. P. Kim and A. Mein (eds.), *Concerning the Nations: Essays on the Oracles against the Nations in Isaiah, Jeremiah, and Ezekiel*, LHBOTS 612, London: Bloomsbury T&T Clark, 179–194.

—— (2017a), 'The Conquest of the Land and Yahweh's Honor before the Nations in Ezekiel', in W. A. Tooman and P. Barter (eds.), *Ezekiel: Current Debates and Future Directions*, FAT 112, Tübingen: Mohr Siebeck, 285–322.

—— (2017b), 'Cosmic Re-Creation', in W. A. Tooman and P. Barter (eds.), *Ezekiel: Current Debates and Future Directions*, FAT 112, Tübingen: Mohr Siebeck, 245–284.

Stuart, D. (1987), *Hosea–Jonah*, WBC 31, Waco: Word.

Stump, E. (2010), 'The Problem of Evil and the History of Peoples: Think of Amalek', in M. Bergmann, M. J. Murray and M. C. Rea (eds.), *Divine Evil? The Moral Character of the God of Abraham*, Oxford: Oxford University Press, 179–197.

Sulzbach, C. (2023), 'Ezekiel's Map of Future Past', in C. Carvalho (ed.), *The Oxford Handbook on Ezekiel*, Oxford: Oxford University Press, 472–491.

Sweeney, M. A. (1996), *Isaiah 1–39, with an Introduction to Prophetic Literature*, FOTL 16, Grand Rapids: Eerdmans.

—— (2012), 'Synchronic and Diachronic Concerns in Reading the Book of the Twelve Prophets', in Rainer Albertz et al. (eds.), *Perspectives on the Formation of the Book of the Twelve: Methodological Foundations – Redactional Processes – Historical Insights*, BZAW 433, Berlin: De Gruyter, 21–33.

—— (2016), *Isaiah 40–66*, FOTL 19, Grand Rapids: Eerdmans.

Sypnowich, C. (2019), 'Law and Ideology', *Stanford Encyclopedia of Philosophy*, 23 April, <https://plato.stanford.edu/entries/law-ideology> (accessed 23 February 2024).

Szpakowska, K. (2014), 'Religion in Society: Pharaonic', in A. B. Lloyd (ed.), *A Companion to Ancient Egypt*, Chichester: Blackwell, 507–525.

Talmon, S. (2001), '"Exile" and "Restoration" in the Conceptual World of Ancient Judaism', in J. Scott (ed.), *Restoration: Old Testament, Jewish, and Christian Perspectives*, SJSJ 72, Leiden: Brill, 107–146.

Tebes, J. M. (2023), 'The Southern Levant and Northern Arabia in the Iron Age', in K. Radner, N. Moeller and D. T. Potts (eds.), *The Oxford History of the Ancient Near East, vol. 5: The Age of Persia*, Oxford: Oxford University Press, 231–298.

Thelle, R. I. (2009), 'Babylon in the Book of Jeremiah (MT): Negotiating a Power Shift', in H. M. Barstad and R. G. Kratz (eds.), *Prophecy in the Book of Jeremiah*, Berlin: De Gruyter, 187–232.

—— (2021), 'The Minor Prophets' Relation to the Torah and Former Prophets', in J. M. O'Brien (ed.), *The Oxford Handbook of the Minor Prophets*, Oxford: Oxford University Press, 186–199.

Thomas, H. A. (2021), 'Hope through Human Trafficking? Theodicy in Joel 4:4–8', in G. Athas, B. Stovell, D. C. Timmer and C. Toffelmire (eds.), *Theodicy and Hope in the Book of the Twelve*, LHBOTS 705, London: T&T Clark, 88–110.

Tiemeyer, L.-S. (2017), 'Death or Conversion: The Gentiles in the Concluding Chapters of the Book of Isaiah and the Book of the Twelve', *JTS* NS 68:1–22.

Tiemeyer, L.-S., and H. M. Barstad (eds.) (2014), *Continuity and Discontinuity: Chronological and Thematic Development in Isaiah 40–66*, FRLANT 255, Göttingen: Vandenhoeck & Ruprecht.

Tiemeyer, L.-S., and J. Wöhrle (eds.) (2020), *The Book of the Twelve: Composition, Reception, and Interpretation*, VTSup 184, Leiden: Brill.

Timmer, D. C. (2009), *Creation, Tabernacle, and Sabbath: The Sabbath Frame of Exodus 31:12–17; 35:1–3 in Exegetical and Theological Perspective*, FRLANT 227, Göttingen: Vandenhoeck & Ruprecht.

—— (2011), *A Gracious and Compassionate God: Mission, Salvation and Spirituality in the Book of Jonah*, NSBT 26, Leicester: Apollos; Downers Grove: InterVarsity Press.

—— (2015), *The Non-Israelite Nations in the Book of the Twelve: Thematic Coherence and the Diachronic-Synchronic Relationship in the Minor Prophets*, BibInt 135, Leiden: Brill.

—— (2017), 'Amos 9 and Jesus Christ's Kingship', *Puritan Reformed Journal* 9.1: 15–26.

—— (2018), 'Reading the Old Testament as Part of a Two-Testament Witness to Christ', in A. Abernethy (ed.), *Interpreting the Old Testament Theologically: Essays in Honor of Willem VanGemeren*, Grand Rapids: Zondervan Academic, 95–108.

—— (2019a), 'Beauty and Glory in Isaiah and in Revelation 21', in J. R. Beeke (ed.), *The Beauty and Glory of the Last Things*, Grand Rapids: Reformation Heritage, 37–55.

—— (2019b), 'Possessing Edom and All the Nations over Whom Yhwh's Name Is Called: Understanding ירשׁ in Amos 9:12', *BBR* 29.4: 468–487.

—— (2020a), *Nahum: A Discourse Analysis of the Hebrew Bible*, ZECOT 30, Grand Rapids: Zondervan Academic.

—— (2020b), 'The Unity of the Book of the Twelve', in A. M. King, R. Osborne and J. M. Philpot (eds.), *The Law, The Prophets, and the Writings: Studies in Evangelical Old Testament Hermeneutics in Honor of Duane A. Garrett*, Nashville: Broadman & Holman, 187–200.

—— (2021a), '"Ah, Assyria Is No More!" Retribution, Theodicy, and Hope in Nahum', in G. Athas, B. Stovell, D. C. Timmer and C. Toffelmire (eds.), *Theodicy and Hope in the Book of the Twelve*, LHBOTS 705, London: T&T Clark, 159–175.

—— (2021b), 'The Construction and Deconstruction of Ethnic/National Othering in the Book of the Twelve', in S. V. Davidson and D. C. Timmer (eds.), *Prophetic Otherness: Constructions of Otherness in Prophetic Literature*, LHBOTS 687, London: T&T Clark, 173–191.

—— (2021c), *Obadiah, Jonah, Micah*, TOTC 26, London: Apollos.

—— (2022a), *Les Livres d'Amos et de Jonas*, CEB, Vaux-sur-Seine: Édifac.

—— (2022b), 'The Material and Immaterial Significance of the Feast in Isaiah 25:6–8', *BibInt* 30: 66–82.

—— (2023a), 'Jonah, Book of', in G. K. Beale et al. (eds.), *Dictionary of the New Testament Use of the Old Testament*, Grand Rapids: Baker Academic, 403–407.

—— (2023b), 'Nahum, Book of', in G. K. Beale et al. (eds.), *Dictionary of the New Testament Use of the Old Testament*, Grand Rapids: Baker Academic, 556–560.

—— (2023c), 'Weeping Turned to Joy by Unmerited Grace (Zech. 12:10–13:9)', in J. R. Beeke and P. Smalley (eds.), *The Grace of Salvation*, Grand Rapids: Reformation Heritage, 41–59.

—— (2024a), 'Election, Israel, and the Nations in the Hebrew Bible/

Old Testament Prophetic Books', in E. C. van Driel (ed.), *T&T Clark Handbook of Election*, London: T&T Clark, 45–62.

—— (2024b), 'Judah, the Remnant, and the Consummation: The People of God in Zephaniah', *Unio cum Christo*, 10.2: 3–16.

—— (2024c), 'Non-Israelite Participation in the Cult in Deuteronomy 23 and Isaiah 56: Dimensions of Intertextual Theological Development', in A. Abernethy and W. de Angelo Cunha (eds.), *Isaiah and Intertextuality*, FAT 2.148, Tübingen: Mohr Siebeck, 41–54.

—— (2024d), 'Prophetic Literature: Book of the Twelve', in H. H. Hardy II and M. D. Carroll R. (eds.), *The State of Old Testament Studies*, Grand Rapids: Baker Academic, 272–286.

—— (2024e), 'Reconsidering Textual Coherence', *VT* 74: 1–22 (advance publication).

—— (2024f), *The Theology of Nahum, Habakkuk, and Zephaniah*, OTT, Cambridge: Cambridge University Press.

—— (2025), 'Constructed Identities and Dueling Ideologies: Reading Ancient Israelite Foreign Oracles as Ideological Critique', *BibInt* 32: 445–466.

Timpe, K., and N. A. Tognazzini (2017), 'Pride in Christian Philosophy and Theology', in J. A. Carter and E. C. Gordon (eds.), *The Moral Psychology of Pride*, London: Rowman & Littlefield, 211–234.

Tobin, V. A. (2002), 'Myths (Overview)', in D. J. Redford (ed.), *The Ancient Gods Speak: A Guide to Egyptian Religion*, Oxford: Oxford University Press, 239–246.

Trueman, C. (2020), *The Rise and Triumph of the Modern Self: Cultural Amnesia, Expressive Individualism, and the Road to the Sexual Revolution*, Wheaton: Crossway.

—— (2023), 'Critical Grace Theory', *First Things*, November: 29–35.

—— (2024), 'The Desecration of Man', *First Things*, January: 21–27.

Tseng, S. K. (2020), *Immanuel Kant*, Great Thinkers, Phillipsburg: P&R.

Tsumura, D. T. (2019), *The Second Book of Samuel*, NICOT, Grand Rapids: Eerdmans.

Ueberschaer, F. (2023), 'Ägypten, Assur und die Wüste im Buch Hosea', *RB* 130.1: 12–40.

Van Bekkum, K. (2017), '"Is Your Rage against the Rivers, Your Wrath against the Sea?" Storm-God Imagery in Habakkuk 3', in K. van Bekkum et al. (eds.), *Playing with Leviathan: Interpretation and Reception of Monsters from the Biblical World*, TBN, Leiden: Brill, 55–76.

Van De Mieroop, M. (2003), 'Revenge, Assyrian Style', *Past & Present* 179: 3–23.

Van der Kooij, A. (1998), *The Oracle of Tyre: The Septuagint as Version and Vision*, VTSup 71, Leiden: Brill.

Van Keulen, P. (2010), 'On the Identity of the Anonymous Ruler in Isaiah 14:4B–21', in M. van der Meer, P. van Keulen, W. T. van Peursen and B. T. H. Romeny (eds.), *Isaiah in Context: Studies in Honour of Arie van der Kooij on the Occasion of His Sixty-Fifth Birthday*, VTSup 138, Leiden: Brill, 109–123.

Van Seters, J. (1989), 'The Creation of Man and the Creation of the King', *ZAW* 101.3: 333–342.

Van Winkel, D. W. (1985), 'The Relationship of the Nations to Yahweh and to Israel in Isaiah XL–LV', *VT* 35: 446–458.

Vanderhooft, D. S. (1999), *The Neo-Babylonian Empire and Babylon in the Latter Prophets*, HSM 59, Atlanta: Scholars Press.

—— (2003), 'Babylonian Strategies of Imperial Control in the West', in O. Lipschits and J. Blenkinsopp (eds.), *Judah and the Judeans in the Neo-Babylonian Period*, Winona Lake: Eisenbrauns, 235–262.

—— (2016), 'Babylonia and the Babylonians', in B. T. Arnold and B. A. Strawn (eds.), *The World around the Old Testament: The People and Places of the Ancient Near East*, Grand Rapids: Baker Academic, 107–137.

VanGemeren, W. (2005), 'Joel, Book of', in K. J. Vanhoozer (ed.), *Dictionary for Theological Interpretation of the Bible*, Grand Rapids: Baker Academic, 389–391.

Vanhoozer, K. J. (2018), 'Toward a Theological Old Testament Theology? A Systematic Theologian's Take on Reading the Old Testament Theologically', in A. Abernethy (ed.), *Interpreting the Old Testament Theologically: Essays in Honor of Willem A. VanGemeren*, Grand Rapids: Zondervan, 293–317.

Vayntrub, J. E. (2020), 'Tyre's Glory and Demise: Totalizing Description in Ezekiel 27', *CBQ* 82.2: 214–236.

Velde, R. te (2007), 'Metaphysics and the Question of Creation: Thomas Aquinas, Duns Scotus and Us', in P. M. Candler Jr and C. Cunningham (eds.), *Belief and Metaphysics*, Veritas, London: SCM Press, 73–99.

Verhoef, P. A. (1987), *The Books of Haggai and Malachi*, NICOT, Grand Rapids: Eerdmans.

Via, D. (2007), *Divine Justice, Divine Judgment: Rethinking the Judgment of Nations*, Facets, Minneapolis: Fortress.

Vlachos, C. A. (2004), 'Law, Sin, and Death: An Edenic Triad? An Examination with Reference to 1 Corinthians 15:56', *JETS* 47.2: 277–298.

Vos, G. (1980), *Redemptive History and Biblical Interpretation: The Shorter Writings of Geerhardus Vos*, ed. R. Gaffin, Phillipsburg: Presbyterian and Reformed.

—— (1994), *Grace and Glory: Sermons Preached in the Chapel of Princeton Theological Seminary*, Edinburgh: Banner of Truth Trust.

Wagner, J. R. (2002), *Heralds of the Good News: Isaiah and Paul 'in Concert' in the Letter to the Romans*, SNT 101, Leiden: Brill.

—— (2005), 'Isaiah in Romans and Galatians', in S. Moyise and M. J. J. Menken (eds.), *Isaiah in the New Testament*, London: T&T Clark, 117–132.

Wallenfels, R. (2008), 'A New Stone Inscription of Nebuchadnezzar II', in M. Ross (ed.), *From the Banks of the Euphrates: Studies in Honor of Alice Louise Slotsky*, University Park: Penn State University Press, 267–294.

Waltke, B. K. (2007), *A Commentary on Micah*, Grand Rapids: Eerdmans.

Walton, J. (2018), *Ancient Near Eastern Thought and the Old Testament: Introducing the Conceptual World of the Hebrew Bible*, 2nd edn, Grand Rapids: Baker Academic.

Waters, M. (2023), 'The Persian Empire under the Teispid Dynasty: Emergence and Conquest', in K. Radner, N. Moeller and D. T. Potts (eds.), *The Oxford History of the Ancient Near East, vol. 5: The Age of Persia*, Oxford: Oxford University Press, 376–416.

Watkin, C. (2022), *Biblical Critical Theory: How the Bible's Unfolding Story Makes Sense of Modern Life and Culture*, Grand Rapids: Zondervan Academic.

Watson, F. (1997), *Text and Truth: Redefining Biblical Theology*, Grand Rapids: Eerdmans.

Watts, J. D. W. (1985), *Isaiah 1–33*, WBC 24, Waco: Word.

—— (1987), *Isaiah 34–66*, WBC 25, Waco: Word.

—— (2015), *Isaiah 1–33*, rev. edn, WBC 24, Grand Rapids: Zondervan Academic.

Watts, R. E. (1990), 'Consolation or Confrontation? Isaiah 40–55 and the Delay of the New Exodus', *TynBul* 41: 31–59.

—— (2004), 'Echoes from the Past: Israel's Ancient Traditions and the Destiny of the Nations in Isaiah 40–55', *JSOT* 28: 481–508.

Wazana, N. (2013), 'War Crimes in Amos' Oracles against the Nations (Amos 1:3–2:3)', in D. Vanderhooft and A. Winitzer (eds.), *Literature as Politics, Politics as Literature: Essays on the Ancient Near East in Honor of Peter Machinist*, Winona Lake: Eisenbrauns, 479–501.

Webb, B. G. (1990), 'Zion in Transformation: A Literary Approach to Isaiah', in D. J. A. Clines, S. E. Fowl and S. E. Porter (eds.), *The Bible in Three Dimensions*, JSOTSup 87, Sheffield: JSOT, 65–84.

—— (2004), *The Message of Zechariah*, BST, Leicester: Inter-Varsity Press.

Webster, J. (2003), *Holiness*, Grand Rapids: Eerdmans.

—— (2014), *The Domain of the Word: Scripture and Theological Reason*, London: Bloomsbury T&T Clark.

—— (2015), *Confronted by Grace: Meditations of a Theologian*, ed. D. Bush and B. Ellis, Bellingham: Lexham.

Weiershäuser, F., and J. Novotny (2020), *The Royal Inscriptions of Amēl-Marduk (561–560 BC), Neriglissar (559–56 BC), and Nabonidus (555–539 BC), Kings of Babylon*, RINBE 2, Winona Lake: Eisenbrauns.

Weinfeld, M. (1986), 'The Protest against Imperialism in Ancient Israelite Prophecy', in S. N. Eisenstadt (ed.), *The Origins and Diversity of Axial Age Civilizations*, Albany: State University of New York Press, 169–182.

Weithman, P. (2001), 'Augustine's Political Philosophy', in E. Stump and N. Kretzmann (eds.), *The Cambridge Companion to Augustine*, Cambridge: Cambridge University Press, 234–252.

Wielenga, B. (2022), 'The God Who Hates: The Significance of Esau/Edom in the Postexilic Prophetic Eschatology According to Malachi 1:2–5 with a Systematic Theological Postscript', *IDS* 56: 1–9.

Wiesehöfer, J. (2009), 'The Achaemenid Empire', in I. Morris and W. Scheidel (eds.), *The Dynamics of Ancient Empires: State Power from Assyria to Byzantium*, Oxford: Oxford University Press, 66–98.

Wildberger, H. (1997), *Isaiah 13–27*, tr. T. H. Trapp, CC, Minneapolis: Fortress.

Williams, R. (2005), 'Introduction', in J. Milbank, S. Žižek and C. Davis (eds.), *Theology and the Political: The New Debate*, Durham: Duke University Press, 1–3.

Williams, T. J. (2023), *Don't Follow Your Heart: Boldly Breaking the Ten Commandments of Self-Worship*, Grand Rapids: Zondervan.

Williamson, H. G. M. (2021), 'Decoding Isaiah 13', in J. Stromberg and J. T. Hibbard (eds.), *The History of Isaiah*, FAT 150, Tübingen: Mohr Siebeck, 539–549.

Willis, J. T. (2012), 'National "Beauty" and Yahweh's "Glory" as a Dialectical Key to Ezekielian Theology', *HBT* 34.1: 1–18.

Wilson, J. R. (2011), 'Pride', in J. B. Green (ed.), *Dictionary of Scripture and Ethics*, Grand Rapids: Baker Academic, 621–622.

Wilson, P. (2014), 'Temple Architecture and Decorative Systems', in A. B. Lloyd (ed.), *A Companion to Ancient Egypt*, Chichester: Blackwell, 781–803.

Winkler, R. (2024), 'Elon Musk Says Neuralink Has Implanted Brain Chip in Human', *Wall Street Journal*, 30 January.

Wiseman, D. J. (1961), *Chronicles of the Chaldean Kings (626–566 B.C.) in the British Musuem*, London: Trustees of the British Museum.

Wodecki, B. (1982), 'Die Heilsuniversalismus bei Trito-Jesaja', *VT* 32: 248–252.

Wöhrle, J. (2008), *Der Abschluss des Zwölfprophetenbuches: Buchübergreifende Redaktionsprozesse in den späten Sammlungen*, BZAW 389, Berlin: De Gruyter.

Wolff, H. W. (1988), *Haggai: A Commentary*, tr. M. Kohl, CC, Minneapolis: Augsburg.

—— (1990), *Micah*, tr. G. Stansell, CC, Minneapolis: Fortress.

Wolters, A. (2014), *Zechariah*, HCOT, Leuven: Peeters.

Woolmer, M. (2017), *A Short History of the Phoenicians*, London: I. B. Taurus.

Wright, C. J. H. (2006), *The Mission of God: Unlocking the Bible's Grand Narrative*, Downers Grove: InterVarsity Press.

Wu, D. Y. (2016), *Honor, Shame, and Guilt: Social-Scientific Approaches to the Book of Ezekiel*, BBRSup 14, Winona Lake: Eisenbrauns.

Xekelaki, G. (2021), 'On Borders and Expansion: Egyptian Imperialism in the Levant during the Ramesside Period', *Heritage* 4: 3938–3948.

Yamauchi, E. M. (1996), *Persia and the Bible*, Grand Rapids: Baker.

Yates, G. E. (2018), 'Hope in the Midst of Wrath: Promises for Outsiders in Jeremiah 46–51', *BSac* 175.697: 67–82.

Younger Jr, K. L. (1990), *Ancient Conquest Accounts: A Study in Ancient Near Eastern and Biblical History Writing*, LHBOTS 98, Sheffield: Sheffield Academic.

—— (2003), 'The Calaḫ Annals (2.117A)', *COS* 1:284–286.

—— (2016), *A Political History of the Arameans: From Their Origins to the End of Their Polities*, ABS 13, Atlanta: Society of Biblical Literature.

Zehnder, M. (2005), *Umgang mit Fremden in Israel und Assyrien: Ein*

Beitrag zur Anthropologie des 'Fremden' im Licht antiker Quellen, BWANT 168, Stuttgart: Kohlhammer.

Zimran, Y. (2021), 'The Prevalence and Purpose of the "Assyria-Egypt" Motif in the Book of Hosea', *JSOT* 46: 3–23.

Zubrin, R. (1996), 'The Case for Colonizing Mars', *Ad Astra*, July, <https://nss.org/the-case-for-colonizing-mars-by-robert-zubrin> (accessed 30 March 2024).

Zukerman, A., and I. Shai (2006), '"The Royal City of the Philistines" in the "Azekah Inscription" and the History of Gath in the Eighth Century BCE', *UF* 38: 729–778.

Index of authors

Abernethy, A., 51, 69, 70
Abo El Magd, A., 124
Abusch, T., 184
Alberta, T., 250
Allen, J. P., 19, 20
Allen, L. C., 84, 87, 98, 106, 107, 109, 115, 116, 127, 128, 130
Amesz, J. G., 83
Andersen, F. I., 141
Anderson, B., 157
Anderson, R. T., 243
Angers, D., 74, 147, 214
Apóstolo, S. S. S., 230
Arnold, B. T., 8, 31, 180
Arthur, D., 114
Aspray, B., 56
Assis, E., 144, 157
Assmann, J., 24, 239
Aster, S. Z., 47, 137, 171
Aubet, M. E., 116
Aufrecht, W. E., 110
Augustine, 237
Averbeck, R. E., 120, 172
Ayali-Darshan, N., 164

Bacon, F., 243
Barba-Kay, A., 243, 244
Barker, J., 144, 145, 146
Barstad, H., 43, 136, 138
Bartholomew, C. G., 53
Barton, J., 144, 146, 148
Bauckham, R., 4, 8, 20, 134, 149, 189, 192, 234, 245, 248
Baugus, B. P., 153
Baumgartner, W., 106, 120, 131, 168, 221
Beale, G. K., 2, 8, 127, 133, 141, 149, 199, 236
Beaulieu, P.-A., 32, 85, 89
Ben Zvi, E., 4, 11, 13, 97, 157, 160, 209, 230
Bergey, R. L., 228
Berlejung, A., 184
Bernays, E. L., 246
Bestock, L., 22, 23
Beuken, W. A. M., 8, 44, 48, 49, 51, 54, 55, 60, 61, 63, 64, 65
Biddle, M. E., 86
Billing, R., 213
Birnie, E., 243
Blocher, H., 75
Block, D. I., 43, 103, 104, 105, 106, 107, 115, 127, 129, 130, 159
Bock, D., 74
Boda, M., 218, 219, 222, 223, 224
Boehmer, R. M., 184
Bosma, C. J., 164
Bosman, H. L., 205
Bowie, A., 203
Braulik, G., 155
Briant, P., 39
Bricker, D. P., 239
Brosius, M., 36
Brueggemann, W., 77, 94, 109
Bryce, T., 62, 114, 116
Buckwalter, D., 156
Bürki, M., 65
Burnett, J. S., 109
Buth, R., 180

Calvin, J., 257, 258
Carley, K., 132
Carroll R., M. D., 154, 187
Carson, D. A., 2, 141
Carvalho, C., 119, 120, 124
Chan, M. J., 7, 212

Chatonnet, F. B., 116, 119
Childs, B. S., 44, 50, 60
Ciftci, M., 237, 253, 254
Claassens, L. J. M., 86
Clarysse, W., 121
Clines, D. J. A., 104, 106, 205, 221
Cogan, M., 35, 153
Cole, G. A., 225
Collins, A. Y., 92
Collins, J. J., 92, 171
Coppens, F., 20
Couey, J. B., 55
Cox, G., 96
Cox, H., 246
Craigie, P. C., 79
Crenshaw, J. L., 144
Crouch, C. L., 26, 31, 85, 103, 104, 105, 106, 123, 128, 166, 184, 188
Curtis, J., 211, 212

Dalley, S., 30
Dandamaev, M. A., 212
David, R., 24
Davidson, S. V., 95
De Blois, R., 109, 115
Dearman, J. A., 138, 173
Dekker, J., 65, 66
Delorme, J.-P., 87, 90
Dempster, S. G., 161, 173, 175, 176, 177
Deneen, P. J., 247, 248
DeRouchie, J. S., 207
Desmond, W., 8
Dewrell, H. D., 136
Dobbs-Allsopp, F. W., 179
Dooley, M., 245, 252
Dow, L. K. F., 149
Doxey, D. M., 58
Drinkard Jr., J. F., 79
Dubovsky, P., 153
Duguid, I., 225

Eck, J., 48, 52, 53
Ehrenberg, E., 231, 232
Ehrlich, C. S., 203
Elat, M., 119, 220

Faulkner, R. K., 243
Favale, A., 242, 243
Ferguson, S., 208
Ferries, R. A. R., 157
Firth, D. G., 2, 188
Fischer, G., 77, 137, 146, 149, 194, 222, 230
Fischer, I., 67
Floyd, M. H., 173
Foster, B. R., 25, 26, 31, 84
Foster, R. L., 209, 210, 213
Frahm, E., 27, 166
Franke, C. A., 52
Freeden, M., 247, 248
Freedman, D. N., 141
Frood, E., 121, 124

Galambush, J., 127
Galter, H. D., 85
García, J. C. M., 23, 24
Garrett, D., 137, 138, 141, 144, 149
Gärtner, J., 206
Gelston, A., 141
George, A. R., 25
Getz, T. R., 250
Geyer, J. B., 123
Gibson, A., 10, 130
Gladd, B. L., 75, 236
Goldingay, J., 68, 79, 91, 137, 154, 167, 172
Goldsworthy, G., 6, 7, 149
Gordon, R. P., 52, 53, 117
Gosse, B., 112
Goswell, G., 56, 228
Graybill, R., 80, 81, 86
Grayson, A. K., 8, 28, 185, 186, 194
Green, G., 241
Greenberg, M., 103, 105, 106, 107, 110, 114, 115, 120, 121, 123, 125
Greenwood, K., 28
Gribben, C., 249, 250
Griffiths, J. G, 58
Gunton, C., 245, 252

Gut, R., 184

Hagelia, H., 66
Hamborg, G. R., 136, 146
Hamilton Jr, J. K., 3
Haney, L., 158
Harrison, R. K., 88
Harvey, B., 8
Hasel, G. F., 19
Hasel, M. G., 19
Hassler, M., 160
Hauser, S. R., 8
Hayes, E. R., 88
Hays, J. D., 134
Hens-Piazza, G., 43
Herring, J., 247
Heywood, A., 247
Hibbard, J. T., 43, 60
Higgs, K., 246
Hill, A. E., 225
Hill, J., 83, 88, 91
Himbaza, I., 232
Hintze, A., 35
Hoffmeier, J. K., 22, 123, 160
Holladay, W. L., 53
Hollis, S. T., 58
Holloway, S., 183
Horton, M. S., 255
Hubbard Jr, R. L., 146
Hwang, J., 77, 94, 97, 100, 136, 137, 138, 139

Innes, D. C., 243
Irsigler, H., 204, 205
Irudayaraj, D. S., 43
Irvine, S. A., 140
Israelit-Groll, S., 59

Jacobs, M., 213, 231
Janák, J., 20
Johnson, D. E., 149

Kähler, S., 89
Kaminsky, J. S., 98, 227
Kant, I., 242
Karlsson, M., 184, 195
Keel, O., 124
Kellermann, D., 219
Kelley, P. H., 79
Keown, G. L., 91, 95
Kessler, J., 210, 213
Kessler, M., 77, 84
Kessler, R., 176, 177, 229
Kilchör, B., 131
Kim, H. C. P., 9, 64, 73, 237
King, A. M., 154
King, D., 248
Klink III, E. W., 6
Koehler, L., 106, 120, 131, 168, 221
Koet, B. J., 74
Kohler, S. R., 37
Koole, J. L., 67, 71, 147
Köstenberger, A. J., 69, 147, 149, 156, 225
Koyzis, D., 249, 250, 251, 252
Kramer, S. N., 96
Kuhrt, A., 36, 38, 39, 85, 90, 114, 183, 211

Lacocque, A., 224
Ladd, G. E., 149
Landy, F., 55
Larsen, M. T., 192
Lee, L., 108, 127
Lee, P. Y., 88, 99
Leichty, E., 21, 153
Leprohon, R. J., 20
Lesko, L. H., 58
Lessing, R., 83
Letham, R., 20
Levavi, Y., 193
Levenson, J. D., 220
Levine, B. A., 164
Lichtheim, M., 21, 22, 24
Lincoln, B., 34, 35, 36, 39
Lints, R., 247
Liverani, M., 27, 114, 166, 182, 183, 250
Lloyd, A. B., 18, 19
Lockett, D., 6

Lukonin, V. G., 212
Lundbom, J. R., 81, 84
Luther, M., 1

McConville, J. G., 47, 61, 70
McDonough, S. M., 141, 199
Machinist, P., 48
McKelvey, R. J., 214
McMuller, S., 245, 247
McNicol, A. J., 100
Maier, A. M., 152
Martin, O., 161
Mason, R., 158
Mathews, K., 2
Mathewson, D., 75
Mattingly, G. L., 98, 116
Mayer, W. R., 118
Mazurel, J. W., 99
Meek, E. L., 245
Melville, S. C., 29
Meyers, C. L., 211, 219, 220, 222, 224
Meyers, E. M., 211, 219, 220, 222, 224
Milbank, J., 241
Millard, A., 25, 96
Minich, J., 238, 241
Moo, D. J., 199
Moore, E., 146
Morgan, C., 30
Morris, E. F., 20, 59, 121
Morris, I., 192
Morrow, W., 184

Naugle, D. K., 125, 239, 252
Naunton, C., 24, 203
Nevader, M., 106, 113, 118, 119, 120, 123, 132
Nguyen, K. L., 67
Nietzsche, F., 255
Noegel, S. B., 21, 23, 30, 31
Nogalski, J. D., 11, 13, 202
Novotny, J., 28, 32, 53, 185

O'Brien, P. T., 69, 147,149, 234
Oded, B., 87, 89, 194
Odell, M. S., 119
O'Donovan, O., 138, 238, 251, 252, 254, 257
Oehler, G. F., 66
O'Kennedy, D. F., 209, 213
Ortlund Jr, R. C., 78
Osborne, W. R., 118
Oswalt, J., 43, 44, 46, 49, 57, 60, 65, 69, 70, 71, 73

Pannkuk, J., 92
Pao, D. W., 142
Paul, S. M., 71, 146
Payne, D., 68
Pearcey, N. R., 242
Peels, H. G. L., 80, 83, 180
Perdu, O., 18, 121
Peter, S., 250
Peterson, D. L., 96, 131, 156, 159
Petterson, A. R., 211, 213, 214, 219, 220, 221, 222, 225
Pfau, T., 241, 244, 245
Phillips, E. A., 149, 164, 177
Pickstock, C., 241
Piotrowski, N. G., 75
Pischikova, E., 138
Plant, R. J. R., 88
Pongratz-Leisten, B., 25
Porter, S. E., 2
Provan, I., 127, 240

Raabe, P. R., 4, 8, 10, 73, 80, 94
Radner, K., 182
Rasmussen, J., 241
Razmjou, S., 212
Reade, J., 184
Redford, D. B., 18, 58, 79, 82
Rendtorff, R., 143
Reno, R. R., 252
Renz, T., 108, 117, 129, 132, 197, 198, 201
Richelle, M., 70, 75
Ricoeur, P., 20
Riecker, S., 169
Ristau, K. A., 213, 214
Roberts, J. J. M., 196

Roberts, R. C., 126, 127
Robertson, O. P., 3
Rogland, M., 284
Romerowski, S., 144
Rosner, B. S., 7, 74
Rossi, B., 43
Roth, M., 147

Sæbø, M., 155
Sals, U., 86–87, 92
Sands, P., 126
Sandy, D. B., 1
Saur, M., 130
Scalise, P. J., 91, 95, 230
Schart, A., 11
Schaumberger, J. B., 167
Scheidel, W., 17, 192
Schmid, K., 91
Schnabel, E. J., 142
Schnittjer, G. E., 47
Schroeder, C. O., 244
Schuele, A., 71
Schulmeister, I., 72
Schultz, R., 10, 43, 44, 67
Schweiker, W., 244
Scolnic, B., 55
Scott, K., 144
Scruton, R., 245
Scurlock, J. A., 52, 53
Sedlmeier, F., 109, 129
Seifrid, M. A., 121, 141, 199
Shai, I., 172, 203
Sharp, C. J., 81
Shead, A. G., 5, 99, 100
Silverman, D. P., 95, 123
Sivanandan, T., 250
Smelik, K. D., 54, 83, 111, 203
Smith, J. K. A., 238, 239, 240, 247
Smith-Christopher, D. L., 172, 173
Smothers, T. G., 56, 80, 83, 91, 95
Snoek, D., 144, 145
Snyman, S. D., 130
Soza, J. R., 100
Spencer, N., 59
Stears, M., 247, 248
Steck, O. H., 96
Stern, E., 111
Sternberg, M., 168
Storrar, W., 251
Strawn, B. A., 123
Strazicich, J., 149
Streets-Salter, H., 250
Strine, C. A., 127
Stromberg, J., 43
Strong, J. T., 102, 112, 115, 116, 129, 132, 133
Stuart, D., 138, 139, 141
Stump, E., 154
Sulzbach, C., 127, 128
Sweeney, M. A., 13, 50, 58, 68, 71
Sypnowich, C., 7
Szpakowska, K., 121, 124

Talmon, S., 96
Tarragon, J.-M. de, 164
Tebes, J. M., 111, 160, 228
Thelle, R. I., 88, 91, 168
Thomas, H. A., 144
Tiemeyer, L.-S., 11, 43, 70, 72, 210, 220, 223, 229
Timmer, D. C., 3, 7, 10, 11, 12, 30, 51, 64, 72, 73, 89, 111, 112, 145, 147, 151, 155, 156, 159, 165, 167, 168, 169, 171, 174, 175, 177, 180, 184, 187, 188, 189, 191, 199, 206, 207, 211, 213, 219, 222, 223, 225, 228, 230, 233, 256
Timpe, K., 126
Tobin, V. A., 58
Trueman, C., 241, 243, 251, 252, 253, 254
Tseng, S. K., 241
Tsumura, D. T., 221

Ueberschaer, F., 139

Van Bekkum, K., 198
Van De Mieroop, M., 85
Van der Kooij, A., 62, 63
Van Keulen, P., 51

Van Seters, J., 118
Van Winkel, D. W., 67
Vanderhooft, D. S., 31, 32, 33, 51, 84, 193, 194, 195, 196, 197
VanGemeren, W., 146
Vanhoozer, K. J., 6, 8, 9
Vayntrub, J. E., 115
Velde, R. te, 254
Verhoef, P. A., 214
Via, D., 187
Vlachos, C. A., 138
Vos, G., 7, 63, 142

Wagner, J. R., 5, 74
Ward, G., 241
Wallenfels, R., 32, 34, 195
Waltke, B. K., 161
Walton, J., 19, 20
Waters, M., 38, 39
Watkin, C., 112, 122, 127, 158, 241, 247, 252, 253
Watson, F., 6
Watts, J. D. W., 58, 60
Watts, R. E., 6, 66
Wazana, N., 153
Webb, B. G., 44, 46, 48, 71, 224
Webster, J., 15, 169, 181, 256
Weiershäuser, F., 32, 53
Weinfeld, M., 7
Weithman, P., 237
Wielenga, B., 228, 231
Wiesehöfer, J., 34, 37, 38, 39, 212
Wildberger, H., 44, 50, 56, 59, 60, 62, 65
Williams, R., 253
Williams, T. J., 122
Williamson, H. G. M., 49
Willis, J. T., 114, 115
Wilson, J. R., 126, 127
Wilson, P., 122
Winkler, R., 244
Wiseman, D. J., 82
Wodecki, B., 73
Wöhrle, J., 11, 12
Wolff, H. W., 47, 213
Wolters, A., 217, 222, 224
Woolmer, M., 62, 116, 117
Wright, C. J. H., 94
Wu, D. Y., 104

Xekelaki, G., 21

Yamauchi, E. M., 40
Yates, G. E., 93, 94, 96
Younger Jr, K. L., 29, 152, 160

Zehnder, M., 69, 132, 184
Zimran, Y., 136
Zubrin, R., 241
Zukerman, A., 172

Index of Scripture references

OLD TESTAMENT

Genesis
1 – 3 *5*
1 – 11 *202*
1:2 *146*
1:21 *120*
1:26 *91*
1:28 *87*
2 *91*
2:7 *146*
2:17 *138*
3 *14, 127*
3:5 *126*
3:14–21 *57*
3:15 *2, 254*
5 *2*
6:12 *146*
6:13 *146*
6:17 *146*
6:19 *146*
9:5–6 *153*
9:6 *221*
9:17 *146*
10:5 *204*
11:10–26 *2*
12 *2, 92*
12:1–3 *57, 61, 110*
12:3 *2, 3, 71, 90, 110, 140, 175, 204, 219*
12:6–7 *60*
14:19 *132*
15 *71, 92*
15:5 *141*
15:16 *159*
15:18 *159*
16:10 *141*
17 *92*
17:1–21 *71, 155*
17:5 *3*
19:21 *213*
19:25 *213*
19:29 *213*
22:18 *93*
25:19–24 *111*
25:23 *227*
26:3 *91*
26:4 *93*
26:5 91
27:28 *175*
28:28 *174*
28:39 *174*
32:12 *141*
35:14 *60*
48:16 *61*

Exodus
1:7 *87*
2:23 *60*
3:7 *61*
3:9 *60*
3:12 *60*
4:22 *231*
4:23 *60*
7 – 12 *60*
12:38 *141*
14:22 *198*
15 *213*
15:1 *213*
15:10–16 *198*
15:17–18 *65, 71, 215*
15:21 *213*
19 *92*
19:1–6 *155*
19:4–6 *167*
19:5 *231*
19:5–6 *3, 140, 141*
19:16–18 *198*
23:31 *159*
24 *65*
24:4–8 *60*
29:45–46 *210*
31:1–11 *117*
31:12–17 *71*
33:19 *180*
34 *167*
34:6 *149*
34:6–7 *11, 167, 180*
40:38 *71*

Leviticus
18:24–25 *159*
26 *132*
26:5 *155*
26:6 *176*
26:12 *210, 219*
26:14–39 *192*
27 *155*

Numbers
6 *136*
11:29 *147*
22 *111*
24:14 *139*
25 *136*
25:3 *136*
25:5 *136*
35:33 *172*

Deuteronomy
2:4–5 *159*
2:4–8 *111*
2:9 *56*
4:6 *3, 117*
4:20 *61, 219*
4:30 *139*
6:5 *233*
6:11 *87*
6:15 *210*
7:1 *155*
7:22 *91*
9:29 *61*
18:12 *159*
20:5–8 *87*
23 *72*
23:1–8 72, *221*
23:2 *221*
23:7 *144*
23:18 *63*
28:9–10 *155*
28:15–68 *192*
28:30 *87*
29:23 *213*
30 *90, 132*
32:2 *174, 175*
33:13–14 *174*
33:28 *174, 175*

Joshua
1:11 *155*
6 – 7 *173*
6:25 *144*
10:12–14 *198*
22:19 *103*
23:9 *155*
24:13 *87*
24:26–31 *60*

Judges
3:12 *111*
5:20 *198*
7:22 *213*

1 Samuel
9:1 *221*
22:3–4 *56*

2 Samuel
1:21 *174*
5:2 *177*
7 *5, 56, 155, 156*
7:1–16 *71*

1 Kings
4:25 *176*
4:29 *117*
7:14 *117*
9:13 *153*
12 *137*
14:25–28 *18*
22:11 *173*

2 Kings
3 *111*
3:4 *56*
14:13–19 *154*
14:25–27 *137*
16:1–9 *78*
16:7–10 *25*
18 – 19 *182*
18:8 *113*
20:12–19 *78*
23:33–35 *79*
24:1 *82*
24:10–17 *82*
25:27–30 *5*

2 Chronicles
7:14 *155*
16:13 *106*
25:27 *154*
35:22–23 *5*

Ezra
1 *34, 40, 211*
1:4 *210*
1:6 *210*
1:7–8 *210*
6:19–21 *5*
7:15–23 *210*

Nehemiah
2:10 *109*
2:19 *109*
10:28–29 *5*
13:1–2 *109*

Job
7:12 *85, 120*
28:28 *117*

Psalms
2 *5, 71*
8:6–7 *91*
9:11 *3*
18:49 *3*
22:27 *94*
22:30–31 *94*
28:9 *61*
33:8 *3*
35:25 *110*
35:26–27 *145*
40:3 *94*
45 *5, 71*
46:10 *3*
49:1 *3*
50:14 *60, 165*
50:16 *165*
57:10 *3*
66:1–4 *3*
67 *94*
66:13 *60*
67:1–7 *3*
68:5 *98*
68:18 *180*
72 *71, 155*
72:6 *175*
72:8 *3*
72:11 *3*
72:17 *3*
74:13 *85, 120*
76:6 *213*
76:11 *60*
83:18 *3*
86 *94*
87 *94*
95:5 *164*
96:3 *3*
96:10 *3*
104:30 *146*
105:1 *3*
106:38 *172*
108:3 *3*
110 *5, 71*
111:10 *117*
115:1 *165*
115:2 *165*
115:3 *165*
115:4–8 *165*
115:9–18 *165*
117:1 *3*
119:46 *3*
126 *94*
133:3 *174*
135:5 *165*
135:15–18 *165*
137:7 *165*
145:6 *3*
145:12 *3*
145:21 *3*

Proverbs
10:5 *164*
15:7 *205*
19:12 *174*
19:15 *164*

Isaiah
1:2 *45*
1:7 *45*
1:10 *46*
1:21–24 *65*
1:24–31 *46*
2 *175, 223, 235*
2:1–4 *72*
2:2 *139*
2:4 *70*
2:6–7 *44*
2:6–22 *44*
2:10 *55*
2:12 *50*
2:19 *55*
2:21 *55*
5:13 *45*
5:26–30 *45*
5:29 *45*
6:5 *205*
7 *44, 45*
7:18–25 *45*
8:5–10 *45*
9:2 *67*
9:7 *56*
9:8–12 *45*
9:9 *55*
10 *182*
10:5 *49*
10:5–6 *4, 47*
10:5–15 *48*
10:5–19 *47–48*
10:6 *173*
10:7 *47*
10:8 *47*
10:9 *47*
10:9–15 *47*
10:10–11 *47*
10:12 *47*
10:12–13 *117*
10:13–14 *48*
10:15 *48*
10:16 *48*
10:16–19 *46*
10:19 *48*
10:20–21 *46*
10:20–22 *48*
10:24–34 *46*
11 *49, 75*
11:2 *117*
11:10 *66*

11:10–11 *5, 75*
11:11–13 *176*
11:15 *59*
12 *15*
13 *48, 49, 51*
13 – 23 *43, 44, 46, 49–51, 57, 64, 73*
13:1 *49*
13:1 – 14:2 *49*
13:2–5 *49*
13:3 *49*
13:4 *49*
13:5 *50*
13:6 *50*
13:6–16 *49, 50*
13:7 *50*
13:9 *50*
13:11 *50, 55*
13:12 *50*
13:17–22 *49, 50*
13:19 *49, 50*
13:20 *50*
13:21–22 *50*
14 *8, 49, 51, 52*
14:1 *219*
14:1–2 *51*
14:2 *51, 203*
14:3–23 *51–54*
14:4–5 *51*
14:6 *52*
14:8 *52*
14:9–11 *52*
14:12–15 *53*
14:16 *53*
14:16–21 *53*
14:22–23 *54*
14:24–27 *47*
14:31 *145*
15 – 16 *54–56*
15:2 *55*
15:2–5 *55*
15:5 *55*
15:7 *55*
16:1 *56*
16:3–4 *56*
16:3–5 *56*
16:4 *56*
16:5 *56*
16:8 *55*
16:9–11 *55*
16:12 *55*
16:13–14 *55*
16:14 *55, 56*
18 *66*
19 *10, 57–61, 235*
19:1 *57*
19:1–4 *57*
19:1–15 *57*
19:2 *57*
19:3 *57*
19:4 *57*
19:5–10 *57, 58*
19:11 *58*
19:11–12 *58*
19:11–15 *57, 58*
19:11–17 *59*
19:14–15 *58*
19:16–17 *59*
19:16–25 *59*
19:18 *59, 60*
19:19–20 *60*
19:19–22 *59, 60*
19:20 *60*
19:21 *60, 165*
19:22 *61*
19:23 *59, 61*
19:24 *61*
19:24–25 *59, 94*
19:25 *61, 219*
20:1–6 *44*
21 *75*
22:1–25 *46*
23 *57, 62, 75, 117*
23:1 *63*
23:1–14 *62, 63*
23:4 *63*
23:6 *63*
23:7–9 *62*
23:9 *62*
23:13 *63*
23:14 *63*
23:15–18 *63*
23:17 *63, 75*
23:17–18 *63*
23:18 *63*
24 *64, 65*
24 – 25 *57, 64–66*
24 – 27 *49, 65*
24:1–22 *64*
24:3 *64*
24:4 *64*
24:5 *64, 66, 172*
24:6 *64*
24:13 *64*
24:14–16 *64, 73*
24:18 *64*
24:19–20 *64*
24:20 *64*
24:21–22 *64*
24:22 *64*
24:23 *64, 65*
25 *64*
25:2 *65*
25:3 *65*
25:4 *65*
25:5 *65*
25:6 *156*
25:6–8 *65*
25:8 *65, 75, 198*
25:9 *73*
25:11 *55*
26:19 *73, 175*
27:1 *85, 120*
29:1–14 *46*
29:10 *164*
29:23 *61*
30:26 *67*
31 *45*
31:1 *45, 46*
31:3 *45*
32:15 *146*
32:15–20 *147, 148*
33:14 *173*
33:18–19 *46*
34 *75*
36 *2*
36 – 37 *44, 182*
37 *48*
37:22–29 *47*
39 *2*
40 – 55 *6, 69*
40 – 66 *43, 66*
40:3–5 *74*
40:5 *73*
41:8–9 *66*
41:8–20 *68*
41:25 *145*
42 *67, 68*
42:1 *67*
42:1–4 *66*
42:1–9 *66, 68*
42:1–12 *66–68*
42:4 *67, 68, 257*
42:5 *67, 68*
42:5–9 *66*
42:6 *67, 68, 73*
42:7 *67*
42:10–12 *67, 68*
42:16 *67*
42:19 *66*
43:17 *76*
44:3 *146, 147*
44:21 *66*
44:28 *34*
45:1 *34, 49, 83*
45:11 *61*
45:13 *66*
45:14 *64, 66*
45:14–26 *66*
45:22–25 *66*
47 *75*
47:8 *204*
47:10 *204*
49 *67, 68*
49:1–6 *66*

49:1–7 *68–69*
49:1–12 *74*
49:1–13 *66*
49:3 *68*
49:6 *69*
49:7 *69*
49:8–21 *71*
49:14–26 *66*
49:21 *75*
49:22–23 *69*
51:5 *66*
51:9 *85, 120*
51:16 *71*
52 *74*
52:1 *224*
52:5 *74*
52:7–10 *74*
52:11 *75*
52:13 – 53:12 *73*
52:15 *66, 73*
53:4 *73*
54:1–4 *71*
55:4–5 *66*
56 *72, 74*
56 – 66 *69–70, 71*
56:1 *72*
56:1–8 *51, 70, 71–73, 75, 221*
56:2 *72*
56:3 *72, 219*
56:3–8 *72*
56:6 *219*
56:6–7 *72*
57:15 *15*
58:8 *67*
59:9 *67*
59:14–21 *70*
59:15–21 *73*
59:20–21 *74*
59:21 *147*
60 *70*
60 – 62 *51, 72*
60:3 *71*
60:4 *71*
60:4–7 *71*
60:5–7 *71*
60:5–11 *64*
60:6 *71*
60:9 *71*
60:10 *71*
60:11 *71*
60:12 *70*
60:13 *64, 71*
60:14 *70, 71*
60:16 *71*
60:21 *61, 73*
61:1–2 *74*
61:1–3 *70, 71*
61:4 *71*
61:5 *71*
61:5–6 *71*
61:6 *64, 71*
61:9 *71*
62 *15*
62:2 *70*
63:1–6 *73*
63:19 *61*
64:8 *61*
64:19 *155*
65:17–20 *76*
65:21–22 *87*
66:7–9
66:16 *146*
66:18–21 *75*
66:18–24 *70, 71–73*
66:19–20 *72*
66:21 *73*

Jeremiah
1:4–12 *99*
1:10 *77, 79, 99*
1:13 *78*
1:13–15 *145*
1:16 *78*
2:2–3 *78*
2:11 *84*
2:13 *78*
2:15 *79*
2:16 *79*
2:18 *78*
2:19 79
2:36 *78, 79*
3 *92*
3:1 *172*
3:2 *172*
3:9 *172*
3:12–15 *93*
3:17 *93*
3:18 *93*
3:22–24 *93*
4:1–2 *93*
4:7 *82*
4:27 *82*
4:30 *78*
5:6 *79*
5:10 *83*
5:15–18 *83*
5:18 *82*
6:6–9 *83*
6:12 *79*
8:10 *79, 83*
8:16–17 *82*
9:26 *99*
10:7 *77*
10:8–9 *77*
10:12 *117*
10:16 *84*
10:25 *79*
12 *94*
12:14 *79*
12:14–17 *93*
12:15 *95*
12:16 *94, 95*
14:9 *155*
16 *94*
16:14–21 *93*
16:19–20 *93*
16:21 *93*
18:7–8 *94*
20:4 *83*
20:5 *83, 88*
21:1–10 *87*
21:4 *83*
21:7 *83*
21:10 *83*
22:1–7 *82*
22:24–30 *213*
22:25 *83*
23:1–8 *87*
23:5–6 *257*
23:5–8 *213*
23:19 *79*
23:31 *79*
24 *87, 88, 91*
24:7 *88*
25 *83*
25:9 *82, 91, 94, 99*
25:11–12 *90*
25:12 *92*
25:12–14 *83*
25:15 *79*
25:17–26 *79*
25:31 *79, 146*
27 *68, 90, 91*
27 – 28 *119*
27:1–11 *111*
27:3 *91, 119*
27:4–11 *82, 87*
27:5 *83, 91, 92*
27:5–6 *92*
27:6 *82, 83, 86, 90, 91*
27:7 *91*
27:8 *91*
27:9–10 *91*
28:14 *83*
29 *89, 91*
29:4 *83*
29:5–6 *87*
29:7 *88, 89, 90*
29:14 *96*
29:16 *87*
29:17 *88*
29:19 *88*
29:21 *83*
30 – 33 *80*
30:3 *96*

30:10 *176*
30:11 *80*
30:16 *80*
30:17 *94*
30:18 *93*
30:18–19 *96*
30:18–22 *96*
30:23 *79*
31 *5*
31:10 *94*
31:20 *93*
31:20–25 *96*
31:31–34 *5*
32:4 *83*
32:28 *83*
32:37–44 *96*
33:1–9 *15*
33:1–13 *94*
33:6–22 *96*
33:7–26 *96*
33:9 *94, 100*
33:26 *93*
34:2–3 *83*
34:6–7 *91*
34:20–21 *83*
37:1–2 *87*
37:5 *82*
37:11 *82*
39:1–10 *82*
42:11–12 *88*
42:12 *93*
43:8–13 *88*
44:30 *83, 88*
46 *95*
46 – 49 *80, 84*
46 – 51 *95*
46:2 *80, 95*
46:8 *80, 95*
46:10 *95*
46:13 *95*
46:14 *95*
46:14–28 *82*
46:15 *80, 95*
46:16 *95*
46:18 *99*
46:19 *95*
46:20 *95*
46:24 *95*
46:25 *95*
46:25–26 *80*
46:26 *95*
47:1–7 *80*
48 *96*
48:1–46 *80*
48:2–4 *96*
48:7 *81, 96*
48:13 *81, 96*
48:14 *81, 96*
48:26–27 *81, 96*
48:29–30 *81, 96*
48:31–32 *97*
48:35 *81, 96*
48:39 *96*
48:42 *81, 96*
48:46 *81, 96*
48:47 *96*
49:1 *81, 97*
49:1–6 *81*
49:2 *97*
49:3 *81*
49:4 *81, 98*
49:6 *97*
49:7–22 *81, 97*
49:8 *97*
49:11 *97, 98*
49:16 *81, 98*
49:18 *213*
49:20 *97*
49:23–27 *80*
49:24–38 *81*
49:26–33 *80*
49:27 *80*
49:34–38 *98*
49:35 *81, 98*
49:37 *98*
49:38 *81, 98*
49:39 *98*
50 – 51 *77, 83, 84, 86*
50:2 *83, 84*
50:4–8 *84*
50:5 *219*
50:11 *84*
50:14 *84*
50:15 *84*
50:17 *84*
50:17–20 *84*
50:19–20 *99*
50:21 *84*
50:23 *82*
50:24 *84*
50:26 *85*
50:28 *84*
50:29 *84*
50:30 *84*
50:31 *84*
50:32 *84*
50:33 *84*
50:33–34 *84*
50:36 *84*
50:40 *213*
51:3 *84*
51:5 *84*
51:6 *85*
51:7 *82, 85*
51:11 *85*
51:17–18 *84*
51:19 *83*
51:20 *82*
51:24 *84*
51:25 *84, 85*
51:34–35 *84*
51:39 *85*
51:42 *85*
51:44 *85*
51:47 *84, 85*
51:48 *85*
51:49 *85*
51:51 *85*
51:52 *84, 85*
51:53–56 *85*
51:57 *84, 85*
51:59 *82, 91*
51:64 *85*
52:1–11 *82*
52:12–23 *82*

Ezekiel

1 – 24 *102–107, 103*
1:1 *103*
1:3 *103*
2:3 *105*
3:5–7 *102*
3:15 *103*
4:3–14 *103*
4:4–8 *105*
4:13 *106*
5:4 *104*
5:6–7 *102*
5:6–9 *104*
5:11 *103*
5:12 *106*
5:14–15 *104*
6 *112*
6:8 *103*
6:8–9 *106*
7:3–4 *106*
7:8–9 *106*
7:21 *106*
7:24 *106*
8 *131*
8:6 *103*
8:13 *103*
8:14 *103*
8:17 *103*
9:7 *103*
10:20 *103*
11:9–12 *106*
11:12 *103*
11:16 *103*
11:17 *103, 130*
12:13 *106*
12:14–16 *103*
12:15 *106*
12:16 *104*
14:7 *103*
16 *134, 235*
16:3 *102*
16:14 *103, 115*

16:15 *115*
16:46–48 *102*
16:49–50 *129*
16:49–63 *101, 129*
16:52–53 *104*
16:53 *111, 129, 130*
16:54 *129*
16:55 *111*
16:57 *104, 110, 113*
16:60–61 *129*
16:61 *129*
16:62 *130*
16:63 *129*
17 *106*
17:5 *106*
20 *102, 103*
20:5 *102*
20:6 *102*
20:7–9 *103*
20:10–26 *102*
20:28–32 *103*
20:34 *103, 130*
20:34–35 *130*
20:41 *103, 105, 130*
20:42 *130*
20:44 *130*
21:18–23 *107*
21:20–22 *109*
21:25 *109*
21:28 *109*
21:28–32 *107, 109*
21:29 *109*
22:3–5 *103*
22:4–5 *104*
22:7 *103*
22:15–16 *103*
22:16 *104*
22:29 *103*
23 *101*
23:3 *103*
23:5–10 *103*
23:11–21 *104*
23:22–24 *101*
23:24 *145*
23:25 *108*
23:25–26 *107*
23:30 *107*
23:38–40 *131*
23:46–47 *107*
24:9–14 *107*
25 *108, 109*
25 – 32 *101, 102, 108, 119, 133*
25:1–7 *107, 109*
25:3 *110*
25:6 *104, 110, 112*
25:8 *110*
25:8–11 *107, 110*
25:10 *111*
25:11 *111*
25:12 *111*
25:12–14 *109, 110, 111*
25:13 *111*
25:14 *111*
25:15 *104, 112*
25:15–17 *109, 112*
25:16–17 *113*
26 – 27 *113, 117*
26 – 28 *108, 113, 114, 119*
26 – 32 *113, 126*
26:1–14 *107, 114*
26:1 – 28:19 *113*
26:2 *110, 114*
26:3 *116*
26:3–4 *116*
26:4 *107*
26:5 *116*
26:7 *145*
26:12 *116*
26:16 *115, 116*
26:17 *114*
26:17–18 *115*
26:20–21 *116*
27 *114, 221*
27:3 *114*
27:3–9 *114*
27:9 *115*
27:10 *115*
27:11 *114, 115*
27:12 *115*
27:12–25 *115*
27:13 *114, 115*
27:18 *115*
27:25 *115*
27:26 *115*
27:26–36 *114*
27:27 *115*
27:28–32 *115*
27:32–36 *115*
27:33 *115*
28 *117, 220*
28:1–10 *107*
28:2 *117*
28:2–10 *117*
28:4 *117*
28:5 *130*
28:6 *117*
28:9 *117*
28:11–19 *118*
28:12–14 *118*
28:14–18 *118*
28:16–20 *118*
28:20–24 *108, 109, 119*
28:24 *104, 110, 119*
28:25 *105*
28:25–26 *128*
28:26 *87, 104, 110*
29 *10, 120, 130, 134*
29 – 32 *108, 113, 119*
29:1–12 *130*
29:1–16 *119, 120*
29:3 *85, 120*
29:4 *120*
29:4–5 *121*
29:6–9 *104*
29:13–16 *95, 101, 112, 119, 123, 128, 130*
29:14–16 *101*
29:15 *158*
29:17–20 *107, 121*
30 *121, 123*
30:1–19 *121*
30:5–6 *121*
30:6 *121*
30:9 *107*
30:10 *107*
30:12 *107, 123*
30:13 *121*
30:13–18 *121*
30:18 *121*
30:20–26 *107, 119, 124*
30:21–22 *124*
30:24 *108*
30:24–26 *124*
30:26 *125*
31 *121, 122, 123*
31:1–18 *119*
31:2 *122*
31:3 *122*
31:3–18 *107*
31:5 *122*
31:6 *122*
31:7 *122*
31:8 *122*
31:8–9 *122*
31:9 *122*
31:14–17 *123*
31:15–17 *108*
31:18 *122, 123, 125*
32 *125, 128*
32:1–16 *119, 121, 123, 124*

32:2 *85*
32:2–3 *120*
32:3 *108*
32:4 *124*
32:17–32 *119, 124, 125*
32:18–32 *108*
32:19 *125*
32:21 *125*
32:23 *125*
32:23–27 *114*
32:24 *125*
32:25 *125*
32:26 *125*
32:27 *125*
32:30 *114, 125*
32:32 *125*
33 *101*
33 – 44 *128, 132*
33 – 48 *101*
33:26 *103*
34:13 *103, 130*
34:14 *130*
34:16 *130*
34:27 *130*
34:28 *176*
34:30 *130*
35 *101, 102, 112, 133*
35:1–15 *109, 111*
35:5 *112*
35:5–6 *112*
35:10 *112*
35:11–12 *112*
35:13 *112*
36 *112*
36 – 37 *128, 132*
36:1–15 *101*
36:2 *105, 110*
36:4 *104, 105*
36:4–5 *105*
36:5 *104*
36:5–7 *105*
36:6 *110*
36:11 *130*
36:13–15 *104*
36:18 *103*
36:23 *105*
36:24 *130*
36:30 *104*
36:34 *104*
36:35–36 *105*
36:38 *130*
37 *134*
37:1–14 *146*
37:6 *130*
37:12 *130*
37:13 *130*
37:14 *130, 146*
37:15–28 *111*
37:21 *130*
37:24–28 *15*
37:28 *105*
38 – 39 *101, 102, 113, 127, 128, 133, 145*
38:11–12 *127*
38:16 *105, 127, 128*
38:18 *128*
38:18–19 *128*
38:21 *213*
38:22 *128*
38:23 *105, 128*
39:1–7 *128*
39:4 *91*
39:4–5 *128*
39:11–16 *128*
39:17–21 *128*
39:21 *128*
39:22 *130*
39:25 *96, 128, 130*
39:26 *176*
39:27 *105*
39:28 *130*
39:29 *146*
40 – 48 *101, 102, 128*
43:12 *131*
44 *131*
44:7 *131*
44:9 *131*
47 *149, 235*
47:1–12 *131, 148*
47:13 *111*
47:13 – 48:29 *131*
47:22 *131*
47:22–23 *101, 103, 130, 131*
47:23 *131*
48:35 *131, 210*
51 – 52 *102*

Daniel

1:4 *117*
4:12 *92*
9:19 *155*
11 *145*

Hosea

1:2 *135*
1:9 *139*
1:10–11 *139, 141*
1:11 *139*
2 *141*
2:1 *141*
2:9 *136*
2:9–20 *140*
2:10 *139*
2:15 *135, 136*
2:16–17 *140*
2:16–23 *135*
2:18 *140*
2:20 *136*
2:20–23 *140*
2:25 *141*
3:4 *139*
3:5 *139, 140*
5:2 *135*
5:11–16 *135*
5:13 *78, 137*
5:15 *139*
7:8–10 *137*
7:11 *78*
7:12 *135*
7:16 *139*
8:7 *138*
8:8–9 *138*
8:9–10 *137*
8:10 *137*
8:11–14 *138*
8:18 *139*
9:1–3 *137*
9:3 *139*
9:6 *138, 139*
9:9 *135*
9:10 *135, 136*
9:17 *139*
10:6 *137*
10:10 *135, 139*
11:1 *136*
11:5 *138, 139*
11:11 *135, 139, 140*
12:13 *136*
12:14 *135*
13:4 *136*
13:5 *136*
13:7–16 *135*
14:1–8 *135*
14:2 *205*
14:3 *137, 140, 141*
14:5 *174, 175*
14:6–7 *141*
14:7 *141*

Joel

1:9 *143*
1:11 *143*
1:13 *143*
1:14 *143*
2 *144*
2:1–11 *145*
2:1–17 *144*
2:2 *143, 144*
2:11 *143*

2:12–14 *12*
2:13 *149*
2:17 *144, 145*
2:18–27 *145*
2:19 *144*
2:20 *145*
2:21 *145*
2:21–24 *146*
2:26 *144, 146*
2:27 *144*
2:28 *146*
2:28–29 *146*
2:28–32 *146, 147, 149*
2:30 *143*
2:30–31 *146*
2:32 *146, 205, 212, 234*
3 *147, 148, 223, 235*
3:1 *96, 143*
3:1–15 *149*
3:2 *144, 147*
3:2–6 *147*
3:4–5 *144*
3:4–8 *144*
3:6 *144*
3:7–8 *144*
3:9–11 *147*
3:9–21 *144*
3:13 *147, 148, 139*
3:14 *143, 148*
3:16 *148*
3:17 *148, 224*
3:19 *144, 148*
3:21 *148*

Amos
1:2 *151*
1:3 *153*
1:3–5 *152*
1:3 – 2:3 *151, 152, 156*
1:5 *80, 153*
1:6–8 *153, 203, 221*
1:9–10 *153*
1:11 *153*
1:11–12 *153, 228*
1:13 *153*
1:13–15 *153*
2:1–3 *153*
2:4–5 *152*
2:4 – 9:6 *156*
2:6 *152, 154*
2:6–8 *154*
2:7 *154*
2:11 *154*
2:12 *154*
3:1 *154*
3:1–2 *152*
3:9–10 *151*
3:10 *154*
3:11 *152*
3:12 *154*
4:1 *154*
4:6–11 *155*
4:11 *154, 213*
5:3 *154*
5:6 *154*
5:10–12 *154*
5:11 *154*
5:12 *154*
5:14–15 *154*
5:16–17 *154*
5:18–20 *154*
5:27 *152*
6:2 *152*
6:7 *152*
6:9 *154*
7:17 *103*
8:4 *154*
8:4–6 *154*
8:6 *154*
9 *154, 156, 157, 235*
9:1–4 *154*
9:7 *152*
9:8–10 *152, 154, 155*
9:11 *56*
9:11–12 *112, 155, 156, 257*
9:12 *151, 155*
9:13–15 *156*
9:14 *87, 156*
9:15 *155*

Obadiah
1 *157*
1–15 *157–159*
2–4 *157*
3 *157*
3–4 *157*
5–6 *158*
5–9 *157*
7 *158*
8 *158*
8–9 *158*
10 *158*
10–14 *157, 158*
11 *158*
11–14 *111*
12–14 *158*
15 *159*
15–16 *159*
15–21 *159*
16 *159*
16–17 *159*
17 *157*
18 *159*
19–20 *159*
21 *159*

Jonah
1:2 *166, 167*
1:5 *163, 164*
1:9 *164*
1:10 *164*
1:14 *165*
2 *169*
3:7–8 *167*
3:9 *12*
3:10 *167*
4:2 *12, 163, 166*
4:6–8 *167*

Micah
1:2 *171*
1:2–9 *171*
1:3–4 *171*
1:4–7 *171*
1:10–16 *171*
1:15 *172*
1:16 *172*
2:12–13 *176*
3:9–12 *172*
3:12 *172*
4 *223, 175, 176*
4:1 *175*
4:1–4 *172, 176, 178*
4:2 *174, 175, 177*
4:2–3 *177*
4:3 *175*
4:3–4 *178*
4:5 *172, 175*
4:9 *172*
4:9 – 5:1 *172, 173*
4:10 *172*
4:11 *172*
4:13 *173, 177, 178*
5 *178*
5:1–6 *173*
5:2–4 *173*
5:3 *173*
5:4 *175, 257*
5:4–5 *176*
5:5 *178*
5:5–6 *173*
5:6 *174*
5:7 *174, 177*
5:8 *174*
5:15 *172, 174*
7 *176, 235*

7:10 *47*
7:11–12 *178*
7:11–13 *176*
7:12 *176*
7:13 *176*
7:14–15 *176*
7:14–17 *176*
7:16 *176*
7:16–17 *173*
7:17 *177*
7:18–20 *12, 174*

Nahum
1 *235*
1:1 *181*
1:2 *12, 180*
1:2–5 *171*
1:2–8 *179–181, 187, 188, 197*
1:3 *12, 180*
1:5 *180*
1:6 *180*
1:7 *179, 180, 187*
1:8 *171, 179, 180*
1:9 – 3:19 *179, 181–186, 182, 186*
1:10–12 *8*
1:12 *187*
1:13 *187*
1:14 *8, 182, 183*
1:15 *186, 187, 224*
2 *185*
2:2 *187, 188, 189*
2:5 *185*
2:7 *185*
2:8 *181*
2:9 *185*
2:10 *185, 186*
2:11–13 *183*
2:11–14 *8*
2:12 *183*
2:13 *184*
3 *185*
3:1–4 *185*
3:4 *8*
3:7 *181*
3:8–11 *185*
3:12 *8*
3:12–15 *185*
3:15–17 *186*
3:16 *8*
3:17–19 *8*
3:18 *181, 186*
3:19 *186, 188, 189*

Habakkuk
1 *192–194*
1 – 2 *191, 198*
1:2–4 *192*
1:4 *191, 192*
1:5–6 *192*
1:6 *193, 199*
1:6–11 *192*
1:7 *193*
1:9 *193*
1:10 *193*
1:11 *194*
1:13 *192, 193, 194*
1:15 *192*
1:15–17 *192, 193*
1:16 *192, 193, 194*
1:17 *192*
2 *194–197, 199*
2:1 *15*
2:4 *198, 199*
2:4–5 *195*
2:6 *195*
2:6–7 *195*
2:6–8 *195*
2:6–20 *195*
2:9–11 *195*
2:10 *195*
2:11 *195*
2:13 *195*
2:14 *196*
2:15–16 *199*
2:15–17 *196*
2:17 *196*
2:18–20 *197*
2:20 *199*
3 *191, 197–198, 198*
3:3–15 *197*
3:6–11 *199*
3:8–15 *199*
3:10 *198*
3:12 *198*
3:12–13 *198*
3:13 *198*
3:14 *198*
3:15 *198*
3:17–19 *15*

Zephaniah
1 *202, 207*
1:2 *201*
1:2–3 *201, 208*
1:3 *201*
1:4–5 *202*
1:4–13 *202, 203*
1:7 *197*
1:8 *202*
1:14–18 *201*
2 *235*
2:1–3 *202, 203*
2:4–7 *202, 203, 204*
2:4–10 *202, 204*
2:4–15 *202*
2:7 *203*
2:8 *203*
2:8–9 *202, 206*
2:10 *203*
2:11 *97, 202, 203, 204, 205, 207*
2:12 *202, 203*
2:12–15 *202, 204*
2:13 *204*
2:13–15 *202*
2:15 *204*
3 *201*
3:1–7 *205*
3:8 *201, 205*
3:8–20 *202*
3:9 *140, 204, 205, 206*
3:10 *206*
3:10–13 *206*
3:11 *206*
3:12 *206*
3:13 *176, 206*
3:14 *207, 208*
3:14–17 *206*
3:14–20 *204, 206*
3:15 *205, 207, 208*
3:17 *15, 205*
3:19–20 *206*
3:20 *203, 206*

Haggai
1 *210*
1:1 *209*
1:10 *174*
2:1–9 *210, 214*
2:3 *210*
2:4–5 *210*
2:5 *213*
2:6 *209*
2:6–7 *210, 213*
2:7 *209, 210, 211, 214*
2:9 *210, 214*
2:10 *209*
2:20–23 *210, 212*
2:21–22 *212*
2:21–23 *209*
2:22 *209, 212, 213*
2:23 *213*

Zechariah
1 *223*
1 – 8 *220*
1:7–17 *217*
1:7 – 2:13 *217*
1:12–13 *218*
1:15 *217, 218*
1:18–21 *218*
1:19 *218*
1:21 *218*
2:1–5 *218*
2:4 *218*
2:5 *218, 222, 225*
2:6 *218*
2:6–13 *219*
2:7 *218*
2:8–9 *219*
2:9 *217, 218*
2:11 *94, 219, 220, 225*
2:11–12 *10*
2:13 *197*
5:5–11 *217, 225*
5:11 *218*
6:1–8 *217, 218*
6:8 *218*
8:1–20 *219*
8:3 *219*
8:4–5 *219*
8:8 *219*
8:12 *174*
8:13 *219*
8:20–21 *219*
8:20–23 *217, 219, 220*
8:22 *219*
8:22–23 *217*
8:23 *219*
9 *220, 222, 235*
9:1 *220*
9:1–6 *220, 224*
9:1–17 *220*
9:2 *220*
9:6 *221*
9:7 *220, 221*
9:8 *222*
9:9 *222*
9:9–10 *225*
9:10 *222, 225, 257*
9:13 *222*
9:13–14 *222*
9:14–17 *222*
10:5 *47*
10:10 *225*
10:11 *224*
12:1–9 *222*
12:3 *223*
12:4 *223*
12:4–6 *224*
12:8–9 *223*
12:9 *224*
12:10 *146, 225*
13:2 *224*
13:7 *225*
14 *223, 224, 236*
14:1 *223, 224*
14:1–11 *222*
14:1–21 *222*
14:2 *223*
14:3 *223*
14:9 *223, 224*
14:12 *223*
14:12–15 *224*
14:12–21 *222*
14:13 *213*
14:13–15 *223*
14:16 *223*
14:16–18 *223*
14:16–19 *222*
14:17–18 *224*
14:21 *224*

Malachi
1 *235*
1:2 *227, 232*
1:2–5 *227–229, 229, 230*
1:3 *228*
1:4 *228, 231, 232*
1:5 *228*
1:6 *229, 232*
1:6–10 *229*
1:6 – 2:9 *229, 230*
1:7 *229, 232*
1:8 *232, 233*
1:9 *12*
1:10 *229, 230*
1:10–13 *257*
1:11 *40, 229, 230, 232*
1:14 *40, 228, 229, 230, 232*
2:5 *232*
2:12 *229*
2:17 *230*
3:3–4 *232*
3:4 *229*
3:5 *232*
3:12 *228, 229, 232*
3:13 – 4:3 *230*
3:14 *230*
3:15 *230, 231, 232*
3:16 *230, 232*
3:16–18 *230–231*
3:17 *231, 232*
3:18 *231, 232*
4:1 *231, 232*
4:1–3 *231–233*
4:2 *231, 232*
4:3 *231*

NEW TESTAMENT

Matthew
2:6 *177*
8:10 *99*
8:11 *66*
10:6 *99*
12:39–40 *168*
12:41 *168*
15:18 *205*
15:24 *99*
15:28 *99*
21:14–15 *214*
24 – 25 *234*
26:29 *156*
28 *177, 234*
28:18–20 *160*

Mark
4:35–41 *169*
7:24–30 *99*
13 *234*
13:10 *234*
14:24 *225*
14:25 *156*
14:58 *214*
15:39 *99, 225*

Luke
1:32–33 *156*
1:54–55 *177*
1:79 *225*
2:32 *74*
2:49 *214*
3:4–6 *74*
4:17–22 *74*
4:23–27 *74*
7:9 *99*
11:29–30 *168*
12:32 *142*
24:47 *74*

John
1:14 *214*
2:1–11 *156*
2:19 *214*
14:23 *207*
14:27 *225*
14:28 *207*
15:4–5 *207*
18:35–37 *160*
18:36 *14*
19:37 *225*

Acts
1:6–8 *160*
1:8 *74*
2 *149*
2:21 *234*
2:32 *149*
2:33–35 *156*
2:36 *234*
2:38 *234*
2:41 *225*
4:4 *225*
4:7–12 *234*
8 *74*
10:36 *225*
10:44–48 *156*
10:47 *147*
11 *156*
11:24 *225*
13:47 *74, 149, 156, 160, 169*
14:21 *225*
15 *112, 177*
15:8 *147*
15:22 *142*
15:36 *142*
17:12 *225*
17:32 *100*
19:6 *147*
26:28–29 *100*
28 *156*

Romans
1:2 *236*
1:16 *100*
1:17 *199*
1:18–21 *153*
2:24 *74*
2:25 *99*
4:13 *132*
4:18 *141, 161*
5:1 *178, 207*
5:6–10 *178*
6:23 *138*
8:18–23 *255*
8:32 *xvii*
9 – 11 *74, 100, 132*
9:23–24 *74*
9:25 *141*
9:26 *141*
9:26–29 *141*
10:10–14 *146*
10:20–21 *74*
11 *161*
11:17 *188*
11:18 *203*
11:25–32 *74*
12:1 *214, 215*
12:1–2 *256*
15 *75*
15:9 *75*
15:12 *5, 75*

1 Corinthians
1:18 *188*
3:16 *208*
3:16–17 *214*
5:5 *188*
6:19–20 *214*
9:16 *169*
15:24–25 *161*
15:25 *257*
25:27 *225*

2 Corinthians
2:16 *178*
3:17–18 *142*
3:18 *207*
5:17 *255, 256*
6:16 *214*
8:3–5 *215*
9:5 *215*
10:1 *256*

Galatians
3:8 *161*
3:11 *199*
3:28 *100*
6:15 *255*
6:16 *100, 160*

Ephesians
1:9–10 *255*
1:12 *215*
1:20–22 *225*
2:1–10 *178*
2:20–22 *214, 215*
3:3–10 *100*
3:6 *100*
5:32 *207*
6:10–12 *14*

Philippians
1:9–11 *215*
2 *86*
2:9 *234*

Colossians
1:6 *225*
1:26–27 *207*
3:11 *100*

1 Thessalonians
1:6 *207*
1:9 *100*
5:2 *188*

Titus
3:3–7 *178*

Hebrews
10:12–14 *207*
11:10 *132*
11:12 *141*
11:14–16 *132*
12:22–24 *208*
12:28–29 *215*
12:29 *215*
13:15 *215*

James
5:13 *215*

1 Peter
1:10–12 *1, 14, 256*
2:9 *177*
3:15 *177*

2 Peter
3:10 *188*
3:13 *251*

Jude
6 *254*

Revelation
5:9 *134, 189, 206*
6:2 *133*
6:4 *133*
6:12–14 *199*
7:9 *141*
8:1 *199*
11:2 *133*
11:9 *133*
11:18 *133, 151*
12:4 *141*
13:3 *199*
14 – 19 *75*
14:8 *199*
14:17–20 *149*
14:20 *149*
15:1 *75*
15:4 *133*
16:1–14 *75*
17 – 18 *133*
17:2 *75*
17:16–17 *133*
18:3 *75*
18:9 *75*
19:1–5 *189*
19:6–10 *189*
19:11–16 *161*
19:17–21 *127*
20:8–10 *127*
20:9 *199*
21:1 *215*
21:1–2 *208*
21:1–5 *76*
21:3 *208, 215*

21:4 *75*
21:8 *189, 207*
21:22 *215*
21:22–27 *189*
21:23 *134, 215*
21:24 *133*
21:26 *133*
21:27 *208*
22:1 *215*
22:2 *131, 133*
22:3 *215*
22:4 *134*

Index of ancient sources

Amman Citadel Inscription *110*
Ashurbanipal royal annal (Cylinders A, B) *29*

Babylonian Chronicle
3 *8, 186*
4, 5 *80, 82*
Behistun relief and inscription *39, 213*

Ctesias, *Persica* *39*
Cyrus 'heirloom' cylinder seal PFS 93* *38*
Cyrus Cylinder *35, 36, 39, 211*

Darius tomb, Naqsh-i Rustam A *36, 37*

Enūma Elish *25, 26, 31, 33, 84, 166*
Esarhaddon royal annal
(Nineveh A) *29*
(Nineveh [Prism] D) *30*
(Nineveh [Prism] S) *183*

Gebel Barkal Stela of Thutmose III *22*
Gebelien wall relief of Mentuhotep *23*
Gilgamesh Epic *118, 123*

Herodotus, *Histories* *39*
Hymns to Sesostris III (hymn 1) *22*

Lamentation over the Destruction of Ur *96*

Mesha Inscription *54, 111, 203*

Nabonidus Chronicle *39*
Nabonidus Sippar Cylinder *38*
Nabopolassar Epic (BM 34793) *194*
Nabopolassar royal inscription 03 (Q005362) *52*
Nabopolassar, Imgur-Enlil wall inscription *32, 85*
Narmer Pallet *23*
Nebuchadnezzar Etemenanki Cylinder *194*
Nebuchadnezzar Prism (EŞ 7834) *33*
Nebuchadnezzar royal inscription 01 (Q005472) *53*
Nebuchadnezzar Sacker Tablet 82.2.8 *32, 33, 34, 196*
Nebuchadnezzar temple building report (CT 37) *193*
Nebuchadnezzar Wadi-Brisa Inscription *196, 197*
Neriglassar Cylinder C21 = Esagil Inscription *32, 53*
Nineveh, Nergal Gate (X) *185*

Prophecy of Neferti *22*

Sargon II Letter to the Gods *47*
Scarabée E 3408 (Louvre), re. Thutmose III *120*
Sefire Inscriptions *144*
Sennacherib Bellino Cylinder *185*
Sennacherib Ki 1902-5-10,2 (Nineveh) *28*

Tiglath-Pileser
I A.0.87.1 *27*
I annal I 01 (Q005926) *28*
III Calaḫ Annals *29*
Tukulti-Ninurta I A.0.78.23 *30*

Victory Stela of Piye (Piankhy) *21, 24*

Titles in this series:

1 *Possessed by God*, David Peterson
2 *God's Unfaithful Wife*, Raymond C. Ortlund Jr
3 *Jesus and the Logic of History*, Paul W. Barnett
4 *Hear, My Son*, Daniel J. Estes
5 *Original Sin*, Henri Blocher
6 *Now Choose Life*, J. Gary Millar
7 *Neither Poverty Nor Riches*, Craig L. Blomberg
8 *Slave of Christ*, Murray J. Harris
9 *Christ, Our Righteousness*, Mark A. Seifrid
10 *Five Festal Garments*, Barry G. Webb
12 *Now My Eyes Have Seen You*, Robert S. Fyall
13 *Thanksgiving*, David W. Pao
14 *From Every People and Nation*, J. Daniel Hays
15 *Dominion and Dynasty*, Stephen G. Dempster
16 *Hearing God's Words*, Peter Adam
17 *The Temple and the Church's Mission*, G. K. Beale
18 *The Cross from a Distance*, Peter G. Bolt
19 *Contagious Holiness*, Craig L. Blomberg
20 *Shepherds After My Own Heart*, Timothy S. Laniak
21 *A Clear and Present Word*, Mark D. Thompson
22 *Adopted into God's Family*, Trevor J. Burke
23 *Sealed with an Oath*, Paul R. Williamson
24 *Father, Son and Spirit*, Andreas J. Köstenberger and Scott R. Swain
25 *God the Peacemaker*, Graham A. Cole
26 *A Gracious and Compassionate God*, Daniel C. Timmer
27 *The Acts of the Risen Lord Jesus*, Alan J. Thompson
28 *The God Who Makes Himself Known*, W. Ross Blackburn
29 *A Mouth Full of Fire*, Andrew G. Shead
30 *The God Who Became Human*, Graham A. Cole
31 *Paul and the Law*, Brian S. Rosner
32 *With the Clouds of Heaven*, James M. Hamilton Jr
33 *Covenant and Commandment*, Bradley G. Green
34 *Bound for the Promised Land*, Oren R. Martin
35 *'Return to Me'*, Mark J. Boda
36 *Identity and Idolatry*, Richard Lints
37 *Who Shall Ascend the Mountain of the Lord?*, L. Michael Morales

38 *Calling on the Name of the Lord*, J. Gary Millar
40 *The Book of Isaiah and God's Kingdom*, Andrew T. Abernethy
41 *Unceasing Kindness*, Peter H. W. Lau and Gregory Goswell
42 *Preaching in the New Testament*, Jonathan I. Griffiths
43 *God's Mediators*, Andrew S. Malone
44 *Death and the Afterlife*, Paul R. Williamson
45 *Righteous by Promise*, Karl Deenick
46 *Finding Favour in the Sight of God*, Richard P. Belcher Jr
47 *Exalted Above the Heavens*, Peter C. Orr
48 *All Things New*, Brian J. Tabb
49 *The Feasts of Repentance*, Michael J. Ovey
50 *Including the Stranger*, David G. Firth
51 *Canon, Covenant and Christology*, Matthew Barrett
52 *Biblical Theology According to the Apostles*, Chris Bruno, Jared Compton and Kevin McFadden
53 *Salvation to the Ends of the Earth (2nd edn)*, Andreas J. Köstenberger with T. Desmond Alexander
54 *The Servant of the Lord and His Servant People*, Matthew S. Harmon
55 *Changed into His Likeness*, J. Gary Millar
56 *Piercing Leviathan*, Eric Ortlund
57 *Now and Not Yet*, Dean R. Ulrich
58 *The Glory of God and Paul*, Christopher W. Morgan and Robert A. Peterson
59 *From Prisoner to Prince*, Samuel Emadi
60 *The Royal Priest*, Matthew Emadi
61 *Life in the Son*, Clive Bowsher
62 *Answering the Psalmist's Perplexity*, James Hely Hutchinson
63 *'Egypt My People . . . and Israel My Inheritance'*, Daniel C. Timmer

An index of Scripture references for all the volumes may be found at http://www.thegospelcoalition.org/resources/nsbt.